LOO2 4575 2-389

DEMOCRACY
IN
LATIN AMERICA

DEMOCRACY IN LATIN AMERICA

Colombia and Venezuela

EDITED BY
DONALD L. HERMAN

New York
Westport, Connecticut
London

Library of Congress Cataloging-in-Publication Data

Democracy in Latin America.

  Bibliography: p.
  Includes index.
  1. Colombia—Politics and government—1946-
2. Venezuela—Politics and government—1958-
3. Representative government and representation—Colombia
—History—20th century.   4. Representative government
and representation—Venezuela—History—20th century.
I. Herman, Donald L.
F2278.D46   1988   320.9861   87–17852
ISBN 0-275-92478-5 (alk. paper)

Library of Congress Catalog Card Number: 87-17852
ISBN: 0-275-92478-5

First published in 1988

Praeger Publishers, One Madison Avenue, New York, NY 10010
A division of Greenwood Press, Inc.

Printed in the United States of America

The paper used in this book complies with the
Permanent Paper Standard issued by the National
Information Standards Organization (Z39.48-1984).

10 9 8 7 6 5 4 3 2 1

Contents

Tables and Figures

FIGURES

Preface

Everywhere in Latin America democracy seems to be dead, dying, or under siege. Twelve of the twenty republics (and the vast majority of the Latin American population) are presently (spring 1978) governed by military regimes, and in five of the remaining countries the military is so close to the surface of power as to make the civil/military distinction nearly meaningless. It has now become commonplace to point to the decline of civilian democracy throughout the continent, the rash of military coups since the 1960s, the rise of corporate-authoritarian regimes in such formerly democratic nations as Chile and Uruguay, the use of torture and repression in Argentina and Brazil, and widespread violations of human rights.[1]

As the 1970s drew to a close, the previously cited syndrome remained intact and only three countries continued to retain civilian-led democratic governments: Costa Rica, Colombia, and Venezuela.[2] Beginning in the winter of 1980, however, most of the dictatorships began to topple like a row of dominoes and constitutionally elected governments under civilian leadership assumed center stage. By the summer of 1986, only Cuba, Chile, and Paraguay were clearly under dictatorial rule.[3] After many years of military dictatorships, such important countries as Argentina and Brazil have once again turned to democratic regimes. In Central America the remaining military dictatorship, Guatemala, held Constituent Assembly elections in 1984 and presidential, congressional, and municipal elections in 1985. In February 1986 the Duvalier dynasty was overthrown in Haiti.

Is democracy sweeping Latin America? Unfortunately, the answer is no. Although it is true that democracies require freely contested elections, they must also establish effective problem-solving mechanisms to deal with socioeconomic deterioration. If democratic institutions cannot solve the most serious problems, they cannot remain viable. The tide can just as easily recede before overwhelming debt burdens, inflation, wealth disparities, official corruption, and the like.[4] Given the recent movement toward Latin American democracy, therefore, and to clarify our understanding of the term, it is most timely to analyze certain countries that have a relatively longer democratic experience in order to better understand what might lie ahead for the younger democracies.

Although several scholars, including the authors of this book, have devoted many years to the study of the democratic regimes in Colombia and Venezuela, no one has treated the two countries in an in-depth comparative macroanalytical framework. We have decided to present such an analysis for several reasons. Geography brings the countries together as Andean neighbors that share a common border in northern South America. Furthermore, their recent political history and political institutions are similar. From 1957 to 1958 both overthrew military dictatorships and established democratic regimes, and in each country two major political parties dominate national and local politics. In addition, with both a democratic and an authoritarian tradition existing within the same country, as exemplified in Colombia and Venezuela, the Latin American concept of democracy may be significantly different from that of such political systems as Great Britain and the United States.[5] It is necessary to look beyond recent elections, therefore, and to consider two questions: (1) Are the form and substance of Latin American democracy similar to the Anglo-American model or are they substantially different? (2) What are some of the important elements we should consider to determine the evolution of specific Latin American democratic countries over a longer time period?

The first chapter (Herman) is concerned with the former question, discussing the reestablishment and early period of the Colombian and Venezuelan democratic regimes. This chapter also presents a dual model of democracy, incorporating the respective countries' democratic and authoritarian traditions. The subsequent chapters address themselves to the second question, analyzing particular topics that are important to an understanding of the political and socioeconomic processes, and focusing on later periods in the development of the democratic regimes. The individual chapters deal with some of the principal components of the respective democracies: political parties and elections (Kline, Hoskin, and Martz), economic development (Berry, Thoumi, and Alexander), the state (Kline), the church (Wilde), the consociational regime (Abente), public opinion (Baloyra), the military/guerrilla movements and pacification (Premo), foreign policy (Hazleton), and the influence of the United States (Myers). In addition, several chapters incorporate discussions of such major interest groups as labor, business, and transnational corporations.

The final chapter (Herman) examines the effect of the drug trade on the respective democratic systems. It also discusses the question of democratization according to the authors' findings and reassesses the validity of the dual model. In offering projections for the remainder of the twentieth century, we consider the components of limited democracy, the driving forces that influence democratic institutionalization, and criteria for measuring the move toward democracy.

NOTES

1. Howard J. Wiarda, ed., *The Continuing Struggle for Democracy in Latin America* (Boulder, Colo.: Westview Press, 1980), p. 3.

2. Some scholars differ concerning Mexico, under the domination of the same political party since 1929, and Panama, in which the army assumes a major institutional role.

3. In Nicaragua the Sandinista-controlled junta that replaced the Somoza dictatorship was, in turn, replaced by an elected government under President Daniel Ortega. The regime's critics and supporters strongly disagree in describing the political system. Their descriptions range from totalitarianism to democracy and pluralism with various political shades in between.

4. North American economists and politicians tend to emphasize the internal causes of the problems, while the Latin Americans usually focus on the external causes. During a conference in Washington, D.C., a Bolivian congressman remarked: "We have inflation of 3,000%. Capital markets have closed. The support to us from abroad has been mostly of a lyrical nature. We have also had wrong internal policies and natural disasters. We seek the understanding of developed countries. We ask that they take into account that we are trying to survive." Suzanne Garment, "U.S. Neighbors Pledge Fidelity to Democracy," *Wall Street Journal*, January 25, 1985.

5. Both traditions were transplanted in Latin America during the colonial period. "We would submit the Latin Americans had received and adapted elements of the monist as well as the pluralist case. The colonies in the 1700s were by no means veiled in ignorance and obscurantism, bound to the teachings of sixteenth-century Spanish theorists. Enlightenment ideas clearly attracted their own advocates, although arriving at a later juncture. They did not displace the earlier tradition; they were in effect superimposed upon it. To understand the Latin American philosophical world view is to recognize the concurrent presence of both traditions." John D. Martz and David J. Myers, "Understanding Latin American Politics: Analytical Models and Intellectual Traditions," *Polity* 16 (Winter 1983): 214–41.

DEMOCRACY
IN
LATIN AMERICA

1

Democratic and Authoritarian Traditions

Donald L. Herman

DEMOCRATIC TRADITION

Elite Accommodation

Today most Latin American countries contain elements of the democratic tradition similar to the Anglo-American practice of liberal democracy, including the procedural norms of freedom of organization and political action, extensive citizen participation, individual rights, political parties, interest-group activity, and a relatively free press. Although many scholars contend that democratic procedures are foreign imports, grafted onto the Latin American societies by political elites who are convinced that modernization requires them, the democratic tradition has a comparatively long history in several of the countries. The basis of that tradition is an accommodation among the elites of the principal political parties. Once they agree that democracy is in their interests and that violent conflicts between them should be brought to an end, they must be prepared to develop a long-term mutually beneficial relationship. Thus, a crucial variable in Latin America is the democratic leaders' attitude toward the political opposition. Not only must they accept the idea of opposition as an abstract principle but also the legitimacy of specific opposition groups and the interests they represent. This requires a degree of tolerance and willingness to compromise that is very difficult, it not impossible, for many Latin American political leaders.[1]

Elite accommodation in Colombia and Venezuela exemplifies varying degrees of consociational practices.[2] According to Lipjhart, the elites in a political system consciously agree to a set of rules to help sustain the democratic regime against threats. Rather than appeals to mass social mobilization that may weaken the tenuous democratic edifice in its early stages, they rely on consultation and accommodation among all major elite groups. Consociationalism contains certain characteristics: (1) a coalition that includes the leaders of all significant societal groups; (2) each group retains a veto on policy issues vital to it; (3) representation in political and governmental office is proportionate to each group's strength; (4) each group has autonomy for its internal affairs. Implementation of consociational practices requires procedural and substantive solutions that will assure continuous support for the democratic regime, not only among the leaders, but among their followers as well.[3] This may take the form of written agreements, continuous dialogue among party leaders, congressional give and take, interparty congressional–executive understandings on policy output, and periodic meetings among party elders. Some or all of these practices may occur during the life of a particular administration.

Venezuela's first experience with democracy lasted only three years (the *trienio* from 1945 to 1948). The civilian–military junta and short-lived elected government, however, did not establish "common rules of democratic coexistence and norms to limit conflict."[4] During the trienio, some individuals among the social democratic majority party leadership–intermediary level, grass roots, and several of the labor leaders–appeared to see political opposition as symptomatic of counterrevolutionary conspiracy rather than as expressions of legitimate critique and alternative policies. On the other hand, the vehement opposition of some of the conservative sectors of the social Christian minority party, particularly in the Andean region, led to further political polarization. The reimposition of military rule (from 1948 to 1958) not only ended the democratic experiment, but it also terminated interparty conflict. Although that conflict certainly did not reach the proportions of La Violencia in Colombia, both situations manifested a lack of consensus concerning interparty legitimacy, as well as acceptance of and commitment to a democratic regime. (In Chapter 2 Professor Kline discusses Colombian consociational democracy during the National Front period [from 1958 to 1974].)

After the dictatorship was overthrown, the Venezuelan elites agreed to a more broadly based government than was the case in Colombia, and three political parties—Acción Democrática (AD), the social Christian party (COPEI), and the Democratic Republican Union (URD)—signed the Pact of Punto Fijo. Although the non-Communist elites decided to exclude the Communist party from the governing coalition, and the URD eventually decided to leave the government, the concept of a multiparty government took root. Thus, certain consociational practices were followed during the administration of AD President Rómulo Betancourt (from 1959 to 1964). Furthermore, the two major parties, AD and COPEI, not only accepted each other's legitimacy, but that of the smaller parties as well. They also agreed to give certain guarantees (particularly important in the case of AD) to such groups as the military, the church, and the business community. For example, the Betancourt government substantially increased the traditional governmental subsidy to the church. Although COPEI remained in the government, the Liberal–Conservative relationship in Colombia was much more formalized, if not institutionalized, than that of AD and COPEI. At the end of President Betancourt's term of office, COPEI left the government and became the principal loyal opposition to the next AD administration of President Raúl Leoni.

Whereas the Pact of Punto Fijo established liberal democracy in Venezuela, the Conservative–Liberal domination in Colombia signified that the National Front Agreement was to be a transitional period because of the limitations placed on other political forces. Colombian liberal democracy was established several years later, at the expiration of the National Front. In both countries the elites acted as autonomous actors in the political process. General economic and social conditions were not a major factor, because the rival elites decided to accommodate one another's special political interest.[5] The Colombian consociational pact excluded all political forces from the governing coalition except the Conservative and Liberal parties. In fact, no other political parties were allowed to participate in elections. Although this stipulation was originally intended for the entire life of the National Front, the Constitutional Reform of 1968 allowed free competition for town councils and municipal assemblies beginning in 1970. Although the Venezuelan version excluded the Communist party from the government, the Communists and other political organizations could legitimately engage in partisan activities.

Popular Participation

It is not easy to compare the concept of democracy in Anglo-American countries with that in other parts of the world for many reasons, including the widespread use and abuse of the term itself and very different cultural contexts in which democracy is practiced. Nevertheless, if we focus on the important concept of mass or popular participation, we can make some meaningful judgments about the extent to which democracy exists in Colombia and Venezuela.[6] In general, defenders of popular participation argue that substantial citizen involvement in meaningful elections (and in various organizations) both reflects and encourages a sense of democratic legitimacy that will help contain violence and channel it into regular competition. The Venezuelan example reflects this view. On the other hand, "democratic elitists" suggest that the involvement of citizens should be minimized to keep the system in the hands of those who are better informed and more supportive of its values.[7] The oligarchical democrats of the Colombian National Front would probably support this position. Among the variables that compose citizen participation, three are particularly germane to Colombia and Venezuela.

For one thing, mass organizations are an important avenue of citizen activism. When the Colombian oligarchical party elites reasserted their predominance over the new social forces by forming the National Front, they did so without any significant mass organization.[8] In Venezuela, however, the political parties, particularly AD, devoted many years to organizing and developing labor, peasant, student, and other groups prior to the reestablishment of the democratic regime. These functional organizations were linked to the national political parties and organized throughout the country. At least during the Punto Fijo period, the developing AD–COPEI two-party system witnessed national party elites who could impose compromises on supporting social forces and interest groups. But a long history of party splits, leading to new parties formed from AD or additional factions within COPEI, has resulted in division within trade unions, peasant syndicates, student organizations, and other party-related groups. Thus, one important sustaining aspect of the Venezuelan system has been weakened.[9]

Second, elections can be a significant manifestation of citizen participation. Voting is not compulsory in Colombia, and the low turnout (50 percent or less) may indicate popular disaffection with the Liberal–Conservative domination. By contrast, voting is required in Venezuela, and 80 to 90 percent of Venezuelans usually cast their ballots. Due to the compulsory nature of Venezuelan elections, the higher voter turnout does not necessarily indicate a greater degree of democratization. Furthermore, although various studies indicate a majority of Venezuelan citizens favor the democratic regime, at the same time they point out specific areas of dissatisfaction: Approximately 40 percent claim they would not vote if voting penalties were removed; increasing numbers of the electorate criticize corruption and bureaucratic inefficiency and suggest a change in the conduct of elections and the political system so that the elected officials represent the interests of the people rather than those of the parties.[10]

Third, whether people vote or join functional political organizations, we assume that the purpose of their participation is to influence governmental policy. Such activities may be manipulated participation, however, engineered or encouraged by a regime in pursuit of its own goals, as distinct from influential participation that refers to activities having a genuine influence over the making of decisions.[11] If governmental manipulation is the principal factor in participatory dynamics, we may be witnessing participation by the government rather than participation by the masses.[12] Perhaps the comparatively high voter turnout in the 1970 Colombian election, when former dictator Rojas Pinilla almost broke the Conservative–Liberal domination by winning the presidency, exemplifies a greater degree of popular influential participation than has occurred in the various Venezuelan elections. Furthermore, the government, party, mass-organization linkages raise another question: Which organizational structures, the Colombian or Venezuelan, indicate a greater degree of autonomy and thereby greater influence over the decision-making process?

Conclusions

As the Colombian and Venezuelan experiences indicate, the components of the democratic tradition compose both the establishment of the liberal democratic regime and the degree of democratization over a period of time. As we have observed, the key to the establishment of the system depends on the elites' choices. Although stability was gained through the principal power contenders' reciprocal restraint and moderation, the two regimes differed in the willingness to accommodate the remaining political opposition. AD and COPEI were significantly more willing to accept the legitimacy of the smaller political parties in Venezuela than were the Conservatives and Liberals in Colombia. One scholar did not include Colombia in a list of democratic systems, because the National Front eliminated the possibility of other political forces winning the presidency.[13]

Further democratization also depends on the elites' choices. Not only must we consider the political variables—developments in the post-National Front and post-Punto Fijo periods—but the socioeconomic variables as well. The substance of liberal democracy may lead to the conclusion that it is more an ideal rather than a day-to-day functioning reality. When inequality indicates that the overwhelming majority of a country's population live in abject poverty while a small percentage enjoy the fruits of a relatively advanced socioeconomic level, if not conspicuous consumption, then the word "democracy" may invite scorn and cynicism by the masses. In Colombia and Venezuela, as elsewhere in Latin America, the substantive norms of economic development and social justice may be severely lacking. Social and economic improvement does not necessarily accompany an enhanced political expression of liberal democracy.

AUTHORITARIAN TRADITION

The Spanish and Portugese conquerors and administrators transplanted a medieval authoritarian tradition from Europe to the New World. That tradition took root in the colonial period, continued to grow among the newly independent Latin American countries during the nineteenth century, and withstood or accommodated challenges in the twentieth century. Most Latin American constitutions include elements of authoritarian rule, as well as constitutional and legal restrictions on human rights. Furthermore, the traditional institutions did not disappear in the wake of "modernization," and the Roman Catholic Church, personalism, militarism, familism, patrimonial societal relationships, and the like form part of the daily reality. Changes take place within this controlled, hierarchical framework as new forces are absorbed into the sociopolitical system. These forces must have enough strength to be taken seriously, but they must also agree to abide by the rules of the game.[14] For analytical purposes we will consider the concept of corporatism, one of the most recent manifestations of the Latin American authoritarian tradition. Other concepts, such as dependency and bureaucratic authoritarianism, are discussed in subsequent chapters.

Corporatism

Essentially a concept pertaining to the relationship between the state and civil society, corporatism is an institutional arrangement for structuring interest representation. Corporate bodies may include labor, farmers and peasants, business, and so forth. In Great Britain and the United States the functionally organized interest groups emerge voluntarily. They are not specifically created, recognized, licensed, or controlled by the state. On the contrary, these groups influence the state. Their spontaneous formation, numerical proliferation, and competitive interaction suggest a horizontal extension.[15] Rather than use the word "corporatism," British and U.S. authors refer to "pluralism."

In Latin America the corporate bodies are usually created by and kept as auxiliary and dependent organs of the state, leading several scholars to refer to the arrangement as state corporatism. This leads to vertical stratification through which the political structure determines the number and type of corporate bodies that will be allowed. The emphasis is on hierarchy, authority, status, and patronage. As Professor Wiarda points out, however, the structure allows for change through the cooptation of new social and political groups into the administrative units of the corporate system. The state preserves the status quo and defuses discontent by keeping the pressures for change in check, thereby minimizing the possibilities for disruption or revolution. Thus, the state responds to modernization and adopts to some of its ways, but it also provides for the preservation of traditional attitudes and institutions.[16]

Some scholars (for example, Wiarda) see corporatism as cultural continuity through traditional institutions such as the *hacienda* (large estate), the village community, and the church. These are challenged by new groups: the development-oriented military, the "new" church, educated "*técnicos*" (technocrats) and various external actors that are seen as ascendant. Other scholars (for example, Stepan) disagree and contend that corporatism is an elite response to crises in which the modern political elites' control of the state apparatus allows them to create new corporate bodies to avoid a perceived threat to societal unity. For example, the military elites may see a connection between internal security and national development and want to use the state to create a new pattern of "integral security."[17] Most agree, however, that there are no fully corporate systems, "but rather there are political systems, in some sections of which (usually the working class) corporatist rather than pluralist patterns of interest representation predominate. The research implications ... are that 'corporatism as structure' is always only a *partial* sectoral phenomenon of the overall political system."[18] In those Latin American countries where corporatism plays a significant role in politics, corporatism is conceptually distinct from but can coexist with democracy. Nevertheless, in theory and practice, corporate representation may be incompatible with democratic principles, because in a sense it counteracts norms of majority rule.[19]

The Colombian example manifests an integrated ruling class in which the same people are very often leaders in parts of the business world, the political parties, and the government.[20] Principal political-party leaders represent families of long-standing and great economic power and a wide diversification of interests. Since all major political factions are represented in the government, any powerful family can be assured that the government will represent its interests.

As might be expected, the upper-income groups, such as the National Association of Industrialists (ANDI) and the National Federation of Coffee Growers (FEDECAFE), are much better organized than the lower-income groups.[21] Although the labor federations are associated with the political parties, they are not *formally* a part of the parties, because the law prohibits membership and Conservative and Liberal party members join the labor federations as individuals. Labor is a weak political force, in part because a small percentage of the work force is unionized, and in part because the labor federations are divided along traditional party lines. The peasants are also associated with the political parties, but they are only slightly organized under elite political leaders. Although scholars may disagree about whether the military has developed a corporate identity as such, its role has increased since the years of the National Front, primarily because of the struggle against the guerrilla movements. The guerrillas, however, have not posed as serious a threat against the status quo as had the *tupamaros* (movement of national liberation) in Uruguay.

The Colombian Roman Catholic Church is one of the most influential in Latin America. After a long period of supporting the Conservative party, it strongly supported the National Front and subsequent governments since then, both Conservative and Liberal. During the last twenty years, however, the church has become more conservative in addressing social issues.

As Professor Kline stated, ''Colombia is not a perfect corporatist society, with the economic and social groups controlled by the political elite. But neither is it a pluralistic system in which groups are formed and operate with nearly complete freedom from government control. Rather it is somewhere between these two ideal types.''[22] Perhaps the same statement could apply to Venezuela. We now should consider which of the two examples is closer to the ''perfect corporate society.''

The Venezuelan situation is very different than the Colombian. Whereas in Colombia the main export, coffee, has been privately owned and the industry integrated into the state corporate structure, Venezuela's great export product (now nationalized) was owned by the large petroleum companies, whose relationship to the decision makers was one of negotiation rather than integration. Furthermore, several years after the signing of the Punto Fijo agreement distrust between AD and the business community, in part a result of AD's seemingly radical program during the trienio, persisted as a significant component of political life. By the 1970s, however, the major business interests concluded that Ad had moderated its program sufficiently and that alternate AD and COPEI governments were capable of directing the overall economy. In turn, the AD–COPEI political elites concluded that they must work closely with business to keep the capitalist economy healthy. In contrast to Colombia, the Venezuelan economy and polity are in quite distinct hands and the government frequently negotiates over policy with the country's leading business organization, the Federation of Chambers and Associations of Commerce and Production (FE-DECAMARAS).[23]

In spite of the fact that Venezuela has been periodically governed by COPEI, a social Christian party, the church is a comparatively weak institution.[24] It is more poorly organized and does not have the money or number of clergy that its Colombian counterpart has. Furthermore, Venezuelan society is more urbanized and secular than that of Colombia, and except for the Andean states, church influence is very limited throughout the country. The discovery and exploitation of petroleum resulted in a much more rapid and complete change of Venezuelan society. Relatively new social, economic, cultural, and political institutions developed accompanied by an aggressive secularism and official indifference to religion.

During the trienio, the church opposed the government, in part because of a decree that proposed to reform the examination system while imposing stricter control over private schools. Although the church supported the 1948 coup that overthrew the AD administration, the ensuing military dictatorship's oppressive policies convinced church leaders to support a democratic regime. Shortly before the dictatorship's overthrow, a 1957 pastoral letter called for social justice, human welfare, democracy, and pluralism.

Guerrilla warfare in the early 1960s persuaded church leaders that they should be neutral and yet continue to support the democratic system. Thus, in Venezuela, as well as in Colombia, violence caused the church to withdraw from partisan politics while accommodating itself to the political system as a whole. Church support in both countries gave a greater sense of legitimacy to the democratic regime.

The armed forces, in particular the army, have not faced a serious guerrilla movement since the early 1960s, and the political elites of Venezuela have not had to call on the army. The army's privileged situation has been sustained through petroleum exports, although the decline in world demand for petroleum has meant that less funds are available. As in most Latin American countries, the army retains relative institutional autonomy and has not developed a corporate identity.

In contrast to Colombia, Venezuela is more highly industrialized and unionized workers are a significant political–economic force. In its early efforts to organize the workers and peasants, the AD political elites allied the labor and peasant movements to their political party. Shortly thereafter, party leaders in Caracas began to set policy, and local power brokers had to adjust accordingly. The other parties followed the same practice. Today, the political parties are represented in the Confederation of Venezuelan Workers (CTV) according to their relative strength. The party leaders determine to what degree the various functional organizations—labor, peasants, professionals, and so forth—will influence party policy. They also decide how many and which functional organization members will be on the party lists to be elected to Congress. In contrast to business associations that primarily articulate their members' interests, therefore, most of the corporate bodies are expected to support their party's positions. Although labor is tied to the political parties in both countries, the Venezuelan movement demonstrates greater autonomy in part due to the higher percentage of organized workers and higher level of skill. Furthermore, the style of Venezuelan collective bargaining is corporatist in that labor organizations need political help, especially from the parties, to gain the crucial support of the labor ministry. The labor movement, however, has some leverage in this relationship because its mass support is essential to the electoral success of the parties.[25]

The comparison of the respective countries indicates that Colombia contains a higher degree of corporatism. The integration of the political–economic elites results in a greater centralization of power. Furthermore, the oligarchical part of the Colombian oligarchical democracy demonstrates considerable power not only within the government and the political parties, but within the corporate bodies as well. Corporatism in Venezuela, on the other hand, is mixed with a higher degree of pluralism. In addition to some leverage by the labor movement, the separation of the business and political elites results in greater business autonomy. In both countries corporatism is not a static condition, and we do witness different degrees of tension between the corporate reality and the pluralistic ideal.

Conclusions

The authoritarian tradition is stronger in Colombia, because the oligarchy controls the political economy. Although Venezuela has its wealthy and powerful families that dominate important parts of the economy, the country does not have an oligarchy as such. Venezuelan elites can be identified, but they can be distinguished from an oligarchy in which a small group controls the government and forces it to follow policies primarily for the benefit of its members. As Professor Bonilla points out, Venezuela has long known a separation between economic and military sectors on the one hand and political and cultural sectors on the other. Throughout its history, Venezuela has experienced a continuous turnover of people in high places. Power has been held for only a short time, and an organic sense has not developed among elite groups.[26]

It is not likely that democratic forces will substantially alter the authoritarian tradition in Colombia and Venezuela in the near future. After all, even the profound revolutions in Mexico, Bolivia, and Cuba made only small gains against this force of great resiliency.

THE DEMOCRATIC AND AUTHORITARIAN TRADITIONS

Populism

Due to the variety of forms or tendencies through which populism appears, the phenomenon cannot be designated as a manifestation of either the democratic or the authoritarian tradition. In some cases populist movements have tended to foster the development of a democratic regime, while in others they have been closer to the authoritarian system. Scholars also find it difficult to define populism. The general consensus, however, focuses on any mass-based multiclass political movement: "a political movement which enjoys the support of the mass of the working class and/or the peasantry, but which does not result from the autonomous organizational power of either of these two sectors. It is also supported by non-working class sectors upholding an anti-status quo ideology."[27] Such a broad definition leads to further analytical difficulty. As Professor Dix has observed, most of the significant existing Latin American political parties can be loosely designated as populist.

We can discern certain elements of the populist style: (1) the assemblage of political coalitions out of disparate interest groups made up mostly of newer economic interests that are not satisfied with their representation through conventional political party structures; (2) the inclusion of social elements from both middle and lower classes; (3) a proclivity for extraparliamentary tactics, such as street demonstrations and threats; (4) personalistic leadership; (5) an assumption of the permanence of capitalism and distributive, rather than redistributive, economics.[28]

From the 1920s through the 1960s populist governments and leaders were one of the main forces in Latin American politics. In recent years the rise of military technocrats and the continual challenge of revolutionary groups, such as in Central America, have led many critics to conclude that populism is dead. Given the demographic changes, however, and the accelerating movement of people to the cities, populism will continue to be an important variable for the understanding of Latin American urban politics. It should be pointed out, however, that although populist movements draw their principal support from the urban areas, they also attract a sizable percentage of rural voters. Because of a commitment to agrarian reform, the democratic populists make greater inroads in the rural areas than do authoritarian populists.[29]

In Colombia authoritarian populism is associated with General Gustavo Rojas Pinilla. During this dictatorship (from 1953 to 1957), good coffee prices on the international market allowed the government to begin an extensive system of public-works projects while improving the system of credits for small farmers.[30] To an extent, he patterned himself after Juan Perón, distributing clothing and food to the poor through an organization called the National Secretariat of Social Assistance (SENDAS). He also raised minimum wages, created public-works jobs, lowered taxes for the poor, and expanded the bureaucracy. Although he tried to capture or create a lower-class constituency, he was either unwilling or unable to realize societal structural change.

A few years after the overthrow of his dictatorship, Rojas Pinilla returned from exile and founded the National Popular Alliance (ANAPO), which became a separate political party in 1971. A high percentage of ANAPO's leadership included retired military officers, landowners, businessmen, and old-line politicians.[31] During the National Front, Rojas tried to present ANAPO as a legitimate critic of Conservative–Liberal domination, as well as an ideological alternative. He attacked the "oligarchs," the "plutocrats," and "official corruption." He borrowed from the communist–socialist lexicon in calling for the nationalization of education, imports, private banks, petroleum, and other natural resources, as well as profit sharing for workers. Regardless of the rhetoric, however, several glaring omissions diluted the Rojas–ANAPO "radical" position. The party did not offer specific proposals for structural change, nor did it advocate redistribution of the nation's wealth. In questions of agrarian reform, land redistribution was hardly mentioned. Of interest was ANAPO's position that the Colombian brand of socialism and Christianity were compatible. Furthermore, if ANAPO assumed power, Rojas promised that both the church and the military would be represented in a corporate National Constituent Assembly that would replace congress.

ANAPO's program and ideology contained an ambivalent mix of populism and traditionalism. It attracted marginalized elements of the elites and the masses in the name of social justice. The party frightened the traditional elites, and Rojas's near victory in the 1970 election drew the Liberal- and Conservative-party leaders even closer together. After Rojas's death in 1975 his daughter, María Eugenia, who was the party's unsuccessful 1974 presidential candidate, assumed the mantle of ANAPO's leadership to confront the Liberal and Conservative parties in the post-National Front period.

Venezuela's experience with democratic mass populism occurred during the trienio (from 1945 to 1948).[32] It consisted of an alliance between the merging middle class and labor, an alliance that had been forged in opposition over the years. Although AD certainly used the resources of the state to reinforce its control, Venezuelan populism assumed less of a clientelistic, personalist form that it did under Perón or Vargas. Most of the party's leaders were either lawyers, doctors, educators, or officials from the labor and peasant movements.

The government introduced many reforms and programs. Thousands of new unions were formed throughout the country, and when the workers engaged in collective bargaining, they received official support for wage increases. The country's first extensive agrarian reform facilitated the formation of numerous peasant unions. Although Venezuelan populism was not limited to labor and the urban population, and included programs and budgetary designations for the rural areas, the newly formed Peasant Federation of Venezuela (FCV), as well as the Confederation of Venezuelan Workers (CTV), were clearly under AD control. The government expanded the suffrage, and Venezuelans voted in the first free elections in the country's history. Additional funds were provided for education and health (antimalaria campaign and new medical facilities), hospitals, sewer and water facilities, and public housing.

As its counterpart in Peru, the American Popular Revolutionary Alliance (APRA), and distinct from the authoritarian populist movements (for example, the one led by Rojas Pinilla), AD was highly institutionalized with strong ties to other organized groups. As a result, AD has continued to flourish since the death of its principal founder, Rómulo Betancourt. On the other hand, it remains to be seen whether the post-Rojas ANAPO effort will have any political significance. Furthermore, AD's durability has also been based on an explicit ideology and a program of democratic reform, while rhetorical criticisms of the Conservative–Liberal dominance have not provided a solid underpinning to the Rojas–ANAPO movement.

The subsequent Venezuelan military dictatorship (from 1948 to 1958) attempted to assume a populist posture. Similar to Perón and Vargas, Pérez Jiménez hoped to expand the economy and attract urban support by focusing on programs in the major cities. This proved to be a typical Latin American dictatorship, however, and showcase projects in Caracas were a poor substitute for economic development and industrial expansion. The wasteful and ill-conceived expenditures, corruption, and brutality led to a severe economic crisis. When civilian leadership returned to power under an AD-led coalition government in 1958, a more diversified, planned economic development program was undertaken.

Both Colombia and Venezuela had populist governments for brief periods of time, but the Venezuelan democratic government of the trienio was much closer to the populist ideal than the Rojas Pinilla military dictatorship and ANAPO in Colombia. In fact, we can say that Venezuela has passed its populist phase of AD radicalism and is now in its bourgeois phase in which the middle class governs with the consent of other social classes.[33] On the other hand, in the event of the demise of ANAPO, the populist strain in the Colombian polity may depend more on the programs and policies of certain traditional Conservative or Liberal party leaders.

Overall, populism had a marginal effect on the establishment of the Colombian democratic regime. The Conservative–Liberal elites were more concerned about bringing La Violencia under control, and the Rojas–ANAPO movement merely reinforced their conviction that they must seek and nurture mutual elite accommodation. Populism was more important to the genesis of the Venezuelan democratic regime because of the trienio experience in building a base for the ideology and program of the post–1958 democratic regime and for avoiding policies that might encourage another coup d'etat.

CONCLUSIONS

Political Factors

In the 1950s the coups that overthrew the Rojas Pinilla and Pérez Jiménez dictatorships had different effects. The Colombian coup returned the Conservative–Liberal elites to power in a very narrowly based government and political–economic structure. Although the National Front leaders made a commitment to universal suffrage and to a more liberal political system, they successfully demobilized and controlled the citizenry. This led to widespread apathy that fit the needs of the oligarchical democracy.[34] The political, ideological, programmatic distinction between the Conservative and Liberal parties was blurred, and the nonloyal opposition was defined as any person or group who opposed the Conservative–Liberal domination. The intent of the Venezuelan leadership was very different. Not only was the government and economic–political structure more broadly based among the various elites, but the distinction between the two principal parties was more clearly expressed. The social democratic AD and the social Christian COPEI joined the Betancourt coalition government but continued to maintain their separate political–ideological identities. Furthermore, for AD, the majority party, COPEI was the loyal opposition. These political choices, rather than petroleum revenue per se, proved to be the major factor in the establishment of Venezuelan liberal democracy. In both Colombia and Venezuela, however, other political forces felt excluded and turned to violent means to express their differences. The guerrilla movements indicated that the elites of the democratic regimes would subsequently have to respond to the demands of several left-wing groups.

Dual Model

In his provocative study Professor Wiarda offers a perspective of Latin American democracy that I believe is applicable, in varying degrees, to Colombia and Venezuela.[35] It represents a blend of both the corporatist, organist, patrimonial features with the liberal, republican, representative ones based on Anglo–American practices. We observe two models that may exist side by side within a given country, sometimes wholly separate and sometimes overlapping, but constantly evolving. In terms of the democratic tradition, this evolution may result in further democratization by increasing electoral participation. Within the authoritarian tradition evolution may take the form of additional power contenders, leading to an expanded corporate framework. (In most Latin American countries the corporate power contenders, rather than Congress or the judiciary, "check" the power of the executive. The Venezuelan Congress, however, and to a lesser degree the Colombian, have frequently asserted their power vis-à-vis the executive branch.)

Although this analysis contends that the National Front placed Colombia closer to the authoritarian, corporatist model and the Punto Fijo agreement placed Venezuela closer to the pluralist, democratic tradition of liberal democracy, further research is required. We must turn to the post–National Front and post-Punto Fijo periods. An in-depth treatment of the topics analyzed in this book will not only allow us to reassess and perhaps modify the dual-model hypothesis, but it will compel us to raise serious questions about the very nature of the democratic regime and its future in Colombia and Venezuela.

NOTES

1. Howard J. Wirada, ed., *The Continuing Struggle for Democracy in Latin America* (Boulder, Colo.: Westview Press, 1980), p. 204. Professor Wiarda discusses extensively both the democratic and authoritarian traditions.

2. See the discussions by Arend Lipjhart, *The Politics of Accommodation* (Berkeley: University of California Press, 1968); "Typologies of Democratic Systems," *Comparative Political Studies* 1 (April 1968); "Consociational Democracy," *World Politics* 21 (January 1969); *Democracy in Plural Societies: A Comparative Exploration* (New Haven, Conn.: Yale University Press, 1977). Also see John A. Peeler, *Latin American Democracies: Colombia, Costa Rica, Venezuela* (Chapel Hill: University of North Carolina Press, 1985), pp. 143–44.

3. Lipjhart also uses the term "consociational democracy."

4. Daniel H. Levine, "Venezuela Since 1958: The Consolidation of Democratic Politics," in *The Breakdown of Democratic Regimes: Latin America*, eds. Juan J. Linz and Alfred Stepan (Baltimore: Johns Hopkins University Press, 1978), p. 92.

5. Peeler, *Latin American Democracies*, p. 93.

6. See Robert H. Dix, "Democracy in Latin America," Books in Review, *Latin American Research Review* 15 (1980):241.

7. G. Bingham Powell, Jr., *Contemporary Democracies: Participation, Stability, and Violence* (Cambridge, Mass.: Harvard University Press, 1982), p. 12.

8. Alexander W. Wilde, "Conversations among Gentlemen: Oligarchical Democracy in Colombia," in *Breakdown of Democratic Regimes*, eds. Linz and Stepan, p. 68.

9. Levine, "Venezuela Since 1958," p. 106. For the purposes of this chapter we will consider the Punto Fijo period as coinciding with the years of the Betancourt government. Some Venezuelan specialists contend that the spirit of Punto Fijo continues to exist.

10. John D. Martz and Enrique A. Baloyra, *Electoral Mobilization and Public Opinion: The Venezuelan Campaign of 1973* (Chapel Hill: University of North Carolina Press, 1976); Enrique A. Baloyra, "Public Attitudes toward the Democratic Regime," in *Venezuela: The Democratic Experience*, eds. John D. Martz and David J. Myers (New York: Praeger, 1977), p. 51; Arístides Torres, "Evaluación y Deterioro del Proceso Democrático," paper presented to the Study Group on Comparative Public Opinion, International Political Science Association, Maracaibo, Venezuela, June 21 to 23, 1984.

11. Thomas A. Baylis, "The Faces of Participation: A Comparative Perspective," in *Political Participation in Latin America*, Vol. 1, *Citizen and State*, eds. John A. Booth and Mitchell A Seligson (New York: Holmes & Meier, 1978), p. 37.

12. Richard Newbold Adams, "The Structure of Participation," in *Political Participation in Latin America* Vol. 2, *Politics and the Poor*, eds. John A. Booth and Mitchell A. Seligson (New York: Holmes & Meier, 1979), p. 16.

13. Powell, *Contemporary Democracies*, pp. 6–7.

14. Wiarda, ed., *The Continuing Struggle*, pp. 12 and 32.

15. Philippe C. Schmitter, "Still the Century of Corporatism?" in *The New Corporatism: Social-Political Structures in the Iberian World*, eds. Frederick B. Pike and Thomas Stritch (Notre Dame, Ind.: University of Notre Dame Press, 1974), p. 97.

16. Wiarda, ed., *The Continuing Struggle*, p. 153.

17. See Howard J. Wiarda, "Toward a Framework for the Study of Political Change in the Iberic-Latin Tradition: The Corporative Model," *World Politics* 25 (1973) 206–35; and Alfred Stepan, *The State and Society: Peru in Comparative Perspective* (Princeton, N.J.: Princeton University Press, 1978), pp. 54–59.

18. Stepan, *The State and Society*, pp. 70–71. Professor Stepan also distinguishes between inclusionary and exclusionary corporatism.

19. Jonathan Hartlyn, "Consociational Practices and Colombian Politics: An Intro-

duction,'' paper presented at the 1985 Meeting of the Latin American Studies Association, Albuquerque, New Mexico, April 18 to 20, 1985.

20. For the difference between Colombian and Venezuelan corporatism, see Peeler, *Latin American Democracies*, pp. 105–6.

21. Harvey F. Kline, *Colombia: Portrait of Unity and Diversity* (Boulder, Colo.: Westview Press, 1983), pp. 79–92.

22. Ibid., p. 92, 1980.

23. Daniel Hellinger, ''Class and Politics in Venezuela,'' paper presented at the 1980 Meeting of the Latin American Studies Association, Bloomington, Indiana, October 17 to 19.

24. See Daniel H. Levine, *Religion and Politics in Latin America: The Catholic Church in Venezuela and Colombia* (Princeton, N.J.: Princeton University Press, 1981), p. 25. Much of the discussion of the church in Venezuela is based on Professor Levine's analysis.

25. Hellinger, ''Class and Politics.''

26. Frank Bonilla, *The Politics of Change in Venezuela*, Vol. 2, *The Failure of Elites* (Cambridge: Massachusetts Institute of Technology Press, 1970), pp. 27, 50–51, 78–79.

27. Torcuato S. di Tella, ''Populism and Reform in Latin America,'' in *Obstacles to Change in Latin America*, ed. Claudio Veliz (London: Oxford University Press, 1965), p. 47, cited by Robert H. Dix, ''Populism: Authoritarian and Democratic,'' *Latin American Research Review* 20 (1985):29.

28. Ronald C. Newton, ''Latin American Populism: Some Notes on Periodization,'' in Wiarda, ed., *The Continuing Struggle*, p. 72.

29. See the article by Lois E. Athey, ''Democracy and Populism: Some Recent Studies,'' *Latin American Research Review* 19 (1984): 172–83.

30. Kline, *Colombia*, p. 52.

31. See the discussion by Robert H. Dix, ''Political Opposition under the National Front,'' in *Politics of Compromise: Coalition Government in Colombia*, eds. R. Albert Berry, Ronald G. Hellman, Mauricio Solaún (New Brunswick, N.J.: Transaction Books, 1980), pp. 140–70. Professor Dix also hypothesizes that the authoritarian populist leaders feel abandoned or threatened by change, and they try to resist or control its consequences. On the other hand, the democratic populist leadership consists of those left behind by change and who aspire to share in it. Dix, ''Populism: Authoritarian and Democratic,'' *Latin American Research Review* 20 (1985): 29–52.

32. Hellinger, ''Class and Politics.''

33. Wiarda, ed., *The Continuing Struggle*, p. 75. Another scholar refers to AD and COPEI as the populist parties. See also David Eugene Blank, *Venezuela: Politics in a Petroleum Republic* (New York: Praeger, 1984).

34. Wiarda, ed., *The Continuing Struggle*, p. 134; and Peeler, *Latin American Democracies*, p. 59.

35. Wiarda, ed., *The Continuing Struggle*, pp. 234–47, 279–85.

2

From Rural to Urban Society: The Transformation of Colombian Democracy

Harvey F. Kline

Colombia has long been considered one of the few Latin American democracies. In a certain sense that categorization is correct, as elections leading to civilian presidents have been the modal pattern of political recruitment. The military has been in power only from 1953 to 1958 in this century, surely less frequently than in most other countries of the region. Yet, on another level the conclusion that the country is a "democracy"[1] is too general, and as such it ignores important historical variations in partisan elite methods of mobilizing voters.

In this chapter I argue that Colombia has gone through three consecutive (save the military hiatus) and related electoral regimes: "sectarian democracy" (late nineteenth century through 1953); "consociational democracy" (from 1958 to 1974); and "democracy" (from 1974 to the present). I show that three forms of mobilizing voters have been common: (1) party members' hatred of the other party, or "*sectarismo*"; (2) direct "machine-oriented" payoffs, or "*clientelismo*"; and (3) programmatic appeals. Although the first two methods correspond especially to the first two periods respectively, and the third has been most notable during the third period, I show that all three methods have existed in each of the three periods.

The chapter is organized into two parts. In the first, I describe the first two historical periods, discussing the partisan dynamics and societal changes that led to alterations of the electoral regimes. In the second, I describe the current period of democracy, exploring the new programmatic mobilization through an analysis of the campaign statements of the Liberal and Conservative presidential candidates in the first three elections of this period.

SECTARIAN AND CONSOCIATIONAL DEMOCRACIES IN COLOMBIA

Before 1974 the modal pattern was for Colombian citizens to vote for their presidents.[2] Yet there were characteristics that prevent the conclusion that Colombia was a "democracy." In the first period these included electoral corruption, the absence of female suffrage,[3] and, most importantly, the "sectarian" nature of the conflict between the parties; in the second, it was the lack of competition between them.

Sectarian Democracy

Elections in Nueva Granada began soon after the dissolution of Gran Colombia (1830); the Liberal and Conservative parties were founded by the late 1840s. Civil wars between the two soon ensued, and in effect the process of building a sectarian democracy started, to be completed by the late nineteenth century. Francisco Leal argued that the decade of 1875 to 1885 was definitive in the parties' development of social integration in two ways. On the one hand, the civil wars of 1876 and 1885 were fundamental in increasing the coverage of bipartisan membership. In addition, the wars were a step toward the reinstitution of religion as a factor of cohesion in politics. On the other hand, civil strife led to a unification of the dominant political interests with the most important economic ones. Regional divisions were left behind.[4] John Peeler suggested that Colombia, by 1886, had hence become very similar to the rest of Latin America in that

[A]n individual often gained control of the national government through the arms of a supporting coalition of allied patrons and their clients. He would then place supporters in all significant positions of power and patronage, from which vantage points they could control violent resistance and determine the outcome of elections. Then a docile constituent assembly could be elected to draft a' new constitution along lines desired by the new leader. The leader could then assure an alternation in the presidency between himself and his supporters, until such time as disgruntled supporters might coalesce with opposition elements to overthrow him.[5]

There was a "peculiarity," however: Personal, patrimonial rule became party hegemony.

That Colombian peculiarity has never been effectively explained through cross-national studies. There is, however, no doubt that it was to be the key characteristic of voter mobilization in Colombian politics from then on, affecting not only the first "sectarian" stage, but also the later electoral variants. Several components of this phenomenon of party hegemony are especially important.

First, the civil wars between the Liberal and Conservative parties, and the alliance of the church with the Conservatives, gave conflicts intensity. As Orlando Fals Borda argued, "This religious struggle—emotional, bitter, and personal—made the consciousness of social class pass to a second level and eliminated the conflicts based on popular self-identification. The Colombian political parties were converted to simple agglomerations in which there remained together both members of the elite and of the lower classes who had their inclinations."[6] Hence, voting became a matter of traditional party loyalties; for the majority of the voters, neither specific program nor candidate image was important in mobilizing voters; nor were direct economic payoffs.

Second, the political system was nevertheless patrimonial, with "natural chiefs" (*gamonales*) at the national level and varying levels of regional and local linkages. Although at the beginning many of the local leaders were *hacienda* (plantation) owners identified with one of the two parties, over the years of the sectarian democracy other kinds of individuals became gamonales. As Fals Borda described them,

Gamonales were petty political leaders whose position in society permitted them to exert influence upon rural voters. Public officials, hacienda owners and overseers, and some priests were counted among them. The machine organized by these leaders was designed to perpetuate them and the higher ranking *caudillos* in power. They saw that their friends, employees, and followers went to the polls and voted "right," paid for the liquor consumed as a reward, and acted as protectors of the constituents.[7]

From the gamonal this system stretched vertically to the pinnacles of power. As Conservative *caudillo* Laureano Gómez once stated, "The regional *caciques* are federated and give their electoral assistance to departmental *caciques*, who pay them back by sustaining them in the municipal barricade. This double game continues in an ascending scale and reaches the highest levels of the State."[8]

Although the key element of this patrimonial exchange dealt with party loyalty and minor rewards at election time, there were also some employment payoffs. With the centralizing Constitution of 1886, the presidential elections became paramount in the changing of office holders. The transition of hegemony from one party to another (such as in 1930 and 1946) meant the removal of the dominating *caciques* at the departmental (the governors) and the local (the mayors) levels. Further, in the absence of civil service, nearly all of the holders of governmental posts were changed.

This situation has led some students of the Colombian system to conclude, as Fernando Guillén Martínez did, that "The history of Colombia since 1828 has been this: a mass of public employees arms in hand faces a mass of armèd aspirants to public office."[9] Or, as Robert Dix stated, "One feature of a weak state, its lack of neutrality, has been evidenced in Colombia by the prevalence of the spoils system. . . . [T]he rule of one party has frequently meant the almost total exclusion of members of the other from government. The parties have treated government as an objective to be seized and, once won, as a bastion in which to entrench themselves like armies of occupation, subsisting on the bureaucratic booty of battle."[10]

Nevertheless, another feature of the weak state—the lack of activities and hence personnel—meant that there was little else that the government could give, and needed to give, of a material sort to the vast majority of its followers. As Leal argued, the institutional state had only small amounts of goods and services. "Clientelism," as it was later called, was thus limited. But this lack of material benefits was not crucial, since there were ideological implications of party triumphs and defeats. These were based on the almost religious feeling of belonging to one of the two parties.[11] Although there have been various academic debates over whether adscriptive ideology or jobs and other material rewards were most important in Colombian sectarian democracy, the important points are (1) for most of the voters, since rewards were unavailable, ideology was more important; and (2) for other people ideology and material rewards were not in conflict, but rather went hand in hand.

The sectarian democracy began to experience changes, including those that included political elements more common in later periods. Party leaders could not prevent the appearance of new social tensions coming from industrialization and the growth of the urban working and middle classes. Sectarismo did not work well with these groups.[12] Neither did it work with the more educated, who desired different kinds of political participation.[13] The country became more geographically integrated, and cities began to grow. Younger groups rebelled against the sectarian system.[14]

The breakdown of the system occurred in the 1940s. While there were some party leaders already considering a change to a consociational system, the two major leaders after the 1946 presidential election, Laureano Gómez and Jorge Eliécer Gaitán, were antagonistic to a bipartisan agreement. Each thought that accommodation with the opposition was betrayal; each believed that his own political future, which was of course synonymous with that of his party as a whole, would be best served by an independent course.[15]

Yet Gaitán, although resistant to the consociational model, mobilized forces that would contribute to changes in sectarian democracy. As Robert Dix pointed out, Gaitán "had challenged for the presidency on a more radical populist platform than had ever been presented in Colombia. His voting strength lay particularly with the lower and lower-middle classes, both urban and rural, in contrast to the traditional multiclass support of both historic parties. He was thus perceived as a somewhat different kind of threat by Conservatives (and by some Liberals as well)."[16]

Sectarian democracy ended with its logical conclusion: La Violencia,[17] although in large part begun by the party leaders, later escaped their control. The Rojas military dictatorship that followed was a system not completely controlled by them. The traumas of these two phenomena were so acute that even the most sectarian of Conservatives—the "angry man of God," Laureano Gómez—came to be a supporter and major author of the agreements that formed the National Front, a coalition of the Liberal and Conservative parties, and led to the sixteen-year period of consociational democracy.

Colombian Consociational Democracy

The National Front[18] was supposed to end all partisan conflict for a sixteen-year period through *paridad* (parity) in legislative and non-civil-service executive positions and *alternación* (alternation) of the presidency between the two traditional parties. This complete lack of competition has led some to call this a "consociational democracy," similar to agreements between ethnic groups in other parts of the world, but in this case between two party groups that were very much alike in all save partisan identification.[19] Two explanations have been given of this coalition.

On one level it has been argued that the party leaders simply were trying to reassert the control that they had lost, first during La Violencia and second with the military government. A study of the national Congress in 1969 showed the importance of this loss of control: When congresspeople were asked what historical event motivated them to initiate political careers, the modal response (48 percent) was "Strong governments, dictatorships."[20]

Others argue that the National Front was more than a coalition of leaders of the two parties. Dix stated that

Underlying such "temporary" or expedient motivations, and giving them particular urgency and impact, were deeper sociopolitical tendencies that increasingly affected Colombia's elites. For as Colombia had become more industrialized, socioeconomic issues have increasingly tended to gain paramountcy over such traditional disputes as church-state relations. . . . Such a coalescence of class interest at the elite level may well have been crucial for the formation of the National Front. A zero-sum conflict over political positions (as well as matters as the role of the church) was increasingly superseded by common stakes in an expanding economy and the need to act jointly to "keep the masses in their place."[21]

Gerardo Molina made the same argument when he stated, "The authors of this compromising declaration were not ignorant that the National Front was nothing more than an agreement of the historical parties, behind which were the dominant economic forces, needing a truce to consolidate their empire and to mold the society which interested them."[22] As Jonathan Hartlyn pointed out, during the crucial, troubled transition from the caretaker military junta to the National Front, one statement favoring the consociational agreement was the "Document of the 14," signed by industrialists in Antioquia calling for a reconstruction of the country without sectarianism.[23]

For whichever of the two reasons (and they are not mutually exclusive), the final decision was to form the consociational agreement. And the agreement came about in the context of "the continued domination of the political landscape by party leaders in control of collectivities with entrenched loyalties."[24]

Party leaders during the National Front period faced a dilemma. They wanted to encourage voting, but they did not want to use the old tactics of sectarian mobilization. They surely could have used these tactics. However, they had made an agreement that they would not do so. Additionally, such tactics would not have been appropriate, since there was no longer any competition with the hated enemies. The role of the gamonal had to change if the National Front was to attain its goal of ending partisan violence.

Politicians did try to encourage voting without using sectarian mobilization tactics. The amount of time the elite spent worrying about abstentionism might be puzzling, given their desire to avoid returning to the sectarian democracy of the past and the military dictatorship to which it led. Yet there were two reasons to encourage voting (in addition to the somewhat cynical explanation having to do with international appearances).

The first reason to mobilize voters was because of the competition within both parties. In each of the four presidential elections during the National Front period, there was at least one important faction of one of the parties that declared itself to be opposed to the major provisions of the coalition agreement.[25] Further, even if all factions agreed on the National Front, the party *de turno* at times had various prospective candidates. This reached its more extreme point in 1970 when, in effect, the Liberal national convention chose the Conservative National Front candidate, because the Conservative convention could not do so. On occasion, the congressional elections were held several months before presidential elections, with the agreement of party leaders that the victorious faction in the former would chose the candidate for the latter.

Even in the absence of the first three causes of intraparty conflict, competition within the parties became extreme. In the *mitaca* (non-presidential-year) Cámara elections of 1968, for example, the average number of lists per electoral district (corresponding to the *departamentos*) was 4.8 Liberal and 4.7 Conservative ones. The most extreme case was that of Nariño in which the number of lists was as follows: ten Official Liberal, two Unionist (Ospina) Conservative, four Independent (Gómez) Conservative, and two Alianza Nacional Popular Conservative (ANAPO, Rojas Pinilla) lists. In other departamentos there were lists also from the Revolutionary Liberal Movement of the People, Liberal ANAPO, and other groups.[26]

One explanation of intraparty competition[27] stresses the freedom that the National Front gave to party factionalism (which had always existed in both parties). During the sectarian democracy, the need to face the opposition party was usually strong enough incentive for eventual party unity. However, during the consociational period, there was no such enemy, and in addition the mechanics of the electoral system encouraged factionalism.

Francisco Leal, in his explanation, emphasized that the two parties were regional coalitions throughout Colombian history. When comparing sectarian and consociational democratic periods, he stated that during the sectarian period,

The "natural chiefs" imposed the authority and the nominal unifying character at the national level of each party, covering, most of the time, the ideological regional archipelago. . . . [W]ith the National Front great traumas were produced at the national level of bipartyism, at the same time as the regional level, which is the properly clientelist one, was being strengthened and modified. In effect, together with the process of bipartisan depoliticization, the role of national leadership as legitimizer of the party collectivities was being weakened. The "natural chiefs" were losing their aureole of superior and unquestionable beings, which went along with party discipline; this discipline was due principally to the fanaticism of partisan affiliation and had made any kind of permanent organization superfluous.[28]

The second reason to mobilize voters during the National Front period was that the termination of the coalition was always foreseeable. Since the National Front was for a specific time period, the return of competition between the two parties could be projected. As Dix stated, "Both the elites and the followers of the respective parties could foresee a tangible end to the constraints of consociational democracy and a return to the competitive politics with which they were more familiar."[29]

Thus there was a strange hybrid situation during the National Front period. Party leaders wanted to mobilize as many voters as possible, but at times it was for one of several congressional lists of their own party and at other times it was for the presidential candidate of the other party. Competition within the party weakened it, but the anticipated competition with the other party made future unity for strength imperative. Party loyalty was used, not for sectarian reasons, but to support the consociational agreement. And finally, at the same time that all of those enigmas existed for party leaders in attempts to mobilize voters, changes in the society and in politics caused additional dilemmas. Some came from economic change and growth; others from unanticipated effects of the consociational agreement.

The role of the gamonal changed dramatically with the transition from sectarian to consociational democracy. Steffen Schmidt argued that "The most far-reaching, but perhaps unforeseen, consequence of this [National Front] arrangement has been to 'devalue' greatly the importance of the *gamonales* and at the same time to constrict the extent to which exchange resources are available."[30]

This suggests yet another enigma of the National Front: At the time that sectarismo had been renounced by all major party leaders, the growth of the economy and the role of the government gave political leaders, much more than ever before, the ability to distribute jobs and other material rewards. Leal argued that urban life and economic growth weakened the need for traditional patronage, and the ability of the parties to deliver it. "But at the same time . . . the rapid growth of the resources of the State served to feed clientelist relations since the devalorization of the ideology of belonging to the parties was replaced with the necessity of affiliation to them as a condition for aspiring to the benefits of that amplified coverage of the State." The budget of the government increased enormously, as did the influence of the government over the economy. Professional politicians had more abundant and varied resources with which they could pay favors to their adherents.[31] In short, what was created was a new bipartisan, notsectarian, patronage system, with many more resources than the old system had ever had at its disposal. While civil-service bureaucrats to a limited degree replaced the old gamonales,[32] no doubt to an even greater degree the old were replaced with new party gamonales. Although in some cases the old and the new were the same individuals, the logic of the two systems had changed. In sectarian democracy the gamonal had mobilized voters against the other party with the adscriptive ideology and a few material rewards; in the consociational period he mobilized voters against other factions of his party with many material rewards. As Leal stated, "The old political relationships of clientelism were becoming more visible to the extent that interest in public jobs and the economic gifts coming from the growth of the State were becoming generalized."[33] One can only hypothesize counterfactually about what would have happened to Colombian politics if the economic growth, and growth of the state, had come without the consociational agreement.

This then was a new form of patronage-based incentives for mobilizing voters, called "clientelismo" by Leal to contrast it with the earlier "sectarismo." Since both systems were clientelist, albeit in different ways, I shall refer to the newer form as machine oriented, given its similarity to certain phenomena in other countries.

These changes led many, Colombian leaders as well as foreign scholars, to be concerned about a return to sectarianism after the National Front. Some of the former thought about an extension of the consociational agreement or even its extension through a single Colombian party, a nonrevolutionary version of the Mexican Partido Revolucionario Institucional (PRI). In the end, neither of these was done, although the agreement was extended in a different version.

At the same time, the forward-focused aspects entered. As Schmidt wrote during the last presidential term of the National Front,

[T]he Liberal and Conservative politicians have begun the difficult process of putting distance between themselves and the National Front. . . . In an effort to politicize the population once again, to build constituencies, and to strengthen their base of support, a recapturing of patronage and a revival of clientelism seem almost unavoidable. This is due to the fact that the Colombian party system has relied so heavily over a long period of time on patron-client loyalties and their accompanying payoff. . . . The traditional politicians, who are virtually the same in ideology, programs, socioeconomic backgrounds of leadership, and constituencies, seem to have no other recourse, although this will create some difficulty.[34]

Of course patronage politics never disappeared, as Schmidt made clear in his later writings,[35] but they changed from a sectarian form to a more machine-oriented form. And the final sentence of the quote, although true in most of the cases of traditional politicians, was not so in all cases, as will be shown in the next section.

DEMOCRACY SINCE 1974

The most certain (and most general) thing that can be said about Colombian democracy since 1974 is that it is a new system of electoral mobilization, which contains elements of the two previous systems. There are still voters who well remember the sectarian stage and can be motivated to vote for the candidates of their historical parties. There are individuals, actual or potential beneficiaries of the machine-oriented clientelism, who make decisions on very pragmatic grounds. But more people than before, no doubt the more educated who do not fall into the second category, look at the different programmatic appeals. And finally, there are Colombians—perhaps the largest group—who fall into none of the above categories.

In this section I analyze the period since 1974 through two related topics. First, I look at the statements of the presidential candidates in the three elections (1974, 1978, 1982). Second, I offer some conclusions about the dynamics of the current period.

Three "givens" of the Colombian system, as of 1974, must first be presented. They deal with the consociational remnants, the return of electoral competition, and the majority status of the Liberal party.

First, one important characteristic of the Colombian electoral system since 1974 is that it is not completely "democratic" because of the vestiges of the consociational period. More specifically, Article 120 of the Constitution (the "*desmonte*" of the National Front, as it is popularly called) extended bureaucratic paridad for the presidential term of 1974 to 1978 and stated that after this term the president has to offer "adequate and equitable" participation to the largest party other than his own. In short, to a certain degree the bipartisan machine-oriented clientelism is continued.

Second, however, the stakes of electoral contests are now greater than they were in the consociational period. In the absence of paridad for legislative bodies (Congress, departmental assemblies, town councils), there is no guarantee that a party or faction will have as many members elected to it as during the National Front. Thus, there is no security that the members of each faction will be involved in the distribution of the *partidas regionales*, the funds voted by the congress for distribution to the various regions of the country.

In the absence of alternación, there is competition for the presidency. Although any president is required to include members of the other party in the executive branch, the operative words "adequate and equitable" are vague. Although the president's cabinet and other posts might be divided equally between the two parties (as they have been in the Betancur years), it is more likely that the party of the president will receive more of the machine-oriented rewards. The importance of this issue was seen when President Betancur did not consult with Liberal leader Alfonso López Michelsen before naming Liberals to his government. For the latter, Article 120 meant more than Liberals in the government; it meant Liberals chosen by the party leader—Alfonso López.

So there is real competition between the two parties, which, *ceteris paribus*, should lead to less factionalism within the parties. Yet intraparty competition has not disappeared, and indeed both parties (more so in the Liberal party) have intense divisions.

The third characteristic of the Colombian system is that for the Conservative party leaders, one clear "bias" of the system is that the sectarian period concluded with their being the minority party. During the National Front period, their congressional lists in every case received fewer votes than the Liberal lists. This suggests that if the consociational remnants had not been carried to the post–1974 period, at least for the first eight years the Conservative regional chiefs would have lost out in the division of the machine-oriented patronage. Further, any Conservative presidential candidate strongly identified with the sectarian period is likely to encounter difficulties in being elected. The opposite, of course, pertains for Liberal party leaders. An election along the lines of apparent party identification would lead to their winning.

The Three Presidential Elections

In this section I analyze the programmatic statements of the Liberal and Conservative candidates in the presidential elections. Each section begins with a description of the election context.

1974: The Period Begins

The 1974 election represented the first opportunity for Colombian voters to choose their president in a competitive contest since 1946. In that hiatus "modernization" changed elections. Fernán González pointed out that the electoral campaign was characterized by publicity techniques and image manipulation. The old rhetoric, which the people applauded without understanding, was replaced with the bombardment of media spots.[36] These techniques were used to create both a negative image of the opposing candidate and a positive one for the favored one. Gómez insinuated a connection between López and Allende, while the Liberals suggested that voting against Gómez was to save the country from fascism.[37]

The 1974 presidential and congressional elections were on the same date; hence the latter were not "primary" elections for the presidential candidate, as were the elections of 1978 and 1982. Each party presented a candidate with some connection with the sectarian period. The father of each had been president during that period, and each had participated himself, although more so in the case of Alvaro Gómez, in a *delfín*-type role. A third major candidate, María Eugenia Rojas de Moreno Díaz, completed the triad of progeny of former heads of state. As the daughter of dictator Rojas Pinilla, she was identified with the breakdown of the sectarian period.

Despite the reliance on the image making of publicity techniques, some programmatic differences appeared between López and Gómez. The three clearest differences, albeit related and slight at times, were concerned with economic models, the role of the government, and agrarian reform.

Alvaro Gómez presented a *desarrollista* (developmentalist) platform. He favored growth of the economy (as all did), but in addition it was to be growth without redistribution. He opined that "to aspire to reforms is a mediocre attitude" that would limit creative capability. His goal, thus, was greater production.[38]

In the case of agrarian reform, Gómez argued that *campesinos* (peasants) were better served by agrarian policies that permitted farmers to earn more, even though they might not have land. He said that "possessing [land] many times signifies a form of dying of hunger on one's own land."[39] Production of food, to the benefit of the producer, should be encouraged. The Gómez proposal was "against the demogogic policy, class conflict, and Byzantine discussions about ownership of the land" that caused lower production.[40]

Therefore, for Gómez the role of the government was to be deemphasized. Rather than the government, which was "a bad investor, a bad partner, a bad patron, and a bad payer," private industry was to be the basic unit of the Colombian economic system. It was the private sector "whose priority goal . . . should be to serve the community better and to contribute to the social promotion of the worker." The government had two basic functions: to encourage development and to administer it.[41]

Nevertheless, Gómez at times tied his economic platform to other themes. At one point he argued that he would destroy the economic dependency that capitalism had imposed on the country, as well as the "mental dependency" that leftist movements wanted to implant.[42]

Winning candidate Alfonso López, on the other hand, placed emphasis on income and salary policies as a way to redistribute wealth more equitably. He criticized Gómez's desarrollista policies for two reasons. First, such policies would lead to a greater concentration of income. Second, they would favor one part of the society—the business sector—to the detriment of others. Rather, López pushed for a quasicorporative "coordinated economy" (*economía concertada*), which, according to him, "tends to substitute the Marxist concept of the State with a conciliation of interests . . . that, taking as its base the fruits of expansion, proposes to socialize the earnings of the collectivity in what we could call a new social contract."[43]

This *concertación* presupposed a strong government. López proposed a strong government that "did not give in to the pressures of minorities." He made it clear that he meant the press, economic associations, and labor groups. None would be stronger than the state.[44] This did not mean that López was an enemy of the business class. Indeed, he was not against any sector, group, or region.

He was in favor of equilibrium,[45] which would come through the government's role in concertación: listening to all sectors of opinion before making decisions, but then making decisions independently. The government would not be just a referee of interest-group conflict.

In response to the agrarian question, candidate López proposed that the latest technological advances should be considered in order to better the situation of the campesinos. He believed that agrarian reform by redistributing land was an "anachronism" and stated that "agroindustrial exploitations demand empresarial capacity, abundant credit, technical knowledge and they cannot be exploited on a small scale; it would be necessary to conceive the forms of organization and ownership that may permit a greater income for the *campesinos* with a modern business criterion . . . but redistributing property without that previous organization is simply a clumsiness."[46] Thus, it is obvious that candidate López, who wanted to "close the gaps" between rich and poor and who criticized desarrollista Gómez, had an agrarian policy that was quite similar to that of his adversary.

López brought a slight return to the sectarian past when he suggested that all religions should enjoy the same property-tax exemptions as the Roman Catholic Church did.[47] Yet the Liberal candidate made it clear that there was to be no return to the sectarian period. He pledged that the Liberal party would be "generous and moderate" with the Conservatives. He stated that "We understand that we are not engaged in a war to the death, but that we will have to govern with the Conservatives." He also said that the election was a civic contest, "a transitory rivalry that can never degenerate into blood-letting."[48]

1978: The Second Liberal Victory

Two structural characteristics were notably different in the 1978 election. First, since economic problems, especially inflation, occurred during the López years, some Liberals found themselves in the position of having to criticize one of their own party, which they did reluctantly. Other Liberals, not so well connected to the López faction of the party, were not reluctant; nor were the Conservatives. The second difference was that congressional elections were scheduled two months before the presidential ones. This allowed various presidential candidates to enter into a kind of "primary," and in this case the Liberal "*precandidatos*" agreed that the "*candidato*" would be he whose congressional lists received the greatest number of votes.

In this context there were four Liberal precandidates, three of whom I will analyze (Hernando Agudelo Villa, Carlos Lleras Restrepo, and the winning candidate, Julio César Turbay Ayala). There was more unity in the Conservative party; hence, I shall analyze only the statements of Belisario Betancur.

The candidacy of Agudelo Villa represented the radical reformist wing of the Liberal party. As he stated about his Frente Liberal, "The Liberal Front will consecrate its efforts to secure that Liberalism . . . assume the responsibility of the government's impelling and executing the reforms that the country demands, . . . oriented to transform society effectively and to correct the immense inequalities that have distorted national life.''[49] Agudelo called for reforms in agrarian, urban, economic, financial, labor, and administrative fields, with the goal of addressing economic concentration.[50]

Agudelo made it clear that he thought that an agrarian reform was needed immediately. He concluded that the rural picture was dramatic, because the peasant population was in worse condition than in previous generations due to the inflation that the country had suffered. Agrarian reform was to be a fundamental policy of development, in order to obtain a better distribution of income and political power and to improve the lives of the peasants. Land redistribution was the only way to reach those goals.[51] In order to carry out this agrarian reform, campesinos needed to be better organized, as did industrial workers and marginal people.[52]

The Agudelo campaign called itself a renovating movement for the Liberal party. Agudelo believed that the party should consider the consociational coalitions cancelled and should struggle for the return of full democracy through modifying Article 120 of the Constitution.[53] Further, the clientelist system should be fought so that the Liberal party could become an ''imminently popular'' organization through the incorporation of unions, cooperatives, artisans, peasants and small-business people.[54]

Although Agudelo agreed with Lleras in the fight against the clientelistic groups, he went further in calling for new leadership. At one point Agudelo stated that the fundamental theme of the election seemed to be the length of time the various candidates had been in public office. This, he continued, showed that Colombia was suffering from ''acute arthritis,'' since ''the same personages have occupied the political scene for more than 30 years.''[55]

The Carlos Lleras campaign was based on his opposition to the López–Turbay *clientela* and on his personal experience. Regarding the former, Lleras talked about the formal character of Colombian democracy, based on a system of captive votes and a gamonal-like structure at all levels, in which personal connections, mutual aid, favors, and services constituted ''the essence of political activity.''[56] He hence stated that ''I believe that the Liberal party is condemned to dissolution if it does not change its political customs radically.'' He proposed for the party— given the high electoral abstention, growing number of people who identified with neither party, and clientelistic politics benefiting only a few—a ''great jolt to liberate itself from that decadence. . . . The country needs a political regeneration.'' If an efficacious democracy was wanted, the Liberals would have to be a well organized party that reflected the opinions of the people.[57]

As far as the problems of the country were concerned, Lleras was less specific than the other candidates. He stated that after a long political life during which he had written over twenty books and numerous laws and decrees, ''I already feel inclined to believe that Colombians know sufficiently my thought.''[58] On this basis Lleras commented on the problem of inflation by stating, ''The important thing is not to say the words, but to know how to do things.''[59]

Lleras did, however, make certain pointed comments. First, he criticized the

growth of financial groups who were controlling more and more of the economy.[60]
Second, as far as agrarian reform was concerned, neither state ownership nor
workers cooperatives were feasible, the former because of the technical nature
of agriculture and the latter because of the state of peasant culture.[61]

But it should be clear what the thrust of the Lleras candidacy was. Clearly
not a desarrollista, the former president stated:

> I interpret the function of government to be the task of forging a modern society in
> Colombia and a modern society characterized by quality of life, by education of people,
> by a redistribution of income that might not establish tremendous differences between
> some that lack everything and others that have an excess of riches. This type of modern
> society is that which the Liberal party has to form and that for which I have always been
> working.[62]

One key thing was different for Julio César Turbay Ayala as a Liberal candidate: He was the "favorite," having the support of the major regional clientelistic groups of the Liberal party. Nor was he a former elected president
(although he had held that position in an "acting" capacity), in a country with
a certain bias against "reelection" even after a term or more of hiatus. Nonetheless, he made many programmatic statements, although at times apparently
more in competition with the Alvaro Gómez of 1974 than the Belisario Betancur
of 1978.

Turbay first tried to differentiate himself from the other Liberal candidates.
This he did by stating that he had been accepted by the party's popular sectors
and by its real leaders throughout the country. Turbay presented his candidacy
as that of an emerging Colombia, including upwardly mobile individuals and
others who found social change incompatible with presidential reelection, as
opposed to the artificial Lleras candidacy, based on exministers, exgovernors,
diplomats, and contractors who owed Lleras favors. Turbay was "the flag-carrier
of a movement of noncomformity, without the dynastic tendencies that the titular
leaders of aberrant privileges demonstrate."[63] It was Turbay himself who represented a change and "the Colombia without coats of arms, without parchments,
without even talking about fathers of the country."[64]

For Turbay competition with the Conservatives was a simple matter: The
Liberals were the majority party, and any of its candidates would win. He would
beat Belisario Betancur, because he was supported by the majority party, not
because he was a better candidate.[65]

Nevertheless, Turbay stated that there were ideological reasons for favoring
him. Although admitting that the National Front had attenuated ideological differences between the parties, he still saw the differences. The Conservative party,
at least in 1974, believed in "developmentalism"—that growth by itself produces
well-being. Liberals considered social justice as the priority element of any plan.
"For Liberalism the social cannot be considered as a simple subproduct of
economic growth; rather it has a higher position in the hierarchy than the latter."[66]

His policy hence was twofold: increase of production and "the diminution of the abyss of the conditions of life between the rich and the poor." Turbay was clear: "I mean by this that my government program is limited to a simple continuation of the current one."[67] He considered employment policy to be fundamental.[68] Yet the government was to be a direct employer not through a large bureaucracy, but through public works projects, especially those that would prevent urban migration.[69]

As far as the problem of inflation was concerned, Turbay urged patience and suggested that increased supply was the solution. At one point he stated, "In developing countries . . . productive capacity is inelastic and does not respond adequately to demand." He urged patience in waiting for market forces. The increase of capital-goods imports would raise the production levels and hence increase supply of goods and services, thereby lessening inflation. Imports of consumer goods would contribute to the resolution of shortages. As imports grew, the international reserves would go down and the growth of the money supply would diminish.[70]

Turbay was against land redistribution, which he said had been a mistake. As he stated, "The cordial relationships between small landowner, worker, owner, and agrarian businesspeople were replaced with a real class confict that still has not been completely extinguished." During land reform, agricultural empresarios and livestock raisers were considered an "authentic social danger." More recently, this situation had begun changing, and as a result, agricultural production was increasing.[71] For workers, land itself was not as important as good salaries. However, other services were also needed by the campesinos.[72]

The Turbay plan, then, had no ideas of structural change in either the countryside or in industry or financial sectors. Further, it had no special emphasis in the industrial, agricultural, financial, or export sector. As Ernesto Parra Escobar concluded, it was "an attempt to offer attractive perspectives to all, in such a way that the hypothesis can be formulated that the Turbay government will not base itself on a special sector of the bourgeoisie, but will seek the support of the entire Colombian capitalist class."[73]

The starting point of the electoral campaign of Belisario Betancur was that the parties no longer had the meaning that they had once had. Therefore, he proposed a Movimiento Nacional. He was "convinced that national problems should be given replies which are also national" and that many Colombians who were abstaining were only waiting for a "different, sincere voice."[74]

This did not mean that the Conservative party had disappeared; rather it was "the axis and impulse" of the movement, against a Liberal party that was led by "those who seek power in order to camp in it like an occupying army in its own territory, with an occupying class and an impoverished community."[75] Further, "The country knows and feels that the Liberal proposal has failed." The only path remaining was the one Betancur had incessantly proposed: to form a great national movement, based in the Conservative party, for the disenchanted, the skeptics, and the uncommitted. This movement would put formulas into effect to get Colombia out of its economic, social, and moral labyrinth.[76] The clear call of the minority Conservative candidate was to the people who did not vote and "to that million of voting Colombians, who are independent, who think before making a decision."[77]

To those voters, Betancur stated that the problem that bothered him most about poverty was "its origin in an unjust distribution of income." The Christian origin of "our political creed and of our social and economic thought imposes on us the duty of declaring emphatically our dissatisfaction with the current models of distribution of income, of wealth, and of the opportunities for well-being."[78] Rather than a desarrollista model such as that of Gómez four years previously, the Movimiento Nacional favored a "contratación de desarrollo" (contracting of development), a model of conditional production in which the state, using its fiscal and monetary powers, "negotiates" a series of agreements with the private sector, both as a whole and in its various parts. In this manner, the goals of the state and of the private sector, in such matters as employment, income distribution, price stability, geographic decentralization, and production of exports, come to coincide.[79] Betancur saw this as a "new style" of politics, which would bring new people into the policy-making process, lead to more effective policies,[80] and put the economy at the service of the people.[81]

This "contracting of development" was the solution to inflation. Using agreements with the different sectors of society would mean that all combined "would not exceed 100 percent of the national income." Any intent to pass that limit would be illusory, because the entire society would pay through inflation. This was the way to avoid an inflation of intolerable levels and to agree to an inflation "of reasonable dimensions."[82] Such a consultation process was also suggested for agrarian policy, about which Betancur was vague: "Whatever the decision that might be taken in agricultural policy, it should be centered on preferential attention on the traditional sector."[83]

1982: The Movimiento Nacional Wins

The 1982 election was similar in many ways to the 1978 one. Once again Belisario Betancur was chosen by the Conservative party convention to be the candidate of a National Movement. The Liberal party was split, this time between former President Alfonso López Michelsen and Luis Carlos Galán, who headed a movement called Nuevo Liberalismo. While the congressional and presidential elections were once again separated by several months, this time the two principal Liberal candidates reached no agreement that the loser of the "primary" would drop out of the presidential race. Thus, Betancur defeated the divided liberals.

As in the previous election, the bad state of the Colombian economy played a key role in the 1982 election. Inflation had increased during the Turbay years. The country was entering its worst recession in fifty years. These issues created an opportunity for candidates not connected to the president but were embarrassing to those who were.

In essence, Betancur's campaign in 1982 was very similar to his 1978 one.

He said, placing the initiation of this movement even earlier, "[I am] carrying out the same commitment that I have presented since 1969, attaching my political survival to the national flag, as a representative of the National Movement, with the conviction that the problems of my people are neither Conservative nor Liberal."[84] His general theme was that things were not going well for Colombians. "Let us say it once and for all: Colombian society is destabilized. . . . There are two economies, the official and the underground one; there are two societies, the one that revolves around the State and the other that does not count on that State for anything; there are various cultures and among them the one that counts for the least is the official culture."[85]

In this context, according to Betancur, the worst thing that could happen would be "that someone arrive to the presidency who is compromised with the current system of things" and who would "continue the clientelistic system of governing and the same economic policy of inflation with recession."[86] Rather, it was time for a change. "[W]hat I offer the country is to maintain myself irreparably at the head of a campaign of purification. . . . I understand that to obtain that moral tone it is necessary to destroy the existing political chieftainships. I can do it because I have no connections to them, because I owe them nothing."[87]

Although Betancur's statements on economic themes were quite similar to the ones he made during the previous campaign, he was perhaps a bit more specific in 1982 than he had been in 1978. He proposed two strategies to obtain more economic growth and employment: "the diminution of uncertainty through contracting for development and the elimination of the fiscal deficit, cause of inflation, high interest rates, and the stagnation of the private productive sector."[88] Within that context he made numerous specific proposals about such matters as houses for the poor with no down payment, university education by correspondence, foreign trade, treatment of foreign multinational corporations, and economic growth. Yet he said little about agrarian reform.

The key objective of Nuevo Liberalismo was the reorganization of the Liberal party. As Galán wrote, in terms similar to those of Agudelo's four years before, one objective

is the reorganization of Liberalism to give a direction to this gigantic popular force that today is found . . . in the hands of interests hostile to economic and social change and enemies of the participation of the people in the control of the State. During a century and a half Liberalism has been the primary creative energy in our society and in each stage of national history there exists a fact generated by the Liberal spirit that resulted decisive for Colombian progress.[89]

New Liberalism had a very detailed program made up of twelve major points: (1) the need to transform the national Congress radically; (2) the regulation and disclosure of financial sources of candidates; (3) the replacement of the political oligarchy that dominated the Congress; (4) the intervention of the state in the growth of large cities; (5) defense of human rights; (6) control of monopolies and oligopolies; (7) the revision of contracts in petroleum, coal, uranium, and other natural resources; (8) the reorganization of the state so that it could defend national sovereignty; (9) cultural identity; (10) the defense of the rights of the indigenous populations; (11) television reforms; and (12) support of the spirit of progressive unionism.[90] This program, according to Galán, could be summarized in four major points: "First, defense of national sovereignty; second, conquest and strengthening of the cultural identity of Colombians; third, struggle against the existing privileges in our society, and fourth, the design of a new strategy to achieve economic growth and social transformation."[91]

Galán, like Betancur, spent much time describing the demographic changes of Colombian society. He placed special emphasis on the new generation, of which he was a member, and which had divided between "help for radical options of guerrilla warfare [and] indifference and skepticism toward all that might have a relationship with the origin, use, and responsibilities of political power."[92]

During the campaign, Galán spelled out a radical reformist program, similar to Agudelo's four years before, but with even greater specificity. This was shown in the case of agrarian reform, about which Galán pointed out that "Latifundia, in certain zones, continue being predominant and even though hundreds of thousands of *campesinos* with lands have migrated to urban slums, the absolute population in our rural zones has grown without any program of land distribution that might mean anything other than the titling of small plots or vacant lands. The Salvadoran experience should lead to certain reflections."[93] Hence, agrarian reform, although placed aside by most presidential candidates, was still a goal for Nuevo Liberalismo.

The official Liberal candidacy was once again that of Alfonso López Michelsen. He characterized himself as a leftist, proposing, for example, that the party join the Socialist International. As he stated in one political rally,

It is very clear: either the party becomes conservative or it becomes socialist. If you want it to become conservative you only have to vote for us to remain being an appendix of the Conservative party under the National Front. If you want it to socialize you only have to vote for those of us who align ourselves to social democracy and who put into practice leftist programs. You have the decision and I am certain that you will decide to vote for the official lists of the Liberal party in the month of May.[94]

Candidate López made various programmatic statements, three of which suggested a return to aspects of the sectarian period. At one point he promised the revision of the concordat with the Roman Catholic Church, with the idea that Colombia could get the church to admit that civil marriage could be ended through divorce. This led to opposition to his candidacy from clerical groups. He also suggested that Article 120 of the Constitution be changed so that Colombia would have a true democracy, stating, "The National Front was prolonged in the last two administrations without a clear government or opposition."[95] On yet a third occasion López suggested that "Peace is Liberal," perhaps the clearest suggestion of the sectarian period.[96]

He also proposed the "federalization" of the country, which was not "decentralization that is pretended through delegation, but rather redistributing incomes and resources and giving power to the officials at all levels." This was not a policy borrowed from the Conservatives, but a Liberal tradition and would be carried out over the first two years of his government.[97]

López also returned to some of the promises that he had made eight years previously. For example, in Antioquia he reminded listeners of what he had promised before: to make Colombia the Japan of South America. That would mean that the departamento would export more manufactured products. At other times he ridiculed the Betancur housing and education proposals, stating, "I offer the country more realistic things."[98]

Clearly, López believed the Liberal party was still the majority one. He finished his presidential campaign with the following statement: "I invite all Colombians, but especially my fellow Liberal party members, that together we might participate in an act of faith in Colombia."[99] The next week López learned that such a partisan appeal would not be successful in 1982.

DYNAMICS OF THE PERIOD

As the preceding analysis shows, since 1974 Colombian politics have approximated "democracy" more than ever before. The political party leaders, when devising their electoral strategies, can use tactics proven over the previous years. However, tactics that worked in the past may not be as effective in the changing political context. To a degree, the "rational" Liberal leader and the "rational" Conservative leader face the same systemic considerations. Yet the system has certain "biases," which have led to differences between the two party leaderships.

Sectarian Tactics

The least used of the three kinds of mobilization tactics were found to be the old "sectarian" ones. This is not surprising since all party leaders have been committed to the idea that sectarian tactics no longer work. However, mainstream Liberal candidates are still likely to call for party loyalty, albeit without hatred and violence. This is a logical tactic for them since, apparently, the Liberal party is a majority one. Intelligent Conservative leaders, on the other hand, have demonstrated that they are better advised to play down their party and pitch their campaigns to something more "national."

Sectarian tactics, hence, seem to be things of the past. They will become even more obsolete with the passing of the years. The other two kinds of tactics—machine oriented and programmatic—are replacing sectarian ones.

Machine-Oriented Rewards

Colombian parties still exhibit extreme factionalism, in great part because they have maintained their regional bases. However, with the continuing growth of the state, the power of the president has changed. This change can be seen most clearly in the cases of the two Liberal presidents of the period, Alfonso López Michelsen (from 1974 to 1978) and Julio César Turbay Ayala (from 1978 to 1982).

López was not a typical finished product of the Liberal party machinery; indeed, he was for a time, during the National Front, in opposition to much of that machinery through his Revolutionary Liberal Movement (MRL), which was against the consociational agreement. However, he later reentered the official Liberal fold, becoming foreign minister during the presidency of Carlos Lleras Restrepo (from 1966 to 1970). It could be argued, nevertheless, that his election in 1974 was that of a "natural chief" (as in the sectarian period), albeit with the assistance of regional leaders of his party.[100]

Yet, because of the logic of nonsectarian, machine-based democracy, this "natural chief" status had new implications. Leal suggested that López cultivated regional clientelism with political gifts. In so doing, he effectively projected provincial clientelism at the national level.[101]

The power of this new machine-oriented clientelist system was shown in the presidential elections of 1978. Although Carlos Lleras carried Bogotá, Turbay won in every departamento. In this election, and in his subsequent presidency, Turbay was the patronage politician par excellence. Leal called him the "greatest triumph of the clientelist system," since he had been able to climb, slowly but surely, all of the steps from the bottom to the top of the political labyrinth by utilizing all of the resources of clientele relationships.[102]

The Liberal party demonstrated similar themes in 1982. Regional *jefes* (chiefs) exerted their influence, first vetoing the candidacy of Virgilio Barco[103] and second falling behind the López candidacy, which was something of a last-minute surprise, and the congressional lists allied with López. Yet they were either unable or unwilling to deliver votes for the presidential candidate López in the number that they had for the lists.

Further, one part of the Liberal party, led by Galán, rejected the clientelistic system of which López formed a part.[104] Galán was thus unwilling to drop out of the presidential race. What the 1982 election, as well as the previous one of the period, shows is that it is no longer certain (1) that the Liberal president will control regional leaders, the opposite being equally likely; and (2) that all Liberal politicians, whether at the national or regional level, will fall behind the party's candidate.

The characteristics of this change were well suggested by Steffen Schmidt when he argued the following:

Clientelism evolves from a series of *socioeconomic exchanges* that create binding ties between client and patron. So long as these exchanges continue, such ties are not easily broken, and enduring political loyalties are consequently formed. On the other hand, precisely because the basic ties are *socioeconomic rather than political*, gamonalismo affords a framework for local politics in which adjustment to changing national political patterns can be made. Motivated by economic need rather than political passion, the clientelist link depends on the continued supply of *material rewards*, however minimal. If ensuring this supply requires shifting with one's gamonal from faction to faction, or even from party to party, the shift will be made. If the gamonal himself will not or cannot shift with prevailing national ties, he may well find his clientele shifting without him, follow *a new gamonal* linked to a *more powerful faction or party*.[105]

The emphasized words suggest the difference of the clientelistic system of the sectarian period from those of the present. In the former, it was inconceivable that dependent campesinos, for example, would attach themselves to a gamonal of the hated party. The consociational period, however, led to a new machine-oriented system in which such changes are possible.

Although Schmidt stresses the level of the gamonal in his analysis, clearly the same kind of arguments could be made about regional or even national caudillos. Politicians of both parties have greater abilities than in the past to deliver with machine-oriented rewards. They also have greater demands for material rewards, not only because sectarismo is no longer enough, but also because there are increasing numbers of poor and marginal Colombians living without the ''protection'' of a traditional *patron*. The gamonal-type machine-oriented payoff is expected in large cities, as well as in isolated rural situations. This is demonstrated by the following words, from a Liberal senator, a follower of Lleras Restrepo in 1978 and Galán in 1982, reporting on his activities in the 1978 election:

One day I was campaigning in the south of Bogotá [the poorer section of the city]. After my speech, in which I talked about what needed to be done in Colombia, an old lady came up and said, ''Look, *doctor*, Senator Echeverri comes here with a few groceries [*un mercadito*] for us. What do you have?'' After I explained that I didn't have any groceries, the old lady went away saying, ''You're not good for anything.'' ... If you look at the 1978 [congressional] results, you will see that Turbay won in the southern part of Bogotá and Lleras from Calle 40 to the North. Politics in the south is still based on what someone can give in an immediate sense.[106]

Clearly, for some *bogotanos* and other city dwellers near starvation, a few groceries are more effective than programmatic promises.

Programmatic Appeals

Another way to mobilize voters is through programmatic appeals. In this the Colombian leaders tread new ground, since such tactics were superfluous during fp both the sectarian and the consociational periods. The analysis of the three campaigns has shown that candidates have disagreed on programs.

One might ask why this is the case, since it appears that there is a lack of strong ideological differences along political party lines. Although there are no mass-level surveys of political attitudes, most Colombian politicians and scholars agree that policy positions do not vary by party affiliation at that level, with the notable exception of those who keep attitudes from the sectarian period. These people no doubt are decreasing in number with the passing of the years. Leal argued, for example, that the generational effects of urbanization began to be seen slowly. The second generation of urban dwellers no longer had the affective, secular ties to the parties nor the "provincial mentality" that was needed for clientelism. The situation was made more complex when, especially in Bogotá, the middle class became larger.[107]

However, party leaders not only have to attract popular support in elections; they also need support from other leaders in their parties to obtain the party's nomination. Of course, the machine-related tactics are one way to do so, but programmatic appeals might be another.

Evidence for the importance of such appeals could be the "partisan obsession" of daily political life. Yet most conclude, as John Peeler, that high-level elite accommodation is hidden by apparent political conflict. Colombian mass media are filled with reports of partisan battles and details of disputes over public policy details. The objects of conflict are loudly proclaimed, but they are less important than the areas of agreement among the antagonists.[108]

When observing the top-level leaders, many Colombians agree with Peeler that there are little or no differences between the two parties. Gerardo Molina, besides reporting that President López Pumarejo thought in 1942 that no differences remained, argued, "In this incessant mixture of ideas and of interests, it is not surprising that there might have been a cross-bartering of doctrinaire positions, in virtue of which men connected to Conservativism, like Alfredo Vásquez Carrizosa and Belisario Betancur, are more advanced in social and political matters than liberals of high rank like Alberto Lleras Camargo and Juan Lozano y Lozano."[109] Indeed, in early 1981, in a "precandidate" speech at the Universidad de los Andes, Belisario Betancur said, "The only difference [between the two parties] is that the color of the Conservative party is blue, the color of the Virgin Mary. The Liberal color is red, color of the Sacred Heart of Jesus."[110]

Systematic interview data at the elite level show slight differences between the two party elites. Ogliastri, in a study of regional elites, found some differences between Liberal and Conservative ideologies, especially in religious, economic, and class ideology. However, he concluded that "Liberals and Conservatives have in common 90 percent of the elements, but they differ in some important things."[111] This is similar to the conclusions reached in elite studies during the National Front of the national Congress[112] and of party elites in Bogotá.[113]

What then should one conclude about programmatic appeals? There certainly is no evidence that a party leader can become president on programmatic appeal alone, as the Agudelo and Galán cases demonstrate. Yet there do seem to be growing numbers of middle-income individuals who look to program. Then there are the majority of Colombians who choose not to vote. Perhaps someone with the right program could mobilize them, it is thought. Thus, the logic is that everyone must make an attempt. Further, since this is a "cheap" mobilization tactic, why would any aspirant not use it?

The 1986 election substantiated, but also modified, the generalizations about the dynamics of Colombian democracy offered here. Luis Carlos Galán found that programmatic appeals were far from sufficient. His lists did so poorly in the congressional elections that he dropped out of the presidential one. The bias of the system in the favor of a Liberal candidate was shown, especially against the Conservative Alvaro Gómez, who was unsuccessful in portraying himself as representing a national movement. But of greatest interest, there was a "new star" of politics in Bogotá, the Liberal Senator Ernesto Samper Pizano, who combined sectarian-like appeals to party tradition for those over forty, on the one hand, with programmatic, class-based appeals to poor people under that age, on the other hand. Whether or not that double strategy could be used at the national level, however, is far from clear.

Yet conclusions about "ideology" or "program" face a problem: On what basis does one conclude whether they are existent and/or important? In the end, an evaluation of policy statements depends on with what they are being compared. There is no Colombian "Pinochet" nor "Castro" shown in the analysis. Hence, an observer from either the extreme left or right might conclude that Colombian politics is not very ideological. The same conclusion, however, might not be reached by people of different, less extreme ideological predispositions. But the important conclusion of this section has been that program since 1974 has been a more important electoral mobilization technique than in previous periods of Colombian history.

CONCLUSION

In this chapter I have argued that Colombian electoral politics has gone through three stages, the last of which is a combination of three electoral mobilization tactics: sectarismo, clientelismo, and programmatic appeal. The first is no longer acceptable to party leaders, and only occasionally are slight uses made of it. The second is anathema to many leaders, although the cynic might argue that it is only the ones who lack the ability to use clientelismo who are so vocal in criticizing it. The third is acceptable to all as the essence of democracy, yet there are doubts about its efficacy and its importance.

The first three elections of the post-National Front period demonstrate that a return to the sectarian past is unlikely. They do not, however, make it clear what the future of Colombian electoral democracy is likely to be. Opinions vary from imminent change of the bipartisan system to a continuing "muddling through" with "incremental changes."

One prediction is that the Colombian system will be an unextreme one. As Hernando Gómez Buendía concluded, after comparing Colombian experience in various "Models of National Construction" with other Latin American countries:

[T]he Colombian version of each one of the Models of National Construction . . . is conditioned by certain structural characteristics of the country, particularly by its "middle" level of economic and social development; by the relative balance between city and countryside, between agrarian and industrial elites; by the comparative weakness of the middle classes; by the nonexplosive and preclass condition of social conflicts; by the bipartisanship which is multiclass and disposed to coalition; by the absence of acute economic, military, or international crises in the immediate past; and by the professional and apolitical character of its armed forces. Perhaps the principal result of this series of characteristics is to give a decidedly "centrist" framework to the Colombian political game, in a manner that the "extreme" options are relatively less so than in other countries of the region.[114]

Others see this centrism as a result of agreements of the dominant classes.[115] As Peeler sees it, "The ideological and policy centrism of the party systems is a consequence of elite accommodation, which presses the competing parties to avoid positions that would be threatening to established interests. In addition, centrism is a direct, strategic response of the parties to the need to build an electoral majority in the context of the winner-take-all character of a strongly presidential system."[116]

Yet there is disagreement about the implications of this centrism. In 1977 Jaime Uribe argued: "The parties of the Right, the Liberal and Conservative . . . will keep losing electoral support each time as long as urbanization and industrialization continue. . . . The new urban class, and the industrial and agrarian proletariat are progressively escaping the domination of the hegemonic class while the traditional parties are only able to conserve . . . the rural clientele and the bureaucratic clientele."[117] Leal agreed: "The old 'political class' finds itself in a trap constructed through its tremendous pragmatism and conservatism: it accepts nothing new out of fear of losing the traditional exercise of its profession, but this rejection can accelerate the fall of its possibilities of future renovation."[118]

Several foreign scholars, however, see vitality in the centrist bipartisan system. After studying the 1974 election, Peeler concluded: "I wish, on the contrary, to suggest that the traditional Colombian party system, though indeed corrupt by widely accepted value standards, is objectively viable and will remain broadly stable in the foreseeable future. Justice is not a precondition of the survival of a political order. The Children of Darkness rule and grow fat in the Earthly City."[119] After the 1978 election J. Mark Ruhl reached similar conclusions, stating that "Colombia's traditional party system is in no danger of collapsing but the 1978 returns do indicate new flexibility in the electorate."[120] No doubt he has seen even more of this after the 1982 election. And Peeler, writing in 1985, concluded:

Thus some of the spirit of power-sharing that characterized the National Front remains, reflecting the continued perception of the elites of the two parties that they are jointly responsible for the political system. Moreover, the public discourse of Colombian politics reveals a continuing awareness, rooted in the experiences of La Violencia and the National Front, that liberal democracy can be maintained only if it is actively tended. . . . Liberal democracy in Colombia is a finely tuned mechanism, assiduously tended by those who operate it, in order to keep it working and to maintain their control of it.[121]

At this point it is difficult to conclude which of the above arguments is more nearly correct. Gerardo Molina saw the difficulties in predicting change: "Will we be present at the final act of bipartyism? We believe so, without that implying that the current parties are going to topple over right away, since in the eighteenth century David Hume saw the phenomenon clearly when he wrote, 'Nothing is more common than to see parties, born when real differences led some to oppose others, continue after the differences had disappeared.' "[122]

I believe that the Hume quote applies to Colombian partisan politics today, yet I am not quixotic enough to predict the imminent demise of two groups with such institutional inertia.

NOTES

1. This chapter makes no pretense of analyzing meanings of democracy beyond its being a system in which leaders are chosen by competitive elections. This is not to belittle the other characteristics needed for a "true" democracy; a discussion of them is simply beyond the scope of the chapter.

2. The best works on the first two periods include John D. Martz, *Colombia: A Contemporary Political Survey* (Chapel Hill: University of North Carolina Press, 1962); Robert H. Dix, *Colombia: The Political Dimensions of Change* (New Haven, Conn.: Yale University Press, 1967); and Orlando Fals Borda, *Subversión y Cambio Social* (Bogotá: Tercer Mundo, 1968). I have summarized the major characteristics in Harvey F. Kline, *Colombia: Portrait of Unity and Diversity* (Boulder, Colo.: Westview Press, 1983).

3. John A. Peeler, *Latin American Democracies: Colombia, Costa Rica, Venezuela* (Chapel Hill: University of North Carolina Press, 1985), p. 24.

4. Francisco Leal Buitrago, *Estado y Política en Colombia* (Bogotá: Siglo Veintiuno, 1984), p. 125.

5. Peeler, *Latin American Democracies*, p. 50.

6. Fals Borda, *Subversión*, pp. 101–2.

7. Orlando Fals Borda, *Peasant Society in the Colombian Andes* (Gainesville: University of Florida Press, 1961), p. 241.

8. Enrique Ogliastri, "Liberales Conservadores versus Conservadores Liberales: Faccionalismos trenzados en la estructura de poder en Colombia," paper presented at the XI International Congress of the Latin American Studies Association, October 1983, p. 9.

9. Martz, *Colombia*, p. 148.

10. Dix, *Colombia: The Political Dimensions*, p. 148.

11. Leal, *Estado y Política*, p. 159.

12. Peeler, *Latin American Democracies*, p. 53.

13. Martz, *Colombia*, p. 12.

14. Fals Borda, *Subversión*, p. 162.

15. Robert H. Dix, "Consociational Democracy: The Case of Colombia," *Comparative Politics* 12 (April 1980):314.

16. Ibid., p. 306.

17. Of the many works on La Violencia, of special note are Germán Guzman Campos, Orlando Fals Borda, and Eduardo Umana Luna, *La Violencia en Colombia*, Vols. 1 and 2, (Bogotá: Ediciones Tercer Mundo, 1962, 1964) and Paul Oquist, *Violence, Conflict, and Politics in Colombia* (New York: Academic Press, 1980).

18. In addition to the works cited in note 2, see R. Albert Berry and Ronald Soligo, "The Distribution of Income in Colombia: An Overview," in *Economic Policy and Income Distribution in Colombia*, eds. R. Albert Berry and Ronald Soligo, (Boulder, Colo.: Westview Press, 1980).

19. Dix, "Consociational Democracy," pp. 303–21, and Jonathan Hartlyn, "Military Governments and the Transition to Civilian Rule: The Colombian Experience of 1957–1958," *Journal of Interamerican Studies and World Affairs* 25 (May 1984): 245–81.

20. Harvey F. Kline, "Selección de Candidatos," in *Estudio del Comportamiento Legislativo en Colombia*, eds. Gary Hoskin, Francisco Leal, Harvey F. Kline, Dora Rothlisberger, and Armando Borrero (Bogotá: Universidad de los Andes, 1975).

21. Dix, "Consociational Democracy," pp. 313–14, emphasis in the original.

22. Leonardo Molina, "Notas sobre el Frente Nacional," *Estrategia económica y financiera* 12 (June 1978):16.

23. Hartlyn, "Military Governments," p. 255,

24. Ibid., p. 273.

25. Dix, "Consociational Democracy," p. 308.

26. Harvey F. Kline, "The Cohesion of Political Parties in the Colombian Congress: A Case Study of the 1968 Session," Ph.D. dissertation (University of Texas, 1970), p. 68.

27. Ibid.

28. Leal, *Estado y Política*, p. 161.

29. Dix, "Consociational Democracy," pp. 316–17.

30. Steffen W. Schmidt, "Bureaucrats as Modernizing Brokers?" *Comparative Politics* 6 (April 1974):435.

31. Leal, *Estado y Política*, p. 160.

32. See Schmidt, "Bureaucrats as Modernizing Brokers?" pp. 425–50, and Steffen W. Schmidt, "Patrons, Brokers, and Clients: Party Linkages in the Colombian System," in *Political Parties & Linkage*, ed. Kay Lawson (New Haven, Conn.: Yale University Press, 1980), pp. 266–88.

33. Leal, *Estado y Política*, p. 147.

34. Schmidt, "Bureaucrats as Modernizing Brokers?" p. 445.

35. Schmidt, "Patrons, Brokers, and Clients."

36. Fernán G. González, *Colombia 1974: I. La Política* (Bogotá: Centro de Investigaciones y Educación Popular, 1975), p. 6.

37. Ibid., p. 160.
38. Ibid., p. 18.
39. Ibid., p. 20.
40. Ibid., p. 21.
41. Ibid., p. 20.
42. Ibid., p. 22.
43. Ibid., pp. 24–25.
44. Ibid., p. 26.
45. Ibid., p. 26.
46. Ibid., pp. 30–31.
47. Ibid., p. 33.
48. Ibid., p. 36.
49. *La Campaña por la Presidencia, 1978–1982: Los Temas en Controversia* (Bogotá: Tercer Mundo, 1978), p. 10.
50. Ibid.
51. Ibid., p. 76.
52. Ibid., p. 59.
53. Ibid., pp. 239 and 183.
54. Ibid., p. 239.
55. Ibid., p. 218.
56. *Elecciones 1978: Legislación, Abanico Político, Resultadose de Febrero* (Bogotá: Centro de Investigaciones y Educación Popular, 1978) p. 66.
57. *La Campaña*, pp. 248–49.
58. Ibid., p. 198.
59. Ibid., p. 52.
60. Ibid., p. 23.
61. Ibid., p. 83.
62. Ibid., p. 22.
63. Ibid., p. 234.
64. Ibid., p. 236.
65. Ibid., p. 256.
66. Ibid., p. 206.
67. Ibid., p. 26.
68. Ernesto Parra Escobar, *Elecciones 1978: Plataformas Econócas* (Bogotá: Centro de Investigaciones y Educación Popular, 1978), p. 51.
69. Ibid., p. 60.
70. *La Campaña*, p. 54.
71. Ibid., p. 91.
72. Ibid., p. 93.
73. Parra Escobar, *Elecciones 1978*, p. 78.
74. *La Campaña*, p. 191
75. Ibid., p. 193.
76. Ibid., p. 194.
77. Ibid., p. 245.
78. Ibid., p. 13.
79. Ibid., p. 16.
80. Ibid., p. 196.
81. Parra, *Elecciones 1978*, p. 11.

82. *La Campaña*, p. 48.
83. Ibid., p. 77.
84. Belisario Betancur, *¡Sí, Se Puede!* (Bogotá: Tercer Mundo, 1982), p. 61.
85. Ibid., p. 8.
86. Ibid., p. 43.
87. Ibid., p. 61–62.
88. Ibid., p. 132.
89. Luis Carlos Galán, "El Nuevo Liberalismo," *El Tiempo*, June 8, 1981, 4D, p. 32.
90. Ibid., 4A.
91. Ibid., p. 32.
92. Ibid., p. 12.
93. Ibid., p. 34.
94. *El Espectador*, Bogotá daily, February 14, 1982, p. 12A.
95. Ibid., February 28, 1982, p. 8A.
96. Leal, *Estado y Política*, p. 165.
97. *El Espectador*, February 28, 1982, p. 8A.
98. *El Tiempo*, April 16, 1982, p. 8A.
99. Ibid.
100. Leal, *Estado y Política*, pp. 161–62.
101. Ibid., p. 161.
102. Ibid., p. 162.
103. Ibid., p. 163.
104. Ibid., p. 164
105. Schmidt, "Patrons, Brokers, and Clients," p. 286, emphasis added.
106. Confidential interview, Liberal senator, Bogotá, May 28, 1981.
107. Leal, *Estado y Política*, p. 163.
108. Peeler, *Latin American Democracies*, pp. 123–24.
109. Molina, "Notas sobre el Frente Nacional," p. 20.
110. Personal notes.
111. Ogliastri, "Liberales Conservadores versus Conservadores Liberales," p. 16.
112. Gary Hoskin, "Dimensiones de Conflicto," in *Estudio del Comportamiento Legislativo*, eds. Hoskin et al., pp. 209–50.
113. Gary Hoskin, "Belief Systems of Colombian Political Party Activists," *Journal of Interamerican Studies and World Affairs* 21 (November 1979):481–504.
114. Hernando Gómez Buendía, "Los modelos del continente y la opción colombiana: reformismos, desarrollismo y Socialismo," *Conyuntura Económica* 7 (December 1977):57.
115. Molina, "Notas sobre el Frente Nacional," and Leal, *Estado y Política*.
116. Peeler, *Latin American Democracies*, p. 123.
117. Jaime Jaramillo Uribe, *La Personalidad Histórica de Colombia y Otros Ensayos* (Bogotá: Instituto Colombiano de Cultura, Subdirección de Comunicaciones Culturales, 1977), pp. 124–25.
118. Leal, *Estado y Política*, p. 170.
119. John A. Peeler, "Colombian Parties and Political Development: A Reassessment," *Journal of Interamerican Studies and World Affairs* 18 (May 1976):223.

120. J. Mark Ruhl, "Party System in Crisis? An Analysis of Colombia's 1978 Elections," *Journal of Interamerican Economic Affairs* 32 (Winter 1978):43.

121. Peeler, *Latin American Democracies*, p. 140.

122. Molina, "Notas sobre el Frente Nacional," p. 20.

3

Colombian Political Parties and Electoral Behavior During the Post-National Front Period

Gary Hoskin

During most of the present century, formal democracy has prevailed in Colombia, and scholars have generated a prolific set of concepts to characterize that political system: (1) a liberal democracy that is restricted, controlled, limited, oligarchical, elitist, pluralist, consociational; (2) an inclusionary authoritarian regime, and (3) a bourgeois democracy resting on a capitalist base.[1] This conceptual maze, resulting from scholarly efforts to understand Colombian politics, has tended to confuse the two basic conceptualizations of democracy: the formal and the substantive.[2] The Colombian model fulfills the requirements of the formal definition with some caveats: a few elections before the National Front that were boycotted by one of the major parties, the military government of General Rojas Pinilla (from 1953 to 1957), the National Front Coalition (from 1958 to 1974), and perhaps electoral fraud (1970). However, since the expiration of the electoral restrictions associated with the National Front in 1974, the only deviation from the formal model, possibly excepting some restrictions on civil liberties, revolves around the status of the opposition party. According to Article 120 of the Constitution, the president shall appoint public officials in such a manner as to give "adequate and equitable" representation to the major party not controlling the presidency. After the termination of the National Front, the sharing of governmental posts between the two traditional parties, Liberal and Conservative, continued during the governments of Presidents Turbay and Betancur, thereby raising some questions about the existence of a true opposition party. But a return to a more competitive party system did occur in 1986 when the Conservative party refused to participate in the Liberal government of President Barco, who had

This chapter is a revised and abbreviated version of a paper presented at the XII International Congress of the Latin American Studies Association Meeting in Albuquerque, New Mexico, April 18–20, 1985.

extended them an invitation as required by the Constitution. Despite these qual-
ifications, mostly past history, classifying the Colombian political system as a
liberal democracy does not violate the integrity of the concept.[3]

Formal democracy in Colombia currently is under siege from virtually every
direction, involving groups that span the social structure from top to bottom, to
the extent that the legitimacy of the system is being questioned seriously. This
is reflected in the attempts to bring various guerrilla groups into the system, the
extensive discontent associated with labor and civic strikes, the unrest within
the military related to the peace initiatives of Presidents Betancur and Barco,
unhappiness with the electoral monopoly of the two traditional parties, the supposedly low rates of electoral participation, the facile resort to a state of siege
to maintain stability, the increasing marginalization of Congress from the policy
process, and the inability—or unwillingness—of policy makers to resolve socioeconomic problems. All of this discontent has been augmented by the worst
economic recession in Colombia since the Great Depression.

Consequently, the severity of the crisis has sparked a national debate in the
country that is oriented toward a restructuring of the political system with the
intention of making it more responsive to citizen demands—a process that has
been labeled "democratic opening." The talks revolve around incorporating the
guerrillas into the system, institutionalizing the political parties, subsidizing
political campaigns, reforming the electoral process, popular election of mayors,
and administrative and judicial reform.[4] Former President Betancur spearheaded
this drive toward opening the system but encountered formidable opposition from
Congress and the military.

Ironically, the national debate in Colombia has reached the point where political reform may well be a necessary condition for system maintenance. However, we should not raise our expectations with respect to the impact of political
reform on the resolution of Colombia's socioeconomic problems, for the Colombian power structure has a long trajectory in terms of preserving its hegemony
and prerogatives. Moreover, I argue in this chapter that Colombian political
structures are not all that inflexible and that resistance to change, although
obviously reflected in the political system, especially in Congress, is embedded
deeply in the country's socioeconomic structures.

This chapter focuses on a pivotal component of the Colombian political system,
namely political party and electoral behavior, with the aim of contributing to
the debate concerning democratic opening. After examining general tendencies
reflected in electoral behavior since 1945 in the next section, the subsequent part
of the chapter analyzes the impact of an increasingly urban electorate, relying
on electoral returns for the lower house of Congress (1974, 1978, 1982). The
fourth section investigates the representativeness of the electoral system, a dimension of the electoral process that impacts on the responsiveness of the political
system to citizen demands. Finally, the last portion offers some generalizations
about Colombian party and electoral behavior.

POLITICAL PARTY AND ELECTORAL BEHAVIOR

The Colombian party system traditionally has been dominated by the two major parties, a generalization that remains as salient for the post-National Front period as during and before it. The two major parties received an average of approximately 97 percent of the total votes cast for the twelve elections shown in Table 3.1. (This percentage includes the National Popular Alliance [ANAPO] vote for 1962 through 1970, when ANAPO utilized both traditional party labels; in 1972 ANAPO became a legal party and did not subsequently use Liberal and Conservative labels.) The two-party proportion of the total vote ranged from a high of 99.9 percent in 1962 to 87.6 percent in 1974. From 1962 through 1974, ANAPO's percentage of the vote averaged 16 percent (ANAPO presented no distinctly ANAPO lists in the 1978 or 1982 legislative elections, although it formed a part of Betancur's National Movement in the 1978 and 1982 presidential elections). Even though displaying a higher degree of intraparty unity than the two traditional parties, as reflected in the number of party lists presented at the polls, the Colombian left received a dismal 2.3 percent of the vote in 1974, 3.9 percent in 1978, 2.6 percent in 1982, and 2 percent in 1986. Although the left is especially weak in rural areas, its strength is somewhat greater in the four major metropolitan areas (5.1 percent in 1974, 6.4 in 1978, and 3.3 in 1982).

Since the 1930s the Liberal party has been the majority party. For the elections shown in Table 3.1, the Liberals received an average of about 55 percent of the vote and the Conservative party 41 percent (once again including ANAPO votes through 1970). The Liberal party obtained an absolute majority of the votes cast in each election. The proportion of the Liberal party's vote ranged between 62.9 percent in 1945 and 51.1 percent in 1970; that of the Conservative party between 48.5 percent in 1964 and 1970, and 32 percent in 1974. (The 1970 percentages, include ANAPO votes cast for either the Liberal or Conservative parties.) The data shown in Table 3.1 clearly indicate that the Liberal party is the majority party, a generalization that also holds for the presidential arena—the combined Liberal vote of López and Galán in 1982 totaled 51.8 percent.

The Colombian electorate is characterized by a very high degree of stability in terms of the percentage of the vote gained by the political parties. The type of election should be held constant, however, for turnouts vary markedly (highest for presidential contests in the post-Frente period, followed by legislative elections, then by off-year departmental and local elections), and considerably more fluctuation in the party vote occurs in presidential elections. As revealed in Table 3.1, the Liberal party received 55.6 percent of the Cámara vote in 1974, 55.1 percent in 1978, 56.3 percent in 1982, and 54.2 percent in 1986; the Conservative party obtained 32 percent in 1974, 39.4 percent in 1978, and 40.3 percent in 1982. The relatively low Conservative vote in 1974 resulted from the attractiveness of the López candidacy (the electoral calendar was unified in 1970 and 1974) and the participation of ANAPO in the campaign. This partisan stability

Table 3.1
National Electoral Returns for the House of Representatives: 1945–1986

	Liberal	Conservative	ANAPO	Total Votes	Participation Rates[a]
1945	551,224(62.9%)	294,237(33.6%)	—	875,856	38.4%
1949	937,600(53.5%)	806,759(46.1%)	—	1,751,804	62.0%
1958	2,132,741(57.7%)	1,556,273(42.1%)	—	3,693,939	68.9%
1960	1,478,403(58.1%)	1,059,370(41.7%)	—	2,542,651	57.8%
1962	1,685,531(54.5%)	1,287,199(41.7%)	115,587(3.7%)	3,090,203	57.9%
1964	1,141,503(50.5%)	802,282(35.5%)	309,678(13.7%)	2,261,190	36.9%
1966	1,529,746(52.1%)	876,423(29.8%)	523,102(17.8%)	2,939,222	44.5%
1968	1,246,332(49.9%)	840,839(33.7%)	401,903(16.1%)	2,496,455	37.3%
1970	1,470,928(37.0%)	1,083,024(27.2%)	1,412,152(35.5%)	3,980,201	51.9%
1974	2,835,245(55.6%)	1,631,926(32.0%)	485,424(9.5%)	5,100,099[b]	57.1%
1978	2,302,230(55.1%)	1,645,496(39.4%)	—	4,180,121[b]	33.4%
1982	3,140,868(56.3%)	2,248,602(40.3%)	—	5,583,219[b]	40.7%
1986	3,746,554(54.2%)	2,558,040(37.0%)	—	6,909,851	42.9%

Sources: The data are taken from Estadísticas Electorales (Bogotá: Registraduría Nacional del Estado Civil, 1975), pp. 373–74; Estadísticas Electorales (Bogotá: Registraduría Nacional del Estado Civil, 1976), p. 93; Angela Gómez de Martínez and Elisabeth Ungar, "Aspectos de la Campaña Presidencial 1974" (Dissertation, Universidad de los Andes, 1974); Estadísticas Electorales: Corporaciones Públicas (Bogotá: Registraduría Nacional del Estado Civil, 1979, 1982); Boletín No. 15 (Bogotá: Registraduría Nacional del Estado Civil, no date). The potential vote (16,126,655) is a Registraduría estimate cited in Consigna (Bogotá: February 7, 1986).

[a] The participation rate represents the total number of voters divided by the number of eligible voters, as estimated by the Registraduría Nacional.

[b] The leftist front, Unión Nacional del Oposición (UNO), received 155,855 votes in the 1974 elections, 3.1 percent of the total vote. The UNO and the Frente Unido del Pueblo (FUP) obtained 178,524 votes, 4.3 percent of the total vote, in the 1978 congressional elections. In 1982, a series of small leftist parties received 2.5 percent of the congressional vote. Although the newly constituted Unión Patriótica (UP) obtained only 2.0 percent of the 1986 congressional vote, a number of electoral alliances, mostly between the Liberal Party and the UP, received 6.4 percent. The Liberal Party vote for both 1982 and 1986 includes those cast for candidates associated with Luis Carlos Galán's Nuevo Liberalismo.

is reflected in terms of the Pearson correlations between the percentage of a party's vote in the first three post-National Front elections for the Cámara, using the twenty-six departmental and provincial electoral districts as the unit of analysis. For the Liberal party the correlations are as follows: .92 between the party percentage of the total vote in 1974 and 1978, .91 between 1978 and 1982, and .81 between 1974 and 1982. The results for the Conservative party are .93 between 1974 and 1978, .91 between 1978 and 1982, and .85 between 1974 and 1982. The correlations are not as pronounced for the left: .92 between 1974 and 1978, .77 between 1978 and 1982, and .66 between 1974 and 1982.

Despite the relatively high rates of partisan stability across elections, this does not mean that changes in party support have not appeared at the departmental level. Taking the Liberal party first, it improved its previous percentage of the vote between 1974 and 1982 by at least 5 percent in the following departments: Atlántico, Cesar, La Guajira, Santander, and San Andrés—all coastal departments except Santander. The Liberal party vote decreased similarly in Cauca, Choco, and the two provinces of Arauca and Caqueta. For the Conservative party, its percentage of the vote increased in Antioquia, Boyaca, Córdoba, Cundinamarca, Meta, Quindio, Risaralda, and Valle; decreases under 5 percent were registered only in La Guajira and San Andrés. Generally speaking, the Conservative party improved its electoral base more than the Liberal party as a consequence of the size of the departments where gains were recorded.

Perhaps the most contentious, as well as significant, dimension of the contemporary Colombian party system revolves around the levels of electoral abstention.[5] As revealed in Table 3.1, the participation rates fluctuate dramatically, from a low of 33.4 percent in 1978 to a high of 68.9 percent in 1958. Caution should be exercised in interpreting participation rates because of the Registraduría Nacional's overestimation of the potential electorate[6] and the fluctuations in turnout associated with the type of election. Assuming constant error in the official estimation of the potential electorate, participation rates can be compared validly across elections listed in Table 3.1, controlling for type of election.

Table 3.2 summarizes the average participation rates for the 1974, 1978, and 1982 Cámara elections according to department and province. The national participation rate for these elections is 47.8 percent, a figure not highly supportive of those arguing that low participation rates reflect a lack of system legitimacy, particularly when considering the overestimation of the potential electorate. Participation rates vary considerably, however, across the departments, with the most urban departments revealing very low rates of participation—Antioquia (35 percent), Cundinamarca (37 percent), Valle (43 percent). The island of San Andrés and Providencia registered the highest participation (70 percent), followed by Córdoba, Sucre, Magdalena (all with 54 percent), Tolima (52 percent), and Nariño (51 percent). The magnitude of urban abstention will become more apparent in the next section of the chapter.

Participation rates affect the political parties differently. Looking at the correlation between participation rate and party percentage of the vote, the higher

Table 3.2
Average Participation Rates for Cámara Elections: 1974, 1978, 1982

Anitoquia	35%	Meta	44%
Atlántico	47	Nariño	51
Bolívar	47	N. Santander	46
Boyacá	48	Quindio	45
Caldas	45	Risaralda	43
Cauca	50	Santander	48
Cesar	47	Sucre	54
Córdoba	54	Tolima	52
Cundinamarca	37	Valle	43
Chocó	49	Arauca	46
Huila	48	Caqueta	43
La Guajira	49	Putumayo	50
Magdalena	54	San Andrés y	70
		Providencia	

Sources: The data are from the Registraduría Nacional. See Table 3.1 for full citation.

the participation, the higher the Liberal percentage of the vote (.15 in 1974, .37 in 1978, .38 in 1982). The opposite tendency prevails for the Conservative party; the higher the participation, the lower the Conservative vote percentage (-.02 in 1974, -.13 in 1978, -.22 in 1982). The left fares considerably better with low participation rates (-.33 in 1974, -.35 in 1978, -.31 in 1982).

Predictions about the Colombian electoral process revolve around the success of the political parties in mobilizing the vote. If the turnout is high, the Liberal party can draw its "majority electoral status," even though that margin is eroding as the Conservative party becomes stronger in urban areas and the number of voters who classify themselves as independents is increasing. When Colombians perceive elections as meaningful—that is, that their vote might make a difference, an attractive candidate is running, or viable policy alternatives are articulated— then they will cast a vote, or at least 50 to 60 percent of them may do so. The 1982 presidential election amply supports this contention.

Are the relatively low turnouts a reflection of the limitations placed on inter-party competition during the National Front? Do the turnouts imply an underlying apathy and/or alienation of the electorate from the political system and the traditional parties? Or does the participation rate depend primarily on contextual factors specific to each election? A satisfactory explanation of electoral abstention in Colombia necessarily is complex and undoubtedly includes variables related to each of the foregoing questions.[7]

THE URBAN VOTE

Colombian society is becoming increasingly urban, with 73.7 percent of its population residing in urban areas in 1982. This trend is not likely to be halted in the near future as the bulk of Colombia's population growth is associated with urban growth.[8] Thus electoral contests are determined more and more by the urban vote. In the 1982 electoral year Bogotá contained 15.2 percent of the potential vote of the country, and the four major metropolitan areas (Bogotá, Medellín, Cali, and Baranquilla) represented 27.5 percent of the nation's electorate. In this chapter the urban vote will be operationalized by examining voting patterns in the twenty-two departmental capitals. This is not a totally satisfactory method of analyzing the urban electorate, for the capitals represent only 56.8 percent of the urban residents (using the 73.7 percent estimate of the Inter-American Developmental Bank). In 1982 Bogotá registered 36.3 percent of the capital-city vote, while the four metropolitan areas contained 65.6 percent.

The Liberal party traditionally has dominated the urban vote. During the National Front period (from 1958 to 1974), the Liberal vote derived from the capitals represented 19.5 percent of the total national vote[9]; for the three post-National Front elections for the Cámara, the figure rises marginally to 20.3 percent (see Table 3.3, column 1). The latter percentage is not indicative of a Liberal trend because it includes the 1974 election, which represented an unusually high Liberal vote, coupled with high abstention rates, particularly in 1978, which work against the Liberal party more than the Conservative party. The Bogotá vote for the Liberals represented 6.4 percent of the total national vote; 2.1 percent came from Cali, 1.7 from Medellín, and 1.6 percent from Baranquilla (for a combined total of 11.8 percent). These data clearly indicate that the electoral fortunes of the Liberal party are not as closely linked to the urban vote as is often though to be the case.

Turning now to the percentage of the national Liberal vote derived from the capital cities, Table 3.3 (column 2) indicates that 36.2 percent of the Liberal-party vote came from urban areas. The four principal metropolitan areas represented 21.3 percent of the Liberal-party vote in the three elections (Bogotá, 11.5 percent; Cali, 3.8; Medellín, 3.1; and Baranquilla, 2.9 percent). Putting it differently, 63.8 percent of the Liberal-party vote came from areas outside the departmental capitals, once again revealing that the fortunes of the party are not totally dependent on the urban vote.

With respect to the Liberal party's percentage of the capital-city vote, Table 3.3 (column 3) reveals that the party received almost 60 percent of the votes cast in these urban areas. Not unexpectedly, Bogotá represents the largest percentage of the capital-city vote for the Liberals (19 percent), followed by Cali (6.2 percent), Medellín (5.1 percent), and Baranquilla (4.8 percent)—a combined

Table 3.3
Average Proportion of Liberal Vote Derived from Capital Cities: 1974, 1978, 1982

	Liberal % of National Vote	Urban % of Liberal Vote	Liberal % of Urban Vote
Bogotá	6.4	11.5	19.0
Cali	2.1	3.8	6.2
Medellín	1.7	3.1	5.1
Baranquilla	1.6	2.9	4.8
Bucaramanga	1.0	1.7	2.9
Cartagena	.8	1.5	2.4
Ibagué	.8	1.4	2.3
Cúcuta	.7	1.3	2.1
Pereira	.7	1.2	2.0
Santa Marta	.5	.9	1.5
Monizales	.5	.9	1.5
Armenia	.5	.8	1.3
Valledupar	.4	.7	1.2
Montería	.4	.7	1.2
Neiva	.4	.7	1.1
Pasto	.4	.7	1.1
Sincelejo	.4	.6	.9
Popayán	.2	.4	.7
Quibdó	.2	.4	.7
Villavicencio	.2	.4	.7
Tunja	.2	.3	.5
Riohacha	.2	.3	.5
Total	20.3	36.2	59.7

Sources: Data are from the Registraduría Nacional. See Table 3.1 for full citation.

total of 35.1 percent. These data suggest that more than a majority of the urban electorate favors the Liberal party. However, the trend seemingly is a downward one for the party, with 73 percent of the capital vote favoring it in 1958, 63.2 percent during the National Front,[10] and 59.7 percent in the post-Frente period. Finally, the fate of the Liberal party should not be overly identified with the urban vote, for in the 1974 to 1982 period the party received 55 percent of the "rural vote" (total national vote minus that for departmental capitals). In comparison, the Conservative party averaged 40.1 percent in "rural" areas.

In contrast to the Liberals, the Conservative party derives a smaller proportion of its votes from urban areas. During the National Front and the three elections thereafter, Conservative votes cast in urban areas represented only 10.2 percent of the total national vote (see Table 3.4, column 1). The Conservative vote in Bogotá provided only 2.6 percent of the national vote. The more rural strength of the Conservative party is revealed by the percentage of the party vote derived from the capital cities—26.7 percent (see Table 3.4, column 2). The four major metropolitan cities constituted only 14.8 percent of the Conservative-party vote in the three elections. However, the party has increased the percentage of its votes stemming from the capital cities in comparison to the early years of the National Front (16.8 percent in 1958; 20.4 percent in 1962).[11] Finally, Table 3.4 suggests that the Conservative party's percentage of the capital-city vote averaged only 29.6 percent during the three elections. For the same period, its percentage of the "rural vote" totaled 40 percent, significantly better than in the capital cities, yet not enough to make the Conservatives highly competitive with the Liberals, at least in congressional elections.

Focusing on electoral tendencies associated with the two traditional parties may well obfuscate one of the most significant dimensions of urban electoral behavior in Colombia, namely the very high rates of electoral abstention. Table 3.5 summarizes the proportion of eligible voters who cast ballots for the Liberals, Conservatives, or abstained. In 1982 the average abstention rate for the capital cities was 59.2 percent, in comparison to 69.3 percent in 1978, and 42.6 percent in 1974. Medellín recorded the highest abstention rate in 1982 (75 percent); followed by Bogotá (73.1 percent), Cali (67.3 percent), and Cartagena (66.5 percent). Only in Quibdo did more people vote than abstain. This scenario suggests that the two traditional parties did not enjoy much success in mobilizing the urban electorate. To take only two examples, in Medellín only 12.7 percent of the electorate voted for the Liberals and 11.1 percent for the Conservatives; in Bogotá the respective figures are 15.9 percent and 8.9 percent. Considering the mounting significance of the urban vote, the traditional parties face a formidable challenge as to how to mobilize Colombia's urban residents.

REPRESENTATIVENESS OF THE ELECTORAL SYSTEM

Allowing for a minimal territorial representation of two deputies in each department (one each for the *intendencias* [provinces] of Arauca and San Andrés),

Table 3.4
Average Proportion of Conservative Vote Derived from Capital Cities: 1974, 1978, 1982

	Conservative % of National Vote	Urban % of Conservative Vote	Conservative % of Urban Vote
Bogotá	2.6	6.9	7.6
Medellín	1.3	3.5	3.8
Cali	1.0	2.6	2.9
Baranquilla	.7	1.8	2.0
Manizales	.5	1.3	1.4
Cartagena	.4	1.2	1.3
Pasto	.4	1.1	1.2
Cúcuta	.4	.9	1.0
Bucaramanga	.4	.9	1.0
Santa Marta	.3	.8	.9
Pereira	.3	.8	.9
Ibagué	.3	.8	.8
Montería	.3	.7	.8
Armenia	.2	.6	.7
Popayán	.2	.5	.6
Villavicencio	.2	.5	.5
Valledupar	.2	.4	.5
Tunja	.1	.3	.4
Neiva	.1	.3	.4
Sincelejo	.1	.3	.4
Riohacha	.1	.3	.3
Quibdó	.1	.2	.2
Total	10.2	26.7	29.6

Sources: The data are from the Registraduría Nacional. See Table 3.1 for the full citation.

Table 3.5
Distribution of the Two-Party Vote and Abstention Rate for Capital Cities: 1982 Cámara Election

	Liberal % of Electorate	Conservative % of Electorate	Abstention Rate
Bogotá	15.9	8.9	73.1
Medellín	12.7	11.1	75.0
Cali	16.3	11.4	67.3
Baranquilla	28.9	12.1	58.2
Bucaramanga	30.6	12.0	56.1
Pereira	24.6	13.7	60.2
Manizales	23.5	22.8	53.0
Cúcuta	21.8	13.7	63.9
Cartagena	21.6	11.0	66.5
Ibagué	28.9	12.5	57.1
Armenia	23.5	13.5	62.3
Pasto	22.0	26.5	50.3
Montería	21.7	14.1	63.9
Neiva	25.0	9.5	63.0
Santa Marta	32.7	15.9	51.2
Popayán	20.7	21.8	55.1
Valledupar	33.7	10.1	56.1
Sincelejo	33.0	13.1	53.9
Villavicencio	19.4	14.9	62.6
Tunja	23.7	19.5	55.2
Quibdó	43.1	13.1	43.8
Riohacha	28.3	14.9	56.7
Average	19.7	11.7	59.2

Note: The row totals do not usually add up to 100 percent because of votes cast for other parties, along with blank and null ballots.
Sources: The data are from the Registraduría Nacional. See Table 3.1 for the full citation.

the Cámara is apportioned on the basis of population. Departments are allotted an additional representation for each 100,000 residents, and the Cámara supposedly is reapportioned after every official census. However, the Colombian Congress has a notorious record with respect to reapportionment—no reallocation of seats took place between 1945 and 1970.[12] Some reapportionment followed the 1973 census; the minimum departmental representation was reduced from three to two, and the number of deputies increased by twenty-three. Because no official census has been implemented since 1973, the same allocation of seats has prevailed since 1974. Consequently the contemporary Cámara is not highly reflective of Colombian society in terms of the territorial distribution of its population. In 1974 the average number of votes required to elect a deputy was 23,375; by 1982 the figure reached 27,023. Even more pronounced is the trend regarding the potential votes represented by each representative—39,306 in 1974 and 60,632 in 1982.

Table 3.6 summarizes the territorial representativeness of the Cámara elected in 1982 by showing departmental deviations from the mean number of actual and potential votes necessary to elect one representative, along with the number of deputies for each electoral district. Departments that are "overrepresented" display a minus sign, and those "underrepresented" have positive values. Regarding the relationship between actual votes and representativeness, the most underrepresented departments are, in descending order, La Guajira, Atlántico, Sucre, Norte de Santander, and Valle. In contrast, the most overrepresented districts, leaving aside the provinces of Caqueta, Putumayo, and San Andrés, are Choco, Antioquia, Boyaca, Cauca, Meta, and Quindio. The following number of votes were required to elect a deputy: 39,574 in La Guajira; 35,385 in Atlántico; 18,359 in Choco; and 9,392 in Putumayo.

Utilizing actual votes to assess representativeness obviously distorts the process as a consequence of the very high abstention rates in major metropolitan areas. The scenario changes significantly if the number of potential votes in a district required to elect a deputy is employed rather than actual votes. The correlation between the participation rate and a department's representativeness based on actual votes is a modest -.09 (the higher the score the more underrepresented a department); but if the correlation is based on potential votes, it rises to -.54. The second column of Table 3.6 assesses representativeness in terms of potential votes represented by each deputy. In descending order, the departments that are most underrepresented are Cundinamarca, La Guajira, Valle, Norte de Santander, Antioquia, and Atlántico. Note that the four major metropolitan areas fall in these departments. Also consider the tremendous underrepresentation of Cundinamarca in relation to Antioquia (almost three times as many potential voters are required to elect a deputy in Cundinamarca). The districts most overrepresented are the three provinces of Caqueta, Putumayo, and San Andrés, followed by Choco, Boyaca, Cauca, Nariño, and Quindio.

The apportionment of the Cámara impacts directly on interparty competition. Thus, the relationship between the Liberal-party percentage of the vote and the

Table 3.6
Representativeness of the Cámara: Number of Actual and Potential
Votes Needed to Elect a Representative: 1982 Cámara Elections

Department	Actual Votes (Deviation from Mean)	Potential Votes (Deviation from Mean)	Number of Elected Representatives
Antioquia	-3,728	14,300	26
Atlántico	8,382	13,110	8
Bolívar	565	4,981	8
Boyacá	-3,629	-13,464	12
Caldas	3,258	-1,735	8
Cauda	-2,717	-10,779	7
Cesar	1,581	4,021	4
Córdoba	1,339	-453	7
Cundinamarca	2,768	37,661	29
Chocó	-8,664	-21,651	3
Huila	-530	-164	5
La Guajira	12,551	25,657	2
Magdalena	3,858	-91	6
Meta	-1,854	1,073	3
Nariño	900	-5,694	8
Norte Santander	6,380	16,383	6
Quindo	-1,273	-2,735	4
Risaralda	1,296	1,667	5
Santander	4,559	4,558	11
Sucre	7,134	2,496	4
Tolima	2,282	130	9
Valle	4,307	18,089	18
Arauca	3,752	9,860	1
Caqueta	-8,926	-16,770	2
Putumayo	-17,631	-35,969	2
San Andrés y Providencia	-15,981	-44,481	1
	27,023 (mean)	60,632 (mean)	199 (total)

Sources: The data are from the Registraduría Nacional. See Table 3.1 for the full citation.

degree of representativeness based on actual votes is -.01 (the higher the score, the more underrepresented) and -.16 for potential representation. For the Conservative party the respective correlations are .12 and .16. The tendency for the left is in the same direction as that for the Liberal party but stronger: -.22 and -.04. However, the relationships change when we control for participation. In those departments where participation is lowest, the correlation between potential representation and the Liberal party's percentage of the vote is .23, in comparison to -.10 for the Conservative party. In those departments where participation is in the average range, the correlation is -.43 for the Liberals and .46 for the Conservatives. For departments with the highest participation, the Liberals score -.19 and the Conservatives .52. Thus, in departments where participation is highest, the Liberal-party percentage of the vote is highest in underrepresented departments. The reverse is true for the Conservative party; the Conservative percentage of the vote is highest in those departments that are overrepresented.

Consequently, the inertia with respect to reapportionment in the Cámara is rooted firmly in interparty competition. If the House were apportioned strictly on the basis of population, the Conservative party would lose legislative seats. Generally speaking, overrepresented departments protect a competitive edge for the Conservative party (if Choco were allotted two rather than three representatives, the Conservatives undoubtedly would lose a seat). The most underrepresented departments tend to be Liberal party strongholds, with the exception of Norte de Santander.

CONCLUSION

This chapter has focused on selected aspects of electoral and party behavior in the liberal democracy of Colombia during the post-National Front period. The system currently is experiencing a legitimacy crisis, perhaps unparalleled since La Violencia of the 1940s and 1950s. To what extent does the crisis stem from the inflexibility of the political system or, more concretely, from the traditional political parties? From a historical perspective the Colombian party system has reflected faithfully the interests of those who dominate the society, but at the same time it has adapted to changing societal conditions, at least in the sense that the two traditional parties have become highly institutionalized and have retained their monopoly in the electoral arena. Empirically speaking, the traditional parties have not been highly innovative or motors of change during and after the National Front. But the process of engineering party reform is considerably easier for academics than for politicians, and the results are not always anticipated (as suggested by the 1972 reforms enacted by the Democratic party in the United States).

Since the end of World War II, the two traditional parties have monopolized the Colombian electoral system, averaging 95 percent of the vote. Even though this two-party hegemony remains, the traditional parties are confronted with uncertainties associated with the changing character of Colombian society. The proportion of the electorate identifying with the two parties has been declining, as a larger segment of the electorate classifies itself as independent, reflecting a more sophisticated issue voting, particularly in presidential elections. An even greater problem for the traditional parties revolves around the phenomenon of electoral abstention, especially in the major metropolitan areas (75 percent abstained in Medellín in 1982, 73 percent in Bogotá).

This failure to mobilize the urban vote is especially acute in light of the increasingly urban composition of the population. By the 1982 elections 27.5 percent of the entire electorate resided in the four major metropolitan areas. The Liberal party traditionally has dominated the urban vote, but the Conservative party has been increasing its share of this vote. The Liberal preponderance in urban areas has tended to disguise the Conservative party's rural strength, which averaged 55 percent in the post-National Front period. This "rural vote" propelled Turbay into the presidency in 1978, but a similar electoral strategy failed for López Michelsen in 1982.

Inequities associated with the apportionment of the Cámara represent one of the most pronounced effects of political-party intransigence. Deviations from an apportionment scheme based on population are pronounced, even though the Constitution dictates otherwise. These representational distortions stem from uneven population growth and the desire of political parties to maximize their electoral opportunities. The present scheme favors the Conservative party, but with its improving support in urban areas, Conservatives may be less reluctant to reapportion.

The process of "democratic opening" in Colombia will be enhanced by a more equitable apportionment and the extension of additional guarantees to minor parties. However, even if the government actively stimulates new forms of political participation, this is not likely to alter drastically the party system. Colombians have tended to adhere to rational voting patterns; they do not support candidates that have little chance of winning, assuming that they decide to vote. In short, minor parties face an uphill struggle. In view of the intensity of the debate surrounding political reform, change is virtually inevitable, but this does not necessarily indicate that the political system will be highly responsive in terms of resolving basic socioeconomic inequities of Colombian society.

NOTES

1. For a bibliographic reference to how scholars have categorized the Colombian political system, see Bruce Michael Bagley, "Colombia: National Front and Economic Development," in *Politics, Policies, and Economic Development*, ed. Robert Wesson (Palo Alto, Calif.: Hoover Press, 1984).

2. See Chapter 1 of this volume for a discussion of the differences between formal and substantive democracy.

3. For the standard-reference work on the Colombian political system, see Robert Dix, *Colombia: The Political Dimensions of Change* (New Haven, Conn.: Yale University Press, 1967). This study should be complemented by three more recent studies: R. Albert

Berry, Ronald G. Hellman, and Mauricio Solaún, eds., *Politics of Compromise: Coalition Government in Colombia* (New Brunswick, N.J.: Transaction Books, 1980); Harvey Kline, *Colombia: Portrait of Unity and Diversity* (Boulder, Colo.: Westview Press, 1983); Francisco Leal Buitrago, *Estado y Política En Colombia* (Bogotá: Siglo XXI y Cerec, 1984); and Robert Dix, *The Politics of Colombia* (New York: Praeger, 1987).

4. Consult Ricardo Santamaría S. and Gabriel Silva Luhan, *Proceso Político en Colombia: Del Frente Nacional a la Apertura Democrática* (Bogotá, Colombia: Fondo Editorial CEREC, 1984), for an excellent analysis of the contemporary debate concerning the opening of the political process in Colombia.

5. For an overview of electoral abstention in Colombia, consult *La Abstención: Libro del Simposio 1980* (Bogotá: Simposio realizado por la Asociación Nacional de Instituciones Financieras, 1980).

6. The official data overestimate the potential electorate because many *cédulas* that appear on the list of eligible voters belong to people who cannot vote—those who have died, members of the armed forces, prisoners, many Colombians living abroad, and those who have moved from where their cédulas were issued and have failed to transfer them or register to vote. Consequently, it has been estimated that a corrected eligibility list would reduce the electorate by around 10 percent. See *La Abstención*, pp. 11–12.

7. For an analysis of electoral participation that emphasizes contextual factors, see Gary Hoskin, "The Colombian Political Party System: Electoral Domination and System Instability," paper presented at the United States State Department, Washington, D.C., November 9, 1981.

8. Inter-American Development Bank, *Annual Report 1983* (Washington, D.C., 1984), p. 106. Between 1970 and 1983 the urban population rate increased by 3.8 percent annually, while the rural rate decreased 1.1 percent yearly.

9. The comparisons with urban voting patterns during the National Front period are taken from the excellent study by Fernando Cepeda and Claudia González de Lecaros, *Comportamiento del Voto Urbano en Colombia: Una Aproximación* (Bogotá: Universidad de los Andes, 1976). The elections analyzed are those from 1958 through 1974 for the Cámara and off-year local elections. The departmental capital of La Guajira, Riohacha, is not included in this study.

10. Ibid., p. 12.

11. Ibid.

12. See Dora Rothlisberger, "La Organización Formal de Congreso," in *Estudio del Comportamiento Legislativo en Colombia* Tomo 2, eds. Gary Hoskin, Francisco Leal, Harvey Kline, Dora Rothlisberger, and Armando Borrero (Bogotá: Universidad de los Andes y Cámara de Comercio de Bogotá, 1975), p. 109.

4

Post-War and Post–National Front Economic Development of Colombia

R. Albert Berry and
Francisco E. Thoumi

The impressive continuity of the main features of Colombia's political system during the post-World War II period (and longer) provides a fascinating test of the implications of its brand of democracy for the process of economic development. No other country in South America has had as little interruption (five years) of at least formally democratic procedures over the last forty years. No other country has had as many deaths broadly attributable to political conflict, these being concentrated in the period of La Violencia beginning in the late 1940s, though this rural violence had surprisingly little impact on the economy.

This chapter reviews the major economic events, trends, and policies of this period, with special emphasis on the decade since the end of the National Front period in 1974. It also provides some comparisons with other Latin American countries and some speculation on the relationships between the political system and economic policies and trends.

POST-WAR ECONOMIC GROWTH AND CHANGE, FROM 1945 TO 1985

Colombia's growth performance from 1945 to 1985 has been about average both for Latin American and for developing countries in general. Real gross domestic product (GDP) grew at an annual average of 4.8 percent or 525 percent for the period as a whole; per capita output rose by an average of 2.1 percent per year or 125 percent for the period. Population growth accelerated to a peak of about 3 percent per year by the early 1960s, then fell to its present level of

The opinions expressed in this chapter do not represent policies or positions of the Inter-American Development Bank.

somewhere between 1.5 and 2.0 percent. Colombia's growth performance falls squarely in the middle range defined by the seventeen major Latin American nations with populations of 3 million or more at present. However, during the depressed early 1980s, the country outperformed all but two of these countries. The Economic Commission for Latin America and the Caribbean estimated a cumulative growth rate for Latin America of zero for the 1980 to 1984 period, while Colombia's was 7.4 percent, a figure comparable to the estimated population growth during the same four-year period. Thus, during this period, Colombia was one of the few Latin American countries in which per capita income did not deteriorate significantly.

The slowly growing Latin countries—Bolivia, El Salvador, Guatemala, Peru, and the Southern Cone—were characterized over at least part of the period by either frequent government changes, violence disruptive of production, or significant changes in economic policy orientations. The Southern Cone countries are also noteworthy for beginning the period much better off than the rest. Although violence and political instability are in all probability both cause and effect of slow growth, the comparison with Latin American countries suggests that when the sort of strife that creates economic chaos can be avoided, growth at the Colombian rate is a quite reasonable expectation, assuming moderate competence in economic management.

Many of the details of Colombia's growth experience are standard features of the development process. The share of agriculture and mining in output and employment fell markedly, while those of manufacturing and services rose. Urbanization proceeded rapidly; the urban population rose from about 32 percent in 1945 to perhaps 70 percent today. Rural population stabilized (more or less) in the 1970s and 1980s, while urban population growth reached 5 to 5.5 percent in the intercensal period from 1951 to 1964 and the rather dramatic figure of 7 percent per year in Bogotá and a few other cities. Educational attainment rose rapidly: In 1951, 41 percent of the labor force had no education and the median amount was probably no more than two years, whereas by 1978 only 16.3 percent had no education and the median level was probably about four years. By 1978, 29 percent had secondary or higher education compared to approximately 9 percent in 1951. Life expectancy has risen from forty years in 1945 to approximately sixty-five years at present.

In many respects this is an impressive performance. The 1970s represented the golden age in terms of growth, at rates significantly exceeding the ambitious Alliance for Progress goals of the early 1960s. The recession of the early 1980s, on the other hand, represented Colombia's worst economic performance since the early 1930s.

The major black mark on Colombia's socioeconomic record is the extremely unequal income distribution, a problem neither new nor specific to Colombia to be certain, but nonetheless central to virtually all the country's other social problems—poverty, malnutrition, tension between the classes and income groups, and so forth. Whether there has been any significant change in income distribution over the last forty years, taken as a whole, is a matter of debate. Although the economic gains of the period clearly have gone to the richer groups in a proportion similar to their income (otherwise one would be able to detect a sharp decline or increase in the level of inequality), they have also substantially raised the living standards of the poor (as best we can measure them), and Colombia's economic growth has not led to observable impoverishment of the lower socioeconomic groups. In the context of Latin American countries, most of which also suffer from very high levels of economic inequality, Colombia's record is, again, near average. Rough evidence suggests that inequality has been least in the Southern Cone countries[1]; in 1970 the income of the top quintile of households in those three countries bottom quintile averaged approximately 11.3 times the income of the bottom quintile (49.7 percent of all income went to the top quintile and 4.4 percent to the bottom one). The three countries whose political regimes have most systematically been democratic over the post-war period, Colombia, Venezuela, and Costa Rica, fall in a middle range; for the three together (using unweighted averages) the top quintile of households had on average 16.4 times as much income as the bottom quintile (55.6 percent to 3.4 percent).[2] In Colombia the ratio was 14.7 (58.0 percent to 3.5 percent). At the other extreme were Brazil, Mexico, Peru, and Panama, for which the un-weighted average figure was 26.6 (61.2 percent versus 2.3 percent). Thus, more equal socioeconomic-class relationships have tended to characterize the relatively advanced and (sometimes democratic) Southern Cone countries of Argentina, Chile, and Uruguay and the less developed but nearly always democratic countries of Colombia, Venezuela, and Costa Rica. Colombia's inequality, although high in absolute terms, is not the worst in Latin America.

THE POST-WAR PERIOD: PROBABLE EFFECTS OF ECONOMIC POLICY ON GROWTH AND INEQUALITY

During most of the period from 1945 to 1985, Colombia has been under civilian government, including the sixteen years of the National Front. During this period, policy can be broadly described as conservative, both to maintain the status quo and to avoid embarking on risky ventures either in the monetary and fiscal domains or elsewhere. As a result of the former conservatism, economic inequalities have remained great. While Colombia has not suffered the extremely high inflation rates of so many other Latin American countries nor built up an unmanageable international debt, the country has also not opted for simplistic economic policies.

The only Colombian president to mount a reasonably serious attack on the socioeconomic status quo was Alfonso López P. in the 1930s. Although a number of his initiatives left a permanent mark (labor legislation, for example), the attack was neither long enough nor strong enough to affect a major change.[3] Since then the pattern has reverted to that described above, though of course with sometimes significant variations from presidency to presidency. The broad outlines of Colombia's economic policy during the last four decades can be described as follows:

1. A fairly standard import-substitution strategy complemented from the late 1960s on by an increasing emphasis on export promotion and outward orientation, which, however, did not lower the protection in the domestic market for many manufactured products;

2. A relatively conservative monetary and fiscal policy, with major budget deficits only appearing around 1980;

3. In spite of great inequality in the distribution of land, a token agrarian reform, which lost impetus as the country became mostly urban and the distributive policy concern shifted to the urban poor;

4. A reasonably conservative labor policy, reflected in a minimum wage set at a level that does not often exceed market rates, a body of labor legislation that does not go very far in providing workers' rights and powers to negotiate compared to some other Latin American countries, and a fairly lax administration of some of the legislation that is on the books;

5. Less state intervention in the economy than has characterized many countries, and frequent dialogue with the private sector so that the large government-financed productive projects complement private ones;

6. A possibly conservative allocation of public expenditures and a possibly low level of both public income and expenditures relative to other developing countries, though on neither count are the data available to confirm this.[4]

Finally, though not primarily viewed as a matter of economic policy, the government's quiet and apparently successful population policy deserves mention because of its possible important longer-run implications for development and for the level of economic inequality.

These generally conservative orientations have been complemented by a considerable continuity and a reasonable level of technical competence in economic policy decisionmaking. That competence has been especially evident since the Carlos Lleras presidency (from 1966 to 1970). The decision to shift toward an outward orientation was probably a major contributing factor to the decade-plus boom of 1967 to 1979, during which Colombia's GDP expanded at a historically unprecedented average rate of over 6 percent per year. Other ingredients contributing to that boom have included factors exogenous to current government policy, such as high coffee prices, a relatively sophisticated industrial sector, and relatively good world markets for Colombia's nontraditional exports.

The modest power of labor (white-collar workers in the public sector, including teachers, seem to have had more power than blue-collar workers) may have contributed to the fairly smooth growth performance of Colombia, in contrast to the Argentine example.

Perhaps the only nonrevolutionary way by which the degree of economic inequality in Colombia could have been quickly and substantially reduced from its historically high levels would have been a major agrarian reform, at a time when the country was still predominantly rural.[5] Alfonso López P. was inclined to move somewhat in this direction during the 1930s and did promulgate new land laws that would have had at least some effect if they had been implemented. But this initiative fell by the wayside, as subsequent administrations did not share his zeal. In 1961 the Colombian Agrarian Reform Institute (INCORA) was founded, partly as a response to the social unrest associated with La Violencia of the late 1940s and the 1950s. But it never had enough political support to be more than a mild palliative; so its overall effect on land distribution was very limited, if not negligible.

The potentially powerful long-run impact of population growth on income inequality merits special attention. Most economists would agree that the faster population grows, the more slowly is per capita income likely to grow. And nearly all would probably agree that the greater the population, the lower are wage rates likely to be in relation to returns to capital, resulting in a worse functional income distribution. One cannot discount the possibility that the relatively progressive attitude of Colombia's recent governments to population control will ultimately have a more favorable impact on the incomes of the poor than any other step the government has taken or perhaps could have taken, short of a near revolutionary set of programs. After the first tentative steps by the government to support population policy in the late 1960s, progress accelerated. By the early 1980s, although not a leader in per capita public expenditure on population programs,[6] Colombia had one of the lowest total fertility rates[7] in Latin America and generally took the population issue seriously. In 1965 former president Alberto Lleras C. agreed to address an international meeting on population held in Cali. By the 1966 to 1970 administration of Carlos Lleras R., the National Front expressed itself cautiously in favor of slower population growth; Lleras R. was the only Latin American president to sign the United Nations Declaration on Population on Human Rights Day, December 10, 1966.[8] At this time Brazil, for example, was still pronatalist.

Income inequality can also be affected by educational policy, labor policy, the level and composition of other social expenditures, and policy affecting the relative conditions of small firms vis-à-vis larger ones. Educational attainment has risen rapidly in Colombia, a phenomenon common to most developing countries in recent decades. It is also obvious that the educational system has been a major mechanism for the maintenance of a high degree of income inequality over time[9]; the income differentials by level of education are large and explain a relatively high share of income differences in Colombia.[10] But again, Colombia is not an extreme case; although inequality of educational attainment is clearly greater than in Chile, for example, it is less than in Brazil. Non-Latin American countries with more equal distributions of income, such as Taiwan and Korea, also have much more complete secondary-school coverage relative to that of higher education.[11]

Had policy provided and supported greater union power,[12] or pushed minimum wages higher and administered them with greater vigor, the impact on income distribution would be difficult to estimate. Higher wages discourage employment. Thus, while raising the income of one group of workers, higher wages are expected to lower that of another group with the overall impact on income distribution depending on the relative magnitudes of these two effects. The positive effect would be likely to dominate if the demand for labor is inelastic or if there is an economic surplus that can be extracted by government (for example, from mineral exports or from export-oriented agriculture, as in Argentina) and transferred to labor via public-sector employment. Obviously, neither condition seems to have held in Colombia. Therefore, it is not likely that a more aggressive ''prolabor'' policy would have significantly improved income distribution; nor is it clear that such a policy would have improved income distribution at all.

The distribution of public expenditures has changed over time, at least judging from those of the central government, where the ''social'' expenditures of the ministries of education, health, and labor, taken together, rose from 12 percent of the total in 1945 to 32 percent in 1984.[13] The ministries of public works and communications showed the largest declines in share of the total. The dramatic increase in the share of the budget going to education reflects the government's response to the needs and pressures of all classes. The social-security system, which is important in providing health care to Colombians, has expanded rapidly since its start in 1949. From a coverage ratio (paying affiliates to the labor force) of 3.2 percent in 1951, it reached 19.6 percent in 1978 and is probably slightly higher in 1987. The combined distributional effect of taxes and expenditures is not easy to assess, but it does appear that as of the period from the mid 1960s to the mid 1970s, that effect was probably positive.[14]

POLITICAL STRUCTURE AND ECONOMIC POLICY THROUGH THE END OF THE NATIONAL FRONT

The absence of a broad base of left-of-center views in the society, and the lack of easy vehicles for such thinking to express itself in the political process, have clearly constrained the socioeconomic options that are taken seriously in the political process. Although in the last few decades that range has not included a program that would effect a major restructuring of the society, policies have varied over time and among administrations in response to which party has the presidency, the characteristics of the president himself, and the changing availability and influence of various types of advisers.

In terms of political arrangements, the postwar period has witnessed four distinct phases. The first, from 1946 to 1953, during which the Conservatives ruled under Ospina Pérez and then Laureano Gómez, and the subsequent 1953 to 1957 dictatorship of General Rojas Pinilla, provides perhaps the biggest contrast. In many respects the Pérez–Gómez period was classic conservatism. It saw a major restructuring on the labor front to the detriment of the Confederación de Trabajadores de Colombia (CTC), which had been founded earlier during López's administration of the 1930s and had grown with the support and protection of the Liberal party. This occurred despite continuous feuding among Communist, left Liberal, moderate Liberal, and other factions. The Unión de Trabajadores de Colombia (UTC) was founded in 1946 and had its origins in several earlier unions and regional federations, founded under church or Catholic lay auspices, to combat Marxist and other leftist influences in the CTC. The UTC grew as the CTC declined because the latter lost government support.

Under Gómez (from 1950 to 1953) austerity measures and tighter budgetary management helped improve the government's fiscal position and foreign investment was encouraged. The government attempted to implement the recommendations of the Lauchlin Currie report—the first such major report in a developing country sponsored by the World Bank—which had been requested and carried out under the previous Ospina administration. Among other things, the report recommended heavy investments in infrastructure, such as transportation and electricity, key sectors in a spatially unintegrated economy, and the government proceeded to obtain large amounts of World Bank and other foreign capital.[15]

Rojas's regime is often seen as an example of a lost opportunity for socioeconomic change. He was fortunate to preside over years of relative prosperity, as coffee prices remained high by both earlier and later standards. Although he was originally supported by a substantial part of the civilian elite, both Rojas's rhetoric and some of his actions focused on social-welfare projects. As time passed, he tried to carve out his own power base by developing organized support within the labor movement, providing an alternative to the traditional elites, and (in 1956) creating a "Third Force," the bases of which were to be the army and labor and which was to be "above the parties." His government pushed various public works, raised land assessments, improved credit for small farmers, exacted a tax on dividends from corporate stocks and bonds, and gave women the vote (1954). But it was not unusually competent from an economic point of view (probably the contrary), and it seemed to lack both the will and the clearheadedness, single-mindedness, and skill to forge a new political equilibrium that could have really provided the social justice Rojas so frequently called for.

The Alberto Lleras administration ushered in the National Front. The National Front owed its existence to the closing of ranks within the elite and was designed to avoid interparty warfare, to school Colombians in the art of political compromise, and to keep power in the hands of the elite during the continuing process of economic development.[16] Although a few "crises" occurred along the way, these goals were all broadly achieved. During the first two administrations (Alberto Lleras and Valencia), economic growth averaged a moderate 5 percent annually, not bad considering the negative shift in the international terms of trade from 1956 to 1959, but uneven as a stop-go cycle involving periodic balance-of-payments crises cum devaluation. At the onset of its 1961 to 1970 development plan, Colombia became the first Latin American country to present such a program in accordance with Alliance for Progress goals. The Alberto Lleras government initiated Colombia's agrarian-reform program. Whether or not it was attributable to a new seriousness of purpose, the government's concern with development appeared to be greater than before, and the sophistication of the *técnicos* in decision-making positions gradually improved despite ups and downs. Valencia (from 1962 to 1966) typified the older-style politician, uninterested and unskilled in technical matters. When a 1962 devaluation produced a surge of inflation the following year, the problems of such periodic sharp devaluations became increasingly manifest. The general emphasis on import substitution to the exclusion of a serious export-promotion policy also did not seem to offer much more hope as a longer-term growth strategy.

The presidency of Carlos Lleras R. marked a turning point in the country's recent economic history. In the context of a dispute with the International Monetary Fund (IMF) over exchange-rate policy, in which that institution argued for a discrete devaluation with continued adherence to a pegged exchange rate, the Lleras government opted for a creeping peg rate. This wise decision was an important factor in ending the balance-of-payment crises that resulted from a downward rigid exchange rate. Lleras also improved public administration and raised government revenues and public investment. The rate of inflation declined to 6 percent in the last two years of his administration. It was the most technocratic and probably the most technically competent government Colombia had had. Although it was primarily oriented toward economic growth, Lleras's government did put some effort into agrarian reform; it also emphasized the need for growth in the agricultural sector, creating the Colombian Agricultural Institute (ICA). During this presidency, other public institutions were strengthened and new ones created. The Industrial Development (IFI), the Export Promotion (PROEXPO), and the Foreign Trade (INCOMEX) institutes are among the most important ones. The proliferation of public institutions, which at the time was seen as a good institution-building program, has added to the fiscal problems of more recent governments by contributing to the inflexibility of public expenditures.

Misael Pastrana's government encouraged economic growth, support for exports, and also a new focus on urban building as motors of growth. While the government believed that the labor intensity of urban building would raise the incomes of the poor, it did nothing on the agrarian-reform front. It also relaxed the traditional monetary and fiscal conservatism, with the result that inflation moved up to an annual rate of 24 percent by 1974. This accelerating inflation rate was probably the main cause of a decline of 15 to 20 percent in most real wage rates, for both blue- and white-collar workers, as their salary increases lagged behind price increases.[17] The urban-building program required changes in the financial system to divert resources to the construction sector, and the first indexed instruments were created, a change that raised real interest rates. These measures can be considered as the first steps in the capital-market liberalization followed by the succeeding governments.

Viewing the National Front period in retrospect, it is evident that public policy had a generally conservative orientation, though middle of the road with respect to the Colombian spectrum. It was also relatively consistent over the four administrations. Given the nature of the political arrangements that constituted the National Front,[18] these orientations are certainly not surprising. But since the consociational patterns of power sharing between the two major parties, formalized in a specific way in the National Front arrangement, have deep roots in the Colombian style of politics, it was not clear how much change in the political process and hence in economic policy was to be expected as open elections returned in 1974.

THE POST-NATIONAL FRONT PERIOD: 1974 TO THE PRESENT

In 1974 López Michelsen became the first president of the post-National Front period. His "Clear Mandate" (Mandato Claro) in the election and his strong technical team created high expectations. The Development Plan Document, entitled "To Close the Gap" (Para Cerrar la Brecha), reflected the incoming administration's plan to improve the situation of the poor. López's history as a member of the left wing of the Liberal party coincided with this plan. Urban construction was deemphasized, and attention switched to integrated rural development programs to assist small farmers, food and nutrition programs, and a more progressive tax system; further encouragement of nontraditional exports was planned. By 1975 the government had introduced a major tax reform, dubbed by some observers as one of the most technically competent and advanced in the world. The reforms were designed to increase the overall tax burden, to eliminate many loopholes, and to make the tax system more progressive. These and other components of the government's plan of action did indeed suggest that post-National Front governments might be more progressive and perhaps also of higher technical competence than the National Front average.

In any event, the economy's growth performance remained reasonably strong, albeit erratic, during this administration and was aided by a dramatic increase in the price of coffee from 1976 and an expanding inflow of drug money. However, the inflation inherited from the Pastrana government proved intractable, especially as the foreign-exchange surplus necessitated monetary sterilization. The need to impose greater expenditure restraint than anticipated led the government to reduce social expenditures below the anticipated level. Although the tax reform allowed the government to increase revenues in the short run, its effectiveness declined significantly from 1976 on; several strikes by ministry-of-finance personnel led to bitter confrontations between their union and the government, which probably weakened the tax collectors' morale and zeal. Moreover, the increase in income-tax rates induced taxpayers to search for legal and illegal ways to avoid taxes, a practice that was morally more palatable at this time when the drug and underground economies were booming.

Only in its last year did this administration show signs of bringing inflation under control. Even at that time some of the decrease may have been the result of the exceptionally high GDP growth rate (nearly 9 percent) in 1978 and a higher production of food crops. Although GDP growth averaged a creditable 5.5 percent from 1974 to 1978, almost identical to the average growth rate during the National Front period from 1958 to 1974 (see Table 4.1), per capita income rose faster than during the National Front period because population was now growing less rapidly, and real wages began to rise after falling during the inflation acceleration of 1971 to 1974. Nevertheless, there was mounting public dissatisfaction toward the end of López's presidency, fostered, it seemed, by the inflation, by the modest growth of the economy prior to the boom year 1978, and by a feeling of unfulfilled expectations.

Julio César Turbay (from 1978 to 1982) provided a strong contrast to López. An old-style politician whose position was based on knowing how to manipulate the patronage system, Turbay had the misfortune to preside over the period during which Colombia's growth slowed gradually from the record level of 1978. By 1982 it was less than 1 percent. This was, of course, mainly the result of the onset of world recession. As a combination of lower coffee prices, reduced drug revenue (probably), and a fall in nontraditional exports due to the recession slashed the country's foreign-exchange revenues, the Turbay government was able to finance very large trade deficits in 1981 and 1982 by foreign borrowing and (in 1982) by a modest drawing down of foreign-exchange reserves that had reached an all-time high of over 5.5 billion dollars in 1980 and 1981. Thus, any serious curtailment of imports and associated deflationary strategy could be and were postponed. As a result, while the manufacturing sector stagnated, overall gross national product (GNP) growth averaged 3.2 percent over the four years and per capita GNP fell only in 1982.

The Turbay administration's development strategy strongly emphasized public-sector investment to improve roads and communication systems. However, dramatic increases in public-sector consumption expenditures in 1979 and 1980, and a mediocre record in raising revenues domestically, severely limited public-sector savings. The government pushed ahead with its large investment program by deficit financing on a level never previously seen in Colombia; in 1981 and 1982 the public nonfinancial sector's deficit averaged over 6 percent of GDP, probably more than twice as high as any level reached earlier.[19] The deficit was mainly financed by foreign borrowing. Inflation returned to a level of about 25 percent, and interest rates rose, partly in response to world trends and partly to government attempts to finance the deficit.

A capital market liberalization, reinforced during the López government, continued under Turbay. The development of new types of financial institutions and activities, in the context of Colombia's concentration of wealth and power, were part of an evolution toward oligopolistic money markets rather than perfectly competitive ones. The government did not understand the dangers of liberalizing interest rates and other controls without taking complementary measures to secure a high level of competition. The result was an unstable system that powerful interests could, at times, manipulate to their own advantage. The high interest

Table 4.1
Average Annual Output Growth Rates by Presidential Periods and by Sector (in percentages)

Sector	National Front 1958-1974	Post-National Front 1974-1978	1978-1982	1982-1984[a]
Agricultural et al.	3.85	5.04	2.06	1.90
Mining	2.37	-1.77	6.47	6.64
Manufacturing	6.67	5.06	0.76	3.37
Public utilities	9.84	6.75	6.07	5.01
Construction	6.22	-2.57	6.16	4.88
Commerce	6.16	5.40	2.34	0.12
Transportation and Communications	7.24	8.97	5.15	0.64
Financial services	11.17	12.29	6.65	2.27
Personal services	5.25	6.91	3.13	3.23
Government services	5.63	4.15	6.21	3.51
Rents and housing	6.65	6.63	3.49	4.13
Total gross domestic product	5.65	5.53	3.16	2.00
National income	6.27	6.10	2.03[b]	1.50[b]
Population	2.70	2.10	1.90[a]	1.80[a]
National income per capita	3.48	3.91	0.13	-0.30

Note: Average annual output is measured in constant 1970 prices for the periods 1958 to 1974 and 1974 to 1978 and in constant 1975 prices for 1978 to 1982 and 1982 to 1984. Presidential periods are approximate since the presidential periods begin on August 7 and the data are for each calendar year.

Source: The average annual output data are from Departamento Administrativo Nacional de Estadística, Cuentas Nacionales de Colombia, several issues, and preliminary DANE 1983 and 1984 data.

[a]Figures are still provisional.

[b]Inter-American Development Bank estimates since 1981, because the official National Income series ends in 1980.

rates, a growing concentration in the financial sector, and the lack of sound rules governing the behavior of financial conglomerates led to a financial crisis.

The long-run implications of Turbay's investment program remain to be seen. His administration did bequeath difficult short-run problems to its successor—a large trade deficit and a large (by Colombia's historical standards, if not by contemporary Latin American standards) foreign debt, a high fiscal deficit and a high rate of inflation, and an impending financial crisis. However, international reserves were still high, and Betancur's incoming administration did have a degree of flexibility, which many other Latin American governments did not have at this time. The Turbay government's own tendencies toward *clientelismo* and pork-barrel practices, together with the temptations created by drug money, produced what was probably the lowest quality of Colombian public administration in recent times.

The Betancur government thus faced economic problems of great difficulty and complexity, not to mention the guerrilla activity and the peace negotiations, which had been the main focus of the president's attention. The government's performance was difficult to judge against this uncompromising setting. During his election campaign, Betancur did not focus on the country's major economic problems except for unemployment and the need to moralize economic activities in the country. Instead, he emphasized two programs with apparent popular appeal but with little potential to improve social justice significantly: a housing system without down payment and a correspondence university program. His catchy campaign slogans of "bread, a roof, and employment" and "it can be done" might have played a role in his victory over the more serious López, who was less willing to make exaggerated promises.

The Betancur government, even with a reasonably competent technical team, not surprisingly had been unable to resolve the problems it faced; Colombia's socioeconomic situation remains tense and problematic. The plan "Development with Equity" (Desarrollo con Equidad) proposed policies to restructure the financial sector, to control inflationary expectations and thereby inflation, to use housing construction to promote growth, to stimulate the demand for domestic products, to increase private-sector financing, and to reduce the fiscal and balance-of-payments (current-account) deficits. Most of these short-term policy goals were set in response to the critical condition of the economy. The plan also revealed long-term programs designed to support sustained growth, involving agriculture, mining, oil, transportation, capital goods, and exports. But the government's main efforts had necessarily been directed to confronting the financial, fiscal, and external sector crises. It delayed a strong austerity program until 1984.

STRUCTURAL CHANGE, POLICY, AND THE IMPACT OF THE FOREIGN SECTOR SINCE 1970

As previously discussed, the National Front period demonstrated that the structure of Colombia's economy moved in typical ways for a developing country;

since then there have been some anomalies. During the National Front, the share of the primary sectors—agriculture and mining—in GDP fell from approximately one third to one quarter (measured in 1975 prices). The share of mining bottomed out in 1979 and has increased since then, a trend that is expected to continue as the recent large investments in oil, coal, and ferronickel mature. Manufacturing's share increased from about 19 percent in 1958 to over 23 percent in 1974. It remained stable at a level of around 22 to 23 percent until the recession pushed it below 21 percent in 1982. In 1958 agriculture's share of GDP was over 50 percent higher than that of manufacturing; by 1980 the two shares were similar, though agriculture again pulled slightly ahead in the 1980s. During the 1970s, the growth sectors—that is, government services, financial services, transportation and communications, and public utilities—were mainly urban. (See Table 4.1.)

These differences in growth patterns reflect the fact that the economic events and the problems faced by Colombia, overall, have differed markedly between the National Front period and subsequent years. What is not clear, however, is whether the formally more open political process of the last decade has made any real difference in terms of public policy. In terms of rhetoric and, it would seem, of intentions as well, the López and Betancur governments appear to have been more progressively oriented (in the sense of their concern with matters of poverty and inequality) than most (perhaps all) of the National Front governments. But it remains uncertain whether this apparent difference has manifested itself in the economic outcomes of the two periods. Public policy has been important to other dimensions of economic life: when the increasingly outward orientation helped to get the economy moving in the late 1960s, and when the Turbay administration's unwillingness to exercise fiscal restraint led to an unprecedented fiscal deficit in the early 1980s.[20] Still, the easily measurable differences in the rate of economic growth are most obviously related to exogenous events like the price of coffee and the world recession of the 1980s.

Most governments arrive in power with a development platform, that is, some ideas about long-term policies to achieve goals of economic development and/or social equality. However, the possibility of achieving their goals depends on the policy leeway allowed by the management of the foreign sector and, since the early 1970s, the battle against inflation. Typically, there has been a conflict between the long-term need for various types of reform and the short-term need for stability. Very frequently, governments have had to devote the bulk of their effort to maintaining a minimum degree of stability but are then accused of disregarding long-term goals and election campaign promises.

The policy area in which the tenor of a government often best manifests itself is the fiscal and monetary. The effects of one government's policies often impinge heavily on subsequent ones. Carlos Lleras R. set a new tone of discipline that raised current revenues of the public sector and slowed inflation, all in the context of an improving growth performance. The Pastrana administration relaxed and let inflation rise, thereby complicating the scenario for all of the administrations that followed. Since the National Front, similar ups and downs have occurred. López M.'s government introduced a modern tax reform that alleviated fiscal stringencies at least temporarily, and Turbay's went to the other extreme as the fiscal deficit grew dramatically.

The prominent role played by the foreign sector in Colombian development is, of course, typical of most developing countries. As the 1970s began, Colombia was a foreign-exchange-constrained country; by the late 1970s foreign exchange was abundant, but by the mid–1980s it was again a constraint. The post–1970 period witnessed several unprecedented events in the world economy, with important impacts on Colombia. These included the sharp increase in oil prices in 1973, the adoption by the OECD (Organization for Economic Cooperation and Development) countries of a flexible exchange-rate system in 1973; the development of the Eurodollar market; the further doubling of oil prices in 1979; and the changes in macroeconomic policies in the United States in 1979 with the resulting extraordinarily high levels of nominal and real interest rates in world markets.

Prior to the late 1960s Colombia had relied heavily on a single primary product export, coffee, and suffered severe fluctuations in foreign-exchange availability when the price of coffee fluctuated. A policy of import-substituting industrialization (ISI) was pursued actively from the end of World War II. But the easier stages of ISI had been completed by the late 1960s; so a continued pursuit of that policy into more and more sophisticated and capital-intensive products did not appear to be a potential motor for much growth. In the late 1960s the Carlos Lleras R. government shifted policy toward export promotion and "minor exports" (that is, exports other than coffee, bananas, petroleum, or sugar) that became important as a source of foreign exchange. The switch in 1967 to a creeping peg exchange rate (noted previously) encouraged exports, as did such other steps as the creation of Fondo de Promociación de Exportaciones (PROEXPO), an institution designed to seek markets and to finance export industries. Between 1967 and 1974 current dollar exports other than coffee and petroleum (which in any case ceased to be a net export in the early 1970s) rose by nearly sevenfold.

Although the relaxing of the foreign-exchange constraint in the late 1960s and early 1970s permitted rapid growth, the cited developments in the foreign sector did create difficult policy problems for the Colombian governments of the period. In the early 1970s manufactured exports grew due to high world demand, domestic subsidies, and an appropriate exchange-rate policy. However, the slow growth of the OECD countries after the first oil price increase, coupled with a coffee boom beginning in 1976 and followed by the boom in illegal drugs, had a markedly negative effect on manufacturing growth as Colombia began to exhibit some of the characteristics of a "Dutch diseased" economy.[21]

Prior to 1970 the country received a substantial inflow of official credit that the government was able to use to finance budget deficits without risking high inflation rates. It was possible to sell the borrowed dollars for pesos to finance the domestic content of projects. As foreign exchange became less scarce and eventually quite abundant,[22] the government faced a new policy dilemma. An accumulation of reserves would have required a budget surplus to avoid inflationary pressures; alternatively, a constant level of reserves would have implied an exchange-rate revaluation, a greater opening of the economy, and substantially lower protection for the nonbooming sectors producing internationally tradeable goods—in this case manufacturing and agricultural products. None of these options was attractive to the government.

The illegal nature of the export boom of the late 1970s also posed special problems, because it entailed a growing underground economy and increasing corruption. Furthermore, given international power politics, the country could not unilaterally legalize the drug industry.

Finally, the world recession of the early 1980s together with U.S. monetary policy raised international interest rates to very high levels, weakened export markets, and limited the country's ability to borrow internationally, eventually forcing it to undertake a fairly severe adjustment. Although the evolution of the foreign sector thus continued to condition the possible economic policies of the country, Colombia's situation as the 1980s began was an enviable one compared to most developing countries.

The ready availability of foreign exchange during the middle and late 1970s contributed to Colombia's cautious external debt management, which resulted in a manageable debt burden. As of 1978 the ratio of debt service to exports of goods and nonfactor services for Latin America stood at 42.2 percent, while Colombia's was only 15.3 percent, the lowest among the large Latin American countries. From 1978 to 1982, however, the total external debt increased at an average annual rate of 22 percent to reach 9,421 billion dollars in 1982. This rapid increase was ironically accompanied by a dramatic accumulation of reserves, which from 1978 to 1981 amounted to 85.5 percent of the increase in total external debt.

Whatever the explanation for what was a process of borrowing to build up reserves, the reserves were soon to be drawn down, a process that began in 1982 and accelerated in 1983 and 1984. Colombian export revenues had grown rapidly over the 1970s. They peaked in 1980 and declined during the world recession that followed, so that in 1983 their level in current dollars was about three quarters that of 1980. Imports, however, continued to grow through 1982 and remained relatively high in 1983, at about 11.3 percent above the 1980 level. Reserves accumulated during the late 1970s were deliberately drawn down as part of a policy to keep the level of imports up and to restrain inflation, while government deficits soared as the peso resources obtained from selling reserves were used to finance the budget deficit without enlarging the money supply. Colombia thereby succeeded in postponing an external sector adjustment; but adjustment eventually became necessary in light of declining exports, a real exchange rate that since 1978 had remained between 30 and 40 percent higher than in 1970, and a deteriorating foreign-debt situation. Had some exogenous event intervened before the foreign exchange ran low, this strategy might in retrospect look like a shrewd one. Maintaining domestic expenditures while not undertaking a real devaluation or taking other steps to close the balance-of-payments gap was made feasible by the high level of reserves, was attractive to a government not anxious to slow or delay its spending program, and was defensible to the extent that the balance-of-payments problem was viewed as temporary and/or world market conditions viewed as not amenable to a quick increase in Colombian exports. In any case the needed stroke of good luck did not appear, and by 1984 a foreign-exchange crisis was developing. It was neither as severe as those in many countries, which entered the world recession without a foreign-exchange reserve cushion, nor as foreboding as it would have been had Colombia not been able to look forward to significant foreign-exchange earnings from its coal reserves by 1986.

The adjustment began in earnest during 1984, as the government restricted imports, tightened the nontariff barriers that had been weakened during the 1970s, and accelerated the devaluation of the peso so that in 1984 the real exchange rate was only about 23 percent above its 1970 level, down from 39 percent in 1982. Although this adjustment has thus far been milder than in most other Latin American countries, there is a great debate as to whether it could have been largely avoided had different policies been followed or had some policies been instituted more expeditiously.

INCOME DISTRIBUTION, UNEMPLOYMENT, AND OTHER SOCIAL INDICATORS SINCE 1970

For the 1970s as a whole, a best guess would be that income distribution did not change significantly; this would mean that all broad income categories (though not, of course, all individuals or occupational categories) tended to share significantly in the growth of per capita incomes during this decade. A worsening of overall distribution probably occurred in the first part of the decade. As previously mentioned, the accelerating inflation from 1971 to 1975 appears to have led to a price–wage lag that contributed to a sharp decline ranging from 5 to 20 percent in the real wages of the major occupational categories for which time-series data are available, at a time when average per capita income (including that from capital) for the population was rising. Although the resulting income shifts hurt some well off as well as poor earners, the overall effects of the shifts on distribution would be expected to be negative if, as seems to be the case, the business income that rose as a share of national income accrues mainly to the rich. In the late 1970s the income distribution probably improved as most real wages were rising. The year 1975 was the low mark for most wage series, and by 1980 or 1981 most groups had gained by 15 to 25 percent relative to 1975; earnings of white-collar workers in manufacturing, the highest income group for which we have data, had however recovered only by 10 percent. For the decade as a whole, though, blue-collar manufacturing wages with fringe benefits rose by about 13 percent, construction wages by about 8 percent, and agricultural wages by something in the range of 20 to 25 percent.[23] Manufacturing white-collar wages showed no change, and in general the paid white-collar category appears to have been the main group that did not share in the improvements during the 1970s. The apparent increase in lower-end incomes was hopefully associated with a tightening market for relatively low-skill labor. The stagnation of income (and the resulting loss in relative terms) for clerical workers suggests an increasing relative supply of workers with basic clerical skills; during the 1970s, the educational level of the labor force continued to increase at a rapid rate. Incomes seem to have risen for a good part of the professional and business groups, which is probably associated partly with the increasing demand for people in these high-skill categories and partly with a rapid growth of small- and medium-size industries that provided high incomes for many successful entrepreneurs.

Urban unemployment rates had fluctuated mainly within the range of 10 to 12 percent between the beginning of the series (1963) and 1974. From the late 1960s or the early 1970s through 1981 there was a downward trend, as the (weighted) average rate approached 8 percent for the four largest cities.

Indicators of welfare, such as life expectancy, housing conditions, and level of education (already mentioned), continued to show improvement in the 1970s. Life expectancy at birth was about fifty-two years in 1970 and about sixty-three years in 1979,[24] with the infant mortality rate having fallen from about 90 in 1970 to 69 per 1,000 live births in 1978.[25] The population growth rate, which was about 3.0 percent per year in the 1960s, fell to an average of 2.3 percent in the 1970s and was down to perhaps 1.8 percent at the end of the decade. Housing conditions continued to improve. Between the population/housing census of 1964 and 1973, the share of houses with running water, electricity, and sewer connection increased markedly as did the quality of construction and the ratio of rooms per person. There is little doubt that these trends continued during the rest of the 1970s.

The economic slowdown of the 1980s has been reflected in a sharp increase of unemployment from under 10 percent at the beginning of the decade to 13.5 percent in 1984 (for the four largest cities). By 1984 employment in factory manufacturing had fallen 10 to 15 percent from its peak in 1979 and 1980.[26] The participation rate has been higher than in the late 1970s, possibly reflecting the entry of secondary workers in response to unemployment or low incomes of primary earners.

No income-distribution data are available to permit a full assessment of which groups bore the brunt of the slowdown, although wage data indicate that agricultural workers were among them (real wages having fallen over 20 percent). The relatively protected workers in manufacturing and large-scale commerce, on the other hand, were not among them, as their wages continued to increase at least through 1983 (for manufacturing, 1984). Probably this increase was related to the decline in the rate of consumer price increases from the peak of approximately 27 percent in both 1980 and 1981 to 16 percent in 1984.

Although the data do not allow a detailed study of social mobility, the large improvement in the social indicators previously discussed, the fast process of urbanization, the changing structure of production, and the high rates of economic growth, as well as the growth of the illegal economy during the 1970s, indicate that there were several channels for social mobility open to Colombians. It could be argued that these channels made the unequal income distribution politically tolerable, and they help us to understand why the income distribution has not led to a political upheaval. As the recession closed some channels of mobility, the frustration generated by unfulfilled expectations increased along with political tensions, in spite of the fact that people were on average richer, better fed and housed, and better educated than ten or twenty years earlier.

A LOOK TOWARD THE FUTURE

Colombia's immediate economic future is full of uncertainty, and the unfolding of the current crisis is hard to predict. The effectiveness of policy measures of the late 1980s depends on many internal and external factors the impacts of which are not well understood or which are beyond the control of the Colombian government. As in all Latin American countries, developments in the international economy are a key determinant of future trends. The level of international demand; protectionist policies of the developed countries, particularly the United States; levels of real and nominal interest rates in international markets; prices of primary products; and the recovery of the Venezuelan economy (an important market for Colombia) will all impinge on the short-run performance of the Colombian economy. Important uncertainties on the domestic front include the timing and prices of the new coal and petroleum exports, the success of the government in eradicating expectations of a large devaluation, and the impact of current restrictive policies.

It is possible, however, to identify some likely characteristics of the Colombian economy in the medium term. Probably the most important structural change will involve the expected surge in coal and oil production, which could turn Colombia into a large exporter of energy. This change will create new policy issues and problems. If the magnitude of energy exports is as large as expected, Colombia will have to deal again with the problems as well as the blessings of a booming export sector, in this case a capital-intensive one, spatially concentrated in sparsely populated areas. As with the coffee and drug boom of the 1970s, the real exchange rate can be expected to appreciate, and other sectors producing internationally traded goods will lose protection as the abundance of foreign exchange creates great incentives to import those goods. In the case of Colombia, the main sectors that will lose protection are manufacturing and, to a lesser degree, agriculture. The service sector can be expected to share in the boom and to become (or remain) the main generator of employment. As this scenario evolves, Colombia's policy makers will face a quandary: If the energy boom is long, say thirty years, it would be too costly to protect the manufacturing and agricultural sectors for such a long time; if it is short, say five years, it would be too costly not to protect them. Since the length of the boom is uncertain, industrial and agricultural policies will clearly be more difficult to design than they have been up to now.

An increasing role for the extractive sector will leave Colombia more vulnerable to terms of trade fluctuations, and since that sector provides virtually no employment, the situation will call for renewed attention to issues of employment and income distribution, variables that will be affected by how much of the rents generated by the mining sector are captured by the government, and by how they are spent. The continued increase in the level of educational attainment will maintain the downward pressure on wages in lower-level clerical jobs and in some more skilled occupations as well, creating the potential for decreasing inequality of earnings but also accentuating the stress associated with such a narrowing of differentials. The general wage level will remain under pressure for some time due to the rapid growth of working-age people, reflecting the rapid population growth of the 1960s.

The decline in family size seems well institutionalized in Colombia and, with further urbanization and education, it is likely to continue at a gradual pace toward a level between 1 and 1.5 percent. Fortunately, Colombia is thus within striking distance of a low enough rate so that population growth is unlikely by itself to sabotage the country's aspirations for economic advancement.

OLIGARCHICAL DEMOCRACY AND DEVELOPMENT: A CONCLUDING NOTE

A review of Colombia's recent economic history in the Latin American perspective does not suggest that the country's oligarchical style of democracy has produced some very special ''model'' of development. It is true, however, as previously noted, that the country seems to have avoided the extremes, by Latin American standards, in both growth rate and income-distribution inequality, as well as in political unrest. Nor does the transition from the National Front structure to the more open political process of the last decade seem to have left clear marks on the pattern of development.[27] Several characteristics of Colombia's economic structure and policies have probably acted to mitigate some of the apparent sources of extreme political repression that arose in other Latin American countries in the 1970s. The fact that the main export product, coffee, is produced mostly on small farms, that Colombian economic policies have not suffered drastic changes,[28] and that the country has not suffered from the high inflation levels of other countries such as Argentina and Brazil,[29] have softened public resentment against the beneficiaries of the export booms and have moderated the reaction of some population groups whose sharp income losses could

have fomented uprisings. In this environment the pressures against income concentration that have resulted from Colombia's democratic forms have not been
strong enough to produce a distribution of income nearly as egalitarian as those
of authoritarian systems like Korea and Taiwan, although it does seem to be the
case that within the Latin American context, the typically democratic regimes
have had somewhat less inequality than ones (like Brazil and Peru) that have
more often been under military rule.

However, some of the economic elements that have contributed to the stability
of the political system in the past have disappeared or weakened. The illegal
nature of the booming drug industry lowers the citizenry's respect for the law,
raises the expectations of quick wealth, and slows the growth of the modern
sector engaged in the production of internationally tradeable goods. The growth
of mineral exports controlled by the government is likely to strengthen and
embitter the fight for the government's spoils and the rents and privileges it can
create. The increased open urban unemployment, particularly among college-
educated individuals with high income expectations, is another factor likely to
contribute to increased social tension and to put stress on the political system.
Thus, it is possible that Colombia, following O'Donnell's suggested stages,[30]
may be entering a period in which the modernization process slows down after
substantial success, economic groups are already well organized and active,
social tensions increase, and political repression becomes more likely. This
scenario, considered possible but unlikely by Sheahan in 1980,[31] is now unfortunately a more serious threat for the near future.

NOTES

The authors wish to thank Mr. Sergio Uribe for comments on a previous version of
this chapter and Mrs. Martha Rountree for her efficient and always cheerful typing
assistance.

1. Cross-country comparisons of income distribution and inequality are risky, as the
available data come from surveys that have diverse methodologies and coverage. To these
problems one must add others that arise from differences in the ways of defining and
measuring income and income recipients; that is, some works measure the distribution
of income among individuals while others measure household-income distribution. The
data problems are compounded by those inherent in the nature of the inequality measures.
In general, there is no one-to-one relationship between income distribution and the inequality measure; that is, it is possible for the distribution of income to change and a
measure of inequality to remain constant. For example, the Gini coefficient could remain
constant when the income share of both the upper and lower classes goes up and the
middle class loses. All these factors make international comparisons of income inequality
difficult. In the comparisons that follow, we use household data for 1970 or the closest
year for which household data were available. We do not compare inequality measures,
such as the variance or the Gini coefficient. Rather, we refer to the income of the different
population quintiles to provide an approximation of the degree of inequality. The source

of these data is S. Jain, *Size Distribution of Income: a Compilation of Data* (Washington, D.C.: World Bank, 1975).

2. The democratic traditions of these three countries are probed and their experiences compared to those of other Latin countries in John A. Peeler, *Latin American Democracies: Colombia, Costa Rica, Venezuela* (Chapel Hill: University of North Carolina Press, 1985).

3. See Robert Dix, *Colombia: The Political Dimensions of Change* (New Haven, Conn.: Yale University Press, 1967), Chapter 4.

4. At least as of the last decade or so, Colombia seems to be a medium case in terms of "tax effort" (that is, tax revenues as a share of GDP and of level of public expenditures). From 1967 to 1979 tax revenues of the public sector fell in the range of 12 to 14 percent of GDP, current income was 21 to 25 percent of GDP, and total expenditure was 25 to 32 percent. Richard M. Bird, *Intergovernmental Finance in Colombia* (Cambridge, Mass.: Harvard Law School, 1984), p. 42.

5. The frequent contrasts made between such countries as Colombia and the few cases where inequality has been markedly reduced over time, Taiwan being the most studied example, quickly light on the presence or absence of agrarian reform and of public policies in support of small farms as key distinguishing features. When income inequalities are reduced significantly at an early stage in the development process, a beneficial inertia may take over, with the effect of keeping the inequalities low. In the case of Taiwan, the level of inequality seems to have followed a nearly continuous downward trend since the reform occurred.

6. World Bank, *World Development Report*, 1984, p. 149.

7. World Bank, *World Development Report*, p. 156. An early start and systematic support lowered the total fertility rate so that in 1982 it was about equal to those of Costa Rica and Argentina. Of the major Latin countries, only Chile had a lower rate. World Bank, *World Development Report*, p. 70.

8. William P. McGreevey, "Population Policy Under the National Front," in *Politics of Compromise: Coalition Government in Colombia*, eds. R. Albert Berry, Ronald H. Hellman, and Mauricio Solaún (New Brunswick, N.J.: Transaction Books, 1980), p. 418.

9. See, for example, Robert Arnove, "Education Policies of the National Front," in *Análisis de un Mito: La Educación como Factor de la Movilidad Social en Colombia*, ed. Rodrigo Parra (Bogotá: Universidad de los Andes, Departamento de Educación, 1973).

10. For example, G. S. Fields, "Income Inequality in Urban Colombia: A Decomposition Analysis," *Review of Income and Wealth*, series 25, number 3 (1979), finds that education differences explain 35 percent of the income inequality.

11. For further details, see R. Albert Berry, "Colombia's Post War Economic Development in Political Perspective" (Toronto: University of Toronto, 1986), mimeo.

12. In a labor-abundant country like Colombia, it is unlikely that unions can have much success in bargaining for the price of labor unless they are supported by the government. This argument is central to the discussion by Miguel Urrutia, *The Development of the Colombian Labor Movement* (New Haven, Conn.: Yale University Press, 1969).

13. See Berry, "Colombia's Post War Economic Development," in *Politics of Compromise*, eds. Berry, et al.

14. See R. Albert Berry and R. Soligo, "The Distribution of Income in Colombia: An Overview," in *Economic Policy and Income Distribution in Colombia*, eds. R. A. Berry and R. Soligo (Boulder, Colo.: Westview Press, 1980), p. 28; A. Berry and M.

Urrutia, eds. *Income Distribution in Colombia* (New Haven, Conn.: Yale University Press, 1976); E. C. Meldau, ed., *Benefit Incidence: Public Health Expenditures and Income Distribution: the Case of Colombia* (North Quincy, Mass.: Christopher Publishing House, 1980); M. Selowsky, ed., *Who Benefits from Government Expenditures?: A Case Study of Colombia* (New York: Oxford University Press, 1979).

15. See John D. Martz, *Colombia: A Contemporary Political Survey* (Chapel Hill: University of North Carolina Press, 1962), pp. 111–15.

16. Dix, *Colombia: The Political Dimensions*, p. 131.

17. R. Albert Berry and Francisco E. Thoumi, "Colombian Economic Policies from 1970 to 1984," in *State and Society in Contemporary Colombia: Beyond the National Front*, eds. B. Bagley, F. Thoumi, and J. Tokatlian (Boulder, Colo.: Westview Press, 1986).

18. For a fuller treatment of Colombia's economic evolution under the National Front, see R. Albert Berry, "The National Front and Colombia's Economic Development,' in *The Politics of Compromise*, eds. Berry et al.

19. Berry and Thoumi, "Colombian Economic Growth and Policies from 1970 to 1984."

20. The importance of domestic policies is shown clearly when cross-country comparisons are made. As shown in the Inter-American Development Bank, *Economic and Social Progress in Latin America* (1982 Report), Chapter 3, during the 1970s, there was, among Latin American countries, no correlation of growth performance with either the evolution of the countries' terms of trade or the availability of oil to them. That is, for a given world economy scenario, domestic policies tend to determine the relative growth success of the different countries. Of course, the better the foreign-sector performance, the better the growth opportunities for each country.

21. When new exports arise or the price of existing ones increases, these sectors have a larger comparative advantage over other sectors than before, and the growth of the latter is discouraged by normal market forces.

22. The dramatic export boom that began in 1975 allowed the country to increase its international reserves to unprecedented levels. In 1974 reserves were 20.5 percent of imports of goods and services, and by 1979 this ratio had reached 104.2 percent in spite of an almost doubling of imports. In absolute terms the increase in reserves was spectacular; at the end of 1968, a year of still serious foreign-exchange constraint, it stood at 28 million dollars, and by 1979 it had reached 4105.9 million dollars en route to a peak of 5630.2 million dollars in 1981.

23. These figures are based on comparisons of the average wages of the 1979–1981 period with those of the 1969–1971 period. For detailed statistics and further discussion, see Berry and Thoumi, "Colombian Economic Growth and Policies."

24. Figures are from *United Nations, Demographic Yearbook*, 1982.

25. Jorge Vivas R., "Evolución de los Principales Indicadores del Sector Salud en Colombia en la década del 70," *Coyuntura Económica* 13 (June 1983):167.

26. DANE's employment survey of a preestablished set of firms shows a decrease by 15 percent during this period; this figure would overstate the true decline if there were net employment growth in newly opened plants, though during the recession this may not have been the case.

27. This is not unexpected, as the relationship between political systems and economic policy types is a very complex and unclear one. See, for example, C. Díaz-Alejandro, "Open Economy, Closed Polity?" in *Latin America in the World Economy: New Per-*

spectives, ed. D. Tussie (Aldershot, England: Grower, 1983), pp. 21–53, and J. Sheahan, "Market-Oriented Economic Policies and Political Repression in Latin America," *Economic Development and Cultural Change* 28 (January 1980):267–91.

28. Sheahan, "Market-Oriented Economic Policies," pp. 267–91.

29. In Díaz-Alejandro's view this is one of the main reasons why the Southern Cone countries had to use strong repression to be able to implement policies.

30. See Guillermo O'Donnell, *Modernization and Bureaucratic-Authoritarianism* (Berkeley: University of California Press, 1973).

31. Sheahan, "Market-Oriented Economic Policies," p. 282.

5

The Colombian State in Crisis: Continuity and Change

Harvey F. Kline

Colombia and the role of its state seem to fit into few of the categories most commonly used in literature about Latin American politics. Indeed, the mixed character of the country's political economy has become part of the ruling mythology. The Bogotá journal, *Estrategia económica y financiera*, applauded this mixed character with the following words:

Economic policy . . . is an eclectic mixture of market economics and of state interventionism in which elements of import substitution coexist with elements of export promotion; protectionism, with international competition; the stimulation of a vigorous private sector, with the deliberate action of the state as an industrial mover and promoter in determined fields; relative financial liberty internally, with exchange controls; stimuli for foreign private investment, with strict limits to its behavior; a prudent monetary and fiscal management, with deliberate efforts to modify the productive structure of the country. . . . In the political aspect, the model has produced legitimacy in the exercise of government; ordered, predictable, and periodic transfer of power; and clear limitations to authority. This in turn has given sufficient continuity to economic and social policy in order to gain experience, develop institutions, and to initiate long-term programs and projects.[1]

Yet, although they are safe, statements that "Colombia is eclectic" do not go very far in describing and analyzing its state system. The purpose of this chapter is to suggest what the state system has been historically and to consider problems and opportunities that *might* soon change it.

We must begin by clarifying terms. Alfred Stepan defines the state as more than the government, suggesting that it is "the continuous administrative, legal, bureaucratic and coercive system that attempts not only to structure relations *between* civil society and public authority in a polity but also to structure many crucial relationships *within* civil society as well."[2]

State relations are often a matter of conflict. Although using different definitions, Joel Migdal argued in 1985:

An understanding of how societies persist and change must start with the organizations that exercise social control, that subordinate individual inclinations to the behavior that these organizations prescribe. These informal and formal organizations, ranging from families and neighborhood groups to mammoth foreign-owned companies, use a variety of sanctions, rewards, and symbols to induce people to behave according to the rules of the game. . . . Indeed, the central political and social drama of recent history has been the battle between the [institutional] state and other social organizations. The dispute is over who makes the rules, who grants the property rights that define the use of assets and resources in society.[3]

Midgal concluded, "The model I am suggesting depicts society as a mélange of social organizations rather than a dichotomous structure. The [institutional] state is seen as one organization which, singly or in tandem, offer individuals strategies of personal survival and, for some, strategies of upward mobility."[4]

I shall use this mélange model in an analysis of the eclectic Colombian state, reserving the term "state" for the broad sense and referring to the specific case as the "institutional state." In the pages that follow, I argue that the Colombian institutional state has historically been weak, because (1) before 1958 it lacked the social need to exist, and (2) even since that date, it has lacked the economic wherewithall to exist in a strong form. Space does not allow a consideration of all the groups within the state. I shall limit my concern to three—the government, local business, and transnational corporations—since the studies done by Stepan and Becker on Peru and Evans on Brazil[5] conclude that the state system, at least in its economic dimensions, is a *tripé* or triad made up of those three parts. In the social dimension of the state, various works on Latin American politics include such "private" groups as the church and the military, not considered here.

THE TRADITIONAL COLOMBIAN STATE SYSTEM AND CONTINUITY

For reasons described in Chapter 2, the beginning of the National Front in 1958 seems to be the watershed of Colombian history. To a certain extent, changes in the traditional state in its social dimensions began in that year. Economic aspects, perhaps because of the importance of exogenous factors, did not change with the political watershed.

The Social Dimension

The social dimensions of the Colombian state before 1958 were built around two principles: (1) political power in the hands of one of the two traditional parties, each of which, in turn, controlled vast numbers of dependent people, primarily through sectarian methods (see Chapter 2); and (2) a social-class system, with a small elite dominating both the economic and political structures. Although many Colombians refer to this elite as *la oligarquía*, it has proved empirically difficult to demonstrate that this elite directly controlled *all* decisions.[6] What is certain, *at a minimum*, is that the well educated dominated the political system. Having the liberty of sending one's children to school (even if it is "free" public education) tended to be the exclusive right of the middle- and upper-income groups. Although the mobilization abilities of the traditional parties declined after 1958, the social-class has remained a strong component of the state.

How this class bias continued in the political system during the National Front is shown in a 1969 study of the national Congress (which is the bottom stratum of the national political elite, rather than the top). In a country in which about 3 percent of the population attempted postsecondary education, 80 percent of the 218 congressmembers reported having completed university education, and another 7 percent reported having attended universities without graduating.[7] Since success as a congressperson is one important route for later positions in the executive branch, clearly this social-class bias exists for the latter also.

This class has been the product of the international division of labor. As one radical Colombian social scientist said to me, "There is a class that runs this country, and that is doing very well under the present dependency system. It is not to their advantage to change things. Why should they go to all the work that change entails?"[8] The dominant sector has included not only those elected and appointed to governmental positions, but also the producer association (the *gremios*) and, to a lesser degree, organized labor. Although there might be disagreements within the dominant sector about public policies, the gremios and organized labor have tended to be united in their support of the state (and the regime, for that matter). All have been granted legal recognition (*personería jurídica*) by the government, on many occasions receive budgetary support from the official sector, and in some cases name ex officio members of governmental committees and agencies. The head of the National Federation of Coffee Growers, to take one notable example, is a member of the ministerial-level National Council of Economic and Social Policy (CONPES), which is supposed to coordinate all economic planning. Yet at least one scholar has concluded that this falls short of corporatism, as the government rarely denies or revokes legal recognition.[9] Generally, new groups are added to the system, but old ones are not eliminated.

Organized labor has been, at the least, on the fringes of the dominant sector in the state system. The first two labor federations were formed respectively by the Liberal and Conservative parties (the Confederación de Trabajadores Colombianos, CTC, and the Unión de Trabajadores Colombianos, UTC). The Liberal confederation was established during a hegemony of that party. Later, the Conservative party was instrumental, along with the Jesuits, in the formation of the UTC—but importantly, without withdrawing recognition from the CTC, although it had less importance.[10] Subsequently, two additional confederations— the Confederación General de Trabajo (CGT) and the Confederación Sindical de Trabajadores de Colombia (CSTC) appeared. The latter was the most radical of all. The union confederations exist in harmony with other groups in the dominant sector, *unless they break the rules of the political game.* Thus, as the result of an illegal strike in June 1985, the CSTC lost its personería jurídica for six months.[11]

The organized groups are consulted by government leaders before certain decisions are made through a process called "concertación." At the ends of calendar years, for example, representatives of organized labor, employer groups, and government officials discuss what the increase of the minimum wage should be, given the inflation of the preceding year. In the early 1980s various producer associations banded together in a Frente Gremial, with the goal of having influence on economic policy in general. Interestingly enough, even a weak president like Julio César Turbay was able to ignore the Frente Gremial for a time.[12]

In August 1985, however, the government of Belisario Betancur proposed a new law, which would give more general functions to a "Consejo Nacional de Concertación Económica y Social." Under this new "social pact" the group would consist of fifteen members, five each from the government, business, and labor (the fifth coming from those on pensions) and would have as its "primary end that of achieving justice in the relations between employers and workers, within a spirit of social equilibrium that might facilitate harmonious national development and secure the well-being of all Colombians."[13]

All the efforts at *concertación* to this point have omitted the unorganized people of the country. While it might be argued that before the National Front most were organized in a sectarian fashion by the political parties, since that time there have been only occasional, most often feeble, governmental attempts to organize them. The first was through Acción Comunal, a government program with two major purposes: to contribute to the material well-being of poor people and to alter the passivity of the peasants (*campesinos*). To a large degree, Acción Comunal worked only as long as Peace Corps volunteers were around to guide it.[14]

The most ambitious effort to organize the campesinos came during the government of Carlos Lleras Restrepo, when the president set up the National Association of Peasants (ANUC), made up especially of those who were beneficiaries of agrarian reform. By the end of the Lleras presidency there were almost a million members. However, under the post-August 1968 presidency of Misael Pastrana, ANUC took actions that went beyond the pale of acceptable behavior. By August 1971 the ANUC board of directors decided to separate itself completely from all existing political parties and factions, as none was judged to be capable of responding to the demands of the peasants. At the same time the board called for the expropriation of large landownings and free land distribution. This radicalization, along with land invasions, occupations of government buildings, boycotts, and demonstrations brought a Pastrana response of divide, coopt, and repress. The major radical ANUC faction was excluded from agrarian policy making and repressed. The moderate wing, on the other hand, was given office space in the ministry of labor and other perquisites.[15]

The Liberal presidencies of Alfonso López Michelsen (from 1974 to 1978) and Julio César Turbay (from 1978 to 1982) made attempts to coopt sectors of the lower class, with the complementary goals of quieting discontent and building personal political empires. However, the relative poverty of the official sector put clear limitations on this cooptation attempt.

THE ECONOMIC DIMENSION

Within the economic dimension of the Colombian state system the government has been the weakest of the three actors. This can be shown by comparing the role of the institutional state to that of the private Colombian sector and to that of the transnational enterprises.

The Institutional State and the Private Sector

Historically, the government has been limited by what the important businesses and gremios think it should be doing. In the 1940s it was decided that the institutional state should take a role in the economy; the way this was structured is illustrative. A decentralized institute, Instituto de Fomento Industrial (IFI), was set up to begin those industrial activities considered to be important for economic development, *but* that private enterprises would not perform because of cost and/or risk. Should the enterprise prove to be profitable, as was to be the case in petrochemicals and automobile tires, it was then expected that IFI would sell to the private sector. This led to one pundit's characterization of the system as "socialism for the rich and capitalism for the poor."

The role of the institutional state in support of the private sector was also shown in 1967, when the government of Carlos Lleras Restrepo issued Decree-Law 444. In addition to collecting information on transnational enterprises (TNEs) for the first time, the law attempted to strengthen the *private* sector. A tax credit (*certificado de abono tributario*, CAT) was established for private exporters of "minor products," that is, all products except coffee and petroleum. Decree-Law 444 also set up an Export Production Fund (PROEXPO), a decentralized institute under the ministry of development, which channels credit under liberal terms to exporting firms and can provide equity capital in special circumstances, among other things.[16]

In economic policy making, the producer associations can usually block policies unfavorable to them, in the long run if not in the short run. These associations have done this in recent years in both land and tax reform.[17] At the time of the initiation of the Andean Pact in the early 1970s, for another example, the gremios objected to the "first option" right of the government.[18] Further, the ideology widely held by government bureaucrats, ministers, and congresspeople[19] is that the private sector can perform economic activities more efficiently than the "official" one.

This upper-class bias of the Colombian state was well described by Jonathan Hartlyn in 1985:

[R]elative to other groups in society, producer associations have far more capacity to influence decisions facilitated by their greater access to arenas of state power. Informal contacts and direct access to key decision makers are often crucial in determining the outcome of policy decisions or in obtaining an administrative ruling or exception favorable to a particular firm or subsector. . . . When these means are not successful, producer groups are also well situated to utilize the democratic aspects of the regime—such as the press, the congress, or the courts—to their advantage.[20]

In the absence of political-party differences, especially since the National Front, the functions of interest articulation and aggregation have been increasingly performed by such groups, usually in representation of their members. Occasionally, they address economic and social problems in general. Since the gremios are primarily employer groups, there is a decidedly upper-class bias in the system.

This bias reflects the relative power of the private sector in capital investment, which continues to be more important than the institutional state. In the mid–1980s the leading export products (coffee and drugs) are controlled by private, albeit different, sectors. This "privatization" is also shown by the fact that the Federación Nacional de Cafeteros collects taxes and has the legal authority to negotiate foreign agreements.

In comparative terms, the Colombian institutional state is weaker than most in Latin America. Why this is the case is explained in different ways by Colombian radicals. Some stress the lack of a nationalist revolution, such as that of the Mexican Revolution or even the Vargas movement in Brazil.[21] Others state that the Colombian government is weak because private capitalists have always been strong. As one said: "Although there are few good studies, the Colombian government is, and probably always has been, one of the weaker ones in Latin America. This is seen in figures of government expenditures as a percentage of Gross Domestic Product."[22] Figures published by the Inter-American Development Bank suggest that such is the case.[23]

Continuing the same reasoning, radicals argue that the dominant classes use the government less in Colombia than their counterparts in most other Latin American countries, because the Colombian dominant classes have been better able to meet their needs for wealth and domination through the private sector.

That the Colombian private sector has traditionally been more dynamic than most in Latin America has long been accepted. Some cultural explanations have been offered in the case of the capitalists around Medellín, the *antioqueños*.[24]

Another line of thought suggests development of the private-sector dominance in the following way: Coffee, produced on small holdings, emerged as the primary export product in the 1870s. It was sold to private merchants, who exported it and made most of the profit. The merchants used the economic surplus to invest in import-substituting industrialization, as early as the first decade of this century.[25] ISI began early in this century, yet it was World War I and, even more so, the Great Depression that led to its growth.

The institutional state, however, almost always has had a legal monopoly in energy-related matters. Since Spanish colonial tradition was that the monarch was the owner of the subsoil, only granting temporary rights for production for a given time period in return for royalties, the Republic governments inherited that right. Although history became a bit complex in this regard in the nineteenth century, generally speaking, the government has retained subsoil rights.

The Institutional State and Transnational Enterprises

Transnational enterprises have never had the amount of investment nor the importance in Colombia that they have had in other Latin American countries. For a time, United Fruit banana production was important, and indeed led to difficulties when the government sided with UFCO against workers. Yet Colombia was never a "banana republic" like some of the Central American countries and Ecuador.

The relatively small importance of transnationals continued during the National Front. In 1970 TNE investment totaled 457 million U.S. dollars, which represented 6.7 percent of the gross domestic product (GDP) and 30.5 percent of the total investment in the Colombian economy.[26] As compared to the rest of Latin America, in 1975 Colombia was seventh in total TNE investment, behind Brazil, Mexico, Venezuela, Panama, Peru, and Argentina. Only 3.9 percent of TNE investment in Latin America (and 0.5 percent of world TNE investment) went to Colombia.[27]

The relative position notwithstanding, the government of Carlos Lleras Restrepo attempted to regulate foreign investment for the very first time in Colombian history. Article 1 of Decree-Law 444 declared that foreign investment would have to be in harmony with the national interest. Any such investment greater than 100,000 U.S. dollars would first have to be approved. A rather complex institutional machinery was set up to enforce this stipulation: Planeación Nacional would analyze and approve investment proposals; the Oficina de Cambios would register and authorize the outflow of capital; the superintendent of foreign commerce (who was the director of Instituto Colombiano de Comercio Exterior, INCOMEX) would grant import licenses; the Advisory Committee of Global

Licenses would be in charge of implementing the governmental policies on capital-goods imports and of avoiding excess unused productive capacity.[28]

In setting up this machinery, the Carlos Lleras government had several goals. First, the government would have accurate data on TNE investments for the first time. Second, using those data, the government hoped to control the remittances of profits, setting a limit of 14 percent on them. Finally, through the approval process the government hoped to prevent TNEs from forcing Colombian enterprises out of business.

Natural resource TNEs always have had different conditions. Although the institutional state had a monopoly over subsoil rights, it did not do the exploration or production itself. When petroleum development began, capital and technology were absent in Colombia. Development was done by the TNEs, and the government remained a rentier partner, first receiving taxes based on the size of the concessions. Later, income and profit-remittance taxes were added.

The government of strongman Rafael Reyes (from 1904 to 1909) set the groundwork for future petroleum exploration and production when the general-president granted concessions to two of his protégés, De Mares and Barco, whose names are still used for the respective concessions. After decades of buying and selling rights, the De Mares concession ended up in the possession of Standard of New Jersey, while the Barco concession became an area in which Gulf Oil was involved. Petroleum production began in 1922, when 900 barrels per day were produced.[29]

During the first fifty years of petroleum production, a number of petroleum laws were written. Subsoil rights were always maintained by the government (with the exception of those cases in which ownership prior to 1873 could be proved), but other provisions changed. Generally speaking, the taxes and royalties went *down* in amount over time. Other inducements were offered to attract foreign TNEs, including the exemption from tariff duties on machinery imported for exploration and production, the right to receive payment in U.S. dollars for 75 percent of the production sold for Colombian consumption, differential exchange rates, depletion allowances, and the right to remit all profits from the enterprises, as well as to repatriate investments. These policies, continually more favorable to the TNEs, extended through the 1970s, during which "in Colombia oil policy became far more pro-producer."[30]

One Colombian radical, Jorge Villegas, interpreted this policy direction (which he considered to be the inverse of the direction of most underdeveloped countries) to be the result of a bargaining process. The "governing oligarchy" ran "persistently to ask the North American companies, again and again, to proceed with extraction." The companies replied that "there are stumbling blocks that prevent it." The oligarchy then took actions "to smooth over such obstacles with new legislation and wait for the turn of events."[31]

On various occasions the government of the United States entered the bargaining, intervening on behalf of the U.S. petroleum TNEs. Some argue that it was well understood that the 25 million U.S. dollar indemnification for the loss of Panama would not be approved by the U.S. Senate until the U.S. petroleum

TNEs had received favorable terms for their concessions.[32] On another occasion the threatened cancellation of the Barco concession led to both quiet diplomatic pressure and a visit from a "bombastic representative" of the U.S. government whose "outspoken criticism" of the Colombian government led to his becoming a "political liability" who was "ostracized until his departure from the city [Bogotá] in the summer of 1928."[33]

Yet none of the above should suggest either that the divisions in Colombia were neatly between "national" actors and "foreign" ones or that all Colombians were united in their support for or opposition to the foreign TNEs. As for the first point, George Philip pointed out that the boundary line between foreign and domestic soon blurred and, by the 1930s, if not before, "successive governments found oil concessions to be an avenue of credit-worthiness and local landowners, lawyers, and so forth continued to trade in concessions. Indeed, successive oil laws continued to be drawn up with an eye to strengthening the position of such local intermediaries."[34]

Many—and perhaps most—Colombian policy makers thought that the petroleum concessions were beneficial to the country. The foreign TNEs brought needed capital and expertise. Petroleum produced was import substitution, giving the country the energy needed for economic development. The foreign TNEs created jobs and paid taxes. Moreover, once Colombia became a petroleum exporter, needed foreign exchange was added to the country's coffers.

From time to time, however, voices were raised against the TNE concessions. Such a debate occurred in the early 1920s, at the time of the development of the De Mares and Barco concessions. In 1931 populist Liberal leader Jorge Gaitán "condemned the contracts as prejudicial to Colombian interests because they were too liberal and posed a threat to national agricultural interests in the concession region." He further stated his fear that the country was in danger of "becoming a pawn in a gigantic chess game between world petroleum powers"; hence it should defend its interests against foreign imperialism.[35]

The same theme was shown in the 1960s when Liberal Enrique Pardo Parra, first as minister of mines and later as senator, questioned their role. As minister, he suggested that profits remitted be limited to 18 percent; the companies replied that they were only making 6 percent on investment.[36] Pardo Parra decreed that companies should register their capital imports in the Oficina de Cambios; by 1968, when as a senator he checked such registrations, he found that none had been made.[37] He made a calculation of gains and losses for the country from the TNE petroleum production. He arrived at the conclusion that the country was receiving about .25 U.S. dollars per barrel and in some cases was not receiving any royalties because of exemptions and depletion allowances.[38]

The reaction to Enrique Pardo Parra was direct and two pronged. First, his figures were said to be incorrect. Second, he was attacked personally. He told the Senate the following in 1968:

And with this technical information—well checked and controlled—I asked the representatives of the foreign companies to modify their voracity a bit and to regulate that unjust situation with the country, although it might be by an adaptation of their contracts to the new Law 10 of 1961. I did not have success, I was slandered, censored by the press, and it was even said to me, by devoted friends of the companies and old lawyers of theirs, that I was causing damage to the nation.[39]

A politician, close to Pardo Parra, and a minister at the time, gave additional details about the case:

The transnationals brought Pardo Parra down as a minister of mines. They spread stories about him, and one day, when the Council of Ministers met, when we entered the room there were copies of a statement at our places accusing him of being a communist. This was because he got tough with them, tried to protect Colombian interests. . . . Later Carlos Sanz de Santamaría [head of the Inter-American Committee for the Alliance for Progress and a Colombian] came back to Bogotá and told President Valencia, "If you want to continue to get Alliance for Progress funds, you'd better do something about Pardo Parra." Valencia told Enrique this and offered him the ministry of education. He resigned rather than taking it.[40]

Yet criticism of petroleum TNEs within the governing system was the exception rather than the rule. In general, ministers of mines did not "rock the boat" as Pardo Parra did. Very importantly, never did either political party use opposition to the TNEs as part of their party program, although at least one presidential candidate (Alfonso López Michelsen) made nationalistic noises before being elected.

Also illustrative is the role of the parastatal petroleum enterprise, Empresa Colombiana de Petróleos (ECOPETROL), which was founded in 1948 with the mandate to work in petroleum and "other hydrocarbons," as well as to "administer and produce in other mining and petroleum fields that the government might assign to it, or that the Enterprise might obtain in any other way."[41] ECOPETROL at first was to administer those TNE concessions that had reverted to the state, and as such, got its real start in 1951 when the Standard of New Jersey subsidiary, Tropical Oil, returned the De Mares concession.

Yet it was a "reluctant institutional state" that founded ECOPETROL in the 1940s. Before establishing a state company, the Mariano Ospina administration offered all of the De Mares area to Colombian private capitalists for 100 million Colombian dollars, an investment that one ECOPETROL official told me they could have recouped in two years.[42] The Ospina government also offered Standard of New Jersey a continued role in the De Mares area, through a service contract. It is not clear which offer the Ospina administration made first. According to one scholar, "after some debate within the company, this offer was rejected for 'reasons of policy.' "[43] So the parastatal petroleum company was the third choice of the Ospina government; not so for his successor, Laureano Gómez, who said: "None of that. I want a state company."[44]

The ECOPETROL policy makers did not tend to be critical of the role of the TNEs. Rather, all evidence suggests that the relationship between ECOPETROL and the foreign companies was good and at times very cordial. A "special relationship" developed between ECOPETROL and the Standard of New Jersey subsidiary, first called Tropical Oil Company and later International Petroleum (Colombia) Ltd. (INTERCOL). One former official, who was in the parastatal enterprise from the time of Laureano Gómez (from 1950 to 1953) to that of Alfonso López (from 1974 to 1978), recalled:

When I went to ECOPETROL in 1950 everything had to be done. There were so many details, so many regulations to work out. Often we began working on a problem that had to be solved at three in the afternoon and saw the sun rise. The biggest problem was the refinery. We just didn't have the technicians to run it. . . . During my ECOPETROL days, the relationship between Tropical and ECOPETROL was like that of mother and child. Tropical was contracted to run the refinery for ten years, but with the understanding the Colombians would be taught the jobs. . . . When there were momentary shortages, these could be made up from INTERCOL. If ECOPETROL needed some diesel fuel, they [INTERCOL] would lend it to us. It was a very good relationship.[45]

Many who were or are involved in the energy field in Colombia reported that such a close relationship did develop. A former minister of economic development told me that "ECOPETROL and Exxon always worked closely together, for good and for bad."[46] Yet, ECOPETROL was perceived as the "prize" of the Colombian institutional state by the 1970s. As one former minister of mines told me, "ECOPETROL is the heart of Colombia. Those little things that the guerrillas are doing are not that important. Much more important is what is going on in ECOPETROL."[47] Further, as a former minister of finance stated in an interview, "In the case of some *institutos decentralizados*, including ECOPE-TROL, they are more powerful than the ministry they report to. The organizational chart may say one thing, but the reality is another."[48] In 1978, 39 percent of the country's petroleum was produced by ECOPETROL directly. Another 24 percent was produced through "*asociación*" contracts between the parastatal and the TNEs (in which the foreign companies were the operators); the remaining 37 percent was still in concessions.[49]

In conclusion, transnational enterprises, such as the Standard of New Jersey subsidiaries, used both punishments (Pardo Parra) and rewards (lending diesel fuel) in their dealings with the Colombian government. "Rational" TNEs were friendly and helpful, even when there were short-term costs for being cooperative, in order to build up "good will" for future relationships. To the extent that government decision makers have come to believe that TNEs are helpful to them in their personal careers (and hence, they no doubt have felt, to their country), the power of the TNEs has increased. This general ideological component of TNE power has complemented other sources of influence—advantages in technology and know-how, willingness to invest and accept risk, and at least allegedly, on occasion, bribes to decision makers.[50]

STATE CHANGES WITH EL CERREJÓN?

In the preceding pages I demonstrated that the Colombian state, in both its social and economic dimensions, has much resiliency and has changed little since the regime watershed of 1958. The one exception to that generalization is that the methods used by leaders to mobilize people for social and political action have changed, because playing upon old sectarian hatreds no longer works. However, the finalizing of a contract with an Exxon subsidiary for the largest coal mine in the world in El Cerrejón, and the agreement with a Spanish–Colombian consortium in an adjacent area, *seemed* in 1980 to protend the promises, and the problems, of a state change.

I have explained the background and magnitude of the El Cerrejón contracts in another publication.[51] Rather than repeating the same material here, my purpose is to discuss the contracts' theoretical ramifications on the Colombian state system.

The Economic Dimension

There seems to be little doubt that there will be economic benefits, for some groups, from the El Cerrejón projects. It was projected that 5,000 people would be employed directly by the two projects. One does not have to accept the International Colombia Resources Corporation (INTERCOR, the Exxon subsidiary) figures as exact to conclude that its royalties and excess profits will go to Carbones de Colombia (CARBOCOL, the parastatal coal enterprise), which will also receive profits from the coal it sells itself from both the northern and central areas. The parastatal enterprise will use those "profits" as stipulated by its statutes, although in the future the Congress, or in some cases the "general assembly" of the enterprise, could change those statutes. The general fund of the government will receive income taxes (currently at 40 percent) from both INTERCOR and CARBOCOL. Further, the general fund will receive the tax on profit remittances (currently at 20 percent). Either of these tax levels could be increased or decreased, under Colombian law.[52]

If we accept the figures of the 1980 INTERCOR projection, this means that the general fund will receive from northern El Cerrejón, in current dollars, between 24.3 billion U.S. dollars (low prices, 15 million tons annually) and 47.3 billion U.S. dollars (high prices, 25 million tons annually).[53] CARBOCOL will have net profits of between 19.8 billion and 44.4 billion U.S. dollars. All of these figures would be higher if central El Cerrejón were included.

Therefore, one key question is, What effects will these new foreign earnings have on the Colombian state? The answer is twofold: It depends (1) on how the earnings are used and (2) on what protection is given to the rest of the economy.

The conclusions in the literature are that the host country would be best advised to use the earnings in capital development, especially since mining projects are likely to be capital, rather than labor, intensive. As Malcolm Gillis argued,

"Rather than seeking employment expansion through uneconomic labor-intensive extractive methods, it is far better to harvest such surpluses through capital-intensive methods, and then channel them into employment-generating programs and projects."[54] James Cobbe made the same point about the use of the surplus in a slightly different way when he argued, "Although it is common to talk in terms of an endowment of three factors of production, capital, labor, and natural resources, it is in some context helpful to view the stock of nonrenewable resources as part of the capital endowment, rather than of the natural resource endowment."[55] In short, these two scholars seem to have recommended that Colombia "sow the coal," as Venezuela has "sowed" petroleum for the long term. David Becker argued that such a policy was generally followed by the Peruvian military "Revolution" (from 1968 to 1980).[56]

It is, of course, impossible at this juncture to predict exactly what the Colombian government will do with its new surplus. Most probably, the profits will be divided between investment and consumption, but this begs the question of, In what proportions? If past history is a guide, however, it might be suggested that there will be actors within the government who will push for consumption of the surplus. As of 1985 the country had suffered from five years of current-account deficits, simply because tax revenues are not sufficient to cover operating expenses. Hence there could be a great temptation to use the coal surplus to cover that deficit. To the extent that this is done, rather than using the profits to promote job-generating investments, Colombia's income distribution, characterized by some as one of the most inequitable in Latin America, would become less equitable. However, this would be an "easier" policy for the government, at least in the short run, than taxing the upper and middle sectors of society at higher rates to diminish the deficit.

Another "consumption" possibility is to use the profits for distribution to lower-income groups who seem likely to cause problems for the state, for example, through a well funded agrarian reform program. The López and Turbay administrations, for example, could have gone much further in their "direct patronage" activities if they had had the El Cerrejón profits. Although this would still be a "waste," it would not be conceived as such by Colombian leaders. Two ex-ministers made this kind of argument when they suggested that bad economic conditions led to unemployment, which in turn led to populism.[57] My inference is that populism leads to problems for la oligarquía.

On the other hand, if the surpluses are to be used in capital investments, the ensuing question becomes, By whom? Logically, there are two policy options: (1) direct investment by the government in nonenergy sectors of the economy or (2) funneling the surplus into the Colombian private sector, through credit policy. Given the history of the Colombian state, the latter seems much more likely. The former policy option would get the government involved in manufacturing and/or agricultural activities traditionally dominated by the private sector.

This Colombian "coal bonanza" is likely to cause two other economic effects.

For one thing, the creditworthiness of the government is likely to increase, since the government will control a greater percentage of both the gross domestic product and the export earnings than before. And Colombia already has a high credit standing. In April 1981 the president of the Inter-American Development bank called Colombia "a rare country among us, a country that in its monetary reserves has the equivalent of all its public debt. I mean that it is a country that has completely open credit, that has not begun to use it."[58] Even three years later, after the Latin American debt crisis, the Colombian situation was enviable. In September 1983 the government announced that private banks would grant loans of 225 million U.S. dollars. These were the first loans to a Latin American government since the debt crisis began.[59] Foreign debt per capita was, at the time, 370 U.S. dollars, one of the lowest in Latin America.[60]

The second economic effect likely to result from the coal bonanza is a modified "Kuwait effect." As Malcolm Gillis explained,

In such countries, per capita export earnings are large enough to provide every family with a high standard of living quite apart from income from labor or capital. In such extreme circumstances, a free market rate of exchange (relative to, say, the U.S. dollar) would tend to be so high that practically everything would be imported; neither export-substituting nor import-substituting industry would be attractive to prospective investors under such conditions.[61]

This is not to argue that the Colombian coal bonanza is ever likely to reach the proportions of the oil bonanza in Kuwait—or even the one in Venezuela for that matter. In Venezuela the national oil company, PETROVEN, paid 12 billion U.S. dollars to the central government in 1980,[62] or about 850 U.S. dollars per capita. My calculations indicate that the *maximum* that northern El Cerrejón earnings will be, with the assumptions (1) of an average population of 35 million over the contract period, (2) of high international coal prices, and (3) of production levels reaching 25 million tons annually, will be 95 U.S. dollars per capita a year.

Yet foreign earnings will be significantly higher than in the past, and Colombia will face a "modified" Kuwait effect, not a completely new phenomenon for the country. Research has shown that as a result of the "coffee bonanzas" of the past century (which did lead to more direct employment than El Cerrejón coal will), the government has tended to lower import tariffs, hence damaging domestic industry, in order to diminish inflation.[63] Devaluation rates for the peso are, in such circumstances, lower than internal inflation. The last such case occurred in the second half of the 1970s, with the combination of bonanzas of coffee, marijuana, and cocaine.

But saying that the Kuwait effect will be less than in other countries and that the country has suffered them before does not detract from the conclusion: El Cerrejón coal might have that effect once again. However much the Kuwait effect occurs, it will work against "sowing the coal" in domestic industry, either manufacturing or agricultural, by the government directly or through credit policy favoring the private sector. Further, the effect will hurt the two parts of the private sector that, at least on occasion in the past, have employed large numbers of Colombians: the export-substituting and the importing-substituting industries. To say that Venezuela failed to anticipate this problem does little to assist Colombian policy makers in "sowing coal."

The Social Dimension

The El Cerrejón bonanza may also have an effect on the elite alliances that dominate the Colombian state and the resultant relationships with the masses. There is considerable controversy in the literature about the effect of TNEs in developing countries. Theodore Moran argued, however, that both dependency (*dependentista*) and nondependency theorists "tend to argue that there is, on some core issues and at some points in time, a fundamental 'reactionary alliance' between foreign investors and host country business groups, landowners, or other conservative groups." These elites share an "abhorrence of radical social change that will destroy them all" and "work together to prevent such an upheaval from taking place."[64]

Moran presented three hypotheses that come from outside the dependentista school and might apply in the Colombian case. The first is that foreign investment threatens the interests of and leads to a reaction from three different host-country groups: "local producers for whom the multinationals mean increased competition, governmental officials (*técnicos*) for whom the multinationals mean a hindrance to the exercise of macro-economic policy, and political leaders for whom multinationals mean a challenge to national sovereignty (and for whom the issue of foreign domination provides a way of gaining public prominence)."[65]

The second hypothesis is that domestic elites can "squeeze" foreign investors as elites "try to take the pressure off themselves as urbanization, industrialization, and social mobilization increase the demand for government programs financed by tax revenues."[66]

The third hypothesis states that different kinds of firms will have distinct self-interests, leading to splits among them. "Extractive companies, which provide for export and are not labor-intensive (and tend to use a labor elite, in any case) would be indifferent to broader social change—or indeed might support progressive legislation for the rest of the society if it tended to provide them with a more stable setting."[67]

David C. Becker, in his study of bonanza development in Peruvian copper, emphasized a change that would be important if it were to happen with the Colombian coal bonanza: the strengthening of state technocrats who "tend to share values and interests with the private-sector managers, both domestic and foreign." These technocrats realize that state revenues and economic power are basically dependent on the modern part of the economy. The health of the economy, they believe, depends on the continuing inputs of capital and technology from abroad. As a result, a "triad of state officials (including military officers), transnational corporate managers, and domestic manager-entrepreneurs captures the heights of the political economy." They are supported by middle-income individuals who "consume the kinds of durable goods that the transnationals specialize in producing and aspire to upward mobility in the managerial-technocratic bourgeois stratum." Opposition comes from other class elements: the more traditional bourgeoisie, whose backward firms cannot compete with modern capitalist enterprise, and the lower classes, whose consumption has to be held in check in order to foster the high rate of capital accumulation that "associated-dependent development" requires. "The dominance of the triad is maintained by resorting to authoritarian rule (necessary because the ruling coalition is numerically small) and by the diversity of the interests among the opposition."[68]

Yet one should not necessarily conclude that similar effects will be seen in Colombia. Carlos Díaz-Alejandro, for example, described quite different results for a country dominated by a more reactionary elite:

If a Southern country is run by a reactionary oligarchy, it is far-fetched to suppose that somehow inducing changes in its trade and finance policies will affect power and wealth distribution in that country in the near future. The oligarchy may or may not allow laissez faire and policies of openness; if it suits the consolidation of its power, the oligarchy may renounce foreign aid and become the ardent self delinker or vociferous Third Worlder. It is more likely than not to be interventionist regarding domestic control over foreign trade; there are few more foolish misconceptions than to suppose that import controls are a badge of progressiveness.[69]

Another foolish misconception might be that the Colombian state will remain, during the El Cerrejón production, just exactly as it was when the Colombian government finalized the El Cerrejón contracts. Just how it will change, however, depends. If the Colombian government uses its surplus for direct capital investment, it would be for the first time in Colombian history, and using the surplus in this way would place the government in direct competition with domestic investors.

The social dimensions of the Colombian state are likely to be greatly changed because of the El Cerrejón bonanza *unless* the government uses most of the surpluses for consumption rather than investment. So the political leaders in the next two decades will be faced with a dilemma, in which they will have to choose among three options: (1) They can use the surpluses for consumption, maintaining the same elite alliances and protecting the interests of the entire upper and middle sectors, but in the process "wasting" the surpluses (although such a "wasting" might be skillful enough to prevent social upheaval). (2) They can use the surpluses in capital investment done directly by the government, thus creating employment sorely needed in the country, but in the process changing the balance between private and official sectors in the state. (3) They can use the surpluses for investments done by the private sector, in the process strengthening the political power of the private sector, while not permitting the growth of the governmental technocrats, as happened in Peru. My suspicion is that the first of the three options will be chosen. The third option is more likely than the second, since the prevailing myth is that the private sector is much more effective than the state sector.

The third option would strengthen one part of the "capitalist class"—the industrialists—and not another part—the financial groups—who, according to radical Colombian economists, have been the ones with political power since 1974, if not since 1965.[70] Hence, the argument might be made that El Cerrejón development will be either (1) if option 3 is chosen, the salvation of the manufacturing sector, which has suffered disastrous times because of an overvalued currency and because of national and international recessions; or (2) if option 2 is chosen, the last "nail in the coffin" of the Colombian manufacturing sector.

So it simply is not clear at this writing whether the El Cerrejón bonanza will lead to a state alliance that is about the same (option 1), that is different because of a weaker private-sector role (option 2), or that is different because of a stronger private-sector role (option 3). A Colombian "tri-pe" (three-legged stool), to use Peter Evans's term, will no doubt continue to exist. Yet that statement is so general as to be meaningless: The real issue is the relative strength of the three parts.

Regarding INTERCOR, my suspicion, based on interviews with five of its officials,[71] is that INTERCOR will be behind progressive legislation in the country, perhaps even more so than most Colombian political leaders, so as to provide themselves with a stable setting. Whatever can be said about high-level employees of transnational enterprises—Colombians as well as foreigners in the case of INTERCOR—one cannot accuse them of not being intelligent. I, therefore, suspect that INTERCOR will support progressive legislation, for purely selfish reasons: (1) The Exxon subsidiary will realize the potential instability that might come from increased national wealth with the same, or even worse, conditions for the poor; and (2) they will realize that such a condition would place their multibillion-dollar investment in jeopardy.

CONCLUSIONS

The first part of this chapter described the Colombian state, with its bias toward the private sector, both domestic and transnational. The conclusion is that the Colombian state is different from others in Latin America. In general, John Sloan argued that "there is no strong ideological limitation on statism in Latin America. The elites are inclined to stress that modernization is essentially an administrative problem rather than a political one."[72] He added, "A second reason for the inclination of Latin American policymakers to pursue a bureaucratically directed style of development is their negative view of the domestic bourgeoisie.''[73] In Colombia there *is* an ideological limitation on statism; policy makers have a *positive* view of the domestic bourgeoisie.

Second, this chapter speculated about some changes that seem likely with the coming "coal bonanza," arguing that state change, in both economic and social terms, might be likely with the dramatic increases of government revenues with El Cerrejón coal development. However, I pointed out that although the new revenues might be *necessary* for state change, they surely were not *sufficient*.

In the end, the Colombian state might not change at all, *not* because the traditional state is so resilient or because the El Cerrejón surpluses would probably be used to maintain the state, but because there are no surpluses. The world energy panorama changed dramatically after the Exxon calculations of July 1980. The technocrats of the world's largest TNE did not, at least in their communications with the Colombian government, consider the possibility that there would be an oil glut, with resulting lower nominal prices. As a result, they grossly overestimated future prices of coal.

Apparently, technocrats of the rentier Colombian institutionalized state accepted INTERCOR's projections of the government's profits, although the projections did not include the cost of paying interest on the loans necessary for northern El Cerrejón preoperational investments. By mid-1985 new projections appeared that did include such costs. Rather than making profits on El Cerrejón coal, some argued, the government would lose 10 U.S. dollars on each ton exported![74] In central El Cerrejón the consortium withdrew, presumably because of marketing difficulties.

The conclusion might best be, then, that the Colombian state will remain the same. If El Cerrejón leads to state changes, it will be because of the financial bonanza that seemed so likely but did not take place, rather than because of the one that did.

NOTES

1. "Observaciones acerca del modelo colombiano de desarrollo, 1958–1980," *Estrategia económica y financiera* 38 (October 1930):9–10.

2. Alfred Stepan, *The State and Society: Peru in Comparative Perspective* (Princeton, N.J.: Princeton University Press, 1978) xi, his emphasis.

3. Joel S. Migdal, "A Model of State-Society Relations," in *New Directions in Comparative Politics*, ed. Howard J. Wiarda (Boulder, Colo.: Westview Press, 1985), pp. 46–47.

4. Migdal, "A Model of State-Society Relations," p. 47.

5. Peter Evans, *Dependent Development: The Alliance of Multinational, State, and Local Capital in Brazil* (Princeton, N.J.: Princeton University Press, 1979); David G. Becker, *The New Bourgeoisie and the Limits of Dependency: Mining, Class, and Power in "Revolutionary" Peru* (Princeton, N.J.: Princeton University Press, 1983).

6. James L. Payne, "The Oligarchy Muddle," *World Politics* 20 (April 1968):439–53.

7. Francisco Leal Buitrago and Harvey F. Kline, "Características básicas y exper-

iencias de cambio de los congresistas,'' in *Estudio del Compartamiento Legislativo en Colombia*, eds. Gary Hoskin, Francisco Leal, Harvey Kline, Dora Rothlisberger, and Armando Borrer (Bogotá: Universidad de los Andes, 1975), p. 140.

8. Interview: Colombian sociology professor, October 7, 1980.

9. John Bailey, ''Pluralist and Corporatist Dimensions of Interest Representation in Colombia,'' in *Authoritarianism and Corporatism in Latin America*, ed. James Malloy (Pittsburgh: University of Pittsburgh Press, 1977), pp. 259–302.

10. Miguel Urrutia, *The Development of the Colombian Labor Movement* (New Haven, Conn.: Yale University Press, 1969).

11. *El Mundo*, Medellín daily, August 21, 1985.

12. Jonathan Hartlyn, ''Producer Associations, the Political Regime, and Policy Processes in Contemporary Colombia,'' *Latin American Research Review*, 20 (1985):119.

13. *El Tiempo*, Bogotá daily, August 7, 1985.

14. Bruce Michael Bagley, ''Political Power, Public Policy, and the State in Colombia: Case Studies of the Urban and Agrarian Reforms During the National Front, 1958–1974.'' Ph.D. dissertation, University of California, Los Angeles, 1979.

15. Ibid.

16. Carlos F. Díaz-Alejandro, *Foreign Trade Regimes and Economic Development: Colombia* (New York: National Bureau of Economic Research, 1974) pp. 61–62.

17. See Bagley, ''Political Power, Public Policy, and the State''; Hartlyn, ''Producer Associations, the Political Regime, and Policy Processes,'' pp. 113 and 125.

18. Miguel Urrutia Montoya, ''Diversidad ideológica e integración Andina,'' *Coyuntura económica* 10 (July 1980):187–203.

19. Interviews: Former minister of mines and energy, April 9, 1981; CARBOCOL official, April 13, 1981, June 4, 1981; Liberal senator, May 8, 1981; Liberal senator, May 28, 1981.

20. Hartlyn, ''Producer Associations, the Political Regime, and Policy Processes,'' p. 127.

21. Interview: Colombian sociology professor, October 7, 1981.

22. Interview: Colombian economics professor, June 5, 1981.

23. *Economic and Social Progress in Latin America: The External Sector* (Washington, D.C.: Inter-American Development Bank, 1982), p. 362.

24. See Everett E. Hagen, *On the Theory of Social Change—How Economic Growth Begins* (Homewood, Ill.: Dorsey, 1962).

25. Francisco Leal Buitrago, ''Social Classes, International Trade, and Foreign Capital in Colombia: An Attempt at Historical Interpretation of the Formation of the State, 1819–1935.'' Ph.D. dissertation, University of Wisconsin, 1974.

26. Franklin Jurado, ''La inversión extranjera en Colombia,'' *Nueva Frontera* 328 (April 20–26, 1981):8.

27. Francois J. Lombard, *The Foreign Investment Screening Process in LDCs: The Case of Colombia, 1967–1975* (Boulder, Colo.: Westview Press, 1979), p. 124.

28. Ibid., p. 41.

29. George Philip, *Oil and Politics in Latin America: Nationalist Movements and State Companies* (London: Cambridge University Press, 1982), p. 11.

30. Ibid., p. 124.

31. Jorge Villegas, *Petróleo Colombiano, ganancia gringa* (Bogotá: Ediciones Peñalosa y Cia. Ltda., 1977), p. 189.

32. Ibid.; J. Fred Rippy, *The Capitalists and Colombia* (New York: Vanguard, 1931).

33. Philip, *Oil and Politics*, p. 35.

34. Ibid., p. 51.

35. Richard E. Sharpless, *Gaitán of Colombia: A Political Biography* (Pittsburgh: University of Pittsburgh Press, 1978), p. 66.

36. Enrique Pardo Parra, *Dos Discursos en el Senado* (Bogotá: Imprenta Nacional), p. 68.

37. Ibid., p. 46.

38. Ibid., pp. 54–55.

39. Ibid., p. 65.

40. Interview: Liberal senator, May 28, 1981.

41. Eduardo Díaz Uribe, *El Carbón en Colombia* (Bogotá: Instituto de Fomento Nacional, 1978), p. 88.

42. Interview: Former ECOPETROL official, April 24, 1981.

43. Philip, *Oil and Politics*, p. 69.

44. Interview: Former ECOPETROL official, April 24, 1981.

45. Ibid.

46. Interview: Former minister of economic development, March 26, 1981.

47. Interview: Former minister of mines and energy, April 29, 1981.

48. Interview: Former minister of finance, April 20, 1981.

49. Miguel Urrutia Montoya and Ricardo Villaveces Pardo, "Reseña de las Perspectivas Energéticas de Colombia," *Coyuntura económica* 4 (October 1979):97.

50. Interviews: Government technocrat, January 8, 1981; Colombian social scientist, March 24, 1981; congressman from minor political party, March 31, 1981.

51. Harvey F. Kline, "The Coal of El Cerrejón: An Historical Analysis of Major Policy Decisions and MNC Activities," *Inter-American Economic Affairs* 35 (Winter 1981):69–90.

52. Interview: CARBOCOL official, June 2, 1981.

53. INTERCOR, "Documento de Declaración de Comercialidad," photocopy stamped "CARBOCOL confidencial," 1980.

54. Malcolm Gillis, "The Role of State Enterprises in Economic Development," *Social Research* 47 (Summer 1980):277.

55. James H. Cobbe, *Governments and Mining Companies in Developing Countries* (Boulder, Colo.: Westview Press, 1979), p. 6.

56. Becker, *The New Bourgeoisie*, pp. 61–62.

57. Interviews: Former minister of mines and energy, April 9, 1981; Former minister of finance, April 20, 1981.

58. *El Tiempo*, April 9, 1981.

59. *El Tiempo*, September 21, 1983.

60. *Latin American Regional Reports: Andean Group*, London quarterly, November 11, 1983, p. 4.

61. Malcolm Gillis, *Taxation and Mining: Nonfuel Minerals in Bolivia and Other Countries* (Cambridge, Mass.: Ballinger Publishing Company, 1978), p. 14.

62. Philip, *Oil and Politics*, p. 48.

63. Alberto Fuentes Hernández and Ricardo Villaveces Pardo, "La Liberación actual de importaciones y su perspectiva histórica," *Coyuntura económica* 6 (June 1976):87–98.

64. Theodore H. Moran, "Multinational Corporations and Dependency: A Dialogue

for Dependentistas and Non-Dependentistas,'' *International Organization* 32 (Winter 1978):93.

65. Ibid.

66. Ibid., p. 94.

67. Ibid., pp. 94–95.

68. Becker, *The New Bourgeoisie*, p. 9.

69. Carlos F. Díaz-Alejandro, ''Delinking North and South: Unshackled or Unhinged?'' in *Rich and Poor Nations in the World Economy*, eds. Albert Fishlow, Carlos F. Díaz-Alejandro, Richard R. Fagen, and Roger D. Hansen (New York: McGraw Hill, 1978), p. 121.

70. Interview: Colombian university professor and journalist, June 3, 1981.

71. Interviews: INTERCOR officials, September 12, 1980, April 6, 1981; INTERCOR officials; May 9, 1981; May 11, 1981; INTERCOR official, June 14, 1981.

72. John W. Sloan, *Public Policy in Latin America: A Comparative Study* (Pittsburgh: University of Pittsburgh Press, 1984), p. 129.

73. Ibid., p. 131.

74. Eduardo Sarmiento Palacio, ''Retorno a la dependencia,'' *El Espectador*, Bogotá daily, November 3, 1985. Another view is that El Cerrejón would lead to new income of 164 million U.S. dollars in 1986. Miguel Fadul, ''La balanza de pagos, el café, el petróleo y el carbón,'' *El Espectador*, November 17, 1985.

6

Creating Neo-Christendom in Colombia

Alexander W. Wilde

The State, in light of the Traditional Catholic sentiment of the Colombian Nation, considers the Roman Catholic Apostolic Religion as a fundamental element of the common good and of the integral development of the national community.

1973 Concordat, Article 1

Colombia confronts in the present moment one of the most acute crises in its history. In addition to profound errors in the political leadership of the State, there is a growing social and economic abyss, with the dislocation of the structures of Colombian society and increasing distance between the classes that compose it. . . . Political structures are inoperative in the realities of the country and neither permit Colombians to participate nor respond to their needs. . . . It is a commonplace in Colombia that democracy is formal and apparent; that election, parties, the parliamentary system have no true popular participation.

The Bishops' Conference, 1978

In Colombia the Catholic Church and oligarchical democracy have survived together. The church was a midwife to the rebirth of the regime in its contemporary form, with the National Front in 1958.[1] In the quarter century since, it has remained a reliable—and many would say, important—support of that regime. For its own part the church has, during the same period, retained its distinctive and prominent place in public life. It is widely regarded as the most powerful church in Latin America and enjoys high regard in the Vatican Curia as a model for the region.

The record is remarkable in light of the political and religious upheaval elsewhere in Latin America during this time. Dramatic discontinuities, and regime shifts, revolutions, and reversals of long historical processes have been the rule. And the Catholic Church has been an important actor associated with these disruptions, in surprising and unanticipated ways. New theological concerns, organizational forms, and political conditions have propelled it into new kinds of social involvement. Although this change has not been uniform, in settings as diverse as El Salvador, Peru, Chile, and Brazil, a certain broad direction of change is discernible. Its most obvious feature is a growing identification of the church with the weak rather than the strong. It has moved away from its historic alliance with the state to become instead the "voice of the voiceless," defender of human rights, champion of democracy. Behind this shift in its relationship to society is a fundamental change in the way that it conceives of itself. Latin American Catholics no longer identify "the church" as just the formal structures of the hierarchical institution. The Vatican Council's metaphor of the "pilgrim people of God" has been conducive to a church that understands itself more as a living community. The authority of bishops is still important, but it is one exercised increasingly in response to and exchange with their flocks, the lower clergy, and Christian laity.[2]

Against this panorama Colombia stands out for its continuities and conservatism. The framework has somehow held. That is not because this has been a tranquil time in Colombia. Socially and economically, the period has been as dynamic—and in many ways, as disintegrative—as that of the rural violence of the 1940s and 1950s. New actors have crowded the political stage—guerrillas from the several sustained insurgencies, an army with increasing autonomy (and often authority), a growing if still divided movement of urban labor—but the play has remained recognizably that of oligarchical democracy. For its part the church has experienced internal conflict unprecedented in its history. The new currents in theology, from the Council and the Latin American bishops' meeting (CELAM) at Medellín, moved many to action in Colombia as elsewhere. The guerrilla-priest Camilo Torres had many successors who believed (though few took up his means of violence) that the church must be allied with those struggling to change the basic structures of society. These "rebel priests," however, did not move the institution as they did in other places. The Colombian hierarchy responded to them largely as a threat, not as an opportunity. The church did change and modernize—but in a characteristically conservative way.

By the 1980s the Colombian church occupied one end of the spectrum of the Latin American church as a whole, with Brazil at the other end.[3] It represented a coherent model for the church, that of "neo-Christendom."[4] Its contrasts with more liberationist churches were clear. The Colombian church expressed some qualified autonomy from the state, but it continued to identify itself overwhelmingly with a larger regime of power. It was willing to preach in general terms in favor of social change but not to permit priests and nuns to be active in popular social movements. Its hierarchy presented themselves as "pastors" but continued to assert the most traditional conception of ecclesiastical authority. Neo-Christendom was a way of blending inherited institutional forms with organizational modernization and a "pastoral" commitment to social reform.

There is a certain elective affinity between Colombia's oligarchical democracy and its neo-Christendom church. That church was shaped by forces peculiar to itself, to its own theology and organization, but also by the context of Colombia's peculiar politics. Most of this chapter deals with the processes by which this occurred since the early 1970s. The neo-Christendom church also played some role in sustaining oligarchical democracy. In other places in Latin America the liberationist church helped mobilize new social forces into politics and distanced itself from government, often in frank opposition. In Colombia, in contrast, the hierarchy set narrow limits on criticism and restricted political opposition from within the church. Its principal service to the regime was in preventing a vertical division in the church's ranks that might have delegitimating effects, a theme that is taken up toward the end of this chapter.

The following section examines neo-Christendom through its most authoritive statement, the 1973 Concordat. That there should be such an international treaty at all is revealing of the church's self-conception, and the parameters of its relationship with the state are elucidated by specific provisions and the hierarchy's commentary on them. The following two sections, the core of the chapter, deal with the 1970s and 1980s and analyze the processes by which the neo-Christendom church was created. The third section examines the pattern of church involvement in political conflict during the period, sets out the bishops' strongest collective critique of the Colombian political system, and then shows how the limits established in that critique were applied to social activists within the church itself. The fourth part describes the institutional leadership that forged Colombia's remarkable episcopal unity, a key to its coherence around neo-Christendom. The final section briefly considers the future stability of such a church and concludes that there are several dynamics, within the church itself and in Colombian politics, that could impel it in quite a different direction.

NEO-CHRISTENDOM IN A CONCORDAT

The character of the neo-Christendom church can be elaborated in many dimensions, ranging from the ethic of salvation to the role of the priest. What is central for our purposes here is the concept of an ecclesiastical institution in an ideal tutelary role toward all of society, in union with the public authority of the state. It differs from historic "christendom" (with its ancient and medieval connotations) in that church and state may be formally separated and that the church accepts the need for social reform. Neo-Christendom, however, represents a distinctly limited modernization of the church's older concept of itself and of its mission in the world.[5]

The character of Colombia's neo-Christendom church is well captured by the Concordat of 1973. A concordat is a rather exceptional regime for a national church in the modern world. Essentially a treaty between the Vatican and a nation-state, it arose as an instrument for defining institutional boundaries and authority between church and state, usually in conflictive situations (as with the first modern concordat, with Napoleon's France in 1801). Colombia's Concordat of 1887 was signed after just such a period of conflict. It was regarded by both the Vatican and the Colombian church itself as quite advantageous at the time and after. (It was subsequently modified slightly by additional agreements, but a more fundamental attempt at reform by a Liberal government failed in 1942.) By the mid–1960s, however, there was considerable sentiment within the Colombian church for a new concordat. The Second Vatican Council (from 1962 to 1965) had promulgated a new understanding of the church and its mission in the modern world, and in Colombia the National Front brought a new political regime, one that guaranteed governments of the historically anticlerical Liberals as well as of the Conservative party.

A major question about the new Concordat was whether Colombia should have one at all. Some politicians, particularly Liberals, believed that the church's influence over social policy (as in marriage and divorce, education, and Indian territories) was too great and should properly be regulated by national government directly.[6] This was a familiar anticlerical position within Colombia's political culture. More startling was opposition from within the church itself. In broad terms this group argued that the church was hindered in its religious and pastoral mission by its ties to a particular political regime, that it was regulated and compromised as a marginal sort of public functionary.[7] In other words, there were Colombian Catholics who believed that the new Concordat—in many of its specific provisions and just in the fact that it existed at all—tended to perpetuate a dependent, preconciliar conception of the church.

The first important fact about the Concordat, then, is that the Colombian bishops unanimously concluded that their church should have one.[8] The bishops made clear in their pastoral communiqué of July 1973, on the occasion of the signing of the new Concordat, that they also regarded it as far more than a "cold, static juridical structure." Their commentary, "as Pastors," was meant to bring out, "more than the letter, the spirit that animates all of its stipulations, and gives it, in the last instance, its reason for being." Anyone, they wrote, who examines the new text carefully "will easily perceive that its essential and indisputable object is man."[9] "Man in his concreteness, as expressed in our times, carrier of worries and hopes, immersed in a changing and at times oppressive world; the whole man, material and spiritual, the subject of rights and duties, citizen and believer, who should carry out his unique vocation on this earth as well as in eternity."[10]

The first article of the 1973 document, the epigraph for this chapter, sets basic parameters for the shift from the old to the new Christendom in Colombia. It guarantees "the Catholic Church and those who belong to it the full enjoyment of their religious rights," while in view of recognizing religious liberty for other confessions. The "consideration" of the state, "the traditional Catholic sentiment of the Colombian Nation," certainly represents a change from the 1887

Concordat (repeated in the 1957 plebiscite), which gave the state the responsibility to "protect and enforce respect" for the church and its ministers, and considered Catholicism quite an official religion, "the religion of Colombia."[11] There is also a shift in language in the 1973 text away from a static to a more dynamic conception of society. The church is no more described in the classic language of the nineteenth century, as "an essential element of the social order," but rather as fundamental to "the common good" and "integral development."

The church presented several images of itself in the Concordat and related documents. One is as "pilgrim," a conciliar metaphor, far from traditional triumphalism. It is related to the new importance the church would give to "service" to man and society and to its "pastoral" relationship to the faithful.[12] In the matter of marriage and divorce, for example, the church moved away from its historical position that Catholic values must be expressed (and indeed are realized) through public authority in favor of a more autonomous pastoral role to Catholics within a liberalized civil arrangement. However, while the "pilgrim" conception is new (and does suggest elements of change), the major image of the church in the Concordat documents is far more ancient—and has quite different implications. It is an image of the church as "Power," (Latin–Spanish *potestad*), in the tradition of the Two Swords, of Two Sovereignties, and of Two Communities, civil and ecclesial, of a church (with its own peculiar "nature") possessing somehow a parallel and coequal jurisdiction over society with the state.[13] This is an image that recalls the church's historical, hierarchical, and institutional character.

In its relationship with the Colombian state, the church was concerned with asserting its "rights" and "autonomy" on one hand, and on the other its sense of shared responsibility, "cooperation," and "collaboration" with the state in its "temporal tasks." The Concordat, the bishops wrote in their Pastoral Communiqué, represented "a cordial and dynamic dialogue between the two societies over an object of common responsibility." They continued in a revealing way, elaborating the character of the relationship:

A dialogue in which one trusts the other and both conjugate their efforts for the integral promotion of man. A dialogue that is translated into juridical formulas to make it stable and to elevate it to the level of a bilateral treaty that guarantees the sovereignty of the contracting parties. A dialogue that excludes subjugation or surrender because those who carry out the dialogue are mutually respectful and are committed to the same people.[14]

The language here conveys the identification the Colombian bishops felt, whatever the formal facts of separation from the state, with a larger regime. This is such a deeply established historical pattern that it seems completely natural to them. The "subjects of the two communities," ecclesial and civil, "almost totally coincide," they noted. The church put greater emphasis than in the past on establishing an active pastoral presence of its "own" structures in society, beyond what was formerly embodied in those of the state. However, the hierarchy did not believe that this new role required the church to divorce itself from civil authority. On the contrary, the hierarchy believed the church should retain the union to which it had always aspired, in new conditions. The autonomy the church claimed, then, was a qualified one. It certainly did not envision itself at a critical distance from the state. It wished to enjoy independence in its own sphere, but at the same time it reaffirmed a larger interdependency.

There are several specific linkages in the Concordat worthy of brief comment. One is the continued government role in nominating bishops. Although the new Article 14 formally recognized that ultimate authority resides in the papacy, it does retain the former right of the Colombian president to raise objections "of a civil or political character" to candidates in advance. Since the hierarchy is crucial to the whole direction of the church (as we will see more fully), this is a significant potential power. It effectively extends the *patronato* in political, if not strictly legal, terms.[15] At the same time that the church sought a wholly new form of governmental cooperation in matters of clerical discipline (motivated rather transparently by problems with social-activist priests), the church declared, "The illegitimate exercise of ecclesiastical jurisdiction or functions by those who lack canonical powers [*mision*] to exercise them, officially communicated by ecclesiastical authority to the appropriate state official, will be considered by him as a usurpation of a public function" (Article 22). The official episcopal commentary explained that this extraordinary "punitive norm" was needed to defend "the right of Catholics not to be deceived by those lacking canonical powers" who would "avail themselves of the ignorance of the people" to carry out "painful and prejudicial acts."[16] In both of these provisions the Concordat reasserted the institutional, hierarchical conception of the church and its intimate interdependence with the national state.[17]

Finally, in light of the growing role of the armed forces within Colombia's traditionally civilian politics, Concordat Article 17, concerning the military chaplaincy, should be noted. The *Vicaria Castrense* was contemplated by the Concordat of 1887 (Article 20) but not actually established until 1949. From that time the archbishop of Bogotá was given an honorary generalship, an act of some symbolic interest.[18] The church's links with the military have expanded with its increasing public influence. In their official commentary the bishops presented this chaplaincy as "indispensible given the maximum importance that the Armed Forces have acquired in all countries in modern times." That importance derives, they went on, not just from the defense of "the sovereignty of national frontiers" but very much also from their "abnegation and sacrifices" as "guardians of internal peace," "*permanently distributed and mobilized*," as they are, "throughout all the territory of the Nation."[19]

THE TRAJECTORY OF THE CHURCH, FROM THE 1960s TO THE 1980s

The Colombian church was not always a neo-Christendom church; it became one. In the early 1970s it still seemed quite possible that its "pastoral" commitments would bring it increasingly into political confrontation with the government and other forms of established power in Colombian society. Priests were actively involved in many different ways in the popular ferment of the times. Members of the Golconda group, inspired by the social-activist ideas of Camilo Torres, had taken part in the 1970 presidential campaign of Gustavo Rojas Pinilla and Alianza Nacional Popular (ANAPO), a serious challenge to the National Front regime. In the countryside priests were present in the rapidly growing peasant movement, often acting in solidarity with their flocks, even in militant initiatives, such as land invasions. Bishops spoke more of the social functions of property and less of the rights of landed interests. The Jesuits, who had since the 1930s represented the activist edge of the church in society, proposed "to give the social problem an absolute priority in [their] apostolate."[20]

In spite of the case of Camilo Torres, laicized for political activities in the mid–1960s, many priests continued to pursue what they took to be the demands of social justice at the grass roots of society. This led to a variety of conflicts with secular authorities. Each such case confronted bishops with choices— whether to accept and support such actions as the work of the church, or disavow them as disruptive or subversive, or just to be silent. In the early 1970s this mechanism of lower-level action and upper-level response within the church seemed to point toward a broadening conception of the church's social–pastoral role. The church "must go beyond the clear exposition of the principles that regulate economic and sociopolitical relationships," said Bishop Darío Castrillón to the Superior War College in 1973, "to the frank and brave denunciation of situations which violate the ethical order."[21] Bishop Raúl Zambrano Camader pointed in 1969 to the need to break with past patterns: "in fulfilling our critical function toward the State, we have perhaps been too aggressive in religious or ecclesiastical questions, [while] in social matters our attitude has been conciliatory, of understanding for the problems the government faces."[22] It seemed possible that the new pastoral commitments of the Colombian church could carry it toward the militant "prophetic" witness associated with the liberationist church in many other places in Latin America.

Nevertheless, that is not what happened. Conflict certainly continued. Since the early 1970s, priests and nuns—and some bishops and lay people as well— were involved in confrontations with political authorities in many regions and at all levels. There have always been parts of the church that have been willing to oppose the policies of the government in power at a given point in a particular situation. Indeed, forces have continued to exist within the church opposed to the whole larger regime of oligarchical democracy (and the church's place in it). However, the church as a whole has never, during this considerable period of time, thrown its institutional weight against either government or regime (in striking contrast to so many other countries of Latin America). Moreover, the church has never experienced a serious vertical split within itself, with one group of more progressive bishops and clergy arrayed against moderates and conservatives. The key here has been the Colombian church's unparalleled episcopal unity, and the concept around which they unified was neo-Christendom.

The reasons for this are to be found both within the church itself and the political context of Colombian democracy. The limits of protest can be seen in the broad trajectory of conflict.[23] There were frequent clashes between the church and the Liberal López Michelsen government (from 1974 to 1978), a period of growing labor agitation. The *toma de templo*—the occupation of a church or cathedral by striking workers—became common, usually encouraged by local priests and nuns and at least condoned by a bishop. At one point during the height of agitation in 1976, some dozen churches were so occupied in different parts of the country. Widely covered by the press, these tomas paralleled similar actions of the church elsewhere in Latin America. They seemed finally to translate into concrete form the general support for the rights of labor that the Colombian church had, since the 1950s, expressed in theoretical terms.[24] Priests, nuns, and lay people were often arrested, in situations ranging from a protest of peasant farmers to alleged complicity with leftist guerrillas. With the coming of the second consecutive Liberal government, of Julio César Turbay Ayala (from 1978 to 1982), episcopal protests over such arrests were increasingly accompanied by accusations of torture, documented by several international missions in 1980.[25]

During both the López and Turbay administrations, the Episcopal Conference issued general statements highly critical of government policy. These sparked several seasons of polemics between the hierarchy and politicians, complementing and framing the outbursts of individual bishops.[26] The character of the episcopal critique, however, is worth closer scrutiny, because it reveals the limits within which the hierarchy chose to operate. The most extensive development of their analysis is found in two documents of 1978 and 1981.[27] The first, which seems not to have been prepared originally as a public statement,[28] employs terms that are not, to say the least, usual in the discourse of the Colombian hierarchy. Indeed, much of the language—of "inoperative" political structures, of merely "formal and apparent" democracy, of social consequences traced to the "ownership of the means of production," of a "growing social and economic abyss" between the "classes" of Colombian society—was softened when the hierarchy issued a more polished version three years later. ("Classes" now appear as "groups" within society, the lack of "true popular participation" becomes one of the "genuine participation of all citizens," and so forth).[29] However, the fundamental frame of the analysis—the projection of the bishops' collective mentality—is the same in both documents.

Their argument runs roughly as follows: Colombia is in the midst of one of the most acute crises of its history. This can be seen in great and growing economic inequalities, a society in which many remain unjustly excluded, a concentration of power and "superpoliticized" partisanship, a state bureaucracy of "generalized corruption" and "vertiginous and parasitic" growth, an excessive statism (which, the bishops noted, can even afflict "so-called democratic states"), all of which adds up to "a crisis of credibility and of confidence": "the Colombian People suffer a grave disillusion with those who govern them, with the national institutions and with the political class." This crisis is "opening the way for the colonization'' of Colombia "by totalitarian ideologies and systems that destroy all liberties with dialectical materialism.'' This can be seen, the bishops argue, particularly in the country's trade unions, which the church has supported when based on "principles of Christian faith and morality, for concord and peace and as instruments of legitimate defense of social justice.'' Instead, Colombian unions demonstrate "dangerous deviations,'' becoming "emerging oligarchies,'' following leaders "without conscience, soul, [or] responsibility,'' abusing the right to strike, paralyzing public services, doing "extremely grave damage to the whole order of society.''

Where, then, did the hierarchy turn for solutions? The whole analysis, it is clear throughout, is addressed first and foremost to Colombia's "ruling class"— to "those who govern," to "the political class," to "the political leadership and social leaders that love Colombia," to the "*fuerzas vivas*" that the hierarchy would convoke "not to feast on favors but share responsibilities.'' The bishops cite provisions from the Puebla documents to support the aspirations of the poor and their right to organize themselves, but their comments are conspicuously general and abstract. There is no sense of the actual fate of popular organization in Colombia since the 1960s—no intrusion of concrete events—save the extended criticism of unions.[30]

The bishops based their hope for action in awakening the consciences of the powerful, not in raising the consciousness of the weak. This is traditional in Colombia and very much part of the concept of neo-Christendom. So, too, is the implicit understanding of how social change should come about: by "civic-political education," by appropriate attention to "human duties" and not just agitation over "human rights," by conciliation and cooperation and not by violence, whether employed by guerrillas or by government (civil authority is requested to "supervise subalterns firmly"). It is a mild recipe that the bishops finally gave for "decisive, sustained, and hopeful action"—particularly in light of the gravity of the national situation they themselves described. There is no reason to doubt their moral fervor or distress—indeed, their statement is a jeremiad—but their message is not a prophetic one. Beneath the lamentation and condemnation was a firm awareness that they defended an institution and the political order of which it is a part. They may have criticized the government, but in Colombia their real wrath was only aroused by "certain ideologies and party programs" motivated by "atheist laicism" and directed against "true religion and the only Church of Christ.'' That is, the hierarchy may indeed rise, when the state threatens to break the pact that gives the church public authority, as represented in "juridical norms" and the "due custody of public morality.'' This is a sociological or cultural Catholicism, and the church will defend it as fundamental to Colombian nationality.

They pretend to bring evolution and progress that clashes with our identity, because we are not Europe, with the decadence of the industrialized countries, while [at the same time], with a sophisticated, somewhat aggressive insolence, they pretend that to be a believer is only a private matter for individuals. . . . The country stands at a crossroads, [its choice] one episode in the permanent antagonism between Good and Evil.[31]

This is classical language of Christendom, and if we return to the political conflicts that involved the church in the 1970s and early 1980s, we can see how it was applied in practice. At the most immediate level the presence of Liberal governments certainly encouraged criticism expressing latent Conservative loyalties. López had campaigned in 1974 in favor of divorce, and Turbay's reforms for secondary education challenged traditional church prerogatives.[32] Morality, whether embodied in public legislation or private corruption (and the latter exhibited orgiastic growth in the period), was a field on which bishops felt free to pronounce. Moreover, even social-activist priests bowed toward traditional church conceptions (as in, for example, their attack on "the liberal mentality" or their innovation of Concordat protections for clerical personnel).[33] Anti-Liberal partisanship was surely only a minor motivation of church political dissent in the period, at least directly, but it was one factor of vertical solidarity between many priests and bishops. That solidarity had existed historically (in the twentieth century notably from 1930 to 1950) but was sorely tried by the new social activism from the mid–1960s on.

The pattern observable from the mid–1970s to the mid–1980s is of a few *individual bishops* sometimes supporting priests and nuns *in particular circumstances* of grievance or protest but of the hierarchy as a whole keeping solidly lined up with the regime. The hierarchy expressed this regime support both directly and indirectly. At the time of every election in the period, it urged all citizens to take part (though not in favor of parties contrary to Christian principles) in order to defend the country's democratic institutions.[34] It consistently anathematized the guerrilla insurgency in the countryside. Other priests might have followed Camilo Torres into the hills,[35] there might have been sympathy for the spirit and sacrifice of this option among a considerable body of other clergy, and individual bishops might have defended priests and nuns they believed were wrongly accused by the government. As a group, however, the bishops never wavered in their choice for oligarchical democracy.

Their indirect support was even more important. This they did by marginalizing, controlling, and purging liberationist elements within the church itself. Their general case for doing so was given in a substantial joint document, "Christian Identity in Action for Justice," issued in 1976.[36] Beyond their theological arguments, however, what was important was their pattern of *action* against liberationist elements in the many separate instances of political conflict. Any and all of the individuals, groups, or organizations of the church that were publically involved came under pressure from the central ecclesiastical institution to curb their activism. They were seen as a threat both to the existing social order and to hierarchical authority within the church. The bishops had many weapons at their disposal—transferring personnel, cutting off funds, reorganizing lines of administration, withdrawing ministerial licenses, and (with the government) deporting foreign clergy—and all of them were brought into play over the course of the period against different offenders of new-Christendom orthodoxy.[37]

The key to achieving this was maintaining episcopal unity. Without that—if there had been bishops willing consistently to support and encourage grass-roots social activism—the centralizing, conservative impulse could have been divisive to the church as a whole. But were there not such bishops who in fact supported "their own" in many specific instances of conflict with political authorities—in Barrancabermeja and Bucaramanga, in Cartagena, Cali, and Cúcuta, in Ibagué, Pereira, Medellín—during these years? There were, and they did—for a while. They may have constituted a somewhat progressive caucus within the Bishops' Conference, which was certainly not without its internal debates. But at the end of the day, none of these bishops—with all the ancient accumulated authority of the Ordinary in his own diocese—was willing to lead those forces that did not want a neo-Christendom church.

Why this was true undoubtedly had something to do with individual biographies, but it is explained to a great extent by collective structures of the church institution—and the surrounding context of Colombia's oligarchical democracy.

EXPLAINING THE NEO-CHRISTENDOM CHURCH: INSTITUTION AND LEADERSHIP

There is a sense of inevitability about the trajectory of the Colombian church toward neo-Christendom since the 1960s. After all, it was long regarded as the most conservative and "traditional" church in Latin America—strong as an ecclesiastical institution identified with a national society and public authority. Nevertheless, the church that had emerged by the 1980s was by no means already formed in the 1960s. Then it was a church with unparalleled internal conflict, sharply divided between longings toward a stable past, associations with a reformist present, and hopes for a transformed future. Its present character may be "traditional," but leaders within it had to wield tradition to bring about the changes that have occurred.

The church's most striking change is organizational modernization and centralization. Long a "national" church, it has only in the last thirty years created a national organization. The key to that process has been a permanent secretariat for the Bishops' Conference (SPEC), begun in the 1950s, one of the first in Latin America. This bureaucracy started modestly, largely as a coordinating group for the bishops' annual meetings. Around the same time the church created many other new structures, such as new seminaries to stimulate clerical vocations and new urban parishes and pastoral groupings for Colombia's swelling cities. It patronized new social initiatives for labor (Union of Colombian Workers, or UTC) and peasants (FANAL, Acción Comunal Popular) and initiated new institutes for sociological research and education (ICODES; Center of Social Research and Action, or CIAS; Institute of Doctrine and Social Studies, or IDES) to interpret social problems and help relate church action to them. This modernization constituted a historic change in the way the church organized itself, but its immediate effects were centrifugal. To control the resulting dispersion, the bishops turned to their new secretariat, Secretariado Permanente del Episcopado (SPEC).

How the SPEC asserted its central control in the 1970s has been described in several studies.[38] What may be less clear is why it succeeded. The Catholic Church had, after all, an ancient pattern of organization relating bishops in their dioceses directly to Rome. In Colombia the canonical independence of each bishop had been fortified historically by realities of regional difference and poor communications. Why should SPEC triumph with a project that, at least in several important respects, clashed precisely with national tradition?

Explanation must begin, as it often does in the Catholic Church, in Rome. For the Vatican Colombia occupied a place of preference within the larger panorama of the Latin American church. Colombia was the first country in the region visited by a reigning pontiff, Paul VI, in 1968 (to inaugurate an International Eucharistic Congress, on his way to the CELAM meeting in Medellín). Bogotá was chosen as the site for the secretariat of CELAM, the new Latin American bishops' organization. So significant in opening the regional church in the 1960s, CELAM became central to reasserting orthodoxy in the 1970s. The fight (clearly supported in Rome) against the whole tendency grouped around "liberation theology" was directed by a young Colombian bishop, Alfonso López Trujillo, CELAM executive secretary from 1972 and its president in 1979. The favor he enjoyed with Rome was displayed in his meteoric ecclesiastical career: He became archbishop of Medellín in 1979 and gained admission to the College of Cardinals as its youngest member in 1983. While heading the CELAM secretariat, López Trujillo continued as auxiliary bishop in Bogotá, thus occupying a key position in the confluence of the Colombian and international churches. Colombian priests and prelates of his confidence received posts in the CELAM machinery. International sources of support from wealthy foreign churches—such as those of the United States and West Germany, which had been so important in financing the new social initiatives of the 1960s—could be redirected toward structures reliably under hierarchical control.[39]

There can be no doubt that the neo-Christendom Colombian church was significantly shaped by conservatism emanating from Rome. However, its character was also strongly molded by aspects of its own national tradition. The Colombian church had long been a clerically dominated institution, one that had never turned to or tolerated autonomous movements of lay Catholics (in contrast, for example, to Brazil or Chile). Moreover, it was, in relative terms, rich in clerical vocations for Colombia itself and so had never requested the large numbers of foreign priests and nuns that had brought "advanced ideas" to so many other countries in Latin America.[40] Above all, the Colombian church had a triumphalist tradition, as described previously—with traditional conceptions of the church as "perfect society" and hierarchical ecclesiastical institution. All these characteristics strengthened the efficacy of ecclesiastical discipline employed on behalf of a conservative conception of church.[41]

These elements of Colombian church traditions were not perpetuated automatically. On the contrary, they had to be chosen and employed in new circumstances in order to create the neo-Christendom church. The man most responsible for doing so was the Cardinal Archbishop of Bogotá, Aníbal Muñoz Duque. The challenge facing Muñoz Duque was somehow to marry the necessary modernization and new social concerns inherited from the 1960s church to the church's traditions of hierarchical authority. The implications of what he achieved—the imposition of episcopal unity and centralized control at the cost of diminishing social influence—are debatable (and are discussed in the concluding section of this chapter). That his leadership was crucial to this outcome is beyond question. His predecessor as Bogotá's cardinal archbishop was Luís Concha Córdoba. Son of a former president of the Republic, Concha was hardly an implacable enemy of Colombia's oligarchical regime. Patron and then prosecutor of Camilo Torres, he was hardly an unqualified friend of liberation theology. But there were more than a few signs, as Concha lingered on as cardinal into the early 1970s, that the Colombian church could have developed quite differently from the direction in which it was taken by Muñoz Duque.[42]

It is not surprising that, as archbishop of Bogotá, Muñoz Duque would have associated the interests of the church with those of the government. Such had been the attitude of all of his predecessors, in a tradition stretching back more than a century. He, as they, headed a national institution, its fortunes linked in myriad ways to the political order. He, as they, had to deal diplomatically with the government of the day (whatever its coloration)—government to which (not incidentally) he, of all the Colombian church, enjoyed privileged access.[43] Nevertheless, as archbishop, Muñoz Duque exceeded all of his predecessors in his steadfastness and zeal in defending oligarchical democracy in difficult times. He stood publicly with the regime in every moment of crisis (most notably following the disputed election of 1970 and in the wave of strikes of 1976 and 1977). Again and again, he defended Colombia's beleaguered political institutions as ''democracy'' itself and rejected any critique that the procedures and consequences of those institutions were undemocratic in practice. He was implacable against social liberationist groups within the church. In addition to employing an impressive range of ecclesiastical discipline against them, he was a master of the public gesture of repudiation. The most spectacular of these gestures came in the midst of the 1976 hunger strike of bank employees who, with clerical and some episcopal support, were occupying various churches throughout the country. Within a period of just a few days Muñoz Duque refused to meet with a large group of priests and nuns supporting the strike, calling the police to have them thrown out of his palace; stepped forward in a blaze of publicity, before a solid phalanx of the capital's financial community, to bless the opening of a new bank; and graciously accepted his honorary title of brigadier general in the armed forces, whom he went on to eulogize in a special mass.[44]

In controlling social-activist priests, Muñoz Duque counted not only with the considerable traditional powers of a bishop but also with the new centralized organization of the Episcopal Conference. That was particularly important in allowing him to maintain unity among the bishops around neo-Christendom. They were, of course, predisposed to conservatism for many reasons, not least of which was their overwhelmingly curial or seminary (rather than pastoral) backgrounds.[45] Nevertheless, they could reach different conclusions about the best course of action in specific conflicts, and many of them did support social militance in particular situations. It was a considerable achievement (with significant consequences) to reach and sustain an unbroken common front. Fate had a hand in it: The country's two most socially progressive bishops, Raúl Camader Zambrano and particularly Gerardo Valencia Cano, the only episcopal member of the Golconda group, were killed in separate airplane accidents in the early 1970s.[46] Muñoz Duque, however, had abundant institutional powers in his own hands. By the early 1980s half of all the bishops in the country had taken office during his tenure, many of them in the new auxiliary positions he had created to strengthen hierarchical organization. Muñoz Duque was not adverse to refuting or reprimanding a fellow bishop on occasion, but that was rarely necessary with the growing strength of the collective Bishops' Conference (and the location of many national ecclesiastical organizations within his own archdiocese). The prominence given the position of individual prelates in the past (and often the public polemics between them) gradually faded before the unified voice of the Bishops' Conference (and SPEC behind it), with its rule of unanimity for collective statements.

The most important reasons for what the Colombian church became in the 1970s are found in the intentions and instruments of ecclesiastical elites. The neo-Christendom church was also shaped, however, by other limitations from the broader political context of the period. It seems appropriate to conclude this chapter with some brief speculations about the staying power both of this model of church and of Colombia's regime of oligarchical democracy.

THE FUTURE OF NEO-CHRISTENDOM

The character of a national church at a given moment in time always represents a kind of equilibrium between different forces within. There may be greater or less coherence among those forces, but there are always tensions (and even contradictions) between them. In the 1970s and early 1980s the Colombian church was led, forcefully, to cohere rather clearly around a conception of neo-Christendom. Those ecclesiastical elites responsible tended to look on this model in terms of continuity and stability—a new synthesis of the church's timeless truths that would permit it to take part in orderly change. It is, however, an equilibrium vulnerable at several points.

Neo-Christendom in Colombia rests on a number of crucial judgements. One of these is that ecclesiastical orthodoxy is more important than social influence; another, closely related, is that the church's social influence is better assured in acknowledged association with a political regime than in frank autonomy from it. This latter depends, in turn, on that regime's effectiveness and legitimacy—

and the strength of the alternatives that exist to challenge or replace it. The odds on all these bets favored neo-Christendom in the late 1970s, and early 1980s, but any of them could shift in the future and upset the existing equilibrium.

The social-activist forces within the church have not disappeared; they are just much more prudent, both ecclesiastically and politically, than when they first appeared. From Camilo Torres in the mid–1970s, they tended to attack the institutional church, and Archbishop Muñoz Duque in particular, frontally and publicly.[47] In time, especially after the events of 1976, they came to realize that such tactics were quixotic and counterproductive. The bishops had weapons and influence much greater than theirs, and popular religiosity was more conservative than they had initially understood it to be.[48] With time they also became more realistic politically. They had begun believing that oppressive social experiences could be transformed rather directly into politically-relevant form. They took a "political option," but what they learned in the political arena—the limitations of popular consciousness, the weaknesses of popular organization, the endless divisions among "progressive forces," not to speak of the effectiveness of government repression—was sobering. Both the religious and the political experiences of church progressives affected them in the same direction. As a result, they have assumed a much lower profile, but they continue to exist in the interstices of the ecclesiastical institution, more cautious but no less committed. Unlike an earlier generation, they will make great efforts to stay within the hierarchical church. They constitute a significant minority of the clergy—and their numbers could multiply rapidly if conditions were to change.[49]

The progressives represent a permanent alternative to the neo-Christendom strategy of attempting to bring about social change by teaching general principles and supporting government reform. That strategy is vulnerable, because at some point it can be judged to have failed. The circumstances that lead to such a political moment of truth are, of course, mysterious, but for the church itself disquieting signs have already appeared. One is the measured decline in religious observance in all its traditional forms, so long a point of pride.[50] Another sign, more diffuse but noted widely, is the church's manifest inability to speak with any effect to Colombia's profound, prolonged "moral crisis." In this of all areas of social life, the church should be able to make a difference. Yet, as in the violence of the 1940s and 1950s, the church seems wholly marginal to the course of events and powerless even to interpret their moral meaning. Reviewing the spectrum of major issues in public life over the last twenty years, it is difficult to find any issue on which the position of the church has made a difference.[51] The hierarchy might regularly urge the citizenry to save Colombian democracy at election times, but that had no discernible influence on massive rates of abstention. The hierarchy may wield ecclesiastical discipline to ensure orthodoxy within their institution, but what is their real authority in society if no one listens to them?

The question will not go away. The Colombian church is extremely proud of its social influence, achieved historically in close association with a political regime. It would be surprising if, at some point, church leaders did not appear who were distressed over the decline of that influence and willing to rethink that association. In that circumstance they, like their counterparts elsewhere in Latin America, might support their clergy acting in solidarity with movements of the poor, even when opposed to the government.

The equilibrium sustaining neo-Christendom, then, could be upset by shifts on the side of church and society. It could also be undone by changes on the side of politics. The continuities of oligarchical democracy in the period were the inescapable context for the successful creation of a neo-Christendom church. They provided the regime stability on which the hierarchy counted (and which they collectively did their part to foster). Several conditions of this regime stand out as particularly crucial. One was the maintenance of a relatively constitutional, relatively open, relatively legitimate politics. The other was the absence of a successful mass-based challenge to the two traditional parties. Either of these conditions could change in the future.

Start with the second. Several generations of developmentalist reform have failed to alter significantly the distribution of power in society or to improve the lot of the poor. This is widely recognized in Colombia, including by the bishops. The reasons such social disparities have not been translated into political terms are complex,[52] but the sheer fact that they have not been is of great importance. The only sustained challenge to oligarchical democracy has come from the rural guerrillas, and even they—whatever their ability to survive—have never succeeded in building a popular base. As long as they remain the only real political alternative, the hierarchy has no difficulty in maintaining its partisanship for the regime. Even in the most liberationist churches in Latin America, bishops have sanctioned insurrectionary violence only in the rarest of circumstances (such as the last stages of the rising against Somoza), when there was some expectation that they could succeed. Those circumstances did not arise in Colombia. The clerical left sometimes appeared to believe that revolutionary triumph was imminent, and guerrilla-priests certainly occupied the highest places in their pantheon of martyrs. But all this had the effect of allowing the bishops to include all forms of social activism in their unwavering condemnation of violence.

The context of oligarchical democracy facilitated the bishops in drawing the line for social action as they did: against social activism and violence rather than between the two, as in more liberationist churches.[53] They lacked the incentive, as it were, of a powerful popular movement that might really alter the premises of the regime. As spokesmen of neo-Christendom, they might offer support for the existing regime, although their declining social authority rendered at least questionable the real effects of such positive legitimation. Their most significant contribution to sustaining the system was to hinder its delegitimation—by maintaining unity among the hierarchy and controlling those social-activist elements that might have split the church. Neo-Christendom is the ecclesiastical dimension of a broader traditional regime, of a general historical type: with ''relatively autonomous collectivities or corporations under the ruler, but controlling their own members, pyramids of authority linked to higher authorities at their apexes, stratified social hierarchies in which each stratum recognize[s] its place.''[54]

In Colombia the corporation most likely to upset this arrangement is the army. The first condition crucial to the regime's survival to date has been the ability of civilian party politicians to retain ultimate (if diminished) authority. Their governments in the last decades have frequently been harsh, arbitrary, and (certainly in social and economic terms) undemocratic. But they have maintained a degree of openness, competition, and legitimacy. In the face of the guerrilla insurgency, however, the power of the army has grown to proportions that have no precedent in Colombian history. Civilian control has been in doubt in all three of the last governments.[55] In the throes of a deep, continuing social crisis— and even with the immense inherited skills of the political class—it is not difficult to imagine circumstances that might lead the army at some point to take power directly.

What would the church do in such a situation? Much would depend on particulars, of course, but it would certainly mean the end of neo-Christendom. Part of the church would undoubtedly support the new regime. It did so after the last army takeover, in 1953, and it would be impelled by the same considerations of *Realpolitik* and its own long historical tradition. Since that era it has considerably strengthened its own ties to the military institution (notably by creating the military chaplaincy, headed by a bishop), in recognition of its "maximum importance" as "guardian of internal peace" (in its words at the time of the 1973 Concordat).

The bishops would have great difficulties, however, in maintaining unity under a military regime. They were divided under the relatively mild dictatorship of Rojas Pinilla in the 1950s and ultimately turned against him. Violations of human rights were one factor even then. Since that time the Colombian military has imbibed a doctrine of "national security" that has been the catalyst of church opposition to authoritarianism wherever it has arisen in Latin America. The Colombian church has also changed since then. Its far greater social consciousness has been tamed within neo-Christendom. Neo-Christendom, however, counted on a stable regime of oligarchical democracy—not with a military government likely to be both more brutal and less predictable.

NOTES

1. See Alexander Wilde, "Redemocratization, the Church, and Democracy in Colombia," in *Colombia Since the National Front*, eds. Bruce Bagley, Francisco Thoumi, and Juan Tokatlian (Boulder, Colo.: Westview, 1987).

2. A short list of the most important studies in English of the new Latin American church in its relation to politics include the following: Phillip Berryman, *The Religious Roots of Rebellion* (Maryknoll, N.Y.: Orbis, 1984); Thomas C. Bruneau, *The Political Transformation of the Brazilian Church* (New York: Cambridge University Press, 1974); Thomas C. Bruneau, *The Church in Brazil* (Austin: University of Texas Press, 1981); Edward L. Cleary, O.P., *Crisis and Change: The Church in Latin America Today* (Mary-

knoll, N.Y.: Orbis, 1985); Daniel Levine, *Religion and Politics in Latin America: The Catholic Church in Venezuela and Colombia* (Princeton, N.J.: Princeton University Press, 1981); Daniel Levine, ed., *Churches and Politics in Latin America* (Beverly Hills, Calif.: Sage, 1980); Scott Mainwaring, *The Catholic Church and Politics in Brazil* (Princeton, N.J.: Princeton University Press, 1986); and Brian H. Smith, *The Church and Politics in Chile* (Princeton, N.J.: Princeton University Press, 1982).

3. The chapters on Brazil by Thomas Bruneau and Scott Mainwaring and on Colombia by Daniel Levine in Daniel Levine, ed. *Religion and Political Conflict in Latin America* (Chapel Hill: University of North Carolina Press, 1986) give a good feel for the contrasts.

4. The concept is both analytical and polemical. It originated among those critical of such a conception of the church's mission; hence, those who hold such a conception do not use the term. However, it is a useful concept to describe certain relations to society and public authority that are manifest both in what the church does and its explanations for that behavior. It is for its analytical utility that the term is used here. A good example of the theological debate, from a liberationist perspective, is Pablo Richard, *Mort des chrétientés et naissance de l'Eglise*, Série Amérique Latine Nombre 3 (Paris: Centre Lebret, 1978).

5. The most extensive efforts to apply the concept of Neo-Christendom to Colombia's church are Luis Alberto Alfonso, *Dominación religiosa y hegemonía política* (Bogotá, Colombia: Punta de Lanza, 1978), especially pp. 84–96 and, following Alfonso, the chapters by Rodolfo de Roux in Comisión de Estudios de Historia de la Iglesia en América Latina [CEHILA], *Historia general de la Iglesia en América Latina*, Vol. 7, *Colombia y Venezuela* (Salamanca, Spain: Ediciones Sígueme, 1981), especially pp. 546–51 and 562–63. See also the thoughtful analysis of Levine, *Religion and Politics in Latin America*, passim, especially pp. 33–34, 304–05. A useful analysis for comparative purposes is Mainwaring, *Church and Politics in Brazil*, Chapter 2, which argues that the Brazilian church cannot be thought of in terms of Neo-Christendom after 1955.

6. See, for example, Andrés Holguín, *Análisis del nuevo concordato* (Bogotá: Revista Derecho Colombiano, 1973) and Pedro Pablo Camargo, *El régimen concordatorio colombiano* (Bogotá, Colombia: Sociedad Colombiana de Abogados, 1971). A defense is given by the Colombian Ambassador to the Holy See, Antonio Rocha, *Matrimonio, educación y actualidad concordatoria* (Bogotá: Editorial Revista Colombiana, 1975).

7. See, for example, "Un Concordato 'con Intencionados criterios,' " *anali-CIAS*, (September 1973):2–17; E. Díaz Ardila, "El Nuevo Concordato," *Revista Javeriana* (October 1973):381–88; de Roux, "La Iglesia Colombiana desde 1962," in CEHILA, *Historia general*, pp. 578–79; and the following prescient publication by one of the members of the Golconda group: Father Manuel Alzate R., *Libertad religiosa en Colombia* (Cali, Colombia: Editorial Pacífico, 1969).

8. Conferencia Episcopal de Colombia, *Concordato de 1973*, third edition, (Bogotá: Secretariado Permanente del Episcopado [SPEC], 1983), pp. 40–41.

9. Colombian ecclesiastical language is invariably sexist and throughout this chapter will be thus rendered into English.

10. Quotations in this paragraph are from Conferencia Episcopal de Colombia, "Comunicado pastoral del comité permanente de la Conferencia Episcopal con ocasión de la firma del nuevo concordato," July 1973, pp. 41, 33. Quotations in the following paragraphs are from either that communiqué or from the text of Conferencia Episcopal de Colombia, *Concordato de 1973*, pp. 9–19.

11. The text of the 1887 Concordat is available most conveniently in English in J.

Lloyd Mecham, *Church and State in Latin America*, revised edition (Chapel Hill: University of North Carolina Press, 1966), pp. 126–31. With all subsequent emendations it may be found in *Constitución política de la república de Colombia*, sixteenth edition (Bogotá: Editorial Voluntad, 1967), pp. 153–200.

12. Conferencia Episcopal, *Concordato de 1973*, pp. 33, 38, 41.

13. Ibid., Article 2, and pp. 34, 36, 41, 52.

14. Ibid., p. 41. The unusual "conjugate" ("to unite sexually, as in marriage," according to *Webster's New Collegiate Dictionary*) has been used to render "conjugan," consistent with the marriage imagery of the passage.

15. The official commentary by the SPEC argues that legally the "last vestige" of the patronato was abolished because the government would no longer formally present candidates. See Conferencia Episcopal, *Concordato de 1973*, p. 59.

16. Ibid., p. 62.

17. The bishop's image of the good Catholic citizen is also apposite here: "The Catholic, faithful subject of the earthly and celestial cities, has a clear consciousness of his duty as member of both societies and in carrying out the laws of both realizes himself as man and as believer." Conferencia Episcopal, "Comunicado," p. 36.

18. See Juan Ignacio Morena, S.J., "Notas históricas sobre el vicariato castrense en Colombia," *Revista Javeriana*, 80 (October 1973):389–92.

19. Conferencia Episcopal, *Concordato de 1973*, p. 60. Emphasis added.

20. For the Jesuit priority, see *anali-CIAS* 10 (September 1972), one issue of a journal that covered church involvement in the countryside in the early 1970s. For information on this church involvement, see also Cristina Escobar, *Trayectoria de la ANUC* (Bogotá: CINEP, 1982?). Concerning agrarian reform, the bishops began talking about the "essential social function" of property in the mid–1960s, although in a highly qualified way. By the early 1970s they had dropped most of their earlier hedging; see, for example, Conferencia Episcopal de Colombia, *La justicia en el mundo* (Bogotá: SPEC, 1972), p. 66. On clerical activism on behalf of ANAPO, see Alfonso, *Dominación religiosa*, pp. 56–57, 191, and Germán Rama, *El sistema político colombiano: frente nacional y ANAPO* (Asunción: Centro Paraguayo de Estudios Sociológicos, 1970). For information on the evolving church relationship with unions in the period, see Kenneth Medhurst, *The Church and Labour in Colombia* (Manchester, England: Manchester University Press, 1984), pp. 95–206. For information on a general treatment of the period, see Alexander Wilde, "The Contemporary Church: The Political and the Pastoral," in *The Politics of Compromise: Coalition Government in Colombia*, eds. R. Albert Berry, Ronald G. Hellman, and Mauricio Solaún (New Brunswick, N.J.: Transaction Books, 1980), especially pp. 222–35.

21. Quoted in "Política y pastoral," *Tierra Nueva* (Bogotá) 2 (July 1973):90.

22. Quoted by de Roux, "La Iglesia colombiana desde 1962" in CEHILA, *Historia general*, p. 576.

23. Useful collections of documentation on the period are the following: SAL [Sacerdotes para América Latina], *Un compromiso sacerdotal en la lucha de clases; documentos 1972–78* (Bogotá: 1978, no publisher listed); the "Documents DIAL," French translations by the Diffusion de l'Information sur l'Amérique Latine [DIAL] (Paris) of materials relating to the Latin American church, with some fifty on Colombia from 1973 to 1984, including the particularly useful "Colombie: dix ans de présence chrétiene dans la société," number D–460 (1978); and from the late 1970s, the left lay monthly, *Solidaridad* (Bogotá). In addition to broader scholarly studies of the Colombian church,

already cited, helpful overviews of the period are Andrés Mendoza, "La Iglesia en Colombia," *América Latina* 20 (Brussels: Informes de Pro Mundi Vita, 1980); "Un pays catholique et conservateur: La Colombie," *Informations Catholiques Internationales* 515 (June 1977):29–36; and "Les deux Eglises de Colombie," *Informations Catholiques Internationales* 558 (January 1981):37–39f. Church involvement in events from 1975 to 1976 is documented and analyzed in *La Iglesia en conflicto?* Controversia 44 (Bogotá: Centro de Investigación y Educación Popular [CINEP], 1976).

24. See Medhurst, *The Church and Labour*, for a history.

25. See "Informe de una misión de amnistía internacional a la República de Colombia" (London: Amnesty International, 1980), and "Informe sobre la situación de los derechos humanos en la República de Colombia" (Washington, D.C.: Comisión Interamericana de Derechos Humanos, Organización de los Estados Americanos, 1981).

26. The years 1976 and 1978 saw the most collective confrontations, which were preceded and followed by the older-style individual encounters.

27. The first was a small part ("Síntesis del diagnóstico de la realidad colombiana") of the very large Colombian statement prepared for the 1979 CELAM meeting at Puebla, Mexico: III Conferencia general del episcopado latinoamericano, *Aportes de las conferencias episcopales*, Auxilliary Book 3 (Bogotá: CELAM, 1978?). The second incorporates this analysis (as "Horizonte sociopolítico") within the hierarchy's general pastoral message following their annual meeting: Conferencia Episcopal de Colombia, "Mensaje pastoral de la XXXVII Asamblea plenaria del episcopado colombiano" (Bogotá: SPEC, 1981). The first aroused a public polemic; the second did not. See the following useful commentaries: "Aporte para la tercera conferencia del episcopado latinamericano," *Aportes* (Bogotá), number 8 (August 1978):5–19; "A propósito el enfrentamiento entre la jerarquiá y los políticos," *Aportes*, number 7 (July 1978):1–16; and "Los sectores populares deberían ser interlocutores de la Jerarquiá," *Solidaridad* (Bogotá), number 30 (November 1981):18–19.

28. See "A propósito," *Aportes*, number 7 (July 1978), pp. 3–4. The document was leaked to the press, quite possibly by more progressive (or anti-Liberal) sectors within the Secretariat of the Bishops' Conference.

29. All quotations that follow in the text are taken from the following document: Conferencia Episcopal, "Mensaje pastoral," 1981.

30. The bishops do express their traditional preference for the country's peasants in terms ("*los más adictos creyentes de la Iglesia*:   the church's most addicted believers") to which Karl Marx could only have smiled in assent.

31. Conferencia Episcopal, "Mensaje pastoral," pp. 30, 31, 37.

32. Anti-Liberal feeling in the church is reflected in the commentary on the period by the reliably reactionary Humberto Bronx [Father Jaime Serra Gómez], *Historia moderna de la Iglesia colombiana*, second edition (Medellín, Colombia: Editorial Argemiro Salazar, 1981?), pp. 451–64.

33. See, for example, CINEP, *Una Iglesia en conflicto?* p. 19 and *Iglesia y justicia militar*, Controversia 74 (Bogotá: CINEP, 1979?). The Conservative background of General Rojas Pinilla was perhaps not wholly incidental in the appeal of ANAPO to the Golconda priests.

34. The 1976 statement was representative, asserting that it was "a solemn duty to vote in order to save Colombia," although it was "not permitted to a Catholic, like any citizen of good faith and good will," to vote for candidates upholding "Marxist doctrines or policies." See DIAL, "Colombie: l'Episcopat et les elections municipales," number

D–303 (May 6, 1976), and the critical reply of left Catholics, "Colombie: á la veille des elections municipales," number D–299 (April 15, 1976). For other examples and other elections, see SAL, *Un compromiso sacerdotal*, pp. 97–102, 189–92, 233–39. The broader analysis of SAL group, "La 'democracia colombiana,' " is an intelligent critique, particularly of party clientelism (SAL, *Un compromiso sacerdotal*, pp. 243–63).

35. Guerrilla-priests subsequently killed in action included the Spaniard Domingo Laín (1974), Florentino Agudelo (1976), and Diego Uribe (1981).

36. Conferencia Episcopal de Colombia, "Identidad cristiana en la acción por la justicia" (Bogotá: SPEC, 1976). The reply from "Numerous Christian Groups," "Identidad cristiana en la acción por la justica; una versión alternativa" appeared the following year (no publication information).

37. Bishops were not shy about laundering dirty linen in public. They name names of offending church groups quite explicitly in, for example, their 1976 "Identidad cristiana" and 1981 "Mensaje pastoral," both cited previously. Among notable examples of administrative reorganization to assert central institutional control were the 1972 take-over of the formerly Jesuit Institute of Doctrine and Social Studies (IDES), the taming of several liberationist catechetical programs (including *Denuncia*, under the Salesian Fathers) from 1973 to 1975, and the closing of the Pastoral Institute for Youth (IPLAJ), involving three different religious orders, in 1975. See Wilde, "The Contemporary Church," pp. 220–23; Levine, *Religion and Politics*, pp. 221–22, 242–48; and Mendoza, "La Iglesia en Colombia," pp. 40–41.

38. In addition to sources in the preceding footnote, see Medhurst, *Church and Labour*, and Juan Botero Restrepo, *Breve historia de la Iglesia Colombiana* (Medellín, Colombia: Editorial Copiyepes, 1983), pp. 170–72.

39. An earlier study of organizational conflict in the Colombian church—which anticipated a rather different direction than what actually occurred—is David Mutchler, *The Church as a Political Factor in Latin America* (New York: Praeger, 1971). Another international ecclesiastical personage who has played an interesting role during this period is Roger Vekemans, S.J. Vekemans was a prominent figure in Chile in the 1960s, especially in church–Christian Democrat relations. He came to Bogotá in 1971 and founded a study center Centro de Estudios para el Desarrollo e Integración de América Latina (CEDIAL) and theology journal (*Tierra Nueva*) that have been conservative redoubts in the battle against liberation theology.

40. Colombia has had historically one of the most favorable ratios of priests to population in Latin America. In 1980 there were 5,330 priests in the country, one for every 5,733 inhabitants. Secretariado Nacional de Pastoral Social (SNPS), *Aproximación a la realidad colombiana* (Bogotá: SNPS, 1971, p. 108. Of the total number of priests, diocesan priests predominated over those of religious orders, 3,284 to 2,046 (SNPS, *Aproximación, p. 103*. Foreign clergy are generally members of religious orders. The unusually national character of the Colombian church is illustrated by the very low proportion of its foreign Religious, 18 percent, as compared to 38 percent in El Salvador, 49 percent in Brazil, 55 percent in Chile, and 68 percent in Peru. See Confederación Latinoamericana de Religiosos [CLAR], *Estudio sociográfico de los religiosos y las religiosas en América Latina* (Bogotá: Secretariado de la CLAR, 1971), p. 40.

41. Even the historic predominance of diocesan rather than Religious priests in Colombia (previous note) facilitated the imposition of hierarchical control. Bishops exercise authority directly over such "secular" priests, rather than through a parallel structure of religious orders.

42. Consider, for example, Concha's sympathy toward the Golconda group in 1969 and 1970; see Alfonso, *Dominación religiosa*, pp. 192–93.

43. This historical pattern is surprising only to those (and they are many) who believe that the Colombian church was monolithically militant on behalf of the Conservative party. In fact, the church had always been divided—progovernment and opposition—whenever the Liberals were in power (as it was often divided by different Conservative factional loyalties when that party held the government). This pattern is described in Alexander Wilde, "Politics and the Church in Colombia" (in progress).

44. See *Iglesia en conflicto?* and the list of grievances of SAL, *Un compromiso sacerdotal*, pp. 195–200.

45. See the analysis of career patterns in Hubert Schwan and Antonio Ugalde, "Orientations of the Bishops of Colombia Toward Social Development, 1930–1970" in *Journal of Church and State* 16 (1974):481–83. Compare with Levine, *Religion and Politics*, pp. 105–6.

46. See *Monseñor Valencia* (Bogotá: Librería Stella, 1972) and "Gerardo Valencia Cano, obispo de los pobres," *Solidaridad* 31 (February 1982):23–34. On Zambrano, see Levine, *Religion and Politics*, pp. 262–85 passim.

47. A typical assertion, part of a lengthy document in 1973 on the fifth anniversary of Medellín, was that "the Hierarchy, part of the clergy, and part of the laity belong to the oppressor class, or are its allies. A sector of the clergy and the great majority of the Christian people are within the oppressed class." SAL, *Un compromiso sacerdotal*, p. 80. Such attacks are a recurrent theme running through the collected documents in the volume. The most elaborate denunciation of Muñoz Duque took the form of an open letter to him in April 1976 and carries a litany of accumulated grievances. Similar messages illustrating this style were sent out of hierarchical channels directly to the Bishops' Synod of 1974 and CELAM meeting of 1976. See SAL, *Un Compromiso sacerdotal*, pp. 115–22, 183–85.

48. See Ibid., p. 282; "Una Iglesia en crisis," *Solidaridad* 20 (November 1980):11–16; and Francisco Zuluaga, S.J., "La religiosidad popular en Colombia," *La Antigua* (Panama), pp. 26, 109–22.

49. SAL, *Un compromiso sacerdotal*, documents this learning process. For the distribution of different groupings within the church at present, see "Una Iglesia en crisis," *Aportes*, and de Roux, "La Iglesia colombiana," in *Historia General*, pp. 586–89.

50. Bronx, *Historia moderna*, pp. 464–66.

51. Divorce is one for which it did, but the exception proves the rule. Not even in family planning—another of the church's most traditional core concerns—was the government prevented from carrying out one of Latin America's most effective programs. See the analysis of defeat by Bronx, *Historia moderna*, pp. 453–59.

52. Bruce Bagley has made an important effort to analyze the patterns of Colombian politics as "inclusionary authoritarianism"—precisely not imperfect democracy—"National Front and Economic Development," in *Politics, Policies & Economic Development in Latin America*, ed. Robert Wesson (Palo Alto, Calif.: Hoover Press, 1984), pp. 124–60.

53. Compare Levine, *Religion and Politics*, on social *activism* versus social *activation*, pp. 139–40, 179–201.

54. Eric Hobsbawn, "Mass-Producing Traditions: Europe, 1870–1914," in *The Invention of Tradition*, eds. Hobsbawn and Terence Ranger (Cambridge, England: Cambridge University Press, 1983), p. 265.

55. See Gustavo Gallón Giraldo, *Quince años de estado de sitio en Colombia, 1958–1978* (Bogotá: Editorial América, 1979) and *La república de las armas*, Controversia 109–110 (Bogotá: CINEP, 1983). The army was a continuing source of opposition to efforts of the Betancur government to achieve an end to the guerrilla insurgency. For relevant documentation, see Luis Villar Borda, ed., *Oposición, insurgencia y amnestía*, (Bogotá: Editorial Dintel, 1982).

7

Politics and Policies: The Limits of the Venezuelan Consociational Regime

Diego Abente

The Venezuelan liberal democratic system is often depicted as the offspring of its oil wealth. As Robert J. Alexander argued in his contribution to this volume, generally, and quite uncritically, petroleum is credited with or blamed for most of Venezuela's successes or failures in the realm of politics. Contrary to that widely held view, this chapter adopts an alternative interpretation that emphasizes, without ignoring the importance of oil, the role that other political and economic factors played in shaping the contemporary political system of Venezuela. This approach is predicated on the assumption that the range of political outcomes that the abundance of oil resources makes possible is just too vast and that therefore more specific variables should be examined to understand why a liberal democratic and not another political system emerged. As a perusal of the twentieth-century history of Venezuela eloquently demonstrates, although the oil wealth set up the broad parameters within which the political process evolved, the specific democratic formulas were determined instead by a complex array of factors that brought about the complete transformation of the Venezuelan polity.

In the early stages of the oil industry, for example, petroleum-related revenues played nicely into the hands of Dictator Juan V. Gómez. They provided him with a steady source of revenue independent from the control of local sectors that strengthened his government and widened his "autonomy" vis-à-vis traditional socioeconomic elites. These revenues also allowed him to bail out factions of the rural elites, especially coffee growers but also sugar growers and cocoa producers, from agriculture and into more profitable operations.[1]

The importance of petroleum increased even more in the following decades. In the 1940s it allowed the short-lived democratic experiment of 1945 to 1948 known as the *trienio* to finance a multitude of social programs. In the 1950s, on the other hand, it provided the dictatorship of General Marcos Pérez Jiménez with the resources needed to embark on massive public works programs. Finally, housing and educational opportunities, health, and other social programs expanded dramatically under the successive democratic administrations of the 1960s, 1970s, and 1980s.

Thus, although it is true that the oil industry reshaped the socioeconomic map of the country in many ways that cannot be fully analyzed here,[2] it would be a mistake, however, to deduce that Venezuela is a democracy solely or mostly or basically because the oil industry provided the "right" social structure or the needed revenues. Oil has coexisted with the old-fashioned dictatorship of Gómez, the transitional governments of Generals Eleazar López Contreras and Isaías Medina Angarita, the trienio, the military junta that overthrew it, the Pérez Jiménez dictatorship, and the democratic period inaugurated in 1958. In all cases petroleum resources have, to a great extent, shaped the levels of public spending and perhaps facilitated regime maintenance but have not explained regime emergence or breakdown; nor have they determined the political formulas.

Furthermore, the contention that the abundance of oil resources makes democracy possible—by easing revenue-expenditure conflicts and financing social reforms without having to increase the tax burden on the domestic sector of the economy—is questionable on other grounds as well. For one thing, that argument wrongly assumes that between 1958 and 1975 it was easier to raise petroleum taxes than to increase domestic levies. In addition, that assertion is at odds with the available evidence that shows that non-oil-related income-tax revenues increased from 1.65 percent of the national income in 1957 to 3.04 percent in 1980.[3]

Finally, even though it is true that before the 1976 nationalization the possibility of increasing oil taxes at least marginally before raising domestic ones has frequently been present, petroleum revenues have not completely substituted for internally generated revenues. In fact, the extractive capability of the Venezuelan government, excluding oil levies, remains average or above average by Latin American standards. For instance, in 1975 non-oil-related income-tax revenues represented 3.04 percent of Venezuela's national income; only Chile and Colombia exhibited higher figures, but in both cases property-tax proceeds were lumped together with income-tax revenues. In 1982 non-oil-related tax revenues represented 12.30 percent of the non-oil-related gross domestic product (GDP). Ratios for other Latin American countries are as follows: Colombia, 7.78 percent; Mexico, 15.46 percent (including oil taxes); Brazil, 6.72 percent; Costa Rica, 12.37 percent; and Argentina, 8.88 percent.[4]

CONFLICT AND ACCOMMODATION: FROM 1958 TO 1986

If petroleum is not the deus-ex-machina, that all-encompassing explanatory factor, how then should the contemporary political system of Venezuela be interpreted? Democracy emerged in Venezuela as a result of the struggle of a broad coalition of diverse forces—from leftist labor leaders to conservative business groups—against a dictatorship that had bitterly fought and alienated them through repression and intimidation. However, the political system installed in 1958 was more than just a rejection of the dictatorial rule of Pérez Jiménez; it also marked a departure from the patterns of the trienio, which conservative sectors blamed for the very emergence of the Pérez Jiménez dictatorship. In terms of a dialectical analogy, the *trienio* had been the ''thesis,'' the Pérez Jiménez dictatorship had been the ''antithesis,'' and the post–1958 regime constituted the ''synthesis'' that overcame that contradiction. To understand the nature of this synthesis, let us first briefly review its thesis and antithesis.

The Trienio: A Taste of Democracy and Change

The coup of October 18, 1945, that brought the social-democratic Acción Democrática (AD) party to power effected not only radical political reforms but also sweeping social and economic changes. In fact, by encouraging social and political participation and later organizing the forces it had mobilized, AD was instrumental in transforming the Venezuelan polity beyond recognition. Three main policy issues dominated the agenda of the AD leadership. One concern was the need to redefine the relations with the oil companies to the advantage of Venezuela. Although some of Venezuela's grievances had been redressed in the early 1940s, these concessions were deemed insufficient, and the leaders of the Junta Revolucionaria moved aggressively toward extracting greater benefits. As a result of the new oil legislation, government revenues jumped from 660 million bolívares in 1945 to 1.8 billion bolívares in 1948.[5] Oil revenues thereby facilitated the implementation of AD's ambitious social and economic programs.

The AD leadership was also concerned with socioeconomic reforms. The organization of the labor movement was strongly encouraged. In 1946 alone, 531 unions were recognized, more than double the number of existing unions (252 as of 1945). Of the over 1,000 unions existing prior to the 1948 coup, almost half, 515 unions, were in the agricultural sector. The total number of unionized workers was estimated by labor sources to have reached 300,000 before the coup that overthrew President Rómulo Gallegos in 1948, although the military junta that ousted AD from government claimed a figure of only 137,313.[6]

The policies of the trienio were strongly supportive of urban and rural labor claims. Approximately 125,000 hectares of land were distributed to some 73,000 peasants between 1945 and 1948.[7] Collective agreements beneficial to workers were signed with the open and decisive support of the Labor Minister, Raúl Leoni. The number of such agreements increased to a high of 575 in 1947 only to decline to 127 by 1950.[8] Labor inspections increased from 1,650 in the January to October 1945 period to 3,423 in 1947.[9] By some accounts, real wages increased by over 60 percent between 1945 and 1948.[10]

In nearly all categories social spending grew dramatically during the trienio.[11]

Legislative initiatives were also strongly prolabor. The Labor Code was amended to include provisions allowing workers to audit their enterprise's books to insure a fair implementation of the profit-sharing clause, and for a bonus when profits were not made. Heavy penalties in case of violation of trade-union immunity were also established.[12] The 1947 Constitution also included a number of sections devoted to guaranteeing the rights of workers. Finally, progressive education, agrarian, and income-tax legislation were being discussed at the time the military coup toppled the Gallegos government.[13]

As was to be expected, business sectors resented virtually all of these policies. According to an International Labor Organization fact-finding mission, businessmen testified that in the hearings of disputes "the evidence of fellow workers submitted by the worker was accepted as absolutely correct . . . [while] the evidence of the supervisory staff brought by the employer was utilized merely as a means of guidance."[14] Businessmen also complained about the profit-sharing clause and about the terms of the collective agreements. They considered the policies of the government too advanced and too ambitious for Venezuela.[15]

The third concern of the AD leadership was political reform. Unlike other prolabor governments in Latin America during the 1940s, the trienio did not exhibit the authoritarian features of populist regimes, such as the ones of Getulio Vargas in Brazil and Juan D. Perón in Argentina. Civil and political freedoms were respected, the franchise was extended to all males and females, and the first free direct election for president took place.[16] The basic organizational framework of modern Venezuelan parties was established during that period.

In spite of AD's commitment to democracy, excesses occurred, particularly in the AD versus Communist party fighting for control of the labor unions.[17] The already-mentioned ILO fact-finding mission, for instance, pointed out AD hostility toward other forces competing for control of the labor movement and toward those unions reluctant to accept AD control; likewise, John D. Martz blamed AD for sectarianism to the point of excluding even minimal accommodation with the other parties.[18] All of this generated distrust at first, deep resentment later, and finally open hostility toward AD from its political rivals. Relations with the church were also strained over the educational policy of the government. In fact, the military coup of 1948 was welcomed by an influential religious magazine as the fulfillment of their hope that "God . . . would intervene with His provident hand and save us."[19]

Furthermore, AD's progressive policies earned it the bitter opposition of the dominant classes. The Venezuelan socioeconomic elites, who had seen their interests challenged but not threatened during the long rule of Juan V. Gómez (from 1908 to 1935), had been unable to develop the political machines that their counterparts in Colombia had. Hence, they regarded the political arena with utmost suspicion, all the more so considering the overwhelming popularity of left-leaning AD. When the trienio began to deliver some of its promises to the popular sectors at their expense, the wealthy threw their support to the 1948 military plotters. The actual extent to which the trienio threatened established interests is, naturally, a matter of debate. What seems beyond doubt, however, is that AD's policies were perceived by broad sectors of the bourgeoisie, the church, military, and rival political parties as a challenge to their very existence. It was on the basis of these perceptions that the socioeconomic and political elites articulated their strategies.

Lessons from the 1940s

The changing domestic and international factors of the 1950s induced the leadership of AD to reassess its strategies. On the domestic front, the military junta that replaced Gallegos evolved into the personalistic and highly repressive dictatorship of Pérez Jiménez and was inflicting severe casualties in AD's ranks. The party's ability to fight back was also impaired by the political isolation that resulted from its policies in the 1940s. On the international front, the Cold War was taking its ugliest face as McCarthyist hysteria was sweeping the area with the consequent strengthening of the most repressive right-wing sectors within the armed forces of the region. As a result, a shift toward a more centrist position took place, and the leadership went a long way toward mending fences with its former foes. In several self-critical statements epitomizing this new attitude, Rómulo Betancourt asserted the need to avoid the ''suicidal'' policies of the past and reiterated AD's commitment not to repeat them.[20]

Just as AD was led to reassess its political strategies, business and other political leaders and even the church were forced to reevaluate their positions as well. The problems created by Pérez Jiménez's consistent policy of alienating every sector, including his friends and advisers, exacerbated the situation. Popular opposition to him was growing stronger,[21] and it became increasingly clear that a solution to the crisis could not be achieved without AD. This realization coincided with Betancourt's attempts at building bridges with both the elites and their political foes and set the stage for meetings between New York exiles Betancourt, Jóvito Villalba of Unión Republicana Democrática (URD), and Rafael Caldera of the social Christian party Comité de Organización Política Electoral Independiente (COPEI) to discuss the return to democracy within a ''grand coalition'' framework. Betancourt also contacted business leaders and made overtures to the Catholic Church.

The agreement reached by the main political forces and socioeconomic elites, based on the experience of the trienio and the Pérez Jiménez dictatorship, transcended the limited scope of the Punto Fijo pact (discussed in Chapter 8 by John D. Martz), and its spirit remained in force well beyond the Betancourt period. It called for a Calhounian political democracy that would ensure the vital interests of all major contenders (the AD, labor, and peasant coalition, other political parties, socioeconomic elites, army, church) through the establishment of an implicit concurrent majority rule. It also lowered political tensions through the deliberate toning down of partisan discourse, although by no means can this be equated to the depoliticization that ensued during the National Front pact in

Colombia in 1958. The fragility of this political arrangement was thus described by Daniel H. Levine: "Political leaders . . . behave as if political institutions might fall apart at any moment, and therefore require constant care. . . . The memory of past conflicts and the fear of renewed military dictatorship arising in response to uncontrollable conflict drove many leaders to handle politics with extreme care."[22]

This political arrangement imposed considerable constraints on the decision-making process. Because every important sector was given a virtual veto power on matters affecting its fundamental interests, lengthy and thorough consultations became the normal way of making policy. While this policy-making pattern insured that the decisions to be adopted would command the acceptance of every important segment of society and therefore enhanced the legitimacy of the system, it generated only slow advances in terms of redistributive legislation.[23]

To summarize, democracy in Venezuela emerged as a consociational or quasi-consociational experiment, and the fact that it has remained such thereafter is the single most important variable to consider in the study of the Venezuelan political system. (For a more extensive treatment of the consociational issue, see Donald Herman's introductory chapter in this volume). Particularly after 1973, an impressive influx of oil revenues strengthened the power of the state vis-à-vis the local economic elites and enhanced its autonomy. This autonomy, however, has not been fully exercised because of the restraining effect of the very consociational nature of Venezuelan democracy. This seeming contradiction illustrates the interplay of economic and political variables and shows how economic factors broaden the spectrum of options opened to political actors. Perhaps more importantly, it reveals how political factors impose limits where the economic sphere does not. The following examination of the six democratic administrations will illustrate this point more clearly. It will also show both the degree to which policies can be said to be fundamentally similar, as well as the extent to which the existing variations did matter.

Betancourt: Laying the Foundations

Although AD's candidate Rómulo Betancourt won the 1958 presidential contest with a comfortable 49.2 percent of the votes, he formed a coalition government in which only two ministers were *adecos* (AD party members). URD and COPEI were given three ministerial posts each, and the rest were offered to independents.[24] The main objective of the Betancourt administration was to establish and consolidate democracy in the face of economic recession and political unrest. Social legislation was not at the forefront of his agenda, although he passed some important pieces, such as the Agrarian Reform Law. The new political climate was favorable to the signing of collective agreements more beneficial to workers. As a result, the percentage of the national income accounted for by salary and wages rose from 55 percent in the 1952 to 1957 period to 59 percent for the 1959 to 1963 period.[25]

On the other hand, the most important economic policy was the import-substitution package. A key instrument in the import-substitution strategy was the Corporación Venezolana de Fomento (CVF), created during the trienio. Between 1949 and 1957 the CVF had made 209 loans for 102 million bolívares. In the first two years of the Betancourt administration alone, by contrast, 266 loans for 205 million bolívares were made.[26] Simultaneously, gross investment in manufacturing more than doubled, jumping from 6.6 percent of total investment in the 1952 to 1957 period to 13.8 percent in the 1959 to 1963 period.[27]

The social and political implications of these policies were far reaching. Betancourt succeeded in the 1960s in reenacting the populist coalition that in the 1940s he failed to consolidate. He did not have to antagonize the rural elites, however, because the resources to finance industrialization were not being transferred from the agricultural sector through exchange-rate manipulations. In any case, the rural elites were already weak, a fact that should be traced back to the already mentioned golden parachute that Gómez extended to them in the 1920s. Thus, the Venezuelan industrialization resembles the Colombian process in that it developed without significant intersectoral strains. Yet, while the Colombian relatively smooth path to import-substituting industrialization has been attributed to the interpenetration of the industrial and agricultural elites and to the composition of the coffee sector, which includes a large number of small- and medium-size growers,[28] the Venezuelan pattern resulted instead from the ability and willingness of the state to transfer resources from the oil to the manufacturing sector.

Betancourt's political accomplishments were as important as those on the socioeconomic front. He successfully managed to head off a number of military attempts at overthrowing him and defeated the leftist guerrilla movements that rose to challenge the consociational arrangement. Finally, he was able to pass on the presidential sash to his freely elected successor. In short, Betancourt was able to consolidate the gains of 1958 by pursuing a policy (1) that assured all significant national contenders—military, church, business, labor, peasants, political parties—that their vital interests would be respected, and granted them a virtual veto power over policies that affected those vital interests; (2) that gave all these sectors a voice in his cabinet and opened other channels of communication with them; and (3) that institutionalized a "grand coalition" type of democracy that, built trust and confidence among contenders and generated firm attachment and loyalty to the democratic system, although it was slow at social reforms.[29]

Leoni: The Limits to Reform

Raúl Leoni, Betancourt's successor, won the 1963 elections with a plurality, 32.8 percent of the votes, and was therefore forced to form a coalition government. These elections further accentuated the trends observed in 1958 regarding AD weakness in the cities, especially Caracas, and its strength in the countryside and provincial towns. In fact, Leoni captured 13 percent of the votes in metropolitan Caracas, 30 percent in other districts with large cities, 37 percent in districts with small towns and cities, and 47 percent in rural districts. His business-sponsored contender, the Frente Nacional Democrático (FND) candidate Arturo Uslar Pietri, on the other hand, won 42 percent of the Caracas vote, 19 percent in districts with large cities, 10 percent in districts with small urban centers, and 4 percent in rural districts.[30]

President Leoni continued Betancourt's policies but departed from his predecessor's tradition in that he included in his agenda issues strongly opposed by business interests, chiefly the 1966 tax reform and the decision to join the Latin American Free Trade Association (LAFTA). In so doing, Leoni risked the still fragile equilibrium achieved by Betancourt, but he did show he knew where the limits stood and backed down, especially in 1966 when the anti-tax-reform coalition rallied forces that could only be defeated at a very high political cost.

Likewise, only after lengthy negotiations with the business community was he able to push through the decision to join LAFTA.[31] When the initiative to participate in the Andean Pact elicited very strong resistance, Leoni retreated to avoid a major confrontation. In spite of these limitations, he managed to pass some prolabor legislation, such as the law creating the Banco de los Trabajadores de Venezuela (BTV) and the law granting workers' participation on the managing board of *institutos autónomos* and state enterprises.[32]

Caldera: A Test of the System

Nineteen sixty-eight marked a watershed in Venezuelan politics, because for the first time an opposition candidate had won an election, and his triumph was recognized by the government. Rafael Caldera, the COPEI candidate, captured some 40,000 votes (a little more than 1 percent of the 3.7 million votes cast) more than his closest rival, Gonzalo Barrios of AD, and became the third president of the democratic period. Caldera did not win a parliamentary majority, however, and had to struggle from the beginning to persuade Congress to approve his legislative initiatives. Caldera rejected the idea of forming a permanent coalition and governed during his entire period with coalitions formed on issue-by-issue bases, which considerably delayed the work of government.

The 1968 elections gave rise to a peculiar scenario, mainly because AD went into them after suffering its major split. Underlying this division was Betancourt's decision to block the presidential nomination of party chief Luis Beltrán Prieto Figueroa whose political position was judged too radical. Eventually, Prieto Figueroa and scores of AD cadres formed the Movimiento Electoral del Pueblo (MEP). Unlike previous splits—those of the Movimiento de Izquierda Revolucionaria (MIR), in 1960, and AD-Oposición (ARS), in 1962 and 1963—the magnitude of this one threatened to alter the whole political arena. Not unexpectedly, MEP's presidential candidate Prieto Figueroa captured 19 percent of the national vote.

The business sector, not as in 1963 when it threw its support to Arturo Uslar Pietri's FND, went to the 1968 elections divided. A significant portion supported Caldera, who had won the backing of the probusiness Movimiento Desarrollista, led by Pedro Tinoco. Many others backed the candidacy of Miguel A. Burelli Rivas, who captured 20 percent of the national vote. Finally, a few supported Barrios.

As the victorious candidate, however, Caldera soon picked up widespread business support. His decision to appoint Tinoco as his minister of finance delighted businessmen who thought that their boys at last were running the government. But the honeymoon between the government and business sectors did not last long. In 1970 Minister Tinoco came up with a tax-reform proposal opposed strongly in many business circles. Later, COPEI was accused of trying to manipulate business organizations, especially Federación de Agricultores (FE-DEAGRO) and Federación Nacional de Ganaderos (FENAGAN). Finally, in a late movement, while already a lame-duck incumbent, Caldera decreed new regulations for rural labor whereby rural workers would enjoy the same benefits as their urban counterparts. The measure elicited the strongest reaction yet, although business sectors claimed that they did not oppose the measure itself but only its timing.

Pérez: The Progressive Populism of the Intermediate Generation

The election of Carlos Andrés Pérez to the presidency in 1973, with 48.6 percent of the votes, signaled a significant shift in party alignments. The highly fragmented party system that had predominated during the 1960s has given way to increasing polarization in the 1970s and 1980s, as AD and COPEI together have captured well over 80 percent of the vote in every election ever since.

Pérez, who had run on a populist platform, moved quickly to insure passage of a number of redistributive measures apparently inspired by his minister of planning, the former *mirista* Gumersindo Rodríguez. A general wage and salary increase was decreed in May 1974, and a minimum wage was established. A law to protect workers facing unjustified layoffs was also enacted. By 1975, however, Pérez adopted a more centrist course. The emphasis shifted to nationalistic policies, chiefly the nationalization of the oil and iron companies. Yet 1976 marked a return to redistribution, as the Pérez administration pushed for the major tax reform of the democratic period. The reform proposal constituted the most ambitious attempt yet to restructure the tax system, but its objectives were only partially attained.

Herrera: The Conservative Version

The election of Luis Herrera Campins in 1978 brought about another significant policy shift. Although Herrera Campins had traditionally been considered a "leftist" within COPEI and half-jokingly, half-seriously likened to the watermelon (green, COPEI's color, on the outside, red on the inside), he pushed forward a conservative economic agenda that included the intention to privatize scores of state-owned enterprises and a recessionary monetary policy. The basic assumption was that the economy was overheated and inflation was reaching dangerous proportions, and that therefore a recessionary "cooling-down" policy was required. The government-induced recession, however, lasted longer and cut deeper than the economic managers anticipated. In 1979 the economy grew at a sluggish 0.9 percent and plunged to negative 1.2 percent in 1980. The economy improved slightly in 1981, when it grew at a 0.6 percent annual rate, but it stagnated in 1982 and fell to new lows in 1983.

The oil price increases of 1979 and 1980 provided the government with an opportunity to revive the economy through budgetary measures. But by the time Herrera decided to change course and embark on an expansionary policy, the oil glut struck and forced the government to review spending plans constantly to adjust them to dwindling petroleum revenues. These difficulties were compounded by heavy pressure on the bolívar during 1981 and 1982. The freeing of interest rates in August of 1981 halted the capital flight only temporarily.[33] Fueled by high interest rates in the United States and the erratic policies of the Herrera Campins administration, billions of dollars continued to flee the country, 22 billion dollars between 1979 and 1982 according to the World Bank.[34] By 1985 that figure increased to 30 billion dollars, according to estimates of the Morgan Guaranty Trust.[35]

In an attempt to stave off the flight of capital, the government adopted a series of measures in September of 1982. They included the taking over of the state-owned oil company's (Petróleos de Venezuela, South America, PDVSA) foreign-currency holdings and the revaluation of gold assets.[36] These measures were geared toward restoring confidence in the health of the bolívar but accomplished the opposite. By February 1983 the situation had reached crisis proportions, and the government was forced to halt foreign-currency operations and establish exchange controls. A week later, the government decreed a four-tier exchange rate: The existing rate of 4.30 bolívares per 1 U.S. dollar was to be applied only to essential imports and the service of the debt; three new and higher rates, including a floating one, were to be used for all other foreign-currency operations.[37] A bitter debate soon followed over whether the private debt would be given the preferential rate. Central Bank President Leopoldo Díaz Bruzual strongly opposed it, while Finance Minister Arturo Sosa favored it. Herrera Campins remained aloof, seemingly unperturbed by the squabbling among his subordinates. A flurry of decisions and counterdecisions ensued, accomplishing nothing except the postponement of the issue until after the election of December 1983. In a limited way that nondecision was a Pyrrhic victory for the Díaz Bruzual camp.

The failure of Herrera's economic policies was compounded by his abrasive style and an equally poor performance in the political field. Herrera alienated business and labor alike with a rhetoric that both sectors considered irritating at best. Grandiose plans, such as the construction of a bridge over the ocean to link the island of Margarita with the mainland and a food-stamp program, the Bono Alimenticio, were high priorities on the agenda and in speeches, but never materialized. The inauguration of the first line of the Caracas metro early in 1983 also failed to improve Herrera's image. Finally, the government attempts at capitalizing on the upsurge of patriotism, which was anticipated in connection with the celebrations of the bicentennial of Simón Bolívar and the Pan American Games, were also unsuccessful. For all the pomp and money—an estimated 500 million dollars for the latter alone, including the cost of new physical facilities[38]— the popularity of the government remained low. Not surprisingly, the AD presidential candidate Jaime Lusinchi won the election of December of 1983 with an overwhelming 56 percent of the votes, the largest margin since 1947. COPEI has not yet recovered from that disastrous loss.

Lusinchi: Picking up the Pieces

Perhaps no other president since Betancourt inherited as many economic problems as Jaime Lusinchi. At the top of the list was Venezuela's 35 billion dollar foreign debt, aggravated by falling oil revenues and the widespread lack of confidence that pervaded the last years of the Herrera administration and spilled over into his successor's term. Accordingly, Lusinchi's main objective was to renegotiate the debt in terms compatible with the need to sustain some economic growth and avoid the worst social consequences of austerity measures.

Lusinchi confronted these problems with a "social pact" approach, which called for business and labor to share the costs of the adjustment process. At the core of the pact lay the business sector's commitment to grant a 10 percent increase in its rosters to offset the high levels of unemployment. In exchange, the government would provide subsidized bolívares for the repayment of the private debt. In addition, the tripartite (business-labor-government) Salary, Wage, and Price Board was established, but business representatives abandoned it at the end of 1984, claiming that their demands were not being considered sufficiently. To help enforce the pact, Lusinchi appointed businessman Manuel Azpurua Arreaza, of Venezuela's largest private economic group, as his minister of finance. Business representatives also played a large role in Venezuela's debt-renegotiation process; former Fedecámaras (the business association) president Carlos Guillermo Rangel was appointed to head the Venezuelan team.

In short, the main thrust of the Lusinchi administration has been the enforcement of a socially acceptable austerity package. (See also the Chapter by Robert J. Alexander in this volume.) Attempts at achieving more ambitious social goals, including improving real wages, were quickly rebuffed, and Planning Minister Raúl Matos Azocar, a strong supporter of these measures, was dismissed. As of early 1986, the Lusinchi administration seems content with having successfully dealt with the debt problem by signing rescheduling agreements generally judged reasonable and that include a contingency clause, already applied once, in the event of further drops in the price of oil.

POLITICS AND POLICIES: THE LIMITS OF THE CONSOCIATIONAL FRAMEWORK

As noted in the previous section, the consociational nature of Venezuelan democracy imposes severe limitations on the range of policy options available to competing political actors. A perusal of the main policies adopted by the six democratic administrations demonstrates that they can all be roughly placed in a fairly narrow band ranging from distributive to mildly redistributive. It would be a mistake, however, to overlook the differences among these six administrations. Just because their policies were not totally different does not mean that they did not vary at all or that they did not entail significant differences. A comparison of the major socioeconomic policies that directly affect domestic actors will allow us to draw a sharper picture, not only of the parameters within which change evolved, but also of the extent to which party control of government made a difference. Table 7.1 lists twenty-three major socioeconomic decisions and classifies them according to whether they were distributive, redistributive, regulative, or regulative with a significant redistributive flavor. Obviously, all regulatory instruments involve a degree of distribution and redistribution. The distinction drawn here, however, aims at tapping an important dimension that tends to go undetected if all regulatory policies are lumped together, and that is whether or not the regulation involves transfer of resources from the elites or elite sector to the nonelites. The category of regulative policies, then, is reserved for those policies with a largely intraelite distributive or redistributive impact.

An examination of the policies listed in Table 7.1 illustrates the extent to which the policies of the first five democratic administrations cover a rather narrow range of redistributive possibilities. All three redistributive policies, as well as those regulative policies with redistributive overtones, were quite mild. The agrarian reform was carried out with the support of most parties at a time when the bulk of the landed elite had already safely moved to more profitable spheres and included enough safeguards for those who had not. The 1966 tax-reform proposal almost brought down the Leoni government,[39] as the elites launched an all-out campaign to defeat it at any cost. Pérez's tax-reform package was somewhat more successful, but after three years of bloodletting the version that passed Congress in 1978 bore little resemblance to the original 1975 package. As for the minimum-wage decree, strongly resented by Fedecámaras, it came about at a time when Venezuela was one of the few countries without such a legal provision. Later, Herrera's salary and wage increase was basically designed to offset the effects of inflation.

All things considered, the redistributive policies adopted in the twenty-five years of liberal democracy, though meaningful, are by no means radical, and they are not radical precisely because the very success of the consociational

Table 7.1
A Classification of Selected Policy Decisions: 1960–1983

Policy	Administration	Nature
Import substitution	Betancourt	distributive
Agragrian reform	Betancourt	redistributive
Tax reform	Leoni	redistributive
LAFTA	Leoni	regulative
Workers' representation in state enterprises	Leoni	regulative
Banking law	Caldera	regulative
Termination of bilateral trade agreement	Caldera	regulative
Capital markets	Caldera	regulative
Andean pact	Caldera	regulative
Rural workers' benefits	Caldera	regulative/redistributive
Minimum salary and wage increases	Pérez	regulative/redistributive
Unjustified dismissals	Pérez	regulative/redistributive
Consumers' protection	Pérez	regulative/redistributive
Financial package[a]	Pérez	regulative
Ayacucho scholarships	Pérez	distributive
Labor code reform	Pérez	regulative
Tax reform	Pérez	redistributive
Salary and wage increases	Herrera	regulative/redistributive
Working conditions[b]	Herrera	regulative/redistributive
Taxable income threshold raised	Herrera	distributive
Dividends exemption extended	Herrera	distributive
Exchange control	Herrera	regulative
Administered pricing system	Herrera	regulative/redistributive

[a]This refers to several decrees that reorganized the financial structure of the country, especially banks and insurance companies. See Gaceta Oficial de la República de Venezuela, Number 1,739, Extraordinary, of May 13, 1975; Number 1,742, Extraordinary and Number 1,743, Extraordinary, of May 22, 1975. These decrees were passed in accordance with a May 31, 1974 law that empowered the president to dictate certain economic and financial measures without congressional approval for a limited period of time.

[b]This refers to a series of laws ratifying several conventions approved by the 1979 International Conference on Working Conditions in Geneva. They include salary protection, maternity benefits, medical services, and equal pay for equal work regardless of sex. See Gaceta Oficial de la República de Venezuela, Number 2,847, Extraordinary, and Number 2,850, Extraordinary, of August 27, 1981.

Sources: Compiled by the author from Centro de Información y Documentación Legislativa, 25 Años de Legislación Democrática (Caracas: Ediciones del Congreso de la República, 1983); Carlos Romero Zuloaga and Luis G. Arcay, Indice de Leyes Vigentes Hasta el 30 de Junio de 1976 (Caracas: Menevan, n.d.); and newspaper coverage.

Table 7.2
Classification of Policy Decisions by Type and Party Control of Government

	AD	COPEI	Total
Regulative	4	5	9
Regulative/redistributive	3	4	7
Distributive	2	2	4
Redistributive	3	-	3

Source: Table 7.1.

model lies on the absence of drastic policy departures from the status quo. A built-in characteristic of the system is that decisions will only be adopted after a broad consensus has developed, that is, after the most innovative aspects of the policies are eliminated.

However, the realization of the multiple constraints that affected the content of social policy should not belittle its significance. During the quarter century of liberal democracy, approximately a third of the budget has been devoted to social programs while another third has gone to economic-development projects that have had a significant impact on the general well-being of the population. Although a systematic comparison of Venezuela's performance vis-à-vis other Latin American countries is yet to be done, the available social statistics demonstrate that it ranks among the better off. (See Robert J. Alexander's chapter in this volume.) Income-distribution figures also consistently place Venezuela among the least unequal countries.[40] In short, within the larger Latin American picture Venezuela's accomplishments, however modest, are significant. Even more importantly, the emphasis on social justice marks a sea of change when compared to the policies of the Pérez Jiménez dictatorship, which is, after all, the referent most lower-class Venezuelans old enough to remember have in mind.

The data provided in Table 7.1 also allow us to explore the issue of the importance of party control of government for understanding policy change. Table 7.2 shows that breaking down the twenty-three policy decisions by party does not affect the basic distribution of regulative and distributive policies.[41] When the redistributive and regulative/redistributive categories are examined, however, the findings are significant. They indicate that while all three redistributive policies were initiated by AD administrations, COPEI has pushed for a far milder regulative/redistributive approach. Furthermore, a comparison of the Caldera and Herrera administrations shows that three out of four regulative/redistributive measures were adopted by the latter and quite early in his period, as opposed to Caldera's decree to extend benefits to rural workers that he enforced as a lame-duck incumbent when his party's presidential hopeful Lorenzo Fer-

Table 7.3
Classification of Policy Decisions by Periods of Time

	1960–1973	1974–1983
Regulative	6	3
Regulative/redistributive	1	6
Distributive	1	3
Redistributive	2	1

Source: Table 7.1.

nández had already been defeated. In the case of AD, two of the four redistributive decisions were adopted by Pérez, which suggests that the so-called intermediate generation adopted a somewhat bolder social policy as compared to the more conservative approach of the old guard.

Still another dimension worth examining is whether the oil boom of 1973 brought about any significant qualitative change in social policy. Table 7.3 shows that the emphasis on regulatory instruments decreased after the oil boom. Perhaps more importantly, the figures demonstrate, contrary to the widespread belief that oil footed the bill for about everything important in the last decade, that policies with redistributive implications did *not* decrease in spite of the additional resources generated by growing petroleum revenues. In fact, the social policies implemented in the post–1973 period are certainly more numerous and more advanced than the ones adopted prior to 1973.

A plausible explanation of this difference is that the additional revenues accrued by the government emboldened the post–1973 administrations and widened their margins for autonomous maneuvering vis-á-vis the dominant economic elites. It could also be interpreted as an indication that the political elites felt the system had consolidated enough to withstand some rough readjustment on the distribution of the payoffs to the supporters of the hegemonic coalition. It may be seen, too, as the natural result of leadership turnover. The intermediate generation could have been not only more committed to social programs, but also could have wanted to differentiate itself from the old guard by having accomplishments of its own. Thus, if Betancourt and Caldera could be credited with the successful installation of a democratic system, then Pérez and Herrera would be credited with extending the benefits of political democracy to the people, thus laying the foundations for economic democracy as well. It is likely that all three sets of factors were at work, but perhaps more important than that is the fact that because, in spite, or regardless of the oil bonanza, the post–1973 period is characterized not by less but by a greater emphasis on redistributive policies.

CONCLUSION

The basic underlying assumption of this study is a distinction, similar to the one made by Fernando H. Cardoso, between the concepts of state and regime that has important implications for understanding the political process.[42] The conceptual status of both categories is, in fact, at the core of this reassessment of certain theoretical issues concerning the nature of the Venezuelan state, the importance of regime type, the characteristics of the dominant coalition, and their policy implications. While the state constitutes an abstract construct that embodied class relations, regime is seen as a set of institutions and institutionalized processes that link government structures among themselves and with civil society. Thus, while the capitalist nature of the Venezuelan state remained unchanged, important transformations took place as Venezuela experienced a short democratic interlude in the mid–1940s, returned to authoritarianism in the 1950s, and finally established a consociational democratic system in 1958 that has lasted until the present day.

Whereas the main actors in the state arena are social classes and fundamental relations are class relations, regimes include both class actors acting as such and political actors whose connection to the former, though undeniable, is often tenuous and whose interactions result in a complex web of relations. Broadly speaking, the constituent units of the regime area are the dominant socioeconomic elites, the subordinate social groups, the "middle classes" or petite bourgeoisie, the political parties, especially AD and COPEI, until 1975 the foreign oil companies, the army, and the church. The complex pattern of relations among these actors defies easy characterization, but certain basic traits can nevertheless be identified.

First, neither the political nor the economic elites are monolithic, single-purpose, cleavage-free, unified entities. They are instead clusters of social actors coalescing around certain fundamental interests but exhibiting nonetheless distinctive ideological and political outlooks and retaining a significant measure of autonomy in the political realm. Furthermore, political actors do not necessarily "re-present" economic actors. Parties, for instance, appeal to or identify with the demands of certain socioeconomic sectors, but the link between one and the other is by no means symbiotic. There is always tension, and not just because political actors are presumably enlightened enough to represent the interest of the whole, thereby occasionally clashing with certain class factions, but because these are independent actors whose interests both coincide and diverge, overlapping at times but moving in opposite directions at other junctures.

This disjuncture between political and socioeconomic actors as they interact in the regime arena is all the more notorious in Latin America in general and Venezuela in particular because of the class structure and the patterns of dependent development that characterized the historical evolution of these societies. The end product of that process has been a weak and relatively small proletariat, and an equally weak and small industrial bourgeoisie (in other Latin American countries challenged from above by an entrenched landed elite). Both developed side by side with an hypertrophic petite bourgeoisie that became, by virtue of sheer numbers, the ''ruling'' class and provided the social bases for the relative autonomy of parties from both the elites and the working class.

In the case of Venezuela, the relative autonomy of political parties, especially AD, was also facilitated by the fact that the patterns of partisan affiliations that the socioeconomic elites developed in the nineteenth century were thoroughly effaced by the thirty-six-year-long rule of dictators Cipriano Castro and Juan V. Gómez. As a result, the Venezuelan political parties that emerged in the 1940s, rather than byproducts of nineteenth century intraelite cleavages, were the expression of rapidly modernizing society. In this new scenario AD provided itself remarkably skillful, and outrunning its rivals to the right and the left, captured the overwhelming support of the popular sector. In contrast, the dominant classes failed to build reasonably well controlled political machineries to process the political demands of the lower strata of the population. This failure increased their dependence on AD and further accentuated the rift between the socioeconomic elites and the political leadership.

By 1958 these rival political and socioeconomic forces reached an impasse as each one of them was unable to develop and sustain a political project susceptible of generating popular support and political legitimacy while retaining the capability to use the coercive resources of the state against attempts at overthrowing it. Both consensus and coercion were needed for success, but neither actor had enough of both resources to enable it to establish a hegemonic role for itself. The regime that emerged in 1958 is both a realization of this limitation as well as evidence of the socioeconomic and political elites' acceptance and/or preference for power-sharing formulae that would avoid the uncertainty of unrestrained competition that usually accompanies the quest for exclusive power. The 1958 formulae consecrated the triumph of a new hegemonic coalition of socioeconomic and political forces that, while imposing severe limits on the scope of social reform policies, also succeeded in bringing about almost three decades of stable liberal democratic rule.

This complex political arrangement was neither the product of chance nor the foretold outcome of factors that were bound to produce it sooner or later. Yet, it would also be a mistake to see it as a ''conspiracy,'' underestimating the conflicts by interpreting them as purely marginal disagreements that did not threaten the overarching loyalty to the system or by judging every crisis as ''functional'' to the maintenance of the system. The Venezuelan political system is a complicated piece of political engineering that has nothing inherently stable except its leadership's ability and will to preserve it. In fact, the evidence examined in this chapter eloquently demonstrates the importance of statecraft as the AD political leadership deftly maneuvered other political sectors, especially COPEI, the business elites, and the military into the system. It also shows the magnitude of the task and the accomplishment, for while certain sectors of the elites were wedded to the system, important political and economic segments of the same elites were challenging it by every possible means. Already in the early 1960s Betancourt pushed for the formation and strengthening of Pro-Venezuela, the association of industrialists that strongly favored and benefited from the import substitution policies of his administration. This emphasis indicated the political leadership's uncertainty about the allegiance of the entrepreneurial elite gathered in Fedecámaras. Similarly, business sectors made several unsuccessful attempts at creating a business political party that would eliminate or lessen their dependence on the two principal political parties, especially AD.

Even though in the 1970s and 1980s the socioeconomic and political elites seemed to resign themselves to coexist peacefully, attempts at redrawing the political map continue. Business groups, for example, vigorously pursued a campaign to weaken the political parties. On the one hand, they used the media to discredit "politics" and the "political" in general; on the other hand, they widely publicized the alleged advantages of a single-member district electoral system. The obvious implication is that single-member district representatives will be much more amenable to pressures by big campaign contributors, whereas in the present system business influence is lessened by the need to deal with whole party machineries. This issue has touched off a big controversy prompting President Lusinchi to set up a presidential commission to study the reform of the state. The commission, Lusinchi warned, was to advise rather than promote, but it has already produced recommendations that call for instituting a uninominal system for municipal contests, the direct election of state governors, and the state financing of political parties. As for congressional elections, AD is on record as favoring the so-called "closed but not blocked slates," which allows the voter to rank the candidates of his chosen slate.[43]

Similar attempts at realignment are observable in the political sphere, and as a result the AD–COPEI competition has turned somehow sour. First, Herrera Campins interpreted his 1978 victory as the beginning of COPEI's one-hundred-year rule. Later, President Lusinchi broke with a long-standing tradition of interparty agreement in the appointment of Supreme Court justices. This trend has led some scholars to suggest that rising levels of interparty competition might indeed endanger the stability of the Venezuelan democracy.[44] However, the increased confrontational nature of AD–COPEI relations may just as well be interpreted as a healthy sign of democratic maturity or perhaps as an indication that the most obviously consociational elements of the political system installed in 1958 have outlived their usefulness. In fact, the most recent developments seem to indicate that fears of "political cannibalism" were indeed unwarranted. For example, reforms to the electoral law and the municipal law are being studied by a Tripartite Commission that includes AD, COPEI, and the Movimiento al Socialismo (MAS).[45] Similarly, in a recent interview Rafael Caldera reassured that the "institutional pact" is alive and well.[46] As John D. Martz convincingly argued, there are indeed strong reasons to believe that "prophecies of pessimism and decay will not prove self-fulfilling."[47]

To summarize, this chapter has pointed out, first, that the role of oil in the

Venezuelan political system has been generally and wrongly overemphasized, thus obscuring the importance of other variables. Second, this chapter has argued that the key to understand the contemporary system is an understanding of its consociational nature. Third, it has highlighted the distinguishing characteristics of the six democratic administrations. Fourth, it has shown how the consociational framework imposes limits on the policy choices available to policy makers but also how, in spite of some basic continuities, differences across parties and administrations do matter. Finally, it has speculated on the theoretical implications of all that, emphasizing the need and usefulness of differentiating state and regime. This distinction and the parallel one between dominant classes and ruling elites, together with the emphasis placed on political engineering, have shed some additional light on the nature and implications of the disjuncture between politics and economics, thus providing a more dynamic and comprehensive understanding of Venezuelan politics.

NOTES

1. B. S. McBeth, *Juan Vicente Gómez and the Oil Companies in Venezuela: 1908–1935* (Cambridge, England: Cambridge University Press, 1983), pp. 129–31.

2. For an interpretation of the relation between petroleum and the quasi-consociational nature of the Venezuelan democracy and of the implications of the pact-making activities of the late 1950s and early 1960s, see Terry Karl's "Petroleum and Political Pacts: The Transition to Democracy in Venezuela" (The Wilson Center, Latin American Program, Working Paper No. 107, 1982).

3. Diego Abente Brun, "Economic Policy Making in a Democratic Regime: The Case of Venezuela," Ph.D. dissertation, University of New Mexico, 1984, p. 67.

4. Ibid., p. 65 for 1975 figures; 1982 figures for Venezuela: calculations by the author based on Banco Central de Venezuela, *Informe Económico 1983* (Caracas: Banco Central, 1983) for other countries: Organización de Estados Americanos [OEA], *Boletín Estadístico 1985* (Washington, D.C.: OEA, 1985). The point made here refers solely to the extractive capability of the state vis-à-vis the domestic sector of the economy.

5. Banco Central de Venezuela, *La Economía Venezolana en los Ultimos Treinta Años* (Caracas: Italgráfica, 1971), p. 259.

6. International Labour Office (ILO), *Freedom of Association and Conditions of Work in Venezuela* (Geneva: ILO, 1950), pp. 104–5.

7. John D. Powell, *Political Mobilization of the Venezuelan Peasant* (Cambridge, Mass.: Harvard University Press, 1971), p. 77. For an analysis of the patterns of socio-political mobilization between 1936 and 1945, see pp. 44–64.

8. *Freedom of Association and Conditions of Work in Venezuela, Observations of the Government of Venezuela* (Geneva: ILO, 1951), p. 66 for the latter figure. For the former, ILO, *Freedom of Association*, p. 129.

9. *Freedom of Association*, p. 146.

10. *Ibid.*, p. 26, and Edwin Lieuwen, *Petroleum in Venezuela, A History* (Berkeley: University of California Press, 1954), p. 110.

11. Tomas E. Carrillo Batalla, *Política Fiscal* (Caracas: Ediciones del Concejo Municipal del Distrito Federal, 1964).

12. ILO, *Observations of the Government of Venezuela*, pp. 84–85.

13. Lieuwen, *Petroleum in Venezuela*.

14. ILO, *Freedom of Association*, p. 165.

15. *Ibid.*, pp. 163–66.

16. Ronald H. McDonald, *Party Systems and Elections in Latin America* (Chicago: Markham Publishing Company, 1971), p. 39.

17. See Steve Ellner, "The Venezuelan Left in the Era of the Popular Front," *Journal of Latin American Studies* 2 (May 1979): 169–84, and "Populism in Venezuela, 1935–48: Betancourt and Acción Democrática," in *Latin American Populism in Comparative Perspective*, ed. Michael L. Conniff (Albuquerque: University of New Mexico Press, 1982), pp. 135–49.

18. ILO, *Freedom of Association*, p. 42; and John D. Martz, *Acción Democrática: Evolution of a Modern Political Party in Venezuela* (Princeton, N.J.: Princeton University Press, 1966), pp. 321–22.

19. Daniel H. Levine, *Conflict and Political Change in Venezuela* (Princeton, N.J.: Princeton University Press, 1973), pp. 38, 40.

20. Arturo Stambouli, "La Crisis y Caída de la Dictadura," *Politeia* 7 (1978): 171. Although the change could have started earlier. See Steve Ellner, "Inter-Party Agreement and Rivalry in Venezuela: A Comparative Perspective," *Studies in Comparative International Development* 19 (Winter 1984–1985): 62, fn. 7. Ellner rightly suggested the precise time of initiation should not obscure the fact that the real impetus developed in the middle and late 1950s. Further elaborations on the same theme can be found in Rómulo Betancourt, *Posición y Doctrina* (Caracas: Editorial Cordillera, 1959).

21. Arturo Stambouli, "La Crisis y Caída"; Winfield J. Burggraaff, *The Venezuelan Armed Forces in Politics, 1939–1959* (Columbia: University of Missouri Press, 1972); and Philip B. Taylor, *The Venezuelan Golpe de Estado of 1958: The Fall of Marcos Pérez Jiménez* (Washington, D.C.: Institute for the Comparative Study of Political Systems, 1968).

22. Levine, *Conflict and Political Change*, pp. 236–37.

23. A point also made by Luis J. Oropeza, *Tutelary Pluralism: A Critical Approach to Venezuelan Democracy* (Cambridge, Mass.: Harvard University Center for International Affairs, 1983).

24. Robert J. Alexander, *Rómulo Betancourt and the Transformation of Venezuela* (New Brunswick, N.J.: Transaction Books, 1982), pp. 421.

25. Banco Central, *La Economía Venezolana*, p. 91.

26. Alexander, *Betancourt*, p. 512.

27. Banco Central, *La Economía Venezolana*, p. 204.

28. Jonathan Hartlyn, "The Impact of Patterns of Industrialization and of Popular Sector Incorporation on Political Regime Type: A Case Study of Colombia," *Studies in Comparative International Development* 19 (Spring 1984):29–60.

29. A study of the "management of conflict" along similar lines is Levine's *Conflict and Political Change*.

30. David E. Blank, *Politics in Venezuela* (Boston: Little, Brown, 1973), p. 144.

31. Robert P. Clark, "The LAFTA Debate in Venezuela: A Test Cast in Building Consensus," Ph.D. dissertation, John Hopkins University, 1968.

32. *Gaceta Oficial de la República de Venezuela*, No. 1023 Extraordinario, July 11, 1966, and No. 1032 Extraordinario, July 18, 1966.

33. *Latin American Weekly Report (LAWR)*, September 4, 1981, p. 4.

34. *World Bank Development Report*, 1985, p. 64.

35. "LDC Capital Flight," *World Financial Markets*, March 1986, p. 13.

36. *LAWR*, October 1, 1982, p. 3. See also Robert J. Alexander's chapter in this volume.

37. Rene Salgado, "Economic Pressure Groups and Policy-making in Venezuela: The Case of Fedecámaras Reconsidered," *Latin American Research Review*, XXII, 3 (1987).

38. Judith Ewell, *Venezuela: A Century of Change* (Stanford, Calif.: Stanford University Press, 1984), pp. 225–26.

39. Lynn P. Kelley, "The 1966 Venezuelan Tax Reform," *Inter-American Economic Affairs*, 21 (Summer 1970):77–92 and Diego Abente, "Policy Formation in Democratic Regimes: The Case of Venezuela," paper delivered at XII International Congress of the Latin American Studies Association, Albuquerque, N.Mex., April 1985.

40. For example, the Venezuelan Gini coefficient of income concentration in the late 1970s was .50, with only Costa Rica (.49), Chile (.48), and Argentina (.44) faring better. James Wilkie, *Statistical Abstract of Latin America*, Vol. 21 (Berkeley: University of California Press, 1981), p. 192. For findings pointing in the same direction, see also the *World Bank Development Report 1985*; see pp. 228–29 for income distribution figures and pp. 218–23 for other social statistics. As for poverty, it is estimated that during the early 1970s, 25 percent of Venezuelan families were living below the poverty line, with only Chile (17 percent) and Argentina (8 percent) doing better. CEPAL, (Comisión Económica para América Latina), *Anuario Estadístico de América Latina*, 1981, p. 84. See also pp. 85–120 and pp. 693–727 for other social statistics. Similar conclusions can be drawn when the income share of the poorest 40 percent of the population is examined. See Claes Brundenius and Mats Lundahl, eds., *Development Strategies and Basic Needs in Latin America: Challenge for the 1980s* (Boulder, Colo.: Westview Press, 1982), p. 4. The slow trend toward decreasing inequality over the last two decades is discussed in Asdrubal Batista, "Más Allá del Optimismo y del Pesimismo: Las Transformaciones Fundamentales del País," in *El Caso Venezuela: Una Ilusión de Armonía?* eds. Moisés Naim and Ramón Pinango (Caracas: Instituto de Estudios Superiores de Administración), pp. 32–35.

41. An obvious limitation of this very preliminary exploration is that the comparisons are based on *numbers* of policies and therefore disregard the qualitative differences between any two policies. Furthermore, this comparison cannot take into full account the extent to which various administrations were pressed into adopting certain pieces of legislation. This is particularly true of the Caldera and Herrera administrations, with a Congress dominated by the opposition. Thus, for example, several of Caldera's policies were indeed the result of highly elaborated compromises with AD, and Herrera's reluctant salary increase came as a mild response to mounting CTV (Confederación de Trabajadores de Venezuela) and congressional pressure. Rough as they are, however, these figures add a new dimension to our outstanding of the contemporary political process.

42. Fernando H. Cardoso, "On the Characterization of Authoritarian Regimes in Latin America" especially pp. 34–40, in *The New Authoritarianism in Latin America* ed. David Collier (Princeton, N.J.: Princeton University Press, 1979). A useful discussion is also in Ralph Miliband "State Power and Class Interests," *New Left Review* 138 (March-April 1983); 57–68. The burgeoning literature on bureaucratic authoritarianism and the relative autonomy of the state addresses this issue in a variety of other ways that cannot be fully explored here. For an overview see William L. Canak "The Peripheral State

Debate: State Capitalist and Bureaucratic Authoritarian Regimes in Latin America,'' *Latin American Research Review* XIX, 1 (1984): 3–36.

43. *El Nacional*, Caracas, May 20, 1986, p. D–1, and May 16, 1986, p. D–14.

44. Ellner, ''Inter-Party Agreement and Rivalry'' and Ewell, *Venezuela*, pp. 225–26.

45. *El Nacional*, Caracas, June 3, 1986, p. D–1.

46. *El Nacional*, Caracas, May 16, 1986, p. D–15.

47. John D. Martz, ''The Malaise of Venezuelan Political Parties: Is Democracy Endangered?'' in this volume.

8

The Malaise of Venezuelan Political Parties: Is Democracy Endangered?

John D. Martz

During his victorious presidential campaign of 1973, Carlos Andrés Pérez reiterated both publicly and privately his conviction that the next five years marked "the last chance for democracy" in Venezuela. Comparing conditions to those prevailing in Cuba of the early 1950s prior to the *golpe de estado* (coup d'état) of Fulgencio Batista, he urged that voters provide the candidates of Acción Democrática *(AD)* with a mandate to correct fundamental ills, advance the cause of social justice and economic equality, and thereby to *rescatar la democracia* (redeem democracy).[1] In five years' time his administration had launched a host of ambitious projects, had further extended the role of the central state in national life, and—buoyed by the extraordinary 1973 and 1974 quadrupling of petroleum prices on the international market—had succeeded in spending more government funds than those of all preceding regimes since the creation of the Republic in 1830. His party was defeated at the polls by the social Christians, whose leader, Luis Herrera Campins, complained bitterly in his 1979 inaugural address of having inherited a "mortgaged" nation.[2]

Herrera initially advocated an austerity program that was intended to cool an overinflated economy and restore a semblance of discipline to the nation. However, when the Iranian Revolution led to dramatic new price increases, he denied his earlier remonstrances, spending in his first three years what Pérez had committed in five. As one Venezuelan observer remarked, "There must be examples of worse fiscal management than that of Venezuela in the last eight or nine years, but I am not aware of them."[3] Following on the heels of a sweeping victory over COPEI that exceeded even the Pérez triumph a decade earlier, Acción Democrática returned to power in February 1984.

The inheritor of a vast economic morass, Jaime Lusinchi uttered familiar language upon his own accession to the presidency. There was a renewed call for sacrifice and austerity—an insistence that Venezuela reject the enslaving chains of exaggerated consumption. He viewed the rapid growth of almost gratuitous petroleum riches as "having unchained in our society radical changes, aggravating unhealthy tendencies of waste, squandering, and illicit profiteering." Reforms were necessary if the nation were to remain a leader of democratic forces in the hemisphere. "We have the conviction that democracy is an experience and a spontaneous, irreversible way of life. . . . But political democracy was not for us a goal in itself; it was an expected stage in our search for social democracy."[4]

With the halcyon years of inordinate petroleum riches behind it, Venezuela has begun to raise more searching questions about the performance of its democractic system. This in turn suggests a probing of the party system, which has come to dominate so powerfully the operations of government and many sectors of society. It has consequently sought to dissect the functioning of Venezuelan parties, and assessments have often been harsh. An alleged *partidocracia* (party-controlled democracy) has become voracious, venal, and incapable of meeting national needs.[5] Discussions of presumed "crises" emanate from divergent definitions of the term. For some, the crisis of the parties presents an apocalyptic vision in which the fabric of society will be torn beyond recognition. Others would suggest that the peril is of a long-range systemic nature, embodied by a state of malaise that need not be fatal.[6] It is the latter vision that orients this commentary. Furthermore, the form of elite accommodation exemplified in 1958 by the Pact of Punto Fijo has been reshaped and restated in more recent times. Tolerance of political opposition has by no means been exhausted; neither has a spirit of consultation been forgotten.

INTELLECTUAL TRADITIONS AND DEMOCRATIC MODELS

If historical patterns and the cultural legacy of past experience are fundamental to an understanding of contemporary Latin American politics, the formulation of these traditions in the literature is diverse. As many observers have noted, there is little consensus on the relative impact of intellectual traditions. Oversimplistic dichotomies between pluralistic democracy and authoritarianism have abounded, with doctrinal and disciplinary fads arising and fading with the varying trends of regimes in Latin America. As John Sloan recently wrote, the 1950s belief in the compatibility of development and democracy was displaced in the 1960s and 1970s by the view that the dependence rooted in the capitalistic economic order assured a more corporatist experience. This in turn is now being questioned, as a host of authoritarian regimes have departed after uniformly unsuccessful rule.

Sloan is not far from the mark in characterizing the study of Latin American politics as an ideological battleground. It is difficult to deny his conclusion that "the diversity of political events in Latin America defies simplistic ideological conclusions."[7] Hopefully, a more helpful and more subtle view is beginning to take shape, one that contends that no single intellectual or cultural legacy can in itself provide an adequate framework for analysis. Wiarda has made this point in a number of his efforts to penetrate the misty complexities of the Latin American experience.[8] A recent essay has further contended that the writings of the *pensadores* (philosophers) have constituted three basic orienting schools of thought: monism, liberal pluralism, and Marxism. As these have coexisted and persisted over time, they have blended together. Indeed, their very "durability and persistence over many generations argue that contemporary analytic models should take into account behavior stemming from all three world views."[9] To examine and assess the state of Venezuelan parties, in turn, one must recognize the existence of these traditions. The tensions and stresses produced by contradictory impulses will help to illuminate the problems confronted by the character and quality of the organizations.

Over the course of the quarter century during which the present Venezuelan democratic system has taken root, the political parties have become ever more central to its very existence. There has developed a strong commitment to democracy in its diverse forms. In terms of Herman's differentiation between formal and substantive norms,[10] party elites have committed themselves to the unqualified realization of both. The record of achievement, however, has been far from flawless. The procedural norms identified by Herman as consonant with liberal democratic pluralism of the Anglo-American mode, at least, have proven reasonably susceptible to the parties.

Beginning with the 1958 contests, Venezuela has held six consecutive national elections marked by uncommon systemic freedom and civic participation. Highly competitive, increasingly intensive and expensive campaigns have been conducted over a period of eighteen to twenty-four months before election day. Indeed, I remarked elsewhere that one of Venezuela's political truisms is the adage that the day after national elections, the campaign starts for the next contest five years distant.[11] Universal suffrage exists in practice as well as theory, with some 90 percent of the eligible population customarily casting a ballot. Even when under threat of terrorist attack in 1963, the drive to vote has been exceptional. Individual rights have been consistently honored through the years, while the vast majority of hemispheric neighbors have struggled to erect systems that respond to the dictates and needs of citizens in democratic societies.

In contrast, what have been termed the substantive norms of economic development and social justice—defined by Herman as typical of the Latin American democratic model—have been resistant to the leadership of the parties. While discussion of these objectives soon goes beyond the purview of the parties alone, it is also true that an enduring commitment to a form of organic statism has been writ large in the Venezuelan experience. The central role of the state has been assumed and rarely challenged as decentralized public agencies have proliferated. Few corners of national life have remained off limits to the intrusions of the state. At the same time, corporatist group representation has further reflected the Hispanic or monist stream in Venezuela's intellectual heritage.

In centering the spotlight on the characteristics of the nation's politics, it is contended that the blend of traditions is present and identifiable. The evolution of the system since 1958 thus reflects both pluralistic and corporatist features. While the parties have promoted the advance of democracy at the public level, they have also responded to monist proclivities in society. Internally, they have also demonstrated patterns of behavior that have emanated from divergent traditions. To review these developments in abbreviated form is to consider the nature of leadership, the organizational operations, and the doctrinal concerns of the parties. For the sake of chronological order, analysis falls into two periods, with the point of demarcation the critical elections of 1973.

SYSTEMIC ORIGINS AND ADOLESCENCE (FROM 1958 TO 1973)

The 1958 competition followed in the wake of ten years of military authoritarianism and corruption. Four parties contested the elections, all of which predated the dictatorial decade. In terms of participatory democratic parties, the origins could be traced back to the student protests later enshrined as the "Generation of '28."[12] Out of this came the leaders who formed the nation's parties. Out of the 1930s—much of which was spent in exile or in underground activities—came the parties of the future. The original Partido Comunista de Venezuela (PCV) was founded in 1931; reformism of the democratic left took the name of Acción Democrática in 1941. Within the next five years, both the social Christian party, Comité de Organización Política Electoral Independiente (COPEI), and the Unión Republicana Democrática (URD) came into being. All four parties were persecuted to varying degrees by the Pérez Jiménez dictatorship, which followed the brief 1945 to 1948 *trienio* under *adeco* (AD) domination.[13]

In the months following the ouster of the dictatorship, party leaders met to lay down the groundwork for a new and potentially more mature party democracy. With the Communist party leadership excluded from talks, representatives of COPEI, the URD, and AD negotiated the so-called Pact of Punto Fijo. This triparty agreement stressed moderation and tolerance in promising cooperation in defense of the democratic system. "The sincere definition . . . of the rights that are held by the parties as representatives of . . . the enduring interests of the Nation . . . are the guarantee that deliberations have recognized . . . presentday urgent needs in Venezuela."[14] Six general principles detailed a defense of the Constitution, an obligation to honor election returns, and the formation of a government of national unity following elections. To guard against possible violations, a tribunal composed of representatives of the three parties was created: the Comisión Interpartidista de Unidad. All three presidential candidates subsequently subscribed to the Pact of Punto Fijo in addition to the parties. As

Herman noted in Chapter 1 in this volume, this demonstration of accommodation among political elites was a hallmark of the newborn democratic system in Venezuela.

The subsequent government under Rómulo Betancourt of the AD functioned for two years until the URD withdrew in November 1960 following a foreign policy dispute in which the *urredista* (URD) minister ignored presidential directives at an Inter-American conference. Although the basic prodemocratic thrust of Punto Fijo held fast, the party system gradually fragmented in the years from 1958 to 1973, by which time no fewer than a dozen presidential candidates and more than twice that number of officially recognized political parties appeared on the ballot.[15] The rapid proliferation of parties in what was from its inception a multiparty system emanated from both the fragmentation of existing organizations and the creation of new ones. At least three impulses were identifiable: doctrinal disputes, generational rivalries, and conflicting personal ambitions.

The dominant party of the 1958 to 1968 decade effectively illustrated the situation, for Acción Democrática experienced three wrenching divisions. In 1960 the youthful left wing departed party ranks. On doctrinal grounds it reflected a neo-Marxist outlook that, stimulated by the new example of the Cuban Revolution, impatiently rejected the gradualism of Betancourt, Raúl Leoni, and the other founding fathers. Ignoring the admonitions of those who argued that in an earlier era, impatience and radicalism had produced a golpe de estado and ten years of barbaric repression and persecution, the so-called *cabezas calientes* (hotheads) broke away, soon to carry their campaign to the mountains in an ill-informed and immature effort to emulate Fidel. Their departure from the AD was also occasioned by an unwillingness to serve at middle-level ranks, rather than elbowing aside the party elders (none of whom were, in point of fact, beyond their early fifties).

Only two years later, the AD was further buffeted by the schism of the so-called *arsistas*. In this instance a substantial number of middle-level leaders—placed generationally between the departed youth and the senior leadership—sought to seize control as a prelude to the 1963 elections. Not all the prominent middle-level figures accompanied the arsistas, whose complaint was personalistic and opportunistic rather than doctrinal. The arsistas ran a separate campaign in 1963, failed dismally, and within a few years had disintegrated organizationally. Some of their leaders left politics, while others joined a variety of different parties, including for a few a sheepish return to Acción Democrática. The gravity of this division was subsequently paled by that of 1967 and 1968, however. On this occasion the senior leadership of the party itself divided over the respective presidential precandidacies of its two remaining founders—AD President Luis Beltrán Prieto Figueroa and Secretary-General Gonzalo Barrios. Contrary to many reports, there were significant programmatic differences. Prieto essentially advocated a more reformist posture, accompanied by a renewal of party commitment to the masses. Barrios pledged a developmentalist continuation of Betancourt and Leoni policies for another five years.

In the end, loyalists rallied by Betancourt enabled Barrios to prevail, while Prieto created his own party, the Movimiento Electoral del Pueblo (MEP). In the 1968 race the two AD leaders polled a total of 47 percent of the vote, enough to have assured yet another party victory. Given the split, however, COPEI's founder Rafael Caldera slipped past for a narrow victory over Barrios while polling 29 percent of the vote. This was of great significance for the entire party system. The previously undefeated AD, viewed by some as moving toward the PRI-type domination seen in Mexico, instead found itself displaced by Venezuela's second party. Had COPEI lost yet another race with Caldera, its preeminent leader, the party might well have receded into the mists of history. As it was, the social Christians were enabled to build a presumably lasting party structure, at the same time assuming national governmental responsibility and strengthening the electoral significance of Venezuelan democracy.

While the AD underwent such internal disputes, there were similar episodes for both the URD and the PCV. With URD they revolved around periodic challenges to party founder and *caudillo* (leader) Jóvito Villalba. First came the 1964 challenge of the party's *ala negra* (black wing), a non-Marxist reformist group, which was too insistent on rapid reforms for Villalba. The second came with Alirio Ugarte Pelayo, a highly talented and upwardly mobile party youth who in time constituted what the defensive Villalba viewed as a questioning of his leadership. Villalba eventually forced Ugarte to depart the URD. Ugarte's creation of a new party was still in process when the overworked and overwrought former *urredista* took his own life.[16] Within a few years, the next would-be heir to the Villalba political mantle—Leonardo Montiel Ortega—was also driven to withdraw from the URD. Not surprisingly, he too formed his own party, which in turn disintegrated after a brief and discouraging electoral venture.[17]

For the Marxist left, divisions and internal dissension also marked both doctrinal and generational problems. There were serious tactical and strategic issues when the youth of the PCV joined former-AD militants in a rural campaign against the system. Once the guerrilla insurgency flagged, it became problematic when the more energetic Communists returned to the party fold and accepted the constraints of parliamentary and electoral activity. This was underlined following the 1968 Soviet invasion of Czechoslovakia. The aftermath saw most of the brightest party intellectuals—predominantly young Communists—leaving the party to create what became the Movimiento al Socialismo (MAS). Once again, a party fission was the result of both doctrinal and generational factors.[18]

Only the social Christians managed to escape the phenomenon of party divisions, although even the redoubtable Rafael Caldera found it necessary to labor long and hard to preserve party unity in the face of profound differences among the party youth in the late 1960s. At the same time, however, it was true that in addition to internal party squabbles that led to departures and fragmentation, there were also "nonparty" movements that compounded the confusion of the system. During the pre–1973 era, this took the form of personalistic campaigns that sought legitimacy as an offshoot of individual charisma. Examples come from Wolfgang Larrazábal in 1958, Arturo Uslar Pietri in 1963, and, ultimately, Miguel Angel Burelli Rivas in 1968.

Although each of these candidacies could be regarded as unique, this was particularly true of Vice-Admiral Larrazábal. Largely as a function of military seniority, he emerged as provisional president in 1958 following the ignominious flight of Marcos Pérez Jiménez. Endorsed by the URD and by the PCV—in acts of consummate opportunism by both Jóvito Villalba and Gustavo Machado— Larrazábal ran first in Caracas but trailed Betancourt elsewhere in the country. By 1963 the retired vice-admiral had organized his own party and had then been buried by the electorate. In later years, with his personalistic movement virtually defunct, he ran for congress on first the *copeyano* (COPEI), and in time the adeco lists.

In 1963, as the AD sought to ride out the impact of both its youth and its arsista divisions, the banner of political independents was purportedly assumed by the prominent writer and essayist Arturo Uslar Pietri. Creating what he dramatically and unequivocally labeled an "antiparty" movement, Uslar ran a respectable race but ended up nationally as a distant fourth. By 1968 antiparty forces sought to unite the remaining personalistic strength of Larrazábal, Uslar Pietri, and the fading URD of Villalba. The result was the candidacy of the political independent Burelli, whose highest position had been Venezuelan ambassador to the Court of St. James under an AD government. The result was yet another strong showing by a quasi-independent candidate who, however, went down to decisive defeat.

While the parties were undergoing the pressures of real or potential divisions and personalistic public figures sought to mount their own campaigns, established organizations were attempting to secure their internal legitimacy. Ideally, this signified institutional over personal control. A striking example came from the AD-party convention, which preceded the nomination of a presidential candidate for 1963. The dominant party elder and President of the Republic, Rómulo Betancourt, presented views reflective of a preoccupation with the survival of systemic democracy in Venezuela. For Betancourt, the spirit of Punto Fijo would ideally be personified by a nonparty eminence acceptable to both COPEI and the AD. Another option was Rafael Caldera of COPEI. For the adecos, however, the two divisions of the past five years suggested the importance of reasserting party hegemony through an avowedly AD nominee. Consequently, Raúl Leoni was named by the party convention shortly after Betancourt had argued for other options. It was significant in demonstrating an important degree of party independence from, and opposition to, the avowed views of the party founder.

During the years from 1958 to 1973, then, the Venezuelan party system in some senses flourished but, unmistakably, divided and proliferated. As already noted, both opportunistic and programmatic elements were involved. Candidates once bitten by the presidential bug insisted on repeating the quest for Miraflores Palace. In most instances the initial failure and subsequent absence of significant party support doomed the effort to ignominy. Provisional president Larrazábal, blessed with URD support in 1958, ran second with 30.7 percent of the vote, then fell to fifth place in 1963 with 9.4 percent from his own Fuerza Democrática Popular (FDP). He was left in 1968 to join with the 1963 phenomenon Uslar Pietri and the fading URD to back the independent Burelli Rivas. The new candidate won 22 percent of the vote in a third-place finish. Five years later, forced to campaign for a minor party, he came in sixth with 0.8 percent of the vote. And although circumstances were fundamentally different, it could also be added that Rafael Caldera's victory in 1968 came in his fifth race for the office. His 1983 quest for a second presidency thereby marked his sixth such effort.

It was the 1973 race that proved to be a critical election in the evolution of the Venezuelan party system. It was not in the strictest definition of the phrase a "realigning" election, for it left the AD and COPEI enjoying hegemonic control. Moreover, 1973 was the third consecutive contest in which the two parties had led all competitors in the ballot. The real significance, then, was the transformation of what had appeared an ever-more fractious and fragmented multiparty system into a dominant two-party arrangement. This did not mean a disappearance of secondary parties—*minipartidos* or *micropartidos* in the Venezuelan political vernacular—but rather this dramatized their swift retreat into the shadows of political ineffectiveness and insignificance.

Three presidential candidates had sought the office in 1958; this number in 1973 reached a round dozen. As a final illustration of the doctrinal, organizational, and personalistic divisions that characterized the party system, let us fill in the scorecard. In addition to the candidates for COPEI and the AD (Lorenzo Fernández and Carlos Andrés Pérez, respectively), there was the former *adeco* Jesús Angel Paz Galarraga, who was the representative of the MEP; he also drew the backing of the PCV. The URD's Jóvito Villalba broke his promise to back Paz and entered the lists on his own. We already mentioned that Burelli Rivas repeated his quest despite the absence of significant party support. The Marxist vote was divided between Paz and the independent leftist José Vicente Rangel, who was backed by two rival Marxist parties, the MAS and the Movimiento de Izquierda Revolucionaria (MIR).

This still leaves another half-dozen candidates to be identified. Several had entered the campaign in hopes of securing the endorsement of former dictator Marcos Pérez Jiménez, at this point ensconced in his luxurious suite in Madrid.[19] Months of embarrassingly sycophantic courting of the pudgy Sybarite proved unsuccessful. On election day would-be suitors of Pérez Jiménez who remained on the ballot included Pedro Segnini La Cruz, Raimundo Verde Rojas, and retired General Martín García Villasmil, a former defense minister under Rafael Caldera. Another former Caldera minister, the wealthy businessman and entrepreneur Pedro Tinoco, also tried his hand. Alberto Solano, unknown to both the public and the media, ultimately brought up the tail end of the competition in polling 1,651 votes, a stunning 0.03 percent of the vote. A highly conservative former copeyano by the name of Germán Borregales repeated his earlier candidacy, standing as something of a folkloric figure for Venezuelan humorists. And by way of footnote, only the last-minute withdrawal of *perezjimenista* Alejandro Gómez Silva avoided the unlucky thirteen as the total of candidates on the first Sunday of December 1973.

CHARACTERISTICS OF PARTY MATURATION: FROM 1973 TO 1983

As the 1973 campaign progressed and the anticipated alliance of minor candidates failed to materialize, the press grew ever more caustic over what was termed a mockery of true democracy. Editorials chided the *políticos* for making Venezuela the laughing stock of genuine democratic systems elsewhere in the world. In the end, the electorate dealt with the matter by casting 85.8 percent of the presidential vote for Pérez and Fernández, while their two parties received 74.6 percent of the congressional votes. In the latter contest, no fewer than thirty-eight separate slates took part; twelve received 0.01 percent or less, while another six received less than 0.1 percent. The results not only reflected the electorate's rejection of extreme multipartyism, but—especially in the presidential election—responded to realistic assessments of "useful" or "wasted" votes. Indeed, by the close of the campaign both the AD and COPEI were enjoining voters not to throw away their exercise of suffrage on a party or candidate without any serious chance for victory.

From 1973 through the decade that includes the 1983 elections, Venezuelan party democracy has thus been reflective of a dominant two-party system. This has also demonstrated a process of maturation in which there has been some diminution of earlier centripetal forces. Among the more important elements of this maturation process are the following: (1) the expense of campaign competition minimizes the realistic chances of minor or of personalistic challenges; (2) the major parties have learned more effectively to control internal conflict without producing outright division; (3) the centrist proclivities of public opinion have helped drive the two dominant parties to the middle of the spectrum, crowding out all competitors; (4) this has also diminished the appeals of parties from either far right or left; (5) the solidification of the democratic system has underlined the commitments of Punto Fijo, to the benefit of COPEI and the AD; (6) party loyalties have overcome the Circean seductiveness of charismatic nonparty personalities; (7) the democratic centralism of both adeco and copeyano organizational dynamics has dominated party organization; and (8) there has been hegemonic turnover of governments.

With the first of these, oil-rich Venezuela has also seen the introduction and development of the most advanced and sophisticated campaign techniques— including the hiring of North American consultants, including such notable practitioners as David Garth, Cliff White, the Squiers, Joe Napolitan, and others. Television advertising contributes to the cost, and from 1973 forward, only the two major parties have been able to bear the cost. Although estimates are impossible to determine with precision, careful analyses have provided ample evidence of the phenomenon. Martz and Baloyra calculated for 1973 that the total expense was some 450 million bolívares (104 million dollars). With some 4.5 million voters, this meant 100 bolívares per voter—some 23 dollars at the existing exchange rate.[20] Five years later, Myers estimated that AD alone may have spent 88 million dollars; the overall total approached 200 million dollars.[21] Myers and Herman have reported the cost of the 1983 campaign as at least 200 million dollars, despite the economic recession and the impossibility of calculating the conversion rate of the sagging bolívar.[22] In short, from 1973 forward, only the AD and COPEI could successfully mobilize the resources necessary to fund a full-blown campaign.

The years from 1973 onward have also seen greater maintenance of internal unity, most notably in the case of Acción Democrática. Following the three schisms of the years from 1958 to 1968, with the last schism costing the party the presidency, the AD has been largely free from serious doctrinal disputes. Moreover, an ordering of its generational leadership has also been accomplished. This dated from the decision of former President Rómulo Betancourt not to seek another presidential term in 1973; his suggestion to his long-time compatriot Gonzalo Barrios that the next generation should have its turn, led to the nomination of Carlos Andrés Pérez. Party struggles for the presidential candidacy, therefore, have reflected personal ambitions rather than more basic doctrinal factors. The AD has moved toward the occasional implementation of primaries as a means of legitimizing its subsequent convention choices. To be sure, the first such effort in 1967 shattered the party, as Prieto won approval of the rank-and-file in defiance of the leadership's preference for Barrios. More recently, however, a vote by party members produced the 1978 candidacy of Luis Piñerúa Ordaz over his rival, Jaime Lusinchi. A somewhat different format in January 1982 then propelled Lusinchi to the nomination over the opposition of David Morales Bello.

COPEI has always stood as an exception to the presumed rules about party fragmentation. It has continued to maintain at least a facade of internal unity, and party dissidence has not led to any important break. This is not to deny rivalry and competition. Disparate ideological views were evident until recent years, when the personal animosity between Rafael Caldera and Luis Herrera Campins has been manifest. The first, undisputed political founder and ideological mentor of Venezuelan Christian democracy helped employ government influence to deny Herrera the 1973 nomination. Herrera doggedly stayed with the party and eventually secured the candidacy in 1978. He in turn sought to block Caldera's 1983 candidacy, without success. In the wake of the 1983 defeat, a struggle between the two camps has again been engaged. Caldera, however, clearly holds the upper hand. Ultimately, Herrera either will have to capitulate or, in leaving COPEI, will be left totally in the political wilderness.

The pronounced centrism of the Venezuelan electorate has also become increasingly evident. A series of data-based analyses by Enrique A. Baloyra—

while providing a richness and subtlety that cannot be reiterated here—amply testify to the orientation of the public.[23] In earlier years memories of 1960s radicalism and *fidelista*-style guerrilla depredations sullied all Marxists and neo-leftists in the eyes of the electorate. More recently, the divisions of the left have rendered even more unrealistic its claims to a meaningful share of power. More-over, the marginally strongest party as of 1987, the MAS, has moved progres-sively toward a quasi-social democratic centrism of its own. In electoral terms, three leftist candidates in 1978 won 7.3 percent of the vote, and five years later two nominees polled 7.5 percent. And from the opposite end of the spectrum, there have been no viable or popular leaders to offer a conservative alternative. Even the more rightist corporate interests in the country chose to cast their lot, their funds, and their interests with COPEI and the AD.

Studies by Baloyra and by public-opinion organizations in Venezuela have documented the extent to which the citizenry regards itself as copeyano, adeco, or—increasingly—as politically independent. This has been demonstrated elec-torally by the turnover of administrations between the two major parties at every election since 1968. One can exaggerate what some would term a public incli-nation to vote for the candidate of the nongovernment party. Conditions have been quite diverse in terms of the COPEI–AD electoral rivalry since 1968. It has also suggested the extent to which the leadership of the two parties has continued to accept democratic competition and, specifically, the principles of the Pact of Punto Fijo. It is striking, for example, that a tacit understanding between the two parties has prevented a gutting of the bureaucracy in the after-math of a change in government. While high-ranking posts are marked for change, to be sure, at middle and lower levels there has been the practice of bringing in supporters of the newly elected party without actually firing those left from the defeated organization. It has been budgetarily expensive and bu-reaucratically inefficient but, at the same time, has helped further to enshrine both systemic democracy and the dominion of the two parties.

Party loyalists, moreover—along with the realism of practically minded Ven-ezuelans over the chances of competing parties and candidates—have further buttressed the strength of the two-party organizations. Periodic efforts to replicate the one-shot electoral phenomenon of Larrazábal in 1958, Uslar Pietri in 1963, and Burelli Rivas in 1968 have foundered. Consider the examples. They appear most strikingly in 1978 when, it is possible, any serious thought of mounting an independent, nonparty or "antiparty" campaign that bore prospects for suc-cess was forever demolished. First, there was Reinaldo Ottolina Pinto, the famed "Renny," a showman, interviewer, entertainment entrepreneur, and salesman par excellence. He announced his candidacy in early 1977 and in time received financing from pro-AD businessmen who calculated that he would take votes away from both COPEI and MAS.

When Ottolina Pinto's candidacy ended in the fatal crash of his private plane in March 1978, the nonparty stage was left for the media-wise, Kennedy-style char-isma of former Caracas governor Diego Arria. A one-time functionary under Rafael

Caldera who later joined the camp of Carlos Andrés Pérez, Arria was a medi-
agenic representative of the younger generation in Venezuela. His presidential
candidacy sought in realistic terms to achieve a position whereby he might hold
the balance between the AD and COPEI. Patrick Caddell, the controversial North
American consultant, was hired after David Garth rejected Arria to accept direction of the Herrera campaign for COPEI. Despite a well-financed campaign,
however, Arria polled only 1.7 percent of the vote.[24]

By 1983 there was little thought that even a congressional delegation offering
votes to either the AD or COPEI was viable. Although there were ultimately
twelve presidential candidates, eight were unable to earn even 1 percent of the
vote. As already noted, the two Marxist nominees won a combined 7.5 percent,
with 91.4 percent captured by the two major candidates. The closest approach
to an individualistic personality in the race was Jorge Olavarría, the maverick
publisher and journalist who had been a thorn in the side of every president
since Rafael Caldera. However, his was a symbolic undertaking, and his eventual
31,909 votes produced but 0.48 percent of the vote. At this juncture, in short,
it staggers the imagination to envisage a protest or antisystem candidate who
could make serious inroads with the electorate. Neither charisma, media styl-
ishness, or a modicum of funding will be adequate to challenge dominant party
leadership.

The practice of democratic centralism within both major parties has also
emerged, not as a new dynamic of internal activity, but as a further buttressing
of organizational domination. For Venezuela, as for the vast majority of Latin
American political parties, the internal functioning of the organization is strongly
reminiscent of western European socialist and social democratic parties. This
produces a form of elitist domination by ranking figures that is only rarely
contradicted by the preferences of the grass roots. This is not to reject the
relevance of party activity at less elevated levels. Recall the teachings of Rómulo
Betancourt about the significance of partisan activity at the lowest levels, lessons
that COPEI later emulated to its own advantage. The effectiveness of party elites
in tapping popular sentiment and incorporating it into policy decisions is one of
the keys to successful democratic leadership in Venezuela. At the same time,
the ultimate centralization control is in the best tradition of Weber, Ostrogorski,
and most certainly Michels.

There are at least two crucial measures that illustrate the point. One has to
do with the role and responsibility of local government in Venezuela. Idealistic
democratic pronouncements have joined to practical enhancing of local authority
in public policy making.[25] The government administration, indeed, has been
somewhat less reluctant than national party elites to transfer some powers to the
local level. In electoral terms, this is tied to the decision to separate municipal
elections from national contests. First in 1979 and then in 1984, the nation
conducted municipal elections several months after the inauguration of new
national governments. Not surprisingly, the latter were still enjoying the initial

honeymoon period; thus, COPEI swept to an impressive victory in 1979 municipal races, and the AD did the same five years later.

The second case involves the necessity for party leaders to construct slates of congressional candidates every five years. The list system of proportional representation employed for legislative contests—also a common practice in Latin America—specifies that party candidates must be placed in a given state and then ranked on the list. It is a means of underlying party discipline; the member who, for instance, violates central party directives in his or her congressional voting may well be eliminated from the list. If not, the individual can easily be dropped well down on the list. Where there are nonparty eminences and independents whose presence will hopefully strengthen the performance of the list, party loyalists must be displaced. In practice, the recommendations of loyal and state party officials must be reviewed and often overridden by the national leadership.

Competing party factions must also be recognized. For example, the most severe tensions in COPEI between the *calderistas* and *herreristas* have occurred when party leaders have attempted to put together these lists. As a recent instance, COPEI's struggle in 1983 was not concluded until September 1983, very late in the campaign. Candidate Caldera designated one third of the names, as did the party Secretary-General Eduardo Fernández. The final third came from the National Committee, which itself was dominated by calderistas. There were substantial protests, with some noting that the party process in 1978 had allegedly been more broadly representative. However, in both instances the national committee, the candidates, and the secretary-general played central roles. This task is not only predictably difficult and controversial, for there are never enough reasonably "safe" positions on the party lists. In addition, it continues to reify democratic centralism even as it produces problems of considerable magnitude.

Finally, let us return to the nature of hegemonic turnover of regimes. As already suggested, it is oversimplistic and unsophisticated to maintain that the electorate is now turning out the rascals every five years. Without engaging in extended electoral analysis, consider a few of the more obvious facts. In 1968 it was the AD split that permitted a superbly organized campaign by Caldera to break the former's monopoly on power. Had the division not occurred, the AD candidate—whether Barrios or Prieto—would have reached power, Caldera would have run his last campaign, COPEI would have receded in importance, and a form of modified one-party domination could have emerged.

Five years later, a reinvigorated Acción Democrática reflected the behind-the-scenes acumen of Rómulo Betancourt, recently returned to Venezuela and the political fray. A strengthened organization worked smoothly and efficiently on behalf of Pérez, arguably the finest political campaigner in recent Venezuelan history. With COPEI running a foolishly overconfident campaign that centered on a capable leader whose skills as a campaigner were quite limited, the AD sweep was scarcely surprising. There were those who believed that true adeco hegemony might be at hand. Five years later, however, the two major parties put forward singularly unexciting campaigners. The Herrera effort was in near-desparate straits when the candidate called in David Garth, paid him extravagant fees,[26] and turned over total control of the campaign. In the end, Herrera defeated Luis Piñerúa, the architect of a somnambulent strategy, by a mere 46 to 43 percent. There is little question that the quality of the campaign itself decided the outcome.

For 1983, although competing analyses are still being formulated and aired, the most basic fact was the extraordinary unpopularity of the Herrera government. Even without the visceral hatred between Caldera and Herrera, the former would naturally have sought to disassociate himself from the administration. The AD campaign, understandably, sought to remind voters that the government was copeyano, while the candidate was the putative founder of the party. It was a situation that even the stature and skill of Rafael Caldera could not overcome. In this instance the losing candidate was indeed weighed down with the sins of the government—conceivably the most inept administration in Venezuelan living memory. Without repeating our point unduly, suffice it to say that the candidate of a governing party in Venezuela need not be consigned automatically to defeat. Although there is an electoral tendency to prefer the "outs"—scarcely an unhealthy attitude for the democratic system—the conditions and circumstances of the particular contest are more decisive.

This factor, in conjunction with the others that stand out in the post–1973 period, helps to delineate more clearly the character of the emergent party system. Moreover, the dynamics of internal party activities remain crucial for an assessment of democratic and nondemocratic qualities. There is clear evidence that there is indeed a blend of these characteristics, as was argued at the outset. It remains to consider these elements for the future, while weighing their impact on the evolving Venezuelan party system.

CONCLUSIONS: CONSISTENCIES AND CONTRADICTIONS

After a quarter century the performance of Venezuelan parties presents both positive and negative elements. At the level of the nation's macrosystemic evolution, the accomplishments are manifest. Political democracy has been enshrined through an observation of procedural norms that has been increasingly beyond reproach. The vigor and intensity of competition, the openness of the process, and the civic conviction that electoral participation is a matter of both pride and necessity—these are hallmarks of systemic achievements. The functioning of the system has been improved by the retrogression of secondary parties and the hegemonic growth of COPEI and the AD. Whatever their many shortcomings, the potential for substantive as well as procedural democracy has been increased by the trend from minority governments and jerry-built coalitions to strong majorities. Whatever the wisdom or folly of policies, they can at least be formulated and implemented without obstructionist opportunism from irresponsible minorities.

In terms of party characteristics at the operational level, the blending of pluralist and monist traditions is more evident. The former is suggested by the organizational structures of the parties and the vitality of local and regional activity. It reaches into segments of the labor, peasant, and student movements as affiliated both officially and informally with the national parties. In some instances it is articulated through convention decisions that contradict the leadership. The introduction of a form of party primary, although flawed in execution, has also brought a further degree of democratization. Offsetting or contradicting these qualities, however, are such proclivities as personal party *caudillismo*, the democratic centralism of the elites, and the resistance of structural changes that would reduce the capacity to shape and ultimately to control the parties.

For the near future, alternatives to the existing system are improbable if less than inconceivable. One scenario foresees, two decades after it was first suggested, the emergence of a PRI-style one-party hegemony under the aegis of Acción Democrática. It is noted that the party believes that the recent Herrera government effectively violated the spirit of Punto Fijo. The putative effort of the Lusinchi administration to create a functioning tripartite *pacto social* based on the comanagement of government, labor, and business might suggest a means of transforming the system. Such an effort would be consistent with the model of organic statism—a version of corporatism rather than democratic pluralism. Granted the magnitude of COPEI's recent defeat, the age of founder Caldera, the extraordinary public rejection of Luis Herrera, and the internal rivalry over future control of the party, it is thus concluded that the AD cannot be stopped. With the political left divided, weakened, and periodically lurching toward the center of the spectrum, the opportunity for Acción Democrática is undeniable.

Such a development, however, flies in the face of the past quarter century. If candidates for government parties do not axiomatically lose the next election, they must nonetheless bear the brunt of unpopularity for the outgoing administration. Lusinchi continues to confront an array of intimidating economic and social problems, ones that will require more than five years to correct. And already, not halfway into his term, the president's rating at the polls has dropped as precipitately as did that of Luis Herrera five years earlier. Moreover, the relative absence of ideological conflict inside the party has not dimmed personalistic ambitions. Carlos Andrés Pérez will be eligible to run for the presidency again in 1988. At this juncture he is undecided, hesitating in part because of the unproven but widely held belief that Caldera's 1983 defeat demonstrates popular opposition to presidential reelection. At the same time, the government is at best unenthusiastic about resurgent *carlosandresismo*. Interior Minister Octavio Lepage is but the most prominent of several ranking leaders who would hope to oppose Pérez. [Editor's note: In 1987, Pérez won the nomination.]

Whatever these eventualities, the AD will be undergoing internal stresses once again. Its candidate will be unable to avoid at least some of the burden of a

Lusinchi administration, which by 1988 will be held in low popular esteem. The AD will also be subject to the traditional conflict between government and government party: This was true of Caldera and COPEI, Pérez and AD, of Herrera and COPEI, and is now taking shape with Lusinchi and the AD. Granted these factors, the other parties cannot be ignored in any speculation about future patterns. COPEI, notwithstanding its grave problems, has overcome similar challenges in the past. The second generation of party leadership is emerging with the blessing of Rafael Caldera, and Secretary-General Eduardo Fernández leads the list of aspirants, which includes Osvaldo Alvarez Paz, ''Pepi'' Montes de Oca, Hilarión Cardozo, and others. Luis Herrera no longer has a real future in the party, and his influence can be discounted.

If the Mexican-style scenario is rejected, then the options for the party system would be two. Either it returns to a more decentralized multiparty state, or it stumbles and staggers along without any major change. The first can result only from the rise of a fresh, new nondoctrinal party headed by a charismatic leader, or from a division of today's dominant parties. Practicalities suggest the difficulty of the former, most recently in the case of Diego Arria. The latter would most logically occur with Acción Democrática, despite the bitter lessons of past divisions. To repeat, the weakening and virtual disappearance of serious ideological battles relegates potential schisms to forces of ambition and personalism. Internal conditions do not support such an occurrence for the AD, at least in the next few years. If Pérez does decide to seek the nomination, it will be difficult for party bureaucrats to stop him. Should he opt out, the rivalry among other, less dominating figures will be susceptible to resolution inside the organizational rules of the game. An AD internal reorganization and party elections in the last half of 1985 provided some decentralization of the apparatus, while encouraging the authority of those who controlled the machinery.

A major division for COPEI would mean its virtual death as a major force in Venezuela. Its leadership recognizes as much and can be expected to act accordingly. Even so, currents within both the AD and COPEI continue to view elite accommodation as a means of preserving the system while avoiding the unpredictabilities inherent in mass social mobilization. To be sure, the intensity and extent of popular participation in Venezuela extends far beyond the sheer act of voting. Perhaps no nation in Latin America demonstrates such participatory vigor. Even so, however, the party elites are reluctant to loosen the control reflected in the democratic centralism of their organizations. Adecos are unlikely to reject the legitimacy of copeyano opposition unless that party splinters, in which case the context for accommodation shifts to internal party linkages and relationships.

In sum, we have argued that the Venezuelan party system and its component members have more fully realized procedural than substantive norms. A blending of pluralist and monist characteristics has been starkly in evidence. Where we have contended in other commentaries that a potential petrification has endangered the system, there is little reason to retract that assessment. There is un-

deniably a malaise that grips contemporary Venezuelan society and politics—
one that appears endemic to the party system. It is a telling if unsurprising fact
that in successive 1985 polls Venezuelans are saying that their *first* electoral
preference is "undecided," followed by Acción Democrática with COPEI and
the parties of the left far in arrears. Past experience suggests that party elites
will not be deaf to such signs. The years since 1958 have permitted a deepening
of democratic roots in Venezuela. The impulse toward elite accommodation has
been accompanied by a stubbornly flourishing practice of participation and of
organizational populism. If party structures mirror democratic centralism, their
leadership is far from insensitive to grass-roots sentiments. It is these well
established qualities that give some hope that the malaise of the mid-1980s will
not endure and that prophecies of pessimism and decay will not prove self-
fulfilling.

NOTES

1. A detailed analysis of the Pérez campaign is included in John D. Martz and Enrique
A. Baloyra, *Electoral Mobilization and Public Opinion: The Venezuelan Campaign of
1973* (Chapel Hill: University of North Carolina Press, 1976), especially in Chapters 5
and 6.

2. Treatments of the 1978 campaign are found in Howard R. Penniman, ed., *Venezuela at the Polls: The National Elections of 1978* (Washington, D.C.: American Enterprise Institute, 1980). Especially see John D. Martz, "The Evolution of Democratic
Politics in Venezuela," pp. 1–30; David J. Myers, "The Acción Democrática Campaign," pp. 91–133; and Donald L. Herman, "The Christian Democratic Party,"
pp. 133–54.

3. Carlos Rangel, "How Venezuelans Squandered their Oil Wealth," *Miami Herald*,
March 20, 1983.

4. Lusinchi's inaugural address appeared in the Caracas press on January 31, 1984.
Also see John D. Martz, "The Crisis of Venezuelan Democracy," *Current History*
(February 1984):73–77 and 89.

5. The phrase was widely used by the muckraking journalist Jorge Olavarría in his
weekly *Resumen*. For example, see his "La partidocracia venezolana" in *Resumen*, July
5, 1981.

6. Characteristic views are presented by John D. Martz, "Los peligros de la petrificación," and by Andrés Stambouli, "La democracia venezolana," in *Iberoamérica en
los Años Ochenta*, eds. Enrique Baloyra and Rafael López-Pintor (Madrid: Centro de
Investigaciones Sociológicas, 1983). Also see Baloyra's reporting of Venezuelan attitudes
in his "Public Opinion and Support for the Regime, 1973–1983," in *Venezuela: The
Democratic Experience*, second edition, eds. John D. Martz and David J. Myers (New
York: Praeger, 1986).

7. John W. Sloan, *Public Policy in Latin America: A Comparative Survey* (Pittsburgh,
Penn.: University of Pittsburgh Press, 1984), p. 4.

8. Several representative statements appear in Howard J. Wiarda, *Corporatism and
National Development in Latin America* (Boulder, Colo.: Westview Press, 1981).

9. John D. Martz and David J. Myers, "Understanding Latin American Politics: Analytic Models and Intellectual Tradition," *Polity* 16 (Winter 1983):214–42.

10. See Donald L. Herman, "Colombian and Venezuelan Democracy: A Model," Paper presented at the Latin American Studies Association Conference, Albuquerque, N.Mex., April 23–25, 1985.

11. John D. Martz. "Venezuelan Foreign Policy and the Role of Political Parties," in *Latin American Nations in World Politics*, eds. Heraldo Muñoz and Joseph S. Tulchin (Boulder, Colo.: Westview Press, 1984), p. 133.

12. Among useful treatments of those of María de Lourdes Acedo de Sucre and Carmen Margarita Nones Mendoza, *La generación venezolana de 1928: Estudio de una élite política* (Caracas: Ediciones Ariel, 1967); Rodolfo Luzardo, *Notas histórico-económicas, 1928–1963* (Caracas: Editorial Sucre 1963); and John D. Martz, "Venezuela's Generation of '28: The Genesis of Political Democracy," *Inter-American Economic Affairs* 6 (January 1964):17–33.

13. A scholarly source for the early period is Steve Ellner, *Los partidos políticos y su disputa por el control del movimiento sindical en Venezuela, 1936–1948* (Caracas: Universidad Católica Andrés Bello, 1980). Historical sections for major parties provide detailed information in Robert J. Alexander, *The Communist Party of Venezuela* (Stanford, Calif.: Hoover Institution Press, 1969); Donald L. Herman, *Christian Democracy in Venezuela* (Chapel Hill: University of North Carolina Press, 1980); and John D. Martz, *Acción Democrática: Evolution of a Modern Political Party in Venezuela* (Princeton, N.J.: Princeton University Press, 1965).

14. Acción Democrática, *Pacto suscrito el 31 de octubre de 1957 y declarción de principios y programa mínimo de gobierno de los candidatos a la presidencia de la república* (Caracas: La Nación, 1958).

15. An intensive examination of the realigning race in 1973 is John D. Martz and Enrique A. Baloyra, *Electoral Mobilization and Public Opinion: The Venezuelan Campaign of 1973* (Chapel Hill: University of North Carolina Press, 1976).

16. For an informative if sometimes anguished account, see Bhilla Torres Molilna, *Alirio* (Caracas: GROMOTIP, 1968).

17. Montiel Ortega, a talented dilettante whose activities in time included a brief stint in a Venezuelan *telenovela*, was among those to focus particular attention on issues of petroleum. See Leonardo Montiel Ortega, *Conflicto en el petróleo venezolano* (Caracas: n.p., 1973).

18. For a statement by the leading Communist intellectual to depart the PCV in ideological protest, see Teodoro Petkoff, *Checoeslovaquia: El socialismo como problema* (Caracas: Editorial Fuentes, 1969). Petkoff eventually fought his way to the party's presidential candidacy in 1983. Another striking statement is that of Freddy Muñoz, *Revolución sin dogma* (Caracas: Ediciones Alcinoo, 1970).

19. For an excellent study that profiles the *perezjimenista* era as well as the Venezuelan campaign later to bring him to justice, see Judith Ewell, *The Indictment of a Dictator: The Extradition and Trial of Marcos Pérez Jiménez* (College Station: Texas A & M University Press, 1981).

20. Martz and Baloyra, *Electoral Mobilization*, pp. 201–3.

21. David J. Myers, "The Acción Democrática Campaign," in *Venezuela at the Polls: The National Elections of 1978*, ed. Howard J. Penniman (Washington, D.C.: American Enterprise Institute, 1980), pp. 106–8.

22. Donald L. Herman and David J. Myers, "The Venezuelan Election," in *The*

World Votes, ed. Howard R. Penniman (Durham, N.C.: Duke University Press/American Enterprise Institute, 1988).

23. Enrique A. Baloyra and John D. Martz, *Political Attitudes in Venezuela: Societal Cleavages and Public Opinion* (Austin: University of Texas Press, 1979); Enrique A. Baloyra, "Criticism, Cynicism, and Political Evaluation: A Venezuelan Example," *American Political Science Review*, 73 (December 1979); and Baloyra, "Public Opinion and Support" in *Venezuela*, eds. Martz and Myers.

24. John D. Martz, "the Minor Parties," in *Venezuela at the Polls*, ed. Penniman, pp. 154–71.

25. See the evolution of municipal power and authority, yielded only slowly and grudgingly by national authorities, in the chapters by Ildemaro Martínez in both the first and second editions of Martz and Myers, eds., *Venezuela*.

26. It was later reported in the Philadelphia *Inquirer* that for Garth and associates, the earnings from Venezuela would finance the college educations of children and grandchildren of the consulting firm. The remark later created some consternation in Venezuela, but not enough to deny Garth a less dominant but significant role with Caldera in 1983.

9

Venedemocracia and the Vagaries of the Energy Crisis

Robert J. Alexander

During the 1970s and the first half of the 1980s, the Venezuelan economy felt the full impact of the dramatic shifts in world demand and supply for petroleum, the country's major export. The four administrations that governed during this period sought to deal with the resulting problems in different ways. But the democratic system that the Venezuelans frequently call the "Venedemocracia" had remained intact since 1958 in spite of the violently shifting economic currents of the period. Orderly elections brought new administrations to power every five years, and the two major parties, Acción Democrática (AD) and Comité de Organización Política Electoral Independiente (COPEI), alternated in power with each election.

President Rafael Caldera, who was in office from 1969 to 1974, presided over the end of one phase of economic development. During the quarter of a century before his coming into power, Venezuela had been undergoing a process in which import-substitution industrialization had been the principal motor force for development. This strategy had been deliberately launched during the *trienio* of 1945 to 1948, in which Acción Democrática had been in power for the first time. The governments of that period had established the Venezuelan Development Corporation and had begun to expand greatly the economic and social infrastructure with the avowed purpose of "sowing petroleum," which in part at least meant expanding the country's industrial base.

Although the dictatorship that ruled Venezuela from November 1948 until January 1958 had nothing that would pass for a deliberate policy of development, the expansion of oil exports during the period helped to expand the internal market, and the process of import substitution went on, rather in spite of the government than because of it. However, with the return to power of President Rómulo Betancourt early in 1959, the Venezuelan government energetically and deliberately pushed import substitution, through expansion of the role of the Development Corporation, direct government investment, and various measures to protect new manufacturing sectors. These policies were continued by Betancourt's successors, Presidents Raúl Leoni and Rafael Caldera.

However, by the early 1970s it became obvious that import substitution, as the principal motor force for development, was reaching its conclusion. The Caldera administration was aware of this and began to take steps to seek to develop markets for new export products, particularly the output of some of the same manufacturing enterprises that had been built up during the import-substitution phase.

THE FIRST "OIL CRISIS"

However, Venezuela's economic development prospects were suddenly drastically altered by what for much of the world was the "first oil crisis," and for Venezuela was "the first oil bonanza" of the 1970s. The administration of President Carlos Andrés Pérez, of the Acción Democrática party, came into office right at the beginning of the new oil boom.

The situation faced by the Pérez administration involved both great opportunities and great dangers. The country was suddenly faced with a many fold increase in oil revenues, which was reflected in a similar increase in the income of the Venezuelan government. This presented the Pérez regime with unprecedented opportunities for development of the economy, but at the same time presented the nation, and particularly the Venedemocracia, with dangers it had not had to face before.

At its inception the Pérez administration developed a program for dealing with the situation that seemed adequate to deal with the sudden increase in national and fiscal income. In the face of the clear fact that the Venezuelan economy could not possibly "absorb" the sudden increase in resources provided by the 1973 and 1974 oil boom, the regime sought to "sterilize" some of the increased income, that is, to keep it out of the Venezuelan economy, at least for the time being.

A new ministry, that of foreign investment, was established, with the veteran economist and politician Manuel Pérez Guerrero as its first chief. The function of this ministry was to invest some of the increased oil revenues outside of the country. Large sums were used to purchase foreign government securities—particularly those of the United States. Smaller amounts were used to help finance development banks in neighboring areas through the Central American and Caribbean Development Banks.[1]

As a consequence of the 1974 oil boom, and particularly of its efforts to extend economic help to neighboring countries, the importance of Venezuela in the Caribbean area, and in Latin America in general, suddenly and drastically increased. For a while, at least, it became customary to refer to Venezuela, along with Brazil, as one of the two most powerful countries in Latin America.

President Carlos Andrés Pérez was exactly the person to try to use the new weight that the oil boom had given to Venezuela in hemispheric—and even world—affairs. On various occasions he presented himself as a spokesman for the Third World, in dealings with the industrial countries of North America and Europe. He also traveled widely abroad, seeking to exert as much personal influence as possible. His personal flair and dynamism complemented Venezuela's new economic power, and certainly Venezuela's voice was listened to with much more attention in world politics than had customarily been the case.

President Pérez's efforts to exert world influence did not go without criticism in Venezuela. Ex-President Rómulo Betancourt, who had long been Carlos Andrés Pérez's patron, was particularly critical of Pérez's ''Third World'' associations, preferring to see Venezuela as a member of Latin America, not as a much more widely diverse ''Third World.''

Also, Venezuela's new influence was not without criticism elsewhere in Latin America. The writer remembers a conversation during this period with a Venezuelan leader who had had occasion to travel widely on offical business in Central America and the Caribbean, and who had been both surprised and shocked to have been confronted on several occasions with charges of ''Venezuelan imperialism.''

Some of the new Venezuelan resources were used to help some of the countries of the region that did not have oil to deal with the crisis that their economies faced as a consequence of the sudden drastic increase in petroleum prices. Agreements were reached with a number of Central American and Caribbean countries for Venezuela to finance through loans, on quite favorable terms, these nations' imports of Venezuelan oil.

However, together with these efforts to ''sterilize'' some of the increased oil income, the Pérez administration also launched a very large development program. In the beginning there were two sectors of the economy for which more or less detailed expansion plans were available and to which the government first turned its attention. These were the steel industry and hydroelectricity. A modest steel industry had first been started in the Orinoco Valley area near the end of the Pérez Jiménez dictatorship, and during the first three democratic administrations, it had been brought into full production. By the early 1970s its capacity was about 1 million tons. The Pérez administration undertook a program to expand its production to about 5 million tons.

The expansion of electric production had always been a high priority of the democratic regimes. Under President Leoni the first stage of the Guri dam on a branch of the Orinoco River had been installed. The Pérez administration undertook a program of greatly expanding this project and of launching other hydroelectric installations in other parts of the country.[2]

Subsequently, the Pérez government expanded its efforts into a variety of other fields. Considerable attention was given to irrigation and generally to the modernization of agriculture. Other considerable sums were spent on various projects to modernize, beautify, and "untangle" the capital city, Caracas. Among these last projects was work on the city's first subway line.

OIL NATIONALIZATION

Another major program of the administration of Carlos Andrés Pérez was the nationalization of the oil and iron ore industries, stimulated no doubt by the sudden oil bonanza.

Acción Democrática had from its inception a well defined oil policy. One aspect of that policy was that no new concessions should be given to foreign firms to explore and exploit Venezuelan oil resources. Another was that the ground should be prepared for the ultimate nationalization of the industry when existing concessions expired. A third was that the Venezuelan government should seek to get the most possible revenue for the country from the oil industry during the remainder of the period in which the industry remained largely in the hands of foreign enterprises.

The first Acción Democrática regime of 1945 to 1948 had first established this petroleum policy. However, during the Pérez Jiménez dictatorship of the 1950s, the policy of no new concessions had been abandoned, and substantial new grants had been made, which contributed greatly to an economic euphoria during the middle years of the Pérez Jiménez regime.

With the return of democracy after the overthrow of the dictatorship in 1958, the AD program of the trienio was reestablished. This time, however, it had the support not only of Acción Democrática, but of virtually all of the other parties as well.

President Betancourt took two major steps in fulfillment of the traditional AD petroleum policy, in addition to reasserting the rule that no new concessions should be made to foreign firms. One of these was the establishment of the Venezuelan Petroleum Corporation, which was to be given areas to exploit that the foreign oil firms had had to turn back to the government from the concessions made during the Pérez Jiménez period. The function of the company was to begin to undertake some oil exploration and exploitation and to train people ultimately to take over the whole of the nation's oil industry. During the Leoni administration, the company had been given preference in the sale of oil in the Venezuelan market.

The second major move of the Betancourt administration with regard to the oil industry was its leadership in the establishment of the Organization of Petroleum Exporting Countries (OPEC). The real "father" of OPEC was Juan Pablo Pérez Alfonso, Betancourt's petroleum minister, who negotiated extensively with oil ministers of several Middle Eastern petroleum-producing nations to bring into existence the new organization. The original purpose of OPEC was to try to prevent the large international oil companies from playing off one petroleum-producing country against another and to try to establish base prices of all oil exports. As a matter of fact, almost fifteen years were to pass before it became possible to put into effect this second objective.

At the same time Betancourt rejected during his presidency all suggestions that the petroleum industry be nationalized. His arguments on this score were several: In due time, with expiration of the concessions, the industry would automatically revert to government control; the bargaining position of Venezuela was not strong enough to resist likely retaliatory action by the companies that would be provoked by precipitate nationalization; Venezuela did not yet have the personnel to take charge of the industry effectively; and Venezuela's interests would be better served pending the end of the concessions by getting the most possible out of the industry from the foreign companies. Interestingly enough, no political opponent of AD, not even the Communist party, urged nationalization during this period.

During the Leoni administration, the government lodged charges against the oil companies that they had for some years not been paying the government the amounts provided by law. Although the oil firms reacted strongly against these charges, long negotiations between the government and the companies finally resulted in the oil enterprises making a substantial lump-sum payment to the government.

Most of the existing oil concessions were due to expire in 1983 and 1984. By the advent of the Caldera administration in 1969, Venezuelan political leaders and oil experts had begun to worry about the possible adverse effects on the oil industry when these concessions expired. It was feared that the foreign companies might begin to dismantle some of the existing installations.

As a consequence of these worries, legislation was passed during the Caldera regime to give the government closer control over the oil industry. After much negotiation in Congress, particularly between the AD and COPEI members of that body, this legislation provided that firms could not make any substantial physical changes in the industry without government approval.

During the 1973 election campaign, Carlos Andrés Pérez, the AD candidate, did not openly promise that he would undertake the immediate nationalization of the oil industry, although he did indicate that this might be a possibility. Undoubtedly, both fear of a deterioration of the industry during the remaining years of the concessions and the vast additional resources made available to the government by the oil boom starting in 1974 stimulated Pérez to undertake nationalization soon after taking office.

Some of the most important and interesting debates in Venezuelan congressional history took place in the process of enacting the oil-nationalization legislation. Both ex-President Betancourt and ex-President Caldera, who were lifetime senators but virtually never attended Senate meetings, participated in this debate. Although no significant group opposed the nationalization, there was very serious criticism by COPEI and other parties of one of its provisions. This was the permission that the law gave the new Venezuelan government petroleum holding company and its subsidiaries to sign contracts with the old foreign oil firms for the provision of technical advice and other help. After bitter controversy this part of the law, and the rest of the bill presented by the Pérez administration, was passed.

The law provided that the existing companies would, for the time being, remain in operation but would be taken over by the Venezuelan government. They would be coordinated by a new holding company, Petróleos Venezolanos (PETROVEN), which would have the overall control of the industry. (The nickname of the holding company was soon changed to PDVSA [Petróleos de Venezuela, South America] when it was discovered that a small private company was already using PETROVEN.)

As well as nationalizing the oil industry, the Pérez government also nationalized iron mining, which had also largely been in the hands of foreign enterprises. Thus, it brought under national ownership and control the country's two most important sources of raw materials and exports.

ORGANIZATION OF NATIONALIZED OIL INDUSTRY

Whereas at the beginning of nationalization the government's petroleum holding company had fourteen subsidiaries, reorganization in 1978 brought into existence four companies. These were LAGOVEN, consisting largely of the former Creole Company holdings of Exxon; MARAVEN, based on the previous subsidiary of Shell; MENEVEN, centered on the former Venezuelan holdings of Gulf; and CORPOVEN, involving the government's former Venezuelan Petroleum Corporation and a small former subsidiary of Mobil.[3]

At the time of consolidation of the industry into four basic firms, PDVSA also became the holding company for two other subsidiaries. One was the trouble-plagued Petroquímica Venezolana (PEQUIVEN), the government's petrochemical firm that had been started late in the Pérez Jiménez dictatorship and had become notorious for inefficiency and waste. The other was the Venezuelan Petroleum Technology Institute, which had a particularly important mission of developing the technology for the use of the Orinoco Heavy Oil Belt, the oil sands of the Orinoco area.[4]

In the early years of oil nationalization there was extensive criticism to the effect that the government firms that were the "heirs" of the former international oil companies were still closely tied to those companies by the service contracts that they had negotiated with them. In 1979 the service contracts were renegotiated, and the provisions for technological information imparted by the multinationals to their former Venezuelan affiliates to remain "confidential" were abrogated. Thus, new technology given to any part of PDVSA became accessible to all of the Venezuelan industry.[5]

Further advances toward making the Venezuelan nationalized petroleum industry more independent of its former owners came in connection with research about exploiting the Orinoco oil sands. After negotiating with the Bechtel Corporation of the United States for research and development of those petroleum resources, PDVSA ended up signing an agreement with the West German company VEBA in 1983.[6] In the next administration the PDVSA–VEBA agreement came in for considerable investigation and criticism from Congress.[7]

Independence from its former owners was not the only significant subject of debate concerning the new nationalized oil industry. James Petras and others have been highly critical of the oil nationalization program because it left the "upstream" parts of the industry to private enterprise. They have seen this as a move to leave the potentially more profitable business of elaboration of the subproducts of the oil industry to the large Venezuelan private economic groups, and particularly to the multinations.[8]

Another important question has been the degree to which the industry should be kept out of politics. Certainly in the beginning there was widespread agreement that the PDVSA should not become the subject of partisan political manipulation and patronage. To this end, President Carlos Andés Pérez named as first head of the nationalzied oil industry General Alfonzo Ravard, who had served for more than a decade as organizer and chief of the Corporación Venezolana de Guayana (CVG), the agency established by President Rómulo Betancourt for the regional development of the Guayana area. He had wide fame as a "no nonsense" administrator who kept at arms length all politicians trying to "interfere" with the work of the CVG.

Ravard remained head of the PDVSA until August 1983. During the last years of his administration, he and the PDVSA were subject to considerable criticism, particularly from the "enfant terrible" of the Herrera Campins administration, Central Bank President Leopoldo Díaz Bruzual, who charged that the oil industry was overstaffed and overpaid, claims that General Ravard rejected.

There was also growing demand that the oil industry become more "integrated" with the rest of Venezuela's economy and polity. Important steps in this direction were undoubtedly taken in the early 1980s. The ex-Shell affiliate of PDVSA, MARAVEN, agreed to help finance a program for urban redevelopment of the eastern shore of Lake Maracaibo. In 1982 the accumulated reserves of the PDVSA, amounting to about 8 billion dollars and until then under its control, were transferred to the control of the Central Bank.[9]

What many people saw as a step toward politicization of the oil industry was the replacement of General Ravard as head of PDVSA in August 1983 by President Herrera Campins's energy minister, Humberto Calderon Berti, a leading figure in the COPEI party.[10] One of the first acts of President Jaime Lusinchi was to remove Calderon Berti.[11]

Whatever the future trends of the Venezuelan nationalized oil industry may be, Professor David Blank has concluded that in its first years it had "been accountable to both the government and the nation." He added that

Between 1976 and 1982, PDVSA taxes paid to the nation's treasury more than doubled. Revenue from oil sales rose despite the need to reduce production to dry up the oil glut.

PDVSA's after-taxes profit in 1981 was $3.1 billion. Part of the 1980 and 1981 profit was from interest earned from its vast reserves and investment funds. More importantly, the nation's proven reserves in crude oil increased by 12 percent after many years of decline. Natural gas reserves increased by 35 percent, and new light oil was discovered.[12]

NEGATIVE ASPECTS OF THE FIRST OIL BONANZA OF THE 1970s

The effects of the first oil boom of the 1970s were not all positive. There were at least four negative elements of some significance that began during the Carlos Andrés Pérez period and were intensified subsequently: inflation, corruption, waste, and foreign indebtedness.

During the 1970s, Venezuela began to suffer for the first time from serious inflation. Although prices had long been high in Venezuela in comparison with neighboring countries, the country had not until the 1970s been faced with a serious problem of rapidly rising prices.

This phenomenon had several causes. One was the fact that in spite of its efforts to do so, the Pérez administration had by no means been able to "sterilize" its new oil income sufficiently to prevent the very rapid growth in purchasing power within the country, which was by no means entirely met by increased domestic production.

One way the government sought to restrain inflation was to allow importation of very substantial amounts of goods. But because there was serious world inflation during this period, to some extent at least increased imports of goods meant simultaneous import of rising prices. The opening of the gates to large amounts of foreign goods was also criticized by some as endangering the country's own industries, which in many cases were discouraged from trying to increase output to meet the new demand.

Another serious effect of the oil boom was the increase in corruption. This had been a growing problem for some years, but there is no doubt about the fact that it was greatly intensified during the Pérez administration.

President Rómulo Betancourt had been absolutely puritanical on the subject of corruption. He insisted on absolute honesty among the high officials of his administration and, insofar as possible, among those working under these high officials, a policy continued by President Raúl Leoni.

One first began to hear complaints about the spread of corruption during the administration of President Rafael Caldera. There is no indication that people high up in that government were involved in corrupt practices, but there was a general acceptance of the fact that in the lower ranks of the administration corruption was indeed spreading.

There can be no question about the fact that corruption grew apace during the Pérez administration. In the following period ex-President Pérez himself was accused of having been involved in at least one incident, and although he was not found guilty by a congressional investigating committee, enough evidence was brought out to indicate that there had been some very shady dealings within the higher reaches of the Pérez government.

Ex-President Rómulo Betancourt was one of the most open critics of the corruption that he felt to be rife in the Pérez government. He strongly supported Luis Piñerúa as Acción Democrática candidate in the 1978 election, because Piñerúa promised that his first effort as president would be to clear out the corruption that he argued was then present in national politics. Both Betancourt and Piñerúa argued that continuation and intensification of corruption might well undermine the Venedemocracia.

The very affluent state of affairs that prevailed during the Pérez administration tended also to generate inefficiency in many government programs. With very large resources available, high priority was not placed on getting the most return for the least expenditure. Ex-Minister Juan Pablo Pérez Alfonso was one of the most acerbic critics of this aspect of affairs during the 1970s, writing articles and even books to lament it.

One clear case of inefficient use of resources was the national steel plant. Although plans at the beginning of the Pérez regime called for expansion of output capacity to 5 million tons, actual production by 1982 was only 2,296,000 metric tons.[13]

Finally, paradoxically enough, foreign indebtedness began to climb rapidly during the Pérez administration. In part, this reflected certain longer-run trends, but in large part, too, it was a function of the oil prosperity of the 1970s.

Nearly fifty years before, during the dictatorship of Juan Vicente Gómez, the tyrant had used part of the vastly increased government revenues resulting from the beginning of large-scale oil exploitation in the 1920s and early 1930s to pay off the foreign debt. For a generation thereafter, it became almost a point of honor for governments of Venezuela not to incur any foreign debt.

This began to break down during the dictatorship of Pérez Jiménez in the 1950s. Although the Pérez Jiménez regime accumulated little if any bonded indebtedness in foreign currencies, that government did build up a great deal of short-term debt arising from huge public-works programs, the bills for which were left unpaid. Evidences of this debt were sold abroad, particularly in New York, and after the fall of Pérez Jiménez, the holders of that paper descended on the provisional government of Admiral Wolfgang Larrazábal, demanding immediate payment. The Larrazábal government, instead of converting these debts into longer-term bonds, hastened to pay them off, draining the country's foreign reserves and helping to generate a recession that continued through the first two and a half years of the Betancourt government.

The democratic administrations of Betancourt and his immediate successors borrowed modestly from abroad for specific development projects. For the most part, these loans came from foreign governmental or intergovernmental lending institutions.

The situation then began to change under Carlos Andrés Pérez. Projecting the vastly increased foreign-exchange income of the 1970s more or less indefinitely into the future, the Pérez government concluded that Venezuela would have little difficulty in meeting payments on whatever foreign debts it might undertake.

The debts that began to be incurred during the Pérez administration differed from those accumulated by its immediate predecessors in at least two respects. For the most part, they arose from commercial transactions rather than from financing of specific development projects. In addition, as was true elsewhere in Latin America in the same period, they were largely debts to private foreign banks rather than to the governmental and intergovernmental institutions, such as the World Bank, Inter-American Bank, or the Export-Import Bank.

THE COLLAPSE OF THE OIL BOOM AND THE HERRERA CAMPINS ADMINISTRATION

Luis Herrera Campins, the COPEI-party candidate who won the 1978 election, came to power at almost the exact time that the second international oil crisis occurred as a consequence of the Iranian Revolution of 1979. However, before Herrera Campins was half way through his administration, the world petroleum situation had been drastically reversed. General overproduction, in addition to reduced demand resulting from the 1981 and 1982 world recession and widespread conservation efforts, provoked serious reductions in petroleum prices, with consequent impact on the economies of the oil-exporting countries, including Venezuela.

President Luis Herrera Campins was unable to deal adequately with the situation with which he was confronted. Soon after taking office, he announced that the economic policy of his administration would seek to control "runaway spending," reduce the balance-of-payments deficit and maintain the value of the bolívar, and ease the price controls that had been instituted by the Pérez government,[14] but he failed to accomplish even the rudiments of this program. The negative aspects of the situation, which had been obtained in the middle 1970s and which we have noted, were intensified. By the end of the Herrera Campins period the situation was assuming crisis proportions.

On the one hand, inflation, which had begun to become serious during the Pérez period, was markedly augmented. On the basis of 1970 as 100, the index number for the general price level had risen from 119.7 in 1974, the first year of the Pérez administration, to 153.0 in 1978, the last year Carlos Andrés Pérez was in office. It then rose from 184.2 in Herrera Campins's first year to 303 in 1983, the last full year of the Herrera period.[15]

At the same time unemployment became a major problem, which it had not been in Venezuela for many years. During the last year of the Carlos Andrés Pérez administration, 1978, the unemployed had amounted to only 4.6 percent of the workforce. But by the last year of the Herrera Campins period, the proportion had more than doubled, reaching 9.8 percent, according to official figures.[16]

Corruption also considerably intensified during the Herrera Campins administration. This was underscored by the fact that during the early months of the following presidential period, Congress and the administration opened official investigations of a wide range of ministries (for example, the ministry of defense) and government-owned enterprises, including the country's international airline, Venezolana Internacional de Aviación, South America (VIASA); the sewer and water company, Instituto Nacional de Sanitarias Obras (INOS); the construction and urban development firm in Caracas, Centro Simón Bolívar; and the domestic airline Aeropostal. Three exministers of defense of Herrera Campins were among those implicated. This series of potential scandals provoked a protest about the corruption that had characterized the Herrera Campins government by ex-President Rafael Caldera, himself a COPEI party leader and the party's candidate in the 1983 election (but admittedly no great admirer of Luis Herrera Campins).[17]

Foreign borrowing also vastly augmented during the Herrera Campins period. President Herrera had announced a few months after taking office that the external debt when he was inaugurated stood at 12.2 billion dollars, or 4.5 billion dollars more than President Carlos Andrés Pérez had claimed it to be.[18] However, by the time Herrera Campins left office, the foreign debt owed by the Venezuelan government and government banks and other enterprises was officially estimated at 27 billion dollars.[19] At the same time, foreign debts owed by the private sector of the Venezuelan economy were said to be about 6 billion dollars.[20] By mid-1985 the total foreign debt of Venezuela was estimated to be about 35 billion dollars.[21]

The Herrera Campins government did not begin to take serious steps to deal with the economic situation, and particularly the foreign debt problem, until about a year before it was scheduled to go out of office. In February 1983 it established a three-tier foreign-exchange-rate system. This was reported as having the impact of effectively devaluing the bolívar (in terms of dollars) by about 78 percent.[22]

This move was followed in May 1983 by an approach to the International Monetary Fund (IMF), to seek help to meet 13 billion dollars in payments soon coming due.[23] However, later in the year President Herrera decided to leave the question of whether to complete negotiations with the IMF up to his successor. Meanwhile, starting in June 1983, the Venezuela government, with the acquiescence of the creditor banks, declared a ninety-day moratorium on repayment of the principal of the national foreign debt.[24] This moratorium was, thereafter, extended each time that it expired.

Overall, the economic policies of the Herrera Campins administration were characterized by confusion. In part, this was undoubtedly due to the role of Leopoldo Díaz Bruzual, president of the Central Bank, whose imperious manner and frequent quarrels with other members of the president's ''economic team'' contributed to the instability of the administration's policy.

The economic and other difficulties of the Herrera Campins administration threatened to become serious enough to endanger the future of the COPEI party and perhaps even the Venezuelan democratic system itself. They intensified factional fighting within the COPEI party. Ex-President Rafael Caldera, who had for long not been a supporter of Luis Herrera Campins within the party, professed to see the need in the 1983 election for him to run again as his party's nominee in order to help retrieve COPEI from the discredit into which he claimed the errors and incompetence of the Herrera Campins government had driven it.[25] In any case, Caldera and COPEI were soundly defeated by Acción Democrática's candidate, Jaime Lusinchi, who became president early in 1984.

THE ECONOMIC POLICIES OF THE LUSINCHI GOVERNMENT

Upon taking office, President Jaime Lusinchi promised to try to come to grips with the economic problems that Venezuela faced. Three weeks later, he announced the details of his immediate economic program. These included a further devaluation of the bolívar, a substantial reduction of general interest rates, and large increases in the price of gasoline sold in Venezuela (thus reducing the subsidy to gasoline users). The Lusinchi program also included continued price controls on those goods that were imported at preferential exchange rates.

Elements of Lusinchi's program that touched the workers aroused some opposition within the labor movement. These included temporary freezing of wage increases, except for those workers receiving the very lowest incomes. However, they also provided that companies with more than ten workers would within six months have to employ 10 percent more workers (in an attempt to deal on an emergency basis with the serious unemployment problem). They also provided that companies would have to distribute 20 percent of their earnings to workers, while managers' earnings would be reduced by 50 percent.[26] In May 1985 President Lusinchi instituted unemployment insurance for the first time, in conformity with a provision of the 1970 social-security law, which had never been put into force.[27] He also returned the Banco de Trabajadores de Venezuela, which had been "intervened" by the Herrera Campins administration when it was threatened with bankruptcy, to the Confederation of Workers of Venezuela and provided that it could again undertake its normal banking activities.[28]

In November 1984 the government liberated all prices from government control except those of basic foods, rent, and education.[29]

In dealing with the problem of the foreign debt, President Lusinchi refused to involve the International Monetary Fund in the situation, dealing directly with the foreign creditor banks instead. In August 1985 Venezuela was reported as being "close to signing a restructuring" of its debt, which "should give it a tolerable debt burden even if oil prices fall slightly."[30]

In his year-end message to the nation, President Lusinchi claimed that 1984 had been a year of "adjustment" and predicted that for the first time in five years the Venezuelan national economy would expand in 1985.[31] He clearly hoped that the private sector would respond favorably to his administration's policies and that new government expenditures for helping to expand the economy would once more become available once the foreign-debt issue had been settled. By the end of 1984 unemployment was officially 13.4 percent and cost-of-living increases were reported having been between 11 and 12 percent in 1984.[32]

OVERALL ECONOMIC AND SOCIAL DEVELOPMENT UNDER VENEDEMOCRACIA

Before turning to the question of the relationship of economic factors to the fate of the Venedemocracia during the rest of the twentieth century, it may be worthwhile to look in somewhat general terms at the nature and extent of the economic and social developments in the six administrations that have held office in democratic Venezuela since 1959. There has undoubtedly been very considerable achievement in both economic and social terms; we shall concentrate particularly on the period since 1970.

In the broadest of economic terms, there has been a marked increase during this period in the Venezuelan gross domestic product. It has grown from 52.3 billion bolívares in 1970 to 291 billion in 1981.[33] Although the advance has been important in all parts of the economy, it is in the manufacturing sector (aside from oil) that most notable economic progress has been made. The index of industrial production rose from 78 in 1970 to 213 in 1982.[34]

In several subsectors of the manufacturing area the increase in output has been particularly striking. Steel production between 1970 and 1982 considerably more than doubled, rising from 927,000 metric tons to 2,296,000 metric tons. At the same time pig-iron and ferro-alloys output rose from 510,000 metric tons in 1970 to 2,440,000 in 1982.[35] Another heavy industry area, aluminum, has shown even more striking growth, rising from 22,700 metric tons in 1970 to 244,000 metric tons in 1982.[36] Cement output has risen somewhat more modestly, going up from 2,318,000 metric tons in 1970 to 5,594,000 in 1982.[37]

Professor David Blank has particularly noted the growth of the automobile industry. A program drawn up by the planning agency Cordiplan in the early 1960s called for the assembly of 70,000 cars a year by 1970, 60 percent of the net weight of each car consisting of parts made in Venezuela. The program was not fulfilled, and the quality of the Venezuelan-produced vehicles left a good deal to be desired. However, a new program developed after Venezuelan adherence to the Andean Pact provided for use of parts coming from other member states of the Pact, and for "hybridization," that is, the use of parts in an assembled car coming from several different manufacturing firms. Under this project Venezuela was producing 182,000 vehicles by 1981, and 75 percent of the components were "local content."

Professor Blank has commented that "While some Venezuelans continue to fear the influence of the transnationals in the industry, suggesting that industrialization has only reproduced dependency, this writer believes that the creation of a viable auto industry, producing close to 200,000 vehicles a year, in 20 years has been a remarkable achievement."[38] I agree with Professor Blank.

The record of production in agriculture is considerably more spotty than that of manufacturing. Overall, cereals production rose from an average of 907,000 metric tons in the 1974 to 1976 period to 1,509,000 metric tons in 1982.[39] However, within this category, sugar production actually fell, from 455,000 metric tons to 382,000 between 1970 and 1982.[40] Corn output also did not do very well, falling from a 1974 to 1976 average of 541,000 metric tons to only 501,000 metric tons in 1982.[41] On the other hand, rice production rose from a 1974 to 1976 average of 289,000 metric tons to a 1982 output of 670,000 metric tons.[42] These figures on balance confirm the judgement that renewed efforts and resources are required for agricultural development.

Social statistics indicate considerable progress in the period of the Venedemocracia with which we are particularly concerned. For instance, in terms of daily food intake, the per capita consumption of calories rose between the 1966 to 1968 period and the 1978 to 1980 period from 2,316 to 2,649. Similarly, the daily consumption of proteins per capita between those same two periods rose from 589 decigrams to 708 decigrams.[43]

Venezuela had come to be relatively well provided for in terms of medical facilities and personnel. By 1978 there were 444 hospital establishments with 41,386 beds. At the same time there were 14,771 medical doctors practicing in the country, and the population per doctor was 888.[44] These figures compare well with most other Latin American countries.

Educational facilities, personnel, and students had also increased substantially during the period under scrutiny. The number of primary schools had risen from 10,509 in 1970 to 12,781 in 1981, and the number of primary school teachers had risen from 50,822 to 97,045 in the same period. The number of students in primary schools had grown from 1,769,680 to 2,591,051.[45]

On the secondary school level the number of students had grown between 1970 and 1981 from 425,146 to 884,233.[46] At the same time the number of teachers on the tertiary school level had jumped from 8,155 to 28,052, and the number of students from 100,767 to 307,133.[47]

Finally, we may note that educational expenditure as a percentage of the gross national product (GNP) had grown significantly during the 1970 to 1981 period, in spite of the very large increase in the GNP during those years. Whereas 4.7 percent of the GNP was spent on education in 1970, the figure was 5.8 percent by 1981.[48]

THE ECONOMY AND THE VENEDEMOCRACIA UNTIL THE YEAR 2000

Clearly, Venezuela's ability to continue to be one of the democratically ruled countries of Latin America through the end of this century will depend to a very considerable degree on what happens to the national economy. In this regard there is substantial ground for sober optimism.

Petroleum will certainly continue to be a major contributor to the national income of Venezuela, to the well-being of its citizens, and to the stability of its governmental structure. However, there are certain complications in this area. The traditional relatively light oils that Venezuela produced are thought to be approaching exhaustion, although new (if limited) life has been given to some of the Lake Maracaibo fields by new technologies of "tertiary" recovery. Also there is at least some hope of finding new sources of lighter oils off shore—a problem complicated by Venezuelan–Colombian border disputes involving some of the areas involved.

But the experts do seem to agree that the longer-range future for Venezuela's petroleum industry is to be found in the heavier oil sands in the Orinoco Valley area. Here, too, there are certain complications, since to make these both accessible and competitive, the development and application of new technologies are still required. As we have noted, steps were taken after nationalization of the industry to foment and acquire those new technologies.

Certain factors outside of Venezuela's control will undoubtedly be very influential in determining the ability of the country to continue to rely heavily on the petroleum industry. One of these, of course, is what happens to the oil industry elsewhere. If new events like the 1979 Revolution in Iran were to occur in one or more of the Middle Eastern oil-producing countries, that might well provoke another world "oil crisis" and give Venezuela the opportunity to obtain much larger revenues even from diminishing oil output. Such occurrences might also give new impetus in oil-consuming countries to help to solve the technological problems of "heavy oil," and to help in financing its exploitation.

In an opposite direction, developments in the United States might conceivably work against Venezuela's oil industry. Were the United States to undertake a serious program to develop its own alternative sources of energy, including oil sands, liquified coal, industrial alcohol, and a variety of others, that might well militate against continued large U.S. demand for Venezuelan oil, for which the United States remains the major market. On the other hand, the Reagan administration has shown what amounts to an utter lack of interest in such possibilities, and it would be foolish to speculate on what the attitude and policies of a successor administration might be.

Venezuela began in the 1970s to seek alternative markets for its oil in Europe and in Latin America. It can be expected that barring unforeseen circumstances, this search will continue with considerable success.

In any case, it seems likely that for the rest of the century Venezuela will remain an important source of petroleum for the United States. Its convenience as a supplier of the East Coast of the United States and Canada, together with the continuing uncertainties of supplies from the Middle East, would seem to confirm this.

It appears dangerous, however, for Venezuela to continue to be as dependent as it has been on petroleum for the last six decades. It is to be hoped that the governments of the rest of the century will return to the process that was just beginning at the end of the Caldera administration but that then was short-circuited by the oil booms of the 1970s, of seeking to develop "new exports." These can include not only some of the products of the manufacturing sector, for which it has at least some advantages, particularly through its association with the Andean Common Market, but also even some products of the land.

Certainly, future democratic governments will want to make a special effort to reduce Venezuela's dependence on outside sources of food. Partly, this growing dependence has been due to greatly increased demands for comestibles resulting from rising incomes—a process that should slow down, if real incomes continue to rise substantially, resulting in a smaller percentage of each increase in income being spent on food. But also it has been due to fumbling policies by recent administrations.

President Lusinchi announced soon after taking office that he would pay special attention to stimulating the expansion of agriculture through particularly favorable interest rates from the Central Bank for agricultural activities.[49] However, undoubtedly much more than that will be required.

Among other observers, David Blank has pointed out that part of the country's agricultural problem is due to the degeneration of the agrarian reform program, which started out so hopefully under the first two presidents of the Venedemocracia. Thereafter, resources for the land-distribution program and financial aid for the beneficiaries of the agrarian reform were drastically cut back, and successive administrations seemed to give it very low priority. President Carlos Andrés Pérez, in particular, according to Professor Blank, quite clearly favored large-scale commercial farming interests over the agrarian reform.

Clearly, several issues are involved in this problem. One concerns agricultural efficiency. In some cases choices may have to be made between less efficient small holdings resulting from agrarian reform and more productive larger rural enterprises—if in fact, they are really more efficient, something that will by no means be clear until peasant farmers have available to them the credit, technical assistance, and other inputs that might make them more efficient agriculturalists, something that in recent years most of them have clearly not had.

On the other hand, the concept of "efficiency" is itself subject to various possible interpretations. It is questionable whether it is really "efficient" for the economy as a whole to have small farmers—agrarian reform beneficiaries and others—give up all efforts to cultivate the land, because of lack of support from official sources, and move to the cities where their usefulness to the output of the economy may quite possibly be very marginal.

In any case it is clear that it will be advisable—in the interest of the soundness of the national economy and of the continuation of the Venedemocracia—for the administrations of the rest of this century to put much larger resources into the development, extension, and improvement of agriculture than has been done in the recent past. Social and political considerations should be of as much importance in determining the nature of such agricultural programs as formal "economic" questions.

The internal market for both agricultural and manufactured products will certainly continue to increase during the rest of the century. The official figures for 1982 gave Venezuela a population of 14,516,735 and showed a relatively rapid population increase rate of 3 percent a year.[50] In fact, both the total population and the rate of increase were probably somewhat more than that, since one of the phenomena of recent years has been an influx of illegal immigrants from neighboring countries, particularly Colombia, a problem that has worried some Venezuelan politicians but about which no effective action has been taken.

Immigration from Colombia is probably one cause of the beginning of what may in the next few years become a serious socioeconomic problem. This is the spread of the drug culture. Attention began to be centered on this problem early in 1984. It was estimated at that time that the value of drug sales in Venezuela in the previous year might have been as high as 3.2 billion dollars.[51] At that point most of the drugs were apparently imported, mainly from the thriving Colombian cocaine business. However, there were also some reports of the beginning of large-scale marijuana cultivation in Venezuela itself. Certainly, one possible source of danger for the future of the Venezuelan economy and polity may well be the spread to that country of the illegal drug business, which has caused so much havoc with its neighbor in recent years.

Another socioeconomic danger to Venezuela that might imperil the Venedemocracia if it is not substantially curbed is corruption. As we have indicated, it grew very considerably during the 1970s and early 1980s, partly as a reflection of the oil bonanza of much of that period. The somewhat more Spartan atmosphere resulting from the end (for the time being at least) of that boom may help to limit corruption. Also, the Lusinchi government has given some indications, as we have noted, of a serious intention to curb the vices of bribery and misuse of public funds. However, it will behoove the political leaders of all democratic parties to take most seriously the problem of corruption, which the major founder of the Venedemocracia, Rómulo Betancourt, warned over and over again might well bring an end to Venezuela's experience with democracy.

CONCLUSION

Venezuela's good fortune in possessing and exploiting one of the world's great sources of petroleum is frequently offered as the explanation for the country's success in establishing and maintaining a political democracy in the quarter of a century following the overthrow of General Marcos Pérez Jiménez in January 1958. Surely, this is a simple-minded argument. The political genius of Rómulo Betancourt, the existence of two well organized major parties, and the ability of the Venedemocracia to make good to a considerable degree on its promises to people of virtually all classes are other major causes of the continuation of a democratic regime in spite of Venezuela's previous dismal history in that regard.

However, it is clear that the exploitation of the nation's oil wealth has provided Venezuela's political leaders of the last quarter of a century or more with resources for developing other parts of the economy, extending the social infrastructure of schools, health facilities, and (to a much lesser degree) housing than would otherwise be the case. However, as we have indicated in this chapter, the vast income from oil has also provided temptations for misuse and even illegitimate use of some of these resources.

Also, the instability of an economy depending as heavily as does that of Venezuela on a single product, petroleum, has presented very serious problems for the country's democratic leaders. The depression that characterized the oil industry and the whole Venezuelan economy during the early 1960s (with which we have not dealt extensively here) was a major challenge to the first president of the Venedemocracia, Rómulo Betancourt. Juan Pablo Pérez Alfonso, Betancourt's petroleum minister, always argued that it was a blessing in disguise, forcing the government to concentrate on the development of other aspects of the Venezuelan economy.

In the period that we have covered in this chapter, it is obvious that the oil industry has presented the Venezuelan democratic leaders with both opportunities and major problems. The boom of the 1970s gave them resources for economic and social development such as had never been dreamed of before. But at the same time it encouraged waste and misuse of those same resources, as we have documented. The sudden collapse of the oil boom in the early 1980s forced on the country's political leaders a challenge to reassess their policies and reorient the whole program of economic and social development. The continuation of the Venedemocracia for the rest of the twentieth century will to a large degree depend on how they meet this challenge.

NOTES

1. Interview with Gumersindo Rodríguez, head of Cordiplan, Caracas, July 31, 1974.
2. Ibid.
3. David Blank, *Venezuela: Politics in a Petroleum Republic* (New York: Praeger, 1984), pp. 157–58.
4. Ibid., pp. 158–59.
5. Ibid., p. 207.
6. Ibid., p. 160.
7. "Caldera Defends the VEBA Contract," *Latin America Weekly Report*, London, August 3, 1984, p. 8.
8. James Petras, Morris Morely, and Steven Smith, *The Nationalization of Venezuelan Oil* (New York: Praeger Special Studies, 1977).
9. Blank, *Venezuela*, p. 173.
10. Ibid., p. 210.
11. *The New York Times*, February 8, 1984, Section 4, p. 2.
12. Blank, *Venezuela*, p. 171.
13. *1982 Statistical Yearbook* (New York: Department of International Economic and Social Affairs, Statistical Office, United Nations, 1985), p. 705. (Hereafter referred to as *UN 1982 Statistical Yearbook*.)
14. *The New York Times*, May 28, 1979, Section 4, p. 4.

15. *1984 Year Book of Labour Statistics* (Geneva: International Labour Office, 1984), p. 726.

16. Ibid., p. 452.

17. "Lusinchi Presents His Package" and "COPEI Scare as Caldera Attacks," *Latin America Weekly Report*, London, March 9, 1984, p. 9, and June 8, 1984, p. 4.

18. *The New York Times*, October 8, 1979, Section 4, p. 3.

19. D. F. Maza Zavala, "La Quincena Económica," *El Nacional*, Caracas, August 17, 1984.

20. Article by Agustín Browes, *El Nacional*, Caracas, August 17, 1984.

21. *Wall Street Journal*, August 1, 1985.

22. *The New York Times*, March 1, 1983, Section 4, p. 15, and *The New York Times*, March 20, 1983, p. 18.

23. *The New York Times*, May 14, 1983, Section 4, p. 2.

24. *The New York Times*, June 14, 1983, Section 4, p. 11.

25. Interview with Rafael Caldera, Caracas, February 3, 1984.

26. "Lusinchi Presents His Package," *Latin America Weekly Report*, London, March 2, 1984, p. 8.

27. "Unemployment Pay Is Introduced," *Latin America Weekly Report*, May 24, 1985.

28. "The CTV Gets Back Its Bank," *Latin America Weekly Report*, June 7, 1985, p. 9.

29. "Social Peace Fears," *Latin America Weekly Report*, January 18, 1985, pp. 6–7.

30. *Wall Street Journal*, August 1, 1985.

31. *The New York Times*, January 1, 1985, pp. 1 and 38.

32. "Social Peace Fears," *Latin America Weekly Report*, London, January 18, 1985, pp. 6–7.

33. *UN 1982 Statistical Yearbook*, p. 108.

34. Ibid., p. 583.

35. Ibid., p. 705.

36. Ibid., p. 707.

37. Ibid., p. 704.

38. Blank, *Venezuela*, p. 184.

39. *UN 1982 Statistical Yearbook*, p. 707.

40. Ibid., p. 658.

41. Ibid., p. 514.

42. Ibid., p. 508.

43. Ibid., p. 568.

44. Ibid., p. 335.

45. Ibid., p. 359.

46. Ibid., p. 380.

47. Ibid., p. 403.

48. *1984 Statistical Yearbook of UNESCO* (Paris: UNESCO, 1984), Section 4, p. 12.

49. *The New York Times*, February 27, 1984, Section 4, p. 4.

50. *UN 1982 Statistical Yearbook*, p. 71.

51. *Latin America Weekly Report*, London, February 3, 1984, pp. 4–5.

10

Public Opinion About Military Coups and Democratic Consolidation in Venezuela

Enrique A. Baloyra

MILITARY COUPS IN VENEZUELA

Gene Bigler recently called our attention to three important facts: (1) between 1811 and 1900 Venezuelan politics turned violent about one third of the time; (2) from 1900 through 1958 military-dominated governments ruled the country for all but one year; and (3) between 1957 and 1963 about a dozen serious barracks revolts resulted in thousands of deaths.[1]

Is acceptance of military interventionism a deeply ingrained feature of Venezuelan politics? What does the Venezuelan public really think about military interventionism today? Under what circumstances would Venezuelans support a coup d'etat?

In 1973 about 50 percent of a national sample that I took of Venezuelan voters believed that there are circumstances in which military coups are justified.[2] An additional 10 percent gave a conditional response that may be interpreted as a qualified yes, and only one third of my respondents rejected coups outright. In 1983 about 53 percent of the respondents in a similar national sample said that they could think of circumstances that justified coups, while an additional 5 percent hedged a conditional response.[3] Once again, about only one third opposed interventionism outright (see Table 10.1). Given these findings, one may imagine that a substantial majority of Venezuelans somehow endorse the idea of military

The author gratefully acknowledges the support of the National Science Foundation (grants SOC7517518, GS38050, and SES8313940), which made possible the collection of the data reported in this chapter.

This is a revised and expanded version of a paper delivered at the annual meeting of the Latin American Studies Association, Pittsburgh, Pennsylvania, April 5–7, 1979.

Table 10.1
Venezuelan Opinions About Interventionism: 1973

Question 1. "Let us move to a somewhat different topic, that of military coups. Do you think, in general, that there are occasions in which military coups are justifiable or not?

	Absolute Frequency	Relative Frequency	Adjusted Frequency
No	482	31.7	34.5
Depends	150	9.9	10.7
Yes	766	50.4	54.8
Refused	9	.6	
Do not know	114	7.5	

Question 2. "Recently, the president of the Republic of Chile, Dr. Salvador Allende, was overthrown by a military coup. Are you aware of this event? (If yes), do you think this was a necessary or an unnecessary measure on the part of the Chilean armed forces?"

	Absolute Frequency	Relative Frequency	Adjusted Frequency
Unaware	209	13.7	
Refused	3	.2	
Do not know	257	16.9	
Unnecessary	645	42.4	61.3
Depends	70	4.6	6.7
Necessary	337	22.2	32.0

Question 3. "Using as an example the case of Venezuela, on November of 1948 President Rómulo Gallegos of Acción Democrática was overthrown by a military coup. Do you recall or are you familiar with this event? (If yes), do you believe that that military coup was justifiable?"

	Absolute Frequency	Relative Frequency	Adjusted Frequency
Unaware	715	47.0	
Refused	7	.5	
Do not know	196	12.9	
Unjustified	457	30.0	75.8
Depends	30	2.0	5.0
Justified	116	7.6	19.2

Table 10.1
Venezuelan Opinions About Interventionism: 1973 (*continued*)

Question 4. "And what do you think of the military coup of January 23, 1958, that overthrew General Pérez Jiménez? Do you believe that the coup was necessary?"

	Absolute Frequency	Relative Frequency	Adjusted Frequency
No	285	18.7	22.3
Depends	64	4.2	5.0
Yes	929	61.1	72.7
Refused	6	.4	
Do not know	237	15.6	

Question 5. "In order to complete this aspect, would you tell me which of the following statements expresses your thinking about the role that the armed forces should best play in the nation's life. That is to say, which of these statements do you agree with most?"

The armed forces should...	Absolute Frequency	Relative Frequency	Adjusted Frequency
...always respect constitutional regimes[a]	466	30.6	32.0
...act in politics only when they think that the Constitution is not being enforced[b]	280	18.4	19.0
...support the popular will when people's aspirations are not being met by the regime[c]	532	35.0	36.5
...intervene whenever they deem it necessary[d]	180	11.8	12.3
Refused	14	.9	
Do not know	49	3.2	

Source: VENEVOTE, June 15, 1978, pp. 113-17.

[a]Civic role.

[b]Constitutionalist role.

[c]Populist role.

[d]Hegemonic role.

interventionism and that the contemporary Venezuelan democratic regime remains vulnerable on this score.

In reality these findings conceal a diverse spectrum of opinion that has more to do with Venezuelan political experience than with a high level of support for coups. In 1973 I asked the study participants to complete a statement with one of four choices, each one reflecting a different type of political role that the military may play.The political roles included were the civic, the constitutionalist, populist, and hegemonic roles. I borrowed the statement and choices from a landmark study of elite attitudes (VENELITE) conducted in the early 1960s by a team of researchers from the Centro de Estudios del Desarrollo (CENDES) and the Massachusetts Institute of Technology (See question 5, Table 10.1.)

The civic alternative was endorsed by about one third of the respondents—a result consistent with the proportion of the public that cannot justify interventionism. They agreed with the proposition that "the armed forces should always respect constitutional regimes." The second or constitutionalist alternative proffered a role that entrusted the military with interpreting when the Constitution is being violated. This second option would conceivably sanction coups against dictatorships, as in January 1958 in Venezuela, as well as against duly elected governments declared "unconstitutional," as in Chile in September 1973. Close to 20 percent of the respondents chose this alternative.

The third alternative may have been designed to measure the degree of support for the "leftist" military insurrections of the early 1960s in Venezuela. I am referring here to the May 1962 revolt staged by marines at their Carúpano barracks and to the naval uprising of June 1962 in Puerto Cabello.[4] The aims of the protagonists of these revolts were, as is frequently the case, unfocused. The Acción Democrática (AD) government presented them as irresponsible elements.[5] It is doubtful that even the most attentive segment of the public understood their motives. The leaders of these insurrections had explored a strategy of collaboration with leftist parties.[6] In retrospective accounts they have identified their goals as similar to those pursued by the Peruvian military after 1968.[7]

In view of the foregoing I would not pretend that my respondents related this third alternative to those movements nor that they established a connection between the failed Venezuelan *porteñazo* (uprising at Puerto Cabello) and the Peruvian military experiment. This is simply the alternative that comes closest to military movements linked albeit vaguely to the "popular insurrections" attempted by the Venezuelan left in the early 1960s.[8] Approximately 35 percent of my respondents chose this alternative in 1973.

The final alternative proffered the most blatant and open-ended form of interventionism, giving the armed forces carte blanche to intervene "whenever necessary." This was the hegemonic option endorsed by only 12 percent of the public.

Analysis of the patterns of opinion about specific coups unveils a more complex picture. For example, opinion about the two most recent successful coups in Venezuela includes strong condemnation of the 1948 coup and wide agreement on the necessity of the 1958 coup. In 1973 a majority of the 30 percent of respondents who had an opinion about the 1948 coup believed that this had been unjustified; only 7.6 percent approved (see question 3, Table 10.1). By contrast, the insurrection of January 23, 1958, is evoked as the act that restored democracy to Venezuela.[9] In 1973 this event was still very fresh in the consciousness of the Venezuelan electorate, 60 percent of which considered that it had been necessary.[10] The figure increases to 73 percent if nonrespondents are excluded (see question 4, Table 10.1).

In essence, then, of the two coups on which I measured opinion, one seems to be regarded as very legitimate, having made possible a democratic transition in Venezuela during 1958 and 1959. The other coup appears to be a more distant event recalled by fewer people and supported by a very small number. By contrast the Chilean coup of September 1973 was very divisive among Venezuelans. Although opponents of the coup outnumbered supporters by a two-to-one margin, roughly 42 to 22 percent, the proportion of supporters was not insubstantial, and there was a sizeable 30 percent of "undecideds."

This first approximation to the data suggests that only about one third of the Venezuelan public are opposed to all forms of interventionism, and the rest would be prepared to support more activist roles on the part of the armed forces. Although a majority of the public can conceive of a legitimate military intervention, the highest level of support was given to the civil–military insurrection of January 1958 and not to right-wing coups. However, the amount of support for the Chilean coup and the proportion of respondents willing to accept a "populist" military intervention are not to be taken lightly. This makes it necessary to determine how these opinions are interrelated, that is, how opinions about the legitimacy of coups in general and about the political role of the armed forces predispose people to support actual coups and how, in turn, these opinions have been shaped by actual historical coups.

This information is presented in Table 10.2, showing the zero-order correlations among the five items. The data presented in Table 10.2 enable me to refine some of the inferences I have made thus far and to establish the implications of the direction of opinion with respect to interventionism. Since the coups of 1948 and 1958 took place long before I asked these questions, it seems more appropriate to treat opinion about them as possible antecedents of opinion about the other aspects of interventionism measured in my survey. Opinion about the Chilean coup, which took place in a different country and shortly before I went to the field, cannot properly be considered an antecedent.

In general, the data presented in Table 10.2 are in line with the scholarly consensus about the historical and political nuances of military interventionism in Venezuela. First, the 1948 Venezuelan coup and the 1973 Chilean coup represented similar kinds of phenomena in the public's mind. Opinions about them are correlated positively and correlate with other opinions in a similar fashion, having the same sign and similar magnitude. Second, agreement with the proposition that "coups are sometimes justified"—identified as "coup legit-

Table 10.2
The Structure of Opinions About Coups

	Favorable Opinion About			
	1948 Coup	1958 Coup	1973 Coup	Coup Legitimacy
and . . .				
Support for the 1948 coup	–	-.08	.25	.18
Support for the 1958 coup	–	–	.00	(.03)
Support for the 1973 coup	–	–	–	.19
Civic role	-.11	(.01)	-.09	-.14
Constitutionalist role	(.07)	.00	.07	.10
Populist role	(.02)	(.04)	.00	(.04)
Hegemonic role	(.05)	-.05	.06	(.04)
All roles combined (item 5)	.09	(-.03)	.07	.20

Note: Correlations among the opinions that sanctioned the different roles that may be played by the armed forces are not reported since these are the result of a statistical artifact, namely, the "dummy variable" procedure that I used to create four variables out of the response categories of question 5 in Table 10.1. Values in parentheses indicate a lack of statistical significance for at least $\underline{P}$ < .05.
Source: VENEVOTE, March 9, 1979, pp. 11-16.

imacy'' in Table 10.2—involves more than a pragmatic recognition that this may be the case. This opinion correlates positively with support for both the 1948 and the 1973 coups while it fails to correlate with opinion about the 1958 coup. This would imply that ''coup legitimacy'' is a proxy of rightist interventionism. Third, exactly the same observation appears pertinent with respect to support for the constitutionalist role, although the magnitude of the coefficients is less robust. It appears that the two propositions tend to identify supporters of rightist modes of interventionism. Fourth, opinion about the 1958 coup does not correlate with anything, except for a very feeble negative relationship with the legitimacy of the hegemonic role. This is a consequence of the large proportion of respondents agreeing to the proposition that coups are sometimes justifiable. But this did not predispose the Venezuelan public to agree to all kinds of military interventionism. Fifth, respondents who sanctioned the civic role for the armed forces can be treated confidently as opposed to hypothetical and to actual forms of interventionism. Support for this role correlates negatively with all measures of support for interventionism. Sixth, support for the populist role is not related to anything; it does not correlate with the other items. Whatever the contextual validity of this option in the early 1960s in Venezuela, it did not seem to elicit a coherent response from the public in the early 1970s. Finally, support for the hegemonic role correlates negatively with opinion about the 1958 coup and correlates positively with opinion about the 1973 coup, but the magnitudes of the coefficients are too small.

One important clarification about the structure of these attitudes is that they are not arrayed on a single dimension or continuum. In a Guttman scale analysis of the 384 different configurations produced by the twelve basic types of scales in which these items may be arrayed, none of these configurations met basic requirements of unidimensionality and cumulativeness.[11] This means that there is not a single underlying dimension at work here, whether left-right or pro-anti military. Instead, one must interpret these attitudes in terms of at least those two, and possibly other, frames of reference.

PATTERNS OF SUPPORT AND OPPOSITION TO SPECIFIC COUPS

The Fading Memories of 1948

The circumstances of the 1948 coup have been described in considerable detail.[12] An uncertain process of political change had been unfolding following the death of Juan Vicente Gómez in 1935. Two Andean generals, Eleazar López Contreras (from 1935 to 1941) and Isaías Medina Angarita (from 1941 to 1945) presided over a controlled process of liberalization. López Contreras treated his opponents more leniently and tried to neutralize them through legal means.[13] Some refer to his regime as a *dictablanda* (soft dictatorship).[14] Medina, on his part, seemed to be more in favor of a process of democratization; his policies were more progressive; he adopted a quasi-populist style during his term; he began to organize a national political party; and he had the support of the left as well as of some conservative nationalists.[15] The social democrats of AD, suspicious of Medina's ultimate intentions and mindful of the clamor for direct elections, which Medina would not entertain, joined in a conspiracy organized by a group of young officers. Together they overthrew Medina on October 18, 1945. AD's Rómulo Betancourt became provisional president and the leading figure of the Junta Revolucionaria de Gobierno.[16] The initiative was vindicated when the government of the "October Revolution" received a very impressive electoral endorsement in the Constituent Assembly election of October 27, 1946, and in the general election of December 14, 1947.

The *adecos* (AD party members) saw little need to compromise with the opposition and much less to slow down implementation of their comprehensive program of reforms. AD leaders saw the new "electoral democracy" as theirs and felt that their substantial triumphs legitimized a hegemonic role that they intended to fulfill.[17] The *copeyanos* (COPEI party members) felt completely left out of everything.[18] By November 1948 the administration of President Rómulo Gallegos was under intense criticism by the opposition, which included the Unión Republicana Democrática (URD) and COPEI parties; *medinista* and *lopecista* sympathizers; important institutional actors like the Catholic Church, organized business, *hacendado* (landholder) groups, foreign oil companies; and other bourgeois and religious elements who viewed the AD reforms with increasing alarm.[19] Eventually the military demanded that Rómulo Betancourt leave the country, that the AD militia be disbanded, and that most cabinet portfolios be given to independents and opposition figures.[20] When Gallegos refused, he was overthrown—on November 24, 1948, less than one year into his term of office.

The coup of 1948 created strong animosities between the social democrats of AD, on the one hand, and the liberals of URD and the Christian democrats of COPEI, on the other. The coup was a very serious setback to the process of democratization begun in 1945, marking the end of the controversial but undeniably democratic experiment of the trienio, and ushered in the decade-long personalistic military dictatorship of General Marcos Pérez Jimenez.[21]

The partisan enmities generated by the 1948 coup were eventually overcome. There is no evidence that these have been passed on to new political generations.[22] What remain are very strong feelings about the protagonists of that era. Basically, the events of 1948 to 1957 changed the antagonistic nature of the relationship between social Christians and social democrats who drew some valuable lessons from the humiliating dictatorship, forgiving one another's conspiratorial intrigues, and coming together in the broad coalition that supported the 1958 coup.[23]

In 1973 only three types of influences remained on opinions about the 1948 coup; two of these may be considered proxies for partisan and ideological preferences. Among older Venezuelans who could still relate to the event, feelings about the Cruzada Cívica Nacionalista (CCN), a movement organized in the late 1960s to promote the Pérez Jiménez legacy, and feelings about Rómulo Betancourt, one of the primary targets of the 1948 coup, remained the more relevant points of reference. These influences are represented in the path-analytic model of Figure 10.1.[24] Gender role, the third independent variable included in the model, is the only other individual characteristic with any kind of measurable impact on opinion about the 1948 coup—except for feelings about the late Raúl Leoni, Betancourt's presidential successor in 1964 and fellow adeco. Although very salient at the time, neither ideology nor social class appeared to have much impact on opinion about the 1948 coup twenty-five years later. The transformation of Venezuelan society may have helped dilute the salience of these factors. In 1948 religious protest against the educational policies of AD and bourgeois misapprehension about adeco reformism helped to create a climate conducive to the coup.[25] But the contemporary insignificance of these factors may also be a result of the homogeneity of the subsample of 238 individual cases for whom we had complete information for all the variables included in Figure 10.1.[26]

Despite this caveat, what is being said here is not that the chroniclers of the events of 1945 to 1948 have exaggerated the degree of polarization that existed at that time but, simply, that twenty-five years after the fact people were polarized in reference to Betancourt and to Pérez Jiménez, not in terms of more fundamental and basic societal cleavages. Even the partisan component, so relevant in what

Figure 10.1
Determinants of Opinion About the Coup of 1948

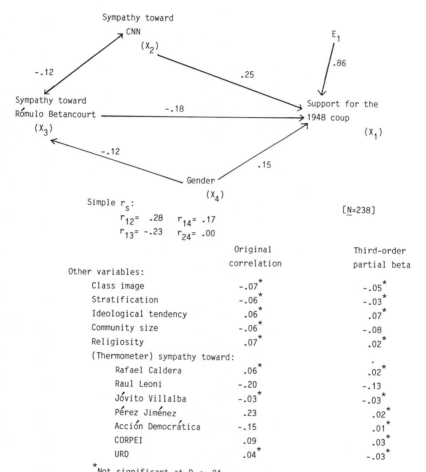

Simple r_s:

$$r_{12}= .28 \qquad r_{14}= .17$$
$$r_{13}= -.23 \qquad r_{24}= .00$$

[N=238]

	Original correlation	Third-order partial beta
Other variables:		
Class image	-.07*	-.05*
Stratification	-.06*	-.03*
Ideological tendency	.06*	.07*
Community size	-.06*	-.08
Religiosity	.07*	.02*
(Thermometer) sympathy toward:		
Rafael Caldera	.06*	.02*
Raul Leoni	-.20	-.13
Jóvito Villalba	-.03*	-.03*
Pérez Jiménez	.23	.02*
Acción Democrática	-.15	.01*
CORPEI	.09	.03*
URD	.04*	-.03*

*Not significant at $P < .01$.
Note: The magnitudes of the causal paths to the dependent variable are standardized (beta) coefficients. Paths among exogenous (independent) variables are measured as simple (zero-order) correlation coefficients.
Source: VENEVOTE, June 14, 1979, pp. 3-5, 27.

was perceived at the time as a struggle over a possible hegemonic one-party rule by AD, has vanished. Despite the antagonism between AD, on one hand, and URD and COPEI, on the other, feelings about these two parties failed to have any significant impact on the overall configuration of opinion depicted in Figure 10.1. The deep cleavages of the day were mended through the Pact of Punto Fijo, which helped stabilize Venezuelan politics after 1958.[27] What remains is a bitter although less extensive antagonism anchored in two diametrically opposed figures: Betancourt, "the single most important individual in determining what the nature of this (post-*gomecista*) system would be"[28]; and Pérez Jiménez, the most formidable obstacle to a possible democratic outcome to the Venezuelan process of political transition initiated in 1935. Basically, in 1973 intense feelings about the 1948 coup was a matter between adecos and *perezjimenistas*.

The Enduring Cleavages of the 1958 Coup

In 1973 a large majority of Venezuelans continued to agree to the necessity of the 1958 coup. Regardless of what they thought about the legitimacy of coups and of the role that the armed forces ought to play, about 60 percent of our respondents supported the coup. This percentage was 62.4 among those saying that coups are justified, 60.7 percent among those saying that this depends on the circumstances, and 62.8 percent among those saying that coups are not justified at all. A high level of support for the 1958 coup is also detectable across all categories of political roles deemed appropriate for the military: 63.3 percent among those endorsing the civic conception, 60 percent of those in favor of the constitutionalist options, 62.4 percent of those in favor of the populist alternative, and 58.9 of the small minority in favor of a hegemonic military. To understand what lies behind contemporary opinion about the fall of Pérez Jiménez, one must understand what he stood for at the time he was overthrown, what overthrew him, and what political options were available in Venezuela in 1958 and 1959.

Following the November 13, 1950, assassination of Lieutenant Colonel Carlos Delgado Chalbaud, Germán Suárez Flamerich was appointed to succeed him as president of the junta, but Pérez Jiménez had become its real leader. The regime was pressured to clarify its institutional intentions. On April 18, 1951, the government published a new electoral statute for Constituent Assembly elections in 1952. On the same day it published Decree Number 120 proscribing the participation of adecos and communists. In June the government organized the Frente Independiente (FEI) to support its own candidates. On election day, November 30, 1952, as it became evident that the URD party would soundly thrash the hastily organized FEI, the government stopped the vote count, imposed a ban on all broadcasts, and declared FEI the winner.[29] On December 2 Pérez Jiménez was designated provisional president, and on April 17, 1953, the Constituent Assembly elected him president for a five-year term. In July 1957 the Venezuelan Congress announced presidential elections for December 15, 1957. As the date approached, it became clear that Pérez Jiménez would not fare any better than in 1952. On November 4 the dictator, in a message to Congress, announced a change in the electoral format: Instead of presidential elections a referendum would be held to determine whether Pérez Jiménez should continue in office.[30] As expected, the government won the referendum.

Under Pérez Jiménez Venezuela enjoyed an economic bonanza brought about by favorable oil prices. A vast program of public works was launched and completed on time. However, the government decided to schedule all this work during only half the year. This brought considerable disruption not only to laborers and wage earners but also to government contractors who had to suffer irrational delays to be paid. The juiciest morsels of these contracts, however, were reserved for the intimate friends of the dictator who were not in the circle of more modern capitalists who chafed under the conditions in which they had to work.[31] At the time he was overthrown, Pérez Jiménez was identified with meaningless elections by a public who had learned to appreciate the suffrage, with union busting by a labor movement that had known better times and that refused to be tame, and with corruption and waste by a new emerging bourgeoisie who demanded a more modern and open version of capitalism.[32] To them, the dictatorship was anachronistic.

The Catholic Church eventually turned against the regime.[33] In a much-celebrated pastoral letter the Archbishop of Caracas, Monsignor Rafael Arias Blanco, blasted the dictatorship for its treatment of the poor, the workers, and the "immense mass of our people living in conditions that cannot be called human."[34] Shortly thereafter, the archdiocesan newspaper, *La Religión*, began to criticize the government, and its editor, Father José Hernández Chapellín, became a collaborator of the Junta Patriótica.[35] At the time of its breakdown, the Pérez Jiménez regime was perceived as a corrupt coterie of friends and relatives, abusing their power, and unconcerned with the fate of most Venezuelans.

What did the dictator really stand for?
One official biographer described the policy orientation of the Pérez Jiménez regime as consisting of "transforming the physical environment and improving the moral, intellectual, and material conditions of people . . . power in today's Venezuela responds to the idea of governing efficaciously [without] the influence of selfish interests and groups, and [without] the intromission of political sectarianism in public administration."[36]

To be sure, there were traces of positivism and of developmentalism in the official rhetoric of the time. There was some intellectual coherence in the writings of one of the intellectual mouthpieces of the dictatorship, Laureano Vallenilla.[37] But it is doubtful that many Venezuelans, either among the elite or at the level of the mass public, took the official "ideology" seriously. In reality, when he was overthrown, Pérez Jiménez was a classical dictator who stood for autocratic, unsupervised rule; for meaningless elections; for politics without parties and without interest groups; for venality and corruption; and for the harsh treatment of his opponents.

Most prominent among these were the political parties who had to sort out their differences, wait for the dictatorship to show its true face and for the society to feel its heavy burden, organize themselves more effectively, and prepare for the final attack against it. Although militants of all stripes paid a heavy price, the adecos felt the wrath of the dictatorship more directly. AD lost some of its top leaders, including Alberto Carnevali and Leonardo Ruíz Pineda. URD and COPEI had some initial respite but moved to a more resolute opposition following the electoral fraud of 1952. Members of the Communist party (PCV) were persecuted from the first.[38] In June 1957 militants of URD and the PCV met to plan a common strategy and invited representatives of AD and COPEI to join them in the Junta Patriótica.[39] The Junta Patriótica played a key role through 1957, particularly during the crucial days of January 1958. In late 1957 AD's Betancourt, COPEI's Rafael Caldera, and URD's Jóvito Villalba met in New York to ratify the agreement that their clandestine operatives had forged.

Dreaded the most as a potential opponent by the dictator was the military. Many officers resented the presence in power of yet another *andino* (Andean) who favored his friends and spied on his colleagues in uniform. Others probably went further, rooting their opposition in feelings and sympathies for more progressive alternatives.[40] As is normally the case when a dictatorship is overthrown, the principal motivations were probably of an institutional nature, namely, mounting concern with being identified with an unpopular regime showing symptoms of deterioration.[41] Many observers suggested that the electoral fraud of 1957 and Pérez Jiménez's subsequent inauguration for a second term of office—on December 20, 1957—were the last straws for many officers.[42]

Eventually, therefore, Pérez Jiménez found himself alone, supported only by his henchmen, cronies, and palace guards and confronted by practically the entire society.

During December 1957, the military conspiracy organized by Colonel Hugo Trejo gathered momentum. In addition to the 360 or so officers implicated, Trejo extended his contacts to prominent civilians and party representatives. Later that month the regime uncovered the plot and began to arrest some officers. The date of the coup was advanced to New Year's Eve, but lack of coordination doomed the initiative; only the Maracay and the Los Teques garrisons responded. Despite this failure, the demands of Trejo and his colleagues remained on the table, reinforced by the support of a number of senior officers. The dictator refused to entertain all of them but had to budge on a few, following a January 9 navy mutiny and the delivery of an ultimatum by Chief of Staff General Rómulo Fernández. Pérez Jiménez tried to reequilibrate by reorganizing his cabinet and ordering the departure of Vallenilla and of Pedro Estrada, the sinister director of the regime's security apparatus.[43] From January 14 to 19 the Junta Patriótica, professional associations, student federations, and prominent citizens denounced the government in a series of manifestos asking for its removal.[44]

On January 21 and 22 the Junta Patriótica took advantage of the impasse and seized the initiative organizing a mass mobilization. A general strike paralyzed the country. Ordinary citizens ran tremendous risks joining in the strike, disputing control of the streets with the police, and storming the headquarters of the much-hated Seguridad Nacional.[45] It was at this point that the script of the Venezuelan events of January 1958 departed radically from the textbook case of a barracks uprising. The civil–military movement that overthrew Pérez Jiménez had different components, including one that had all the characteristics of a popular insurrection.[46] During the rest of 1958, the revolutionary option remained very much alive.

Sensing this climate, the leaders of the dominant parties moved quickly to recover the initiative, demobilize the citizenry, ship the more problematic officers out of the country, and steer the new regime in a reformist direction. These initiatives represented a successful effort by senior party leaders to reassert themselves and thereby reimpose their authority on a younger group of leaders who had gained prominence during the period of clandestine party activity. These senior leaders agreed to a blueprint sanctioned by the Pact of Punto Fijo, a tripartite agreement among AD, COPEI, and URD that served as a pact of political transition and was very instrumental in the consolidation of the new democratic regime.[47] That democracy, however, excluded the parties of the left from this "consociational" agreement.

Memories of the 1958 coup among Venezuelan leftists, therefore, evoke feelings of a missed opportunity.[48] Basically, the left did not realize the extent to which the country was in revolutionary ferment, and when it tried to emulate the Cuban example, in 1959 and 1960, it was too late.[49] The options of 1958 included radical populist and even revolutionary alternatives. The former sought expression through the figure of Admiral Wolfgang Larrazábal, a leader of the military conspiracy, who developed a considerable popular following, was courted assiduously by different parties, and became the presidential candidate of a URD–PCV ticket.[50] However, the admiral was not interested in radical politics, and his star faded eventually.

The revolutionary alternative found a responsive audience among some of the younger militants of the PCV and URD parties, the *arsista* faction that split from the AD, and a number of young military officers. They kept the country in considerable turmoil with barrack uprisings in the early 1960s and a guerrilla campaign that lasted through the end of the decade. But they had to be content with a coalition government anchored by a party with impressive reformist credentials (AD), including some of its more formidable adversaries of yesterday (COPEI and URD), and now in power as a result of a mechanism that was probably one of the most legitimate features of the new regime and that had given a majority to the AD once again, although not as ample as in the 1940s.

Inspection of the model presented in Figure 10.2 shows that feelings about Pérez Jiménez in 1973 remained the most important determinant of opinion about the 1958 coup. Repudiation of the dictator is one aspect of the plebiscite nature of the "spirit of January 23." A second element is clearly partisan and ideological and apparently linked to the disenchantment of supporters of leftist parties with the nature of the new regime. The third element of some causal importance refers to opinion about the institution of elections, suggesting a link between the coup and the restoration of elections in Venezuela. In short, the model presented in Figure 10.2—which boasts a smaller error term and a larger number of cases than the one presented in Figure 10.1—suggests that perezjimenistas, leftists, and persons very critical of elections were in 1973 the ones most opposed to the notion that the coup had been necessary. This combination of causal factors is explicable in terms of the contextual and historical circumstances of the coup, reviewed previously, and is congruent with patterns of political criticism found in Venezuela at the time of my survey. At that time sympathizers of the leftist parties were more critical of the government and of the regime and also more critical of the institution of elections. On the other hand, it is clear that there is no connection between the perezjimenistas and the other two groups of critics of the 1958 coup—note the magnitude and lack of statistical significance of the coefficients among these three variables, r_{23}, and r_{24}. Therefore, although support for the coup cut across a broad spectrum of opinion, it is possible to identify three different groups of people opposed to the coup: the partisans of the dictator, sympathizers of leftist parties, and critics of the institution of elections. These findings, strange though they may seem, must be interpreted in terms of the meaning of January 23. The civil–military revolt against Pérez Jiménez gave Venezuelans a choice between a regime without parties and without elections, and one anchored in those intermediary institutions. Venezuelans opted for the latter, and a substantial majority of them continued to ratify in 1973 the instrument that made that choice possible.

However, it is a matter of historical record that most leftists not only supported but also took an active part in overthrowing the dictatorship. Therefore, how is it possible that they opposed the coup fifteen years later? Since most of the cases included in the model of Figure 10.2 are not of young individuals, it is not likely that they were socialized to repudiate the coup but that they came to repudiate it ex post facto.

We have hypothesized that this resulted from their effective exclusion from power as well as from their violent disagreement with the direction of the new regime. What we are measuring in their case, therefore, cannot be their initial attitude toward the coup but their change of heart about it, as a result of the events of the intervening years. This shows that coups and their aftermath are important influences on the formation of other political attitudes, including loyalty to the new regime, and possible criticism of the suffrage as well. Given their inability to capitalize on the cycle initiated on January 23, 1958, leftist Venezuelans no longer regard that coup favorably. In addition, their criticism

Figure 10.2
Determinants of Opinion About the Coup of 1958

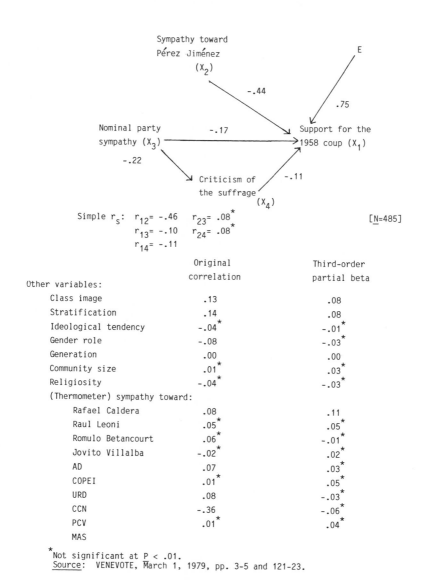

Other variables:	Original correlation	Third-order partial beta
Class image	.13	.08
Stratification	.14	.08
Ideological tendency	-.04*	-.01*
Gender role	-.08	-.03*
Generation	.00	.00
Community size	.01*	.03*
Religiosity	-.04*	-.03*
(Thermometer) sympathy toward:		
Rafael Caldera	.08	.11
Raul Leoni	.05*	.05*
Romulo Betancourt	.06*	-.01*
Jovito Villalba	-.02*	.02*
AD	.07	.03*
COPEI	.01*	.05*
URD	.08	-.03*
CCN	-.36	-.06*
PCV	.01*	.04*
MAS		

*Not significant at $P < .01$.
Source: VENEVOTE, March 1, 1979, pp. 3-5 and 121-23.

of elections could be linked to their limited success in the electoral arena as well as to a more ideological aversion to the "electoralism" of the new regime. In other words, they repudiate the mechanism that brought about the new regime as well as the mechanism that continues to reproduce it.

OPINION ABOUT COUPS IN 1983

The decade between 1973 and 1983 witnessed major changes in the Venezuelan polity. The electoral dominance of the social democratic (AD) and social Christian (COPEI) parties was confirmed in a series of elections. Both parties took turns running the national government, as approximately nine of every ten voters favored them. But a series of scandals, policy immobility, and the onslaught of economic deterioration seemed to be creating a great deal of public discontent. Despite the absence of civil protests, observers of Venezuelan politics grew increasingly concerned with a malaise affecting the democratic regime. In 1982, John D. Martz described the crisis in terms of " . . . a detectable and growing cynicism toward political parties and their leaders in the land; incredulity about the integrity of public officials, and skepticism about their capacity to shape and implement an effective national policy in years to come."[51] Martz believed that both AD and COPEI have to redefine themselves and their programs and that they must avoid the myopic, opportunistic, and selfish policies that they have put in practice. He thought that AD, then in opposition, had a more urgent need to face these challenges and that COPEI would be able to gain new impetus from the presidential candidacy of its founder, Dr. Rafael Caldera.[52] Ironically, AD was able to assimilate the death of Rómulo Betancourt and inflict a decisive defeat upon Caldera in the elections of 1983, sending COPEI into one of the worst crises in its history.

Andrés Stambouli echoed these concerns, describing the contemporary Venezuelan model in terms of two fundamental traits: "an undeniable institutional stability based on a widespread diffusion and acceptance of the rules of representative democracy . . . [and] a special filial-paternal relationship between state and society that . . . is now in crisis and . . . [that] could jeopardize what it once helped establish."[53] Stambouli believed that the dominant parties have to address the challenge of furthering the legitimacy of the regime through the increased efficacy of its institutions.[54]

To be sure, other critics of the regime are much less thoughtful in their style and less pure in their intentions. As a matter of fact, from 1981 to 1983 the Venezuelan media were saturated with caustic and relentless attacks against the regime, the dominant parties, and the policy outcomes of their administrations. Elsewhere I have dealt with these criticisms and with the extent to which they have made an impact on the consciousness of the public.[55]

Has this crisis affected the manner in which Venezuelans think about interventionism?

Discontent with a paralysis of government, cynicism about the integrity of

Table 10.3
Opinions About Military Interventionism in 1983

Items	No	Depends	Yes	Do not know	Refused
Coups sometimes justified[a]	31.6	4.9	52.9	9.8	.8
Current situation in Venezuela justifies a coup[b]	52.1	3.8	34.2	9.4	.4
If things continue as they are the possibility of a coup would be . . .[c]	22.9[d]	17.0[e]	35.5[f]	21.0	1.9

[a]"Do you think, in general, that there are occasions in which military coups are justifiable or not?"

[b]"Do you believe that, at the present time, there is a situation in Venezuela that justifies a military coup, or not?"

[c]"Do you believe that, if things continue to go this way, the possibility of a military coup . . .

    [d] . . . will decrease?"
    [e] . . . will remain the same?"
    [f] . . . will increase?"

Source: VENEDEMO, June 10, 1984, pp. 104-5.

political leaders and public officials, and impatience with the shortcomings of the regime are, after all, the stuff that supposedly leads to coups d'etat in Latin America. Is the Venezuelan public immune to these? The data suggest a very complex answer.

In a nutshell, analysis of the modes of public criticism found in 1983 leads to the conclusion that Venezuelans remain very supportive of democratic norms, are increasingly dissatisfied with the performance of the government, and want to allow the suffrage to correct these shortcomings in the future.[56] As a matter of fact, most dimensions of public evaluation of the Venezuelan regime and its institutions are mediated, that is, constrained, by predominantly partisan considerations.[57]

Concerning interventionism, the first impression derived from the data is disturbing. In the fall of 1983 about 53 percent of Venezuelans continued to believe that there are occasions in which coups are justified, and about 34 percent believed that the situation prevailing at the time justified a military coup.[58] In addition, about 36 percent of respondents in the VENEDEMO sample believed that the probability of a coup would increase during the next two years (see Table 10.3).

To be sure it is always possible for surveys to impute (nonsalient) attitudes to the public. One may contend that all of the opinion items presented in Table 10.3 address the realm of conjecture. In addition, one must bear in mind the historical specificity in which opinion about coups has been shaped in Venezuela.

After all, Venezuelan democracy became possible, in part, as a result of a military insurrection. But it would be foolhardy to dismiss these finds altogether.

If the three VENEDEMO items measuring opinion about coups are combined into a composite measure, identified as "predisposition to support coups" in Figure 10.3, we find that the causal determinants of that measure do not include partisan or ideological factors.[59] This is disturbing since one would expect that after twenty-five years of democratic politics, sympathies toward the two dominant parties would correlate strongly with opposition to military interventionism. They do not. But neither do the measures of sympathy for the Socialist (MAS) and Communist (PCV) parties. Nor is there a robust correlation between ideology, measured as preference for types of economic system (capitalism, socialism, or communism) and as ideological tendency (right, center, left), and predisposition to support coups (see bottom of Figure 10.3).

The model depicted in Figure 10.3 is congruent with previous descriptions of patterns of political criticism in Venezuela.[60] Venezuelans more predisposed to support a coup at the time of the VENEDEMO survey included those more critical of the democratic regime, residents of poor neighborhoods, the young, members of families with below-average incomes, and apolitical people. The lack of any partisan or ideological constraints on this attitude has been previously highlighted. In other words, salient or not, a predisposition to support coups is not linked to the main axes of partisan and ideological oppositions in Venezuela.

The best predictor of "predisposition to support" is another attitude, namely, a more negative evaluation of the democratic regime—variable X_2 in Figure 10.3. This attitude correlates somewhat strongly with sympathy toward MAS ($r = .20$) and toward PCV ($r = .17$), and also with a leftist ideological tendency ($r = .14$). However, these links become irrelevant once the other predictors of predisposition to support are included in the model (see bottom of Figure 10.3). It would appear that while sympathizers of the MAS and the PCV are more critical of the regime, they remember the lessons of the failed insurrectionist campaigns of the 1960s. A negative evaluation of democracy appears to be an attitude that characterizes the young and the apolitical, precisely two types of individuals who appear more predisposed to support coups than the rest of the public. Consequently, one would have to point to important gaps in the socialization process, regarding the young, and to a certain aversion to democratic politics—rooted not so much in ideology and party as, quite the contrary, in apoliticism—as principal stimulant of predisposition to support coups.

This picture would be incomplete without at least some reference to the impact of the social circumstances of individuals. This is present in the model both in an ecological and in an existential way. Basically, one's share in the fruition of the economic model has an impact on the extent to which one is willing to support coups. Family income, a determinant of neighborhood of residence, appears to be the more salient socioeconomic characteristic of individual respondents more predisposed to support coups. Family income and neighborhood of residence clearly have a shaping influence on "predisposition to support."

Figure 10.3
Determinants of the Predisposition to Support Coups

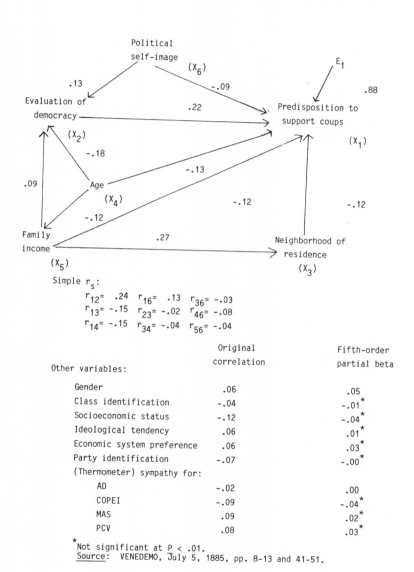

Simple r_s:

r_{12}= .24 r_{16}= .13 r_{36}= -.03
r_{13}= -.15 r_{23}= -.02 r_{46}= -.08
r_{14}= -.15 r_{34}= -.04 r_{56}= -.04

Other variables:	Original correlation	Fifth-order partial beta
Gender	.06	.05
Class identification	-.04	-.01[*]
Socioeconomic status	-.12	-.04[*]
Ideological tendency	.06	.01[*]
Economic system preference	.06	.03[*]
Party identification	-.07	-.00[*]
(Thermometer) sympathy for:		
AD	-.02	.00
COPEI	-.09	-.04[*]
MAS	.09	.02[*]
PCV	.08	.03[*]

[*]Not significant at P < .01.
Source: VENEDEMO, July 5, 1885, pp. 8-13 and 41-51.

What you earn and where you live have independent and combined causal effects on potential support for military coups. It is not simply whether your family makes a lot or not enough money but also whether you live around others who share your circumstances.

One final clarification is in order. A battery of questions comparing democracy and dictatorship was administered in the VENEDEMO survey. Respondents overwhelmingly chose democracy over dictatorship (82 percent), considered that it could resolve problems better (67 percent), that it can produce more well-being (69 percent), and that it would be better for Venezuela (76 percent). The only unfavorable comparison involved democracy being considered more corrupt than dictatorship (by 47 to 23 percent).[61] All of these items correlate with evaluation of the democratic regime, but not with one item inviting the more critical respondents to identify the kind of regime that they would prefer (only 86 of 1,789 respondents mentioned a military dictatorship).[62] In other words, there is a disconnection between dissatisfaction and alternatives.

A similar disconnection may be at work between many people considering that conditions under President Herrera justified a coup, that is, that President Herrera *deserved* a coup, and these people not being supportive of a military dictatorship. This would imply that coups remain in the mind of the Venezuelan public because they are efficient instruments of government change, not because they are associated with a kind of regime considered better than democracy. In essence, most Venezuelans believe that circumstances could arise that may justify the extreme remedy of a military coup. That they do not seem to associate this with a return to dictatorship is some consolation, but the fact that they continue to entertain the option is disturbing.

NOTES

I am indebted to John Martz, Frederick Turner, John Booth, Mitchel Seligson, Peter McDonough, Gene Bigler, and Juan del Aguila for their comments and criticisms.

1. Gene E. Bigler, "Professional Soldiers and Restrained Politics in Venezuela," in *The New Military Politics in Latin America*, ed. Robert Wesson (New York: Praeger, 1982), p. 175.

2. This was a multistage national probability sample of 1,521 adult Venezuelans that I took during October and November 1973. These data will be cited as VENEVOTE.

3. The 1983 data were gathered from a questionnaire that I administered to a multistage national probability sample of 1,789 adult Venezuelans interviewed during October and November of that year. Data from these interviews will be called VENEDEMO.

4. For details see Alí Brett Martínez, *El Porteñazo, Historia de una Rebelión* (Caracas: Adora, 1973), pp. 24–26; Ramón J. Velásquez, "Aspectos de la evolución política en Venezuela en el último medio siglo," in Ramón J. Velásquez (ed.), *Venezuela Moderna* (Caracas: Fundación Eugenio Mendoza, 1976), pp. 222–32.

5. Gene E. Bigler, "The Armed Forces and Patterns of Civil-Military Relations," in *Venezuela, The Democratic Experience*, eds. John D. Martz and David J. Myers (New York and London: Praeger, 1977), p. 127; John D. Martz, *Acción Democrática: Evolution*

of a Modern Political Party in Venezuela (Princeton, N.J.: Princeton University Press, 1966), pp. 311–13.

6. Pompeyo Márquez, in *La lucha armada, Hablan cinco jefes*, ed. Agustín Blanco Muñoz (Caracas: Universidad Central de Venezuela 1980), pp. 86–88, 131–35.

7. Víctor Hugo Morales, *Del porteñazo al Perú* (Caracas, 1971), pp. 40–44, 69–71, 124–29, 178–80, and 192–94.

8. Velásquez, "Evolución política," pp. 212–15, 228–31.

9. Robert J. Alexander, *Rómulo Betancourt and the Transformation of Venezuela* (New Brunswick, N.J.: Transaction Books, 1982), pp. 385–98; Luis Herrera Campins, *Conversaciones con Luis Herrera Campins* (Caracas: Editorial Ateneo, 1978).

10. There are, to be sure, dissenting opinions not only from the right but also from the left. For illustration, see Domingo Alberto Rangel, *La revolución de las fantasías* (Caracas: Ediciones OFIDI, 1966).

11. See the optimal scale values for the twelve different configurations.

12. Glen L. Kolb, *Democracy and Dictatorship in Venezuela: 1945–1958* (New London: Conn.: Archon, 1974), pp. 41–59; Andrés Stambouli, *Crisis política, Venezuela 1945–58* (Caracas: Editorial Ateneo, 1980), pp. 70–93; Velásquez, "Evolución política," pp. 69–99.

13. Velásquez, "Evolución política," pp. 32–37.

14. Alfredo Tarre Murzi, *López Contreras, De la tiranía a la libertad* (Caracas: Editorial Ateneo, 1982), pp. 253–92.

15. Luis Cordero Velásquez, *Gómez y las fuerzas vivas* (Caracas: Lumego, 1975), pp. 32–34; Velásquez, "Evolución política," pp. 36–39.

16. Rómulo Betancourt, *El 18 de Octubre de 1945* (Barcelona: Seix Barral, 1979), pp. 301–61.

17. Martz, *Acción Democrática*, pp. 62–72.

18. Donald L. Herman, *Christian Democracy in Venezuela* (Chapel Hill: University of North Carolina Press, 1980), p. 35.

19. Winfield J. Burggraaff, *The Venezuelan Armed Forces in Politics, 1935–1959* (Columbia: University of Missouri Press, 1972), pp. 87–111; Herman, *Christian Democracy*, pp. 31–36; Daniel H. Levine, *Conflict and Political Change in Venezuela* (Princeton, N.J.: Princeton University Press, 1973), pp. 37–41; Martz, *Acción Democrática*, pp. 81–87.

20. Stambouli, *Crisis política*, pp. 81–84.

21. Herman, *Christian Democracy*, pp. 31–36; Kolb, *Democracy and Dictatorship*, pp. 43–65; Martz, *Acción Democrática*, pp. 84–85; Stambouli, *Crisis política*, pp. 240–54.

22. The fact that younger Venezuelans cannot really relate to this event is borne out by the results of a cross-tabulation between age of respondent and percentage of "nonresponses" (do not know, not aware) to question 3, Table 10.1, reproduced as follows:

Age	18–24	25–29	30–34	35–39	40–44	45–49	50–54	55–59	60+
Percentage of nonrespondents	80.1	79.7	71.0	57.3	43.4	40.5	24.1	28.4	28.5

eta = .43

23. Kolb, *Democracy and Dictatorship*, pp. 165–66, 174–75; Levine, *Conflict*, pp. 46–47.

24. Notice that the zero-order correlation between the "thermometer measure" of sympathy toward Pérez Jiménez and opinion about the 1948 coup is very similar in magnitude to the correlation between the thermometer measure for the CCN and opinion about the coup. Exactly the same observation applies to feelings about AD with respect to feelings about Betancourt. Essentially, the measures are interchangeable.

25. Levine, *Conflict*, pp. 38–39, 62–93.

26. Path analytic models are normally derived through stepwise regression techniques. Among many decisions, one must choose between a "pairwise" approach, which maximizes the number of cases included in the analysis while making its results less reliable, or a "listwise" approach predicted on exactly the opposite strategy. The approach utilized here is the latter, and therefore, anyone with no opinion about the 1948 coup, that is, a majority of the sample, was excluded.

27. For a capsule summary of the Pact of Punto Fijo and its implications, see Humberto Njaim, Ricardo Combellas, Eva Josko de Guerón, and Andrés Stambouli, *El sistema político venezolano* (Caracas: Editorial Arte, 1975), pp. 13–15. For the text of the pact, see Presidencia de la República, *Documentos que hicieron historia* Vol 2 (Caracas: Editorial Arte, 1962), pp. 443–49.

28. Alexander, *Betancourt*, p. 17.

29. Kolb, Democracy and Dictatorship, Chapter 8.

30. Ibid., pp. 167–70.

31. Ibid., Chapter 9.

32. Velásquez, "Evolución política," pp. 149–51.

33. Helena Plaza, *El 23 de Enero y el proceso de consolidación de la democracia representativa en Venezuela* (Caracas: Garbizu & Todtmann, 1978), pp. 73–77.

34. Presidencia, *Documentos*, pp. 423–26.

35. Kolb, *Democracy and Dictatorship*, p. 168.

36. Ladislao Tarnói, *El nuevo ideal nacional de Venezuela* (Madrid: 1954), pp. 142–43.

37. To be sure, he was the most literate and interesting figure in Pérez Jiménez's entourage. See Laureano Vallenilla, *Cesarismo democrático* (Caracas: Imprenta Garrido, 1952).

38. Alexander, *Democratic Revolution*, pp. 47–48; Stambouli, *Crisis política*, pp. 141–51.

39. Plaza, *Proceso de consolidación*, pp. 78–90.

40. Stambouli, *Crisis política*, pp. 134–36.

41. For a discussion of this topic, see Federico G. Gil, Enrique Baloyra, and Lars Schoultz, "The Peaceful Transition to Democracy: Elections and the Restoration of Rights," paper no. 1 in *Democracy in Latin America, Prospects and Implications*, Department of State Contract 1722-020083, mimeo (Chapel Hill, N.C.: August 1981), pp. 35–46, 91–107.

42. Velásquez, "Evolución política," pp. 151–53.

43. Stambouli, *Crisis política*, pp. 136–41; Velásquez, "Evolución política," pp. 153–54.

44. Presidencia, *Documentos*, pp. 433–42.

45. Alexander, *Democratic Revolution*, p. 50; Kolb, *Democracy and Dictatorship*, Chapter 11.

46. Velásquez, "Evolución política," pp. 157–61.

47. See note 27.

48. Rangel, *Fantasías*, pp. 86, 253–58.

49. Blanco Muñoz, ed., *Lucha armada*, pp. 18–21, 39–50, 92–104.

50. Plaza, *Proceso de consolidación*, Chapter 3.

51. John D. Martz, "Los Peligros de la petrificación: El sistema de partidos venezolanos y la década de los ochenta," in *Iberoamérica en los ochenta, Perspectivas de cambio social y político*, eds. Enrique A. Baloyra and Rafael López-Pintor (Madrid: Centro de Investigaciones Sociológicas e Instituto de Cooperación Iberoamericana, 1982), p. 149. My translation.

52. Ibid., pp. 157–63.

53. Andrés Stambouli, "La democracia venezolana, De los requisitos de estabilidad a las exigencias de eficacia," in *Iberoamérica en los ochenta*, eds. Baloyra and López-Pintor, p. 167.

54. Ibid., pp. 172–73.

55. Most recently in Enrique A. Baloyra, "Public Opinion and Support for the Regime, 1973–1983," in *Venezuela, The Democratic Experience*, second edition, eds. John D. Martz and David J. Myers (New York: Praeger, 1986).

56. Ibid., Tables 10.1, 10.2, and 10.3.

57. Also Enrique A. Baloyra, "Public Opinion and Support for Democratic Regimes, Venezuela 1973–1983," paper presented at the Annual Meeting of the American Political Science Association, New Orleans, Louisiana, August 29 to September 1, 1985, Appendix C.

58. For all practical purposes, the 3 percent difference between VENEVOTE (1973) and VENEDEMO (1983) respondents saying that coups are sometimes justified may be treated as sampling error. Although I cannot conclude that this has become an item of contemporary Venezuelan political culture, I would suggest that it has been a fixture of Venezuelan public opinion during the democratic regime. VENEDEMO, question: "Do you believe that, *at present*, there is a situation in Venezuela that *justifies* a military coup or not?"

59. "Predisposition to support coups" is one of ten dimensions of public evaluation of the Venezuelan regime. This configuration was derived from a factor analysis of the VENEDEMO data discussed in Baloyra, "Venezuela 1973–1983," Appendix B. The three variables identified in Table 3 "loaded" on the factor with magnitudes of .69, .71, and .58, respectively, following the order in which they appear in the table.

60. Compare with Enrique A. Baloyra, "Criticism, Cynicism, and Political Evaluation: A Venezuelan Example," *American Political Science Review*, 73 (December 1979), pp. 987–1002. Also Baloyra, "Public Opinion and Support for the Regime," especially Table 4; and Arístides Torres, "Factores relacionados con el desencanto de la democracia en Venezuela," paper presented at the roundtable of Venezuelan politics, University of Connecticut, Storrs, October 31, 1984.

61. See Baloyra, "Public Opinion and Support for the Regime," Table 3.

62. As following:

	item1	item2	item3	item4	item5
coups justified . . .	.13	.20	.13	.15	.19
coup justified now . . .	.26	.17	.22	.28	.21
coup possibility . . .	.18	.18	.16	.15	.14
critical of democracy . . .	.31	.32	.22	.27	.33
substitute it with . . .	− .04*	− .03*	− .12*	− .03*	− .06*

*not significant at P<.01.

item1: prefer dictatorship . . .

item2: dictatorship solves national problems better . . .

item3: dictatorship is more corrupt . . .

item4: dictatorship produces more well-being . . .

item5: dictatorship better for Venezuela . . .

11

Coping with Insurgency: The Politics of Pacification in Colombia and Venezuela

Daniel L. Premo

A recent work on liberal democracy in Latin America lists Venezuela, Colombia, and Costa Rica in its subtitle, currently the three countries in the region with the longest tradition of continuous democratic rule.[1] Prior to 1973 Venezuela and Colombia undoubtedly would have been preempted by Uruguay and Chile in any ranking of democracies in the region, a not so subtle reminder that even the most democratic societies in Latin America are subject to relatively sudden, radical shifts in their civil–military relations.

Colombia and Venezuela themselves emerged from a period of highly personalistic, repressive military dictatorship as recently as 1957 and 1958; the former to resume a tradition of civilian authority spanning most of the twentieth century, and the latter to renew the struggle to establish the first precedent of civilian supremacy in its national history.

Both Colombia and Venezuela found their efforts to establish democratic government threatened in the 1960s by insurgency movements. By 1970 Venezuela had for all practical purposes resolved its guerrilla problem. Colombia, on the other hand, has only recently engaged in a pacification program that holds forth some promise of bringing an end to over two decades of almost continuous guerrilla activity.

This study examines the origin of guerrilla violence in each country and the respective government's political and military response to the threat of insurgency. Special attention is given to the "politics of pacification," which culminated in the resolution of Venezuela's guerrilla problem and which characterize the Colombian government's present efforts to achieve a negotiated settlement with various guerrilla organizations. Throughout the study the role of counterinsurgency is examined as a military concern and as a source of friction between the armed forces and civilian authorities. The chapter concludes with an assessment of why the pacification process pursued in Venezuela was relatively more successful and was achieved within a shorter time period than in the case of Colombia.

ORIGINS OF THE GUERRILLA VIOLENCE IN VENEZUELA

From the political history described elsewhere in this volume, there was little reason to believe that the coup that overthrew Pérez Jiménez in 1958 and the subsequent election of Rómulo Bentancourt in 1959 would lead to one of the region's most stable, functioning democracies. For most of the nineteenth century Venezuela had provided a textbook study of caudillism, followed by the long and often ruthless dictatorships of Cipriano Castro (from 1898 to 1908) and Juan Vicente Gómez (from 1908 to 1935).[2]

Even prior to Pérez Jiménez's ouster, the principal leaders of Acción Democrática (AD), (COPEI), and Unión Republicana Democrática (URD) had agreed on many of the principles and mechanisms of coalition government that were to be formalized in the Punto Fijo Pact of October 21, 1958.[3] Among the agreements reached was the decision to exclude the Venezuelan Communist party (PCV) from the governing coalition. While the Pact of Punto Fijo doubtlessly served to diminish conflict and dissent among the future coalition partners and established the basis for a democratic system, the decision to exclude the PCV had serious repercussions for the AD government. In recognition of the Communists' role in overthrowing Pérez Jiménez, the provisional military government had restored the PCV's legal status and allowed the party to expand its influence in labor unions, student groups, and in the *barrios* (poor areas) surrounding Caracas. When Betancourt declared in his inaugural address that communism was "incompatible" with the development of Venezuela, the PCV was at the peak of its political respectability and popular support.[4]

Leftist opposition to Betancourt's government included splinter movements within AD and URD. In May 1960 many of the younger leaders of AD split to form the Movement of the Revolutionary Left (MIR). Inspired by the Cuban Revolution, MIR proclaimed itself a Marxist movement and challenged the PCV's leadership for control of the Venezuelan left, especially among university students. Student and worker demonstrations against the Betancourt government were met with increasing police repression.[5]

Betancourt's decision to break diplomatic relations with Cuba increased tension between the government and its left-wing opponents. By November 1960 armed extremists and pro-Castro students affiliated with the PCV and MIR were attacking police and property from their privileged sanctuary on the campus of the Central University of Venezuela in Caracas (UCV).[6] These early insurrectional attempts led to intermittent suspension of constitutional guarantees and renewed denunciations of "Castro-Communism" and the local Communists. Throughout this period government supporters and the left argued vehemently over who was responsible for the violence. Those sympathetic to the left insisted that the Betancourt government initiated the violence by its attempts to repress its leftist opposition and that the radical left launched its own insurgency only in response to this repression. Those sympathetic to the Betancourt government insisted that the PCV and MIR leadership failed to maintain firm control over its youth membership, which called for increasingly radical responses to government actions.[7] By 1961 a number of guerrilla groups, made up mostly of university and secondary-school students, had begun to operate. PCV and MIR leaders concluded that a strategy of guerrilla warfare in the major cities would undermine the government's legitimacy and precipitate a proleftist military coup.

INSURGENCY UNDER BETANCOURT AND LEONI

Throughout most of 1961 the insurgency was primarily an urban phenomenon. By the end of the year rural guerrillas had made an appearance in the state of Falcon. After April 1962 guerrilla activities were reported in at least eight of the country's twenty states. Hastily recruited from the youthful membership of the PCV and MIR and university students, the initial guerrilla bands were poorly organized and militarily inept. Only in Falcon and Trujillo states did they survive the military's counterinsurgency operations. After the military uprisings at the Carúpano and Puerto Cabello naval bases in May and June 1962, a number of disgruntled officers joined the guerrilla ranks.

Following the uprising at Puerto Cabello, the military increased the pressure on Betancourt to take stronger action against extremists. Some senior officers were sensitive to the accusations by their rebellious colleagues at Carúpano and Puerto Cabello that Betancourt had disregarded military rank in choosing his minister of defense and politicized the military to the extent that "party loyalty had become the determining factor in promotions."[8] Most officers had little sympathy for the leftist views that apparently motivated most of the rebels. They were indignant, however, that while the military ringleaders were promptly tried and given stiff sentences, many left-wing civilian leaders remained untouched because of their congressional immunity. Working under a limited suspension of constitutional guarantees, Betancourt suspended the PCV and MIR from any further activity, closed their offices, and banned their publications.[9] No longer permitted to operate legally, the PCV came out officially in support of armed insurrection in December 1962. By then, the National Guard and civil police had successfully contained, although not eliminated, the urban guerrilla tactical units operating in Caracas, while the army had defeated most of the rural guerrilla bands. The leaders of the surviving opposition movements, drawn primarily from the PCV, MIR, and disaffected officers, met in Caracas on February 20, 1963, to establish formally the Armed Forces of National Liberation (FALN).

The FALN represented the disparate opposition groups' most serious attempt at unification and imbued the insurgency effort with a more clearly defined military organization and program of action. The FALN's national commander,

Manuel Ponte Rodríguez, had been one of the leaders of the Puerto Cabello uprising. Although the FALN established numerous rural camps in the early months of 1963, most of its activity was concentrated in Caracas in an effort to disrupt the December 1963 national elections. Operating in small tactical units, the FALN carried out an urban campaign of terrorism in 1963 that brought it worldwide attention. A turning point came on September 29 when FALN commandos attacked a suburban train, killing five national guardsmen and wounding several women and children. Faced with rising demands by military leaders for sterner action against terrorism, Betancourt responded to the attack with a violent campaign against the left. Eight senators and deputies long identified as the intellectual authors of much of the urban terrorism were stripped of their congressional immunity and turned over to military courts for trial. Although Betancourt denied rumors that the harsh measures taken against Communist leaders had been dictated by the military, it seems more than coincidental that regular army troops were used in Caracas to restore and maintain order for the first time since late 1960.[10]

The FALN's failure to disrupt the 1963 elections was a major political defeat and prompted some guerrilla leaders, especially those in prison, to question the wisdom of further armed struggle. In January 1964 the secretary-general of MIR, Domingo Alberto Rangel, came out openly in favor of abandoning the armed struggle.

In March Betancourt stated that he would not as a final presidential act grant amnesty to the Communists in prison. Although during the presidential campaign both major party candidates had opposed any reinstatement of the leftist parties suspended in 1962, President Raúl Leoni announced in his inaugural speech on March 11 that as a gesture of national reconciliation the ban on the PCV's activities would be removed if the party renounced violence. The PCV did not at first support Rangel's position. However, in May the Central Committee indicated for the first time that an end to the fighting was "negotiable" with the government.[11]

Following the 1963 elections, the FALN shifted the center of its guerrilla activities to the countryside.[12] Despite frequent governmental claims in 1964 that the FALN "no longer existed," separate guerrilla fronts reappeared in eight states. Estimates of their strength ranged from 200 to 1,500, but army reports seldom indicated more than a few hundred full-time, active guerrillas. While the guerrillas continued to suffer from chronic disorganization and lack of funds, the military's lack of training in counterinsurgency operations hampered antiguerrilla operations. Under Betancourt no special units or organizations had been established to deal with the insurgency, although Venezuelan military leaders had sounded out the possibility of U.S. assistance as early as September 1963. After the discovery of a Cuban arms cache in November, Betancourt formally requested U.S. advice on surveillance, infiltration intercept tactics, and counterinsurgency.[13] Under President Leoni U.S. Special Forces and Air Commando training teams began working directly with Venezuelan forces. The Venezuelan military rapidly developed an increasing sense of urgency and professionalism in its approach to the guerrilla problem and the application of unconventional tactics to combat it.

By mid–1965 some 9,000 troops—nearly one third of the country's armed forces—were engaged in antiguerrilla operations. Elite units of *cazadores* ("hunters") effectively reduced the extent of guerrilla activity. The Leoni government's reforms in urban and rural areas further eroded the FALN's base of popular support, as did the military's civic action and various public-relations programs. Leoni's modest amnesty campaign under which PCV and MIR leaders were released from prison in March 1966 proved remarkably successful in intensifying political dissension among rebel leaders. Some continued to embrace guerrilla warfare, while others such as Rangel, the Machado brothers, Teodoro Petkoff, and Pompeyo Márquez were now prepared to abandon armed struggle in favor of political action. By the end of 1966 the only major guerrilla movement left was that of Douglas Bravo and Luben Petkoff.[14]

As the rural guerrilla threat receded, a new wave of violence broke out in Caracas. Following the near assassination of the army's chief of staff in December, President Leoni suspended constitutional guarantees and ordered the military occupation of the UCV campus, probably at the insistence of the armed forces.[15] By 1967 the guerrilla movement had sunk to its lowest ebb, with both the scattered *mirista* guerrillas and those of Bravo in a state of decline. Encouraged by Leoni's conciliatory policy, the PCV adopted measures in April that paved the way for the party's eventual return to electoral politics. The PCV condemned terrorism, formally expelled Bravo for "factionalism," set aside armed struggle (without renouncing it), and announced plans to take part in the 1968 elections.[16] In April 1968 Teodoro Petkoff wrote that the "armed struggle in the true sense of the word no longer exists in Venezuela; there are simply armed bands, those headed by Douglas Bravo and the *miristas*, who carry out sporadic operations."[17]

CALDERA'S PACIFICATION POLICY

Although guerrilla activity had declined dramatically, the question of what to do about the insurgents still at large and the broader issue of stability figured prominently in the 1968 campaign.[18] Although COPEI had been part of the Betancourt coalition and shared responsibility for its antiguerrilla policy, the party's candidate, Rafael Caldera, intimated that both Betancourt and Leoni had relied principally on repression in dealing with the insurgents. Critics of AD's policy argued that the government's hard line forced many of the moderate left into open rebellion and generated sympathy for the guerrillas that allowed them to sustain their opposition longer than otherwise would have been possible. For its part, AD boasted that its antiguerrilla policy had succeeded, since Bravo's guerrilla group was the only one left of any consequence. Caldera campaigned for amnesty for the remaining guerrillas. His AD opponent also called for their reincorporation into national political life.[19]

Caldera came into office on March 11, 1969, with a pledge to legalize the PCV and pacify the remaining guerrillas. In his inaugural address Caldera immediately set out to make peace with an offer of amnesty to those guerrillas who would renounce violence and lay down their arms. He also promised to initiate discussions with the Soviet Union to reestablish diplomatic relations.[20] On March 26 Caldera fulfilled another electoral promise by lifting the ban on the PCV's political activity, an action subsequently repeated for the MIR. At the same time he set in motion a pacification policy by offering to negotiate with the guerrillas. He appointed the Archbishop of Caracas, Cardinal José Humberto Quintero, head of a special mediation commission.

Bravo's faction of the FALN temporarily suspended its activities after the government's amnesty offer, although the original proposal was rejected as "unconditional surrender." In late March the guerrillas in Falcon issued a set of conditions (ranging from the elimination of the police and army organizations that had dealt with the guerrillas to demands for diplomatic relations with all socialist countries), which would have to be met before they would lay down their arms. Although the FALN subsequently resumed its activities, a number of the estimated 200 to 300 guerrillas still at large turned themselves in to the government.[21]

Caldera's pacification program is viewed by most observers as the hallmark of his administration. Although isolated guerrilla bands remained after 1969, producing occasional acts of violence, his presidency marks an effective end to insurgency in Venezuela. His policies persuaded many of the government's leftist opponents to abandon the insurrectionist path in favor of legitimate participation in the political system. Several of the Communist leaders freed from prison in 1969, notably Teodoro Petkoff and Pompeyo Márquez, were instrumental in organizing the independent Communist Movement Toward Socialism (MAS) in 1971.[22] By the end of his presidency the left had returned to parliamentary politics through the PCV (1969), MAS (1971), and MIR (1973).

Not all military officers supported Caldera's pacification initiative. For almost a decade the military's primary preoccupation had been with internal security. As Gene Bigler pointed out, by linking insurgency to Castroite foreign intervention, Betancourt successfully undermined the social and political legitimacy of radical opposition. In the process "he legitimized a military role in the maintenance of stability and succeeded in reorienting the mission of the armed forces." In short, the government had given the military a mission and the resources to carry it out.[23]

Some officers doubtlessly feared that civilian authorities would be less inclined to sustain the accustomed level of appropriations for modern weaponry and enviable personal benefits in more peaceful times. However, like his predecessors, Caldera combined a policy of force and flexibility in dealing with the military. He immediately asserted his authority as commander-in-chief by passing over a senior general to pick his defense minister. He reaffirmed military obedience to civilian authority by purging disaffected elements within the officer corps. In August 1969 Caldera ordered the arrest of three high-ranking officers who had publicly criticized government policy. He then ordered military authorities to prosecute the inspector general of the armed forces for conspiracy in seeking support to protest Caldera's criticism of military discipline.[24] In the course of carrying out its counterinsurgency mission, the military acquired a heightened sense of institutional cohesion and an increased level of professionalism. The factionalism and interservice rivalries that had divided the officer corps and hampered antiguerrilla operations in the early 1960s had largely disappeared by the end of the decade.

Another faction of the military conveyed its concern to political leaders over the slow pace of Venezuela's social and economic development. They feared that rising inflation and unemployment would lead to a resumption of guerrilla warfare by radical groups if the country did not accelerate reforms. For the most part, however, officers have tended to view insurgency in Venezuela as an external threat, rather than as a consequence of frustrations with underdevelopment.[25]

Caldera's minister of defense, General García Villasmil, provoked a congressional demand for clarification when he announced that the armed forces could intervene to restore order without civilian authorization. García Villasmil was one of the few officers who succumbed to the sins of higher political ambition. After his retirement he issued a statement about the need for a "decisive change in political procedures," explaining afterward that he had not been seeking to instigate a coup.[26] He later criticized the "decadence" of political parties and expressed dismay over the lack of political rights of officers on active duty. Although some officers may have desired a larger political role for the military, they were unprepared to support García's campaign for the presidency in 1973.[27] For the most part, the military seemed content with its rising professional status. As Donald Herman observed, the armed forces under Caldera were "more apolitical than ever."[28]

A resurgence of guerrilla activity in the spring of 1971, especially in Caracas, worried the Caldera administration enough for it to adopt sterner measures. However, the guerrillas responsible for occasional kidnappings, temporary occupation of small towns, and assaults on police stations lacked any appreciable support from political or popular sectors. According to one source, the number of guerrillas killed by government forces during Caldera's term in office did not exceed ten.[29] Nonetheless, as part of AD's opposition to the Caldera administration, Carlos Andrés Pérez, who as Betancourt's minister of the interior had directed the counterinsurgency campaign in the early 1960s, attacked the government's pacification policy, charging that the state had been left without sufficient force or adequate intelligence services to deal with the guerrillas.[30] In December Caldera pardoned 200 prisoners, including some political leaders and army officers. As further indication of how dramatically the guerrilla ranks had declined since 1969, when guerrillas hijacked a small plane in May 1973 in an effort to revive national interest in their activities, the government simply ignored their demands.

Caldera viewed better relations with Cuba as an essential component of his domestic pacification program. After his inauguration the two countries tacitly agreed to avoid verbal attacks on each other. Venezuela resumed contacts with Cuba, including official exchanges, as part of an effort to develop new relations short of diplomatic recognition. In December 1972 Caldera issued an amnesty to one of two Cuban guerrillas arrested in 1963. For its part, Cuba refrained from intervening overtly in support of Venezuela's few remaining guerrillas.[31]

GUERRILLA ACTIVITY IN VENEZUELA SINCE 1974

Since 1974 Venezuela's remaining guerrillas have had neither the manpower nor the minimum public support necessary to exercise any noticeable impact on the country's general political situation. Although armed attacks were particularly troublesome just before the inauguration of Carlos Andrés Pérez in March 1974, only sporadic reports of guerrilla actions appeared in the press during the first years of his administration. An increase in kidnappings and renewed guerrilla activity, especially by the Bandera Roja (Red Flag) in the mountainous eastern part of the country, forced Pérez to mobilize counterinsurgency units in late 1977. Spokesmen for his administration refused to acknowledge publicly that the country was experiencing a resurgence of guerrilla activity and attributed the various incidents to "irregular" troops or criminal bands.

Although pacification of the guerrilla threat was no longer as intense an issue as it had been in 1969 when Caldera took office, it received some attention from Herrera Campins after his inauguration in 1979. Herrera pardoned a number of the remaining guerrillas in an attempt to complete the reincorporation of the revolutionary left into Venezuela's political life. Among them was Douglas Bravo, who returned to legal status in November 1979 after eighteen years of clandestine operations.

The sudden resignation of Army Commander General Arnaldo Castro Hurtado in May 1979 led to speculation about discord between the government and the military and even to rumors about a possible coup. One source reported that disagreement with the government's pacification program figured largely among the causes of his resignation. Castro was particularly critical of the Chamber of Deputies for paying tribute to the PCV's secretary-general, Gustavo Machado, on the occasion of his retirement from Congress in June. He accused Machado of responsibility for "the death and sacrifice of almost a generation" in the guerrilla warfare of the 1960s.[32]

There has been little evidence of a renewed guerrilla struggle in the 1980s. Sporadic raids have occurred in the eastern states of Monagas and Anzoategui and in the western states of Lara and Falcon, where the military reports that the Red Flag maintains ties with the Colombian Movimiento 19 de Abril (M–19) and the Ejército de Liberación Nacional (ELN). In addition to the Red Flag, other guerrilla groups still thought to be operational include the Revolutionary Organizations (OR), and the Américo Silva Front (FAS). Official estimates of combined guerrilla strength seldom exceed 200 to 300 men.

A more immediate problem facing the Lusinchi administration is how to deal with growing drug use and trafficking. Although military officials have consistently denied charges that the armed forces are involved, the evidence of their increasing complicity is mounting. Venezuela's defense minister, General Humberto Alcalde Alvarez, met with his Colombian counterpart in February 1984 and signed an agreement to increase military cooperation to combat drug trafficking and guerrilla activity along the border.[33]

Lusinchi's government has also discussed normalization of relations with Cuba, which were strained on several occasions during the Herrera administration. According to David Myers, Cuba continues to figure prominently in the Venezuelan military's calculations concerning problems associated with the defense of the Caribbean coastline and with the possibility that guerrilla insurgency might again become a threat to democratic stability.[34] Although there is not likely to be a resurgence of subversion in Venezuela in the foreseeable future, it is one of the factors capable of producing a dramatic shift in the present balance in civil–military relations.

THE ORIGINS OF GUERRILLA VIOLENCE IN COLOMBIA

Guerrilla warfare has been a feature of Colombian life since the late 1940s. Although no precise date can be given to the beginning of the violence, most would agree that partisan rural violence intensified after the election of Conservative President Mariano Ospina Pérez in 1946. Ospina organized special police forces to cope with rising social and political unrest, but these forces were later transformed into repressive agents at the service of the Conservatives. Liberals were widely persecuted, while their own counterattacks, directed by local leadership and confined largely to the rural areas, contributed further to the outbreaks. Thousands of persons sought refuge in the cities, where partisan clashes also began to occur.

On April 9, 1948, the assassination of popular Liberal leader Jorge Gaitán sparked an explosion of mob violence known as the *bogotazo*.[35] Extremist elements within both traditional parties undermined collaborative efforts, and rural violence continued unabated. By the time Conservative chieftain Laureano Gómez returned from his self-imposed exile in June 1949, partisan hostilities had reached new limits.

The breakdown in Colombia's social and political order after 1946 led to the growing involvement of the military in political affairs and the use of the army and National Police as partisan political instruments by Conservative administrations.[36] As the situation worsened, Ospina increased his use of the National Police and the army to harass the Liberals. The reorganization of the former was used as a pretext to purge Liberals remaining in the force, while discrimination adopted against Liberal officers in the army resulted in many of them deserting to the rural areas, where they undertook partisan warfare against the government.[37] Thus, there gradually emerged a pattern of organized guerrilla skirmishes between Liberal guerrillas and government forces and between Liberal and Conservative guerrilla units. Both the military and the National Police became increasingly involved politically as repressive instruments of the central government after Gómez's election on November 27, 1949. By the end of 1952 the rural violence had reached such proportions that many who had initially supported Gómez, including the Conservative followers of Ospina, openly criticized his imposition of dictatorial measures. On June 13, 1953, the armed forces, with their corporate survival threatened and their commander-in-chief, Lieutenant General Gustavo Rojas Pinilla threatened with dismissal, forcibly removed Gómez from office.

Unlike Venezuela, where the guerrilla violence after 1959 was linked directly to the PCV and other leftist parties, it is difficult to assess the extent of the Colombian Communist party's (PCC) involvement in the violence of this period. Although some guerrilla leaders were known Communists, it is much less certain that the violence they pursued was motivated by ideological as opposed to economic or partisan political reasons. Communist influence was evident in several areas involved in the insurgency, especially in the so-called "independent republics." However, the reasons for the violence that brought virtual civil war to much of Colombia's countryside between 1946 and 1953 are extremely complex.[38]

The military's role during the Rojas regime (from 1953 to 1957) was dictated initially by the immediate problem of settling the internecine violence. In early July 1953 Rojas offered a general amnesty to all guerrillas. The military also played an important role in essentially nonmilitary, developmental activities. While measures taken to restore order were highly successful in certain departments, especially the Llanos region, other sections of the country remained in turmoil. Rural violence continued throughout Rojas's dictatorship, although it never duplicated in scope nor in intensity the level at which it operated from 1950 to 1953.

By the mid–1950s politically motivated violence had declined. The military's role in counterinsurgency was overshadowed by a return to interparty agitation, Colombia's mounting economic problems, political corruption, and the repressive practices of Rojas's design to perpetuate his tenure. Internal security under Rojas remained a priority mandate to the National Police. However, in practice both the police and the armed forces in general were called upon to implement repressive political orders.

The 1956 Pact of Benidorm between Gómez and Liberal leader Alberto Lleras Camargo confirmed the union of both parties to oppose Rojas and contained a dramatic appeal to all party members to abandon partisan sentiments. In July 1957 Lleras again consulted with Gómez to work out details for a program of national political conciliation. The resulting Sitges Agreement provided the basis for Colombia's unique experiment in controlled democracy known as the National Front.[39]

GUERRILLA VIOLENCE DURING THE NATIONAL FRONT

With the establishment of the first National Front government of Alberto Lleras (from 1958 to 1962), the major political factor in the insurgency of the period from 1946 to 1958—the interparty rivalry between Liberals and Conservatives—was replaced by intraparty competition. Although another offer of amnesty led to a decline in the level of violence, pockets of guerrilla resistance and widespread banditry remained.

With the rise of Fidel Castro a new threat to Colombia's internal security emerged in the form of ideologically based guerrilla groups intent on overthrowing the government. The first of Cuban-inspired groups to spring up in the early 1960s were organized primarily by idealistic students and intellectuals associated with the Workers, Students, and Peasants Movement (MOEC) and the United Front of Revolutionary Action (FUAR). Although the Partido Comunista de Colombia (PCC) condemned the adventurist activities of these youthful revolutionaries, their appearance prompted the government to mount a campaign against the Communist "independent republics."[40]

In the decade prior to the National Front it had become obvious to authorities that the National Police were incapable of coping with the problems of internal security and public order on a scale associated with La Violencia. As a result, under Lleras the army was given primary responsibility for the planning and implementation of counterinsurgency. The National Police were designated members of the armed forces, placed directly under the command of the minister of defense, and given a supportive role to the army in internal security affairs. Militarily, the change made sense by assigning primary responsibility for counterinsurgency activities to the armed force best organized, trained, and equipped to carry them out. Politically, however, the shift marked a significant change in the definition of the military's traditional role. In effect, it made the armed forces a legitimate political instrument responsible for defending the National Front coalition. Since under the terms of the National Front agreement neither presidential nor congressional elections were actually contested between opposing parties, one of the dominant issues in politics between 1958 and 1974 was the question of the National Front's survival.

The historic change in the military's mission was also influenced by the decision of the United States to shift the basis for its military assistance program to Latin America from hemispheric defense to internal security. By mid-1962 evidence of this shift can be seen in the Colombian military's approach toward the control of guerrilla activity. With some technical assistance from U.S. officials, a counterinsurgency plan was conceived and implemented under the direction of the minister of war, Major General Alberto Ruíz Novoa. "Plan Lazo" called for special training in antiguerrilla operations, intelligence techniques, and the development of military civic-action programs. Military civic action became an integral part of the army's mission during the 1960s, especially after the emergence of the pro-Castro National Liberation Army (ELN) in 1964 and the Communist-dominated Revolutionary Armed Forces of Colombia (FARC) in 1966.[41]

With the appearance of the ELN, the Conservative administration of Guillermo León Valencia (from 1962 to 1966) found itself dealing with a new type of insurgency group. Unlike the Liberal–Conservative banditry, the existence of self-contained "independent republics" and the short-lived actions of the MOEC and FUAR during the early years of the National Front, the ELN and the FARC placed primary focus on the seizure of national power.[42] The new guerrilla threat resulted in a quantum jump in military manpower. Between 1964 and 1966 the army more than doubled in size from under 23,000 to an estimated 53,500.[43]

In contrast to the Castroite character of the ELN, the FARC emerged under the tutelage of the PCC in what amounted to a defensive reaction to the military's attacks on the "independent republics." Under the leadership of Manuel Marulanda Velez, the FARC recruited some 500 active guerrillas and several thousand peasant supporters during its first years of activity. However, the PCC withdrew much of its economic support after the Liberal administration of Carlos Lleras Restrepo (from 1967 to 1970) established relations with the Soviet Union in 1968.[44]

Unlike their Venezuelan counterparts, Colombia's major revolutionary guerrilla movements survived the military's counterinsurgency operations of the late 1960s, although heavy casualties and the mass arrest of suspected urban supporters reduced substantially their organizational strength.[45] All three groups experienced further setbacks during the final National Front presidency of Conservative Misael Pastrana Borrero (from 1970 to 1974).

Military operations carried out against guerrilla units operating in the middle Magdalena region were particularly successful in late 1973. Two of the ELN's founders were killed and a third captured, leading Colombia's defense minister to claim that the ELN had suffered its "greatest setback in eight years."[46] The Ejército Popular de Liberación (EPL) also suffered critical losses that led to predictions of its "imminent elimination," while the FARC's relative inactivity led to speculation in early 1974 that Marulanda had left the country.[47]

During Pastrana's presidency, the essential role of the military remained unchanged. In addition to its counterinsurgency priority, special military units continued to work in conjunction with the National Police to suppress occasional urban disorders involving students and workers and to eliminate networks of urban support for the surviving guerrilla fronts.

GUERRILLA VIOLENCE IN THE POST-NATIONAL FRONT PERIOD

Under Liberal President Alfonso López Michelsen (from 1974 to 1978) the military once again became deeply involved in counterinsurgency offensives. Despite extensive operations, the government was unable to eliminate rural guerrilla groups. The ELN belied periodic army reports of its "eradication" and celebrated ten years of armed struggle in January 1975 with several major attacks. Similarly, the FARC displayed its ability to regroup and conduct sporadic actions on an increasing number of fronts. Only the EPL failed to sustain its viability as a rural guerrilla movement. By 1974 it had turned almost exclusively to acts of urban violence.

The M–19, a new revolutionary group claiming to be the armed branch of the National Popular Alliance (ANAPO), made its first appearance in January 1974. The M–19's theft of Bolívar's sword brought the movement notoriety, but authorities did not consider the group a serious urban guerrilla threat until it kidnapped and murdered a prominent labor leader prior to the 1976 midterm elections.

The resurgence of guerrilla activity in 1975 forced the army to increase counterinsurgency actions, spurring debate within the officer corps over the most appropriate means of dealing with the guerrilla problem. One faction, headed by army commander General Alvaro Valencia Tovar, advocated widespread social reforms as the best means of eliminating popular resistance to the government. A second tendency, represented by Defense Minister Abraham Varon Valencia, perceived the solution to popular discontent in military terms through the repression of "subversive" groups. As the leader of the military reformists, Valencia believed that the guerrillas could be contained militarily but could only be defeated through political action. Like Ruíz a decade earlier, Valencia became openly critical of the civilian administration and his military superiors for failing to implement basic structural changes rather than rely on new antiguerrilla offensives. Amid widespread rumors of a coup attempt, President López and his defense minister engineered the forcible retirement of Valencia and several of his principal supporters in June 1975.

General Valencia's removal was broadly interpreted as a victory for the hard-line faction that had been pushing for increased military action against the guerrillas and a firmer stand by the government against continuing labor and student unrest. Guerrilla and terrorist activities remained a cause of concern throughout López's term in office, although at no time did they constitute a direct threat to the stability of the government. Military spokesmen maintained the position that neither the government nor the armed forces would negotiate with the rebels. The notion of amnesty for guerrilla groups was rejected within official circles at this time, although the idea appeared to receive some support from retired military officers in 1976.[48]

During the presidency of Liberal Julio César Turbay Ayala (from 1978 to 82), the armed forces increased their assigned responsibiltiy for maintaining internal security to assume a greater role in the administration of justice. Within a month after assuming office, Turbay's defense minister, General Luis Carlos Camacho Leyva, announced an ''unrestrained offensive'' against guerrillas in keeping with Turbay's campaign promise to ''wage war against crime and subversion.'' On September 6, 1978, Turbay decreed a controversial security statute that gave military courts jurisdiction over many ''political'' crimes. During his term in office, Turbay was careful to repudiate charges of human-rights violations brought against the military and praised military leaders for ''not allowing their institution to be lured by the temptation of power.''[49]

The military's continued inability to eliminate guerrilla activity was a major factor leading to increased military influence during the Turbay administration. The M–19's widely publicized theft of weapons from a Bogotá barracks in late 1978 and its seizure of diplomatic hostages at the Embassy of the Dominican Republic in February 1980 underscore the military's tendency to overstate its ability to bring the guerrilla situation under control. The latter incident also exposed a continuing struggle between Turbay and the military high command over the formulation of antiguerrilla policy. While Turbay worked through Congress to secure some form of limited amnesty for the guerrillas, the military hard-liners headed by General Camacho pursued a policy intended to demonstrate that the guerrillas still represented a threat requiring a military solution.

The military also adopted a strident anticommunist stance during Turbay's presidency, claiming that Colombia's guerrillas were receiving tactical and financial support from Cuba and the Soviet Union. Cuba's alleged training of Colombian guerrillas strained relations between the two countries in early 1981, culminating with President Turbay's decision on March 23 to suspend diplomatic relations. The action followed an invasion attempt by M–19 guerrillas in southern Colombia, many of whom were known to have spent time in Havana. Although the M–19's invasion was a military disaster, it marked the movement's transition from a predominantly urban guerrilla movement to one that since 1981 has been engaged more actively in rural struggle.[50]

The military's reaction to the M–19's invasion and the subsequent break in diplomatic relations with Cuba were followed closely by a warning from army commander General Fernando Landazabal Reyes about a prolonged battle against subversion and an appeal for socioeconomic and political changes. In an editorial appearing in the *Army Review*, General Landazabal revived political and developmental concerns previously articulated by Ruiz Novoa and Valencia Tovar. Expressing the army's deep concern over the situation in 1981, Landazabal stated:

Subversion survives, with greater strength than before, and with the souls of patriotic and loyal soldiers, we have the vague premonition of worse days to come. We are convinced that the army can militarily destroy the guerrillas, but we are also convinced that . . . this subversion will continue as long as the objective and subjective conditions in the economic, social, and political fields, which daily impair and disrupt stability, are not modified.[51]

It is a measure of the military's increased political influence under Turbay that Landazabal was not officially reprimanded, much less cashiered, for espousing a position that had been politically unacceptable during earlier administrations.

The failure of the government's initial amnesty proposal led Turbay to appoint an ad hoc peace commission headed by former president Carlos Lleras. There is some indication that the commission was close to a peace settlement with the M–19 when it became embroiled in electoral politics, prompting Turbay to curtail its activities.[52]

Guerrilla groups greeted the 1982 campaign and election of Conservative Belisario Betancur (from 1982 to 1986) with an undeclared suspension of armed activity. In June the M–19's leaders asked the president-elect for a general amnesty for all political prisoners and the "demilitarization" of the country. Marulanda Velez announced that the FARC was prepared to initiate a peace dialogue with the new government. The prospects were encouraging that the new president, who had campaigned vigorously on a pledge to bring peace to the country, would act quickly to negotiate a settlement of Colombia's long-standing insurgency problem.

BETANCUR'S PEACE INITIATIVES

In his inaugural address on August 7 President Betancur appealed to the guerrillas to accept the "white flag of truce" and reincorporate themselves into national life. By the end of 1982 he had established an all-party peace commission (including a representative from the PCC) and persuaded Congress to approve a new amnesty, which dropped most of the conditions attached to the government's previous offers under Turbay. Guerrilla leaders began meeting openly with senior government officials.

In the spring of 1983 Betancur made a rapid tour of Central America and assumed the lead in pursuing the regional peace initiative previously championed by Venezuela and Mexico. From the beginning Betancur linked the Contadora Group's approach to Central America to his domestic strategy in dealing with the M–19 and FARC, that of negotiated settlement. His pacification policy thus took on an international dimension directly related to the relative success or failure of the Contadora's efforts to alleviate tensions in Central America.

Betancur's hopes for an early peace settlement in Colombia failed when the M–19 announced in April 1983 that it was returning to armed struggle. Although an estimated 250 to 1,000 guerrillas had accepted the government's amnesty offer, there were few leaders among them. The fact that some 20 guerrillas who did turn themselves in were murdered in early 1983 and another 50 or so "disappeared" attested to the general climate of violence that existed in mid–1983.[53] Nevertheless, contacts between the government and guerrilla leaders continued. In October a presidential spokesman confirmed that Betancur had met with M–19 leaders in Madrid and agreed to hold further talks in early 1984. The EPL, which had previously opposed the government's amnesty and pacification initiatives, also announced its willingness to meet with government representatives.

For their part, military leaders made no secret of their displeasure that the amnesty did not provide for disarming the guerrillas. They also complained that troops continued to be ambushed with alarming frequency—144 times in 1983—and that several score of the guerrillas amnestied since November 1982 had rejoined guerrilla ranks.[54] In congressional testimony Defense Minister Landazabal stated that the military would not yield to guerrilla demands that the army withdraw from the main areas of conflict, nor would it agree to dialogue with the rebels. In a New Year's message to the Colombian people General Landazabal indicated that the military ''respected'' Betancur's efforts to establish peace talks with the guerrillas, but it did not support a cease-fire. He warned that the guerrillas were preparing to launch new actions in 1984 and emphasized that the military would continue to use force in dealing with subversion. In a document delivered to Betancur in early January, the top commanders of the armed forces expressed support for Landazabal's position on the need to take stronger action against the guerrillas.

Betancur responded to the military's complaints by reprimanding Landazabal and his supporters for publicly criticizing the efforts of the Peace Commission to reach an agreement with the guerrillas. He ''persuaded'' Landazabal to resign, reaffirming that the government would continue to pursue talks with the guerrillas and reminding the armed forces to adhere to their constitutional role as a non-deliberative body.[55]

With military opposition muted, Betancur's persistent negotiations culminated in 1984 in historic truce agreements with three of Colombia's four major guerrilla movements. The FARC agreed to a one-year cease-fire, effective May 28, while the M–19, the EPL, and the small Workers Self-Defense Movement (ADO) agreed to suspend armed activity indefinitely after August 30. Neither accord required the guerrillas to surrender their weapons, nor did the government make any explicit commitment to withdraw troops from guerrilla strongholds. The pact with the FARC affirmed the government's willingness to encourage adoption by the Congress of agrarian reform and laws designed to broaden the electoral representation of opposition parties and their access to news media. The agreement with the M–19, EPL, and ADO called for the convening of a ''national dialogue'' in which the country's various political forces would participate.[56] The ELN and splinter groups within the FARC and M–19 refused to negotiate with the government and continued guerrilla operations in an effort to sabotage the peace agreements.

Betancur managed to keep the peace throughout 1984 largely by force of his persuasive personality and negotiating powers. However, internal dissension and long-standing ideological differences between the country's guerrilla movements complicated the peace process in 1985.

Drawing on the organizational and financial support of the PCC, the FARC announced plans to reconstitute itself as a political movement and engage in legal political activity with the Patriotic Union, a coalition of leftist parties including the PCC and the Workers Socialist party. On March 31, 1985, the FARC's directorate met with members of the National Verification Commission to affirm its participation in the 1986 elections. The FARC established political headquarters in major cities and began publication of a weekly newspaper. Marulanda consistently praised Betancur's peace policy. In July he assured the government that the FARC would continue to honor the truce agreement as it moved closer to launching its political campaign. In August Marulanda announced that FARC representatives would join the national dialogue in an attempt to revitalize the peace process.

In contrast, the M–19 has lacked a consistent policy regarding the cease-fire, the national dialogue, or its political future. Unlike the FARC, the M–19 lacks the tutelage of an established political party. Throughout the early months of 1985 various M–19 spokesmen asserted they would neither surrender their arms nor participate in the 1986 elections in protest over the government's lack of progress in implementing social and economic reforms. The M–19's leadership appeared to be irrevocably divided over the question of its political future, leading the government to complain of numerous "irregularities" in M–19's compliance with the truce. In December and January the army surrounded M–19 troops in Valle del Cauca and forbade the guerrillas from establishing armed camps similar to the "independent republics" of the early 1960s. In June the military moved forcefully against M–19 columns in central Valle, prompting a guerrilla spokesman to proclaim that the M–19's truce with the government was "broken."

With the FARC committed to upholding the peace process, government officials adopted a firm stance in dealing with the unpredictable M–19 leadership. The military repeatedly warned that no new talks should be held with the M–19 as long as it persisted in armed struggle.[57] With President Betancur claiming that 90 percent of Colombia's estimated 10,000 guerrillas had accepted the government's truce and would participate in the 1986 elections as a political force, the military was given a free hand to deal severely with the remaining insurgents. At the opening of Congress in July Betancur reaffirmed his support for the armed forces in their struggle against the guerrillas, stating that in Colombia's case, the groups up in arms could be overcome "with a minimum cost."[58]

During the final year of Betancur's presidency, the army inflicted heavy casualties on M–19 columns operating in Antioquia, Valle de Cauca, Cauca, and southern Quindio. Ivan Marino Ospina, the M–19's top leader who had met with Betancur in Mexico City in December 1984, was killed during a shootout in

Cali on August 28, 1985. The M–19's attack on the Palace of Justice in Bogotá on November 6 brought universal opprobrium to the movement and intensified the military's resolve to eliminate the surviving members of the M–19's leadership. Marino's successor, Alvaro Fayad, was killed on March 13, 1986, during a military operation in Bogotá. The army subsequently confirmed the death of Israel Santamaría and Gustavo Arias Londono, both members of the M–19's high command. By mid–1986 the army firmly believed that it was militarily and psychologically winning the war against the M–19.

Although Betancur encountered numerous obstacles in advancing his peace proposals, both domestically and in Central America, he refused to back away from them on either front during his final year in office. From the beginning, Betancur's peace initiatives assumed a highly personalist, improvisational character, thereby ensuring necessary flexibility but risking ephemerality. Neither of Colombia's major political parties took a firm stand in support of Betancur's peace program during the 1986 election campaign. The Liberals appeared willing to abandon the bipartisan peace process on the assumption that an opposition role would help them defeat the Conservatives. None of the three major candidates for the 1986 presidential election adopted an unequivocal position in support of Betancur's initiatives. The victorious Liberal candidate, Virgilio Barco Vargas, campaigned on a platform promising greater firmness against guerrillas and more economic and social assistance for the country's poor.[59]

The lack of political consensus, accentuated by the recent change in administration, brings into question the continuity of Colombia's pacification program after August 1986. The Congress, which voted in September 1984 to reject participation in the "national dialogue" with guerrilla leaders, passed legislation in 1985 to pardon political criminals and to allow for the popular election of mayors. The implementation of both measures is vitally important if the guerrillas are to reincorporate themselves into national political life.[60] During Betancur's term in office, Congress failed to approve any of the substantive social and economic reforms he pledged to put forward under the truce accords. The promise of a land distribution program and improvements in health, housing, and education conditions went unfulfilled—a failure that by mid–1985 had cost Betancur most of his original support for the peace initiative.

Some critics charge that Betancur's government failed to institutionalize the mechanisms through which a lasting peace could be attained. Others point out that the government's failure to establish clear guidelines for political participation by the guerrillas has created confusion and threatens to destroy the entire peace process. Although there may be some validity to such criticism, even Betancur's harshest critics do not fault him for lack of good intentions. Although the prospect of total pacification in Colombia remains distant, Betancur set in motion a process that, combined with effective counterinsurgency operations, has the potential to reduce the country's long-standing guerrilla problem to a few isolated, dissident groups.

As the Venezuelan case suggests, a successful pacification process requires the transformation of the guerrillas into a legal political movement. In March 1986 the FARC signed a peace document that adds to the 1984 agreement of La Uribe. The Patriotic Union's poor showing at the polls in the 1986 general and presidential elections, together with scattered but persistent reports of clashes between the army and FARC fronts operating in Antioquia, Caqueta, and Meta, underscore the fragility of the truce agreement. Nevertheless, at least for the moment, the FARC remains committed to pursuing the implementation of peace accords with the new government.

CONCLUSIONS

There is a beginning and a reasonably clear end to the guerrilla violence in Venezuela that one does not find in the case of Colombia. The origins of La Violencia in Colombia are considerably more complex, although the guerrilla movements that emerged in the 1960s shared the same overall objective as their Venezuelan counterparts—the overthrow of the national government.

Unlike Colombia, where the guerrilla violence predates the rise of Castro and has incontrovertibly indigenous roots, the Venezuelan insurgency was treated as Cuban inspired and external in its origins. This had important consequences in defining the military's role. The armed forces' primary mission defined for it by civilian authorities after 1959 was to defend the nation from external threat originating from Cuban support and training of Venezuelan guerrillas. The targeting of predominantly U.S. firms, missions, and personnel reinforced the external character of the Venezuelan violence, especially during its urban phase. Consequently, the Venezuelan military has been less preoccupied with the possible social and economic causes of guerrilla violence and less prone than its Colombian counterparts to embrace a developmental or reformist ideology. The Venezuelan military has also been less directly involved in civic-action programs.

The Venezuelan insurgency began as an urban movement dominated by students affiliated with the MIR and PCV. Betancourt acted with considerable restraint confronting urban violence from 1960 to 1962 in deference to AD's tenuous relationship with the moderate opposition parties, the left, and the military. The government relied mainly on the civil police and the national guard—not the army—to cope with the urban insurgency.

When urban terrorism intensified in 1962 and 1963, the Venezuelan government was able to capture, imprison, or otherwise "neutralize" most of the leaders involved. It was aided in this by the fact that a number of the most militant leftists served in Congress. Also, urban guerrillas made extensive use of the National University of Caracas as a center of operations and sanctuary. Much of the Communist leadership abandoned the tactic of armed struggle after the killing or capture of key guerrilla leaders. To the degree that Venezuela's guerrillas were an extension of leftist political parties, they were less able to sustain themselves, especially in rural areas, once the party leadership had withdrawn their support.

In contrast, Colombia's guerrilla movements, which originated in the countryside, have no formal party ties, although the FARC arguably receives its directives through the PCC, and the M–19 claimed, at least initially, to be the armed wing of ANAPO. The lack of any political ties has been one of the inherent weaknesses of the insurgent movement in Colombia. On the other hand, the guerrillas' lack of domestic or international political support may account in part for their longevity, since the various groups have long been accustomed to financing themselves locally through kidnappings, extortion and assaults.

On balance, Venezuela has been more successful than Colombia in coopting guerrilla demands for social and economic reform. The country's vast oil revenues have allowed it to institute agrarian reform and provide other forms of social assistance that have helped to erode the base of popular support for guerrilla movements. Colombia, despite basically prudent fiscal policies during the recent period of debt crisis, simply does not have the necessary financial resources to implement a massive social rehabilitation plan for amnestied guerrillas. Nor has the Colombian political elite been as responsive in meeting the demands of nonrevolutionary groups for broader social, economic, and political reform.

Venezuela's success in combating insurgency in the early 1960s was due in no small part to the inherent organizational and tactical weakness of the guerrilla movement. The PCV, for example, followed what one writer called an "incoherent" policy in 1962 and 1963 of promoting urban terrorism, rural insurgency, military coups, and parliamentary activity. In 1964 a badly weakened party shifted to a strategy of "prolonged" rural guerrilla warfare, without taking into account the relatively small size of the Venezuelan peasant population or its pro-AD leanings.[61] In short, the guerrillas were unable to establish a firm base in the countryside or to achieve a positive public image in the urban areas. Most important, at no time did the guerrilla bands in Venezuela grow strong enough to become a real military threat to the government. Compared to Colombia, there were fewer guerrillas operating on fewer fronts. Although size in numbers is not the sole determinant of guerrilla strength or effectiveness, it affects a movement's credibility and ability to survive. At no time did the rural-based guerrillas in Venezuela number more than 2,000. By 1966 the guerrillas had ceased to be a factor in Venezuelan life. Although their members, numbering at most 300, still continued sporadic attacks on towns and army patrols, their political and numerical importance was negligible. Clearly, the guerrillas in Venezuela had been soundly defeated militarily several years before Caldera undertook his pacification program.

If there is a lesson to be learned from the Venezuelan example, it is that guerrillas must be militarily defeated or so severely disillusioned through attrition and exhaustion that insurgency is no longer an acceptable alternative to the legal expression of discontent. Guerrilla leaders must be able to rationalize abandoning their revolutionary rhetoric for amnesty and a partial stake in the system, or at least the promise of being allowed to compete for one.[62] Venezuela defeated the guerrillas in Caracas and elsewhere and then provided them with the opportunity for legitimate representation.

In Colombia the insurgent groups have never been as close to physical elimination as their Venezuelan counterparts were by 1969, although they may have approached that point during the period from 1969 to 1971. However, given the electoral restraints imposed by the National Front and ANAPO's narrow defeat in the 1970 presidential elections, the Pastrana government had neither the inclination nor the constitutional means to reincorporate the guerrillas.

"Pacification" as understood by the Colombian military during the National Front was synonymous with counterinsurgency. Since the National Front's constitutional arrangement prohibited the electoral participation of leftist parties that would not attach themselves to either the Liberal or Conservative label, it was not until after the formal expiration of the National Front in 1974 that the governing coalition might have considered the political reintegration of the guerrillas. The resurgence of guerrilla activity in 1975, especially the emergence of the M–19, discouraged reconciliation during the López presidency and for most of Turbay's administration. Only since 1982 have most of Colombia's insurgents had the option of amnesty and the opportunity to establish a legal political movement. In much the same manner that Caldera, free from the AD's hardline, anticommunist approach toward insurgency, found himself able to enact a pacification program in 1969, Belisario Betancur, an "independent" Conservative, was able to devote himself to a bipartisan peace initiative that none of his predecessors found politically feasible.[63] The resignation of General Landazabal and most of Colombia's high command in January 1984 eliminated, at least temporarily, overt military resistance to ending the insurgency by amnesty. To achieve total pacification, the Colombian political system at some point will have to move beyond a two-party system in order to accommodate leftist dissent. The popular election of mayors can be viewed as a cautious, initial step in that direction.

Counterinsurgency has been a key factor in accelerating professionalism, modern weapon procurement, and a dramatic increase in the size of the armed forces in both Venezuela and Colombia. Evidence of civilian dominance is apparent in both countries in the examples of forced retirement, courtmartial, and even incarceration of officers, although democratic leaders have been careful to maintain the military's institutional prerogatives.

The military establishment poses no threat to liberal democracy in either Venezuela or Colombia at the present time. Betancur curbed some of the repressive tendencies of the Colombian military, as well as the fears of "creeping militarism" that surfaced during the Turbay administration. It would require a dramatic breakdown of the political process or an economic collapse to bring about an active military intervention in either country.

Civilian political elites will be severely tested in the next several years, especially in the economic arena. It is likely that the recent pattern of civil–military relations will undergo major strains but continue essentially in balance as long as civilian authorities can maintain existing levels of competency and legitimacy.

NOTES

1. John A. Peeler, *Latin American Democracies: Colombia, Costa Rica, Venezuela* (Chapel Hill: University of North Carolina Press, 1985).

2. The classic studies in English on caudillism and the Venezuelan military are Robert L. Gilmore, *Caudillism and Militarism in Venezuela, 1810–1910* (Athens: Ohio University Press, 1964), and Winfield J. Burggraaff, *The Venezuelan Armed Forces in Politics, 1935–1959* (Columbia: University of Missouri Press, 1972).

3. For a discussion of the negotiations and their outcome, see José Antonio Gil Yepes, *The Challenge of Venezuelan Democracy*, transl. Evelyn Harrison I., Lolo Gil de Yanes, and Danielle Salti (New Brunswick N.J.: Transaction Books, 1981), pp. 50–51.

4. Howard I. Blutstein, et al., *Area Handbook for Venezuela* (Washington, D.C.: U.S. Government Printing Office, 1977), p. 225. Robert J. Alexander places the PCV's membership in 1961 at 40,000; see his *The Communist Party of Venezuela* (Stanford, Calif.: Hoover Institution Press, 1969), p. 138.

5. For a concise analysis of the role of university students and their interactions with political parties in the period of insurrectionary violence, see Daniel H,. Levine, *Conflict and Political Change in Venezuela* (Princeton, N.J.: Princeton University Press, 1973), especially Chapters 6 and 7.

6. Philip Taylor notes that the privilege of university autonomy was of particular significance in Venezuela because of the size of the UCV campus and its location in the heart of the capital. See his chapter on Venezuela in D.M. Condit, et al., eds., "Venezuela," *Challenge and Response in Internal Conflict*, vol. 3, *The Experience in Africa and Latin America* (Washington, D.C.: American University, 1968), p. 474.

7. For an account sympathetic to the left, see James Petras, "Revolution and Guerrilla Movements in Latin America: Venezuela, Colombia, Guatemala, and Peru," in *Latin America: Reform or Revolution?*, ed. James Petras (Greenwich, Conn.: Fawcett Publications, 1968), pp. 337–43. For an account of the period favorable to the government, see Robert J. Alexander. *The Venezuelan Democratic Revolution: A Profile of the Regime of Rómulo Betancourt* (New Brunswick: N.J.: Rutgers University Press, 1964), pp. 118–36.

8. Steve Ellner, "Political Party Dynamics and the Outbreak of Guerrilla Warfare in Venezuela," *Inter-American Economic Affairs* 34 (Autumn 1980):11.

9. Alexander, *The Communist Party*, pp. 80–81.

10. Taylor, "Venezuela," p. 485.

11. Richard Gott, *Guerrilla Movements in Latin America* (Garden City: N.Y.: Doubleday, 1972), p. 149.

12. Talton Ray provides an interesting analysis of why the extremist strategy of the PCV and MIR did not produce more support among Venezuela's urban marginals. In addition to the left's serious miscalculations concerning the barrio residents' "ripeness" for revolt, the government's positive social measures were effective in weakening leftist influence. Most important, urban guerrilla warfare proved to be a grave tactical error. Feelings of hostility toward the Betancourt government's methods of repression were more than offset by the mood of revulsion that developed in the barrios against terrorist

actions, many of whose victims, for example, policemen, were barrio residents. See Talton F. Ray, *The Politics of the Barrios of Venezuela* (Berkeley: University of California Press, 1969), pp. 130–36.

13. It was apparent to one U.S. team member that one of the great deficiencies, if not the greatest, within the Venezuelan military establishment was the lack of a joint concept of operations. The lack of facilities for interservice communication and the absence of personnel trained in any facet of intelligence further weakened the military's counterinsurgency capability. See Immanuel J. Klette, "U.S. Assistance to Venezuela and Chile in Combatting Insurgency, 1963–1964," *Conflict* 3 (1982):227–44.

14. According to Mario Menendez Rodríguez, who interviewed Douglas Bravo and Luben Petkoff in December 1966, Bravo commanded a guerrilla force numbering some 110. For Menendez's account, see "Guerrillas At War," *Atlas* 13, (June 1967):19–23.

15. David Eugene Blank, *Politics in Venezuela* (Boston: Little, Brown, and Company, 1973), p. 219.

16. Alexander, *The Communist Party*, p. 106. Leoni permitted the PCV to propose a slate of candidates for the 1968 elections under the banner of the Unión Para Avanzar.

17. Teodoro Petkoff, as quoted in Luigi Valsalice, *Guerrilla y Política: Curso de Acción en Venezuela, 1962–1969* (Buenos Aires: Editorial Pleamar, 1975), p. 78.

18. For an analysis of the 1968 campaign, see David J. Myers, *Democratic Campaigning in Venezuela: Caldera's Victory* (Caracas: Editorial Sucre, 1973).

19. Ibid., p. 131.

20. The best summary in English of Caldera's pacification policy is by Donald L. Herman, *Christian Democracy in Venezuela* (Chapel Hill: University of North Carolina Press, 1980), pp. 132–34.

21. The only exceptions to Caldera's pacification program were people accused of specific crimes. However, it was reported that even in such cases few who sought amnesty were prosecuted. H.J. Maidenberg, "Venezuela Finds Terror Abating," *The New York Times*, July 19, 1970, p. 19.

22. According to David J. Myers, MAS has since become Venezuela's third political force, "the only one with even a remote chance of breaking the domination over Venezuelan politics currently exercised by COPEI and AD." See his "Venezuela's MAS," *Problems of Communism* 29 (September–October 1980):16–27.

23. Gene E. Bigler, "Professional Soldiers and Restrained Politics in Venezuela," in *New Military Politics in Latin America*, ed. Robert Wesson (New York: Praeger, 1982), p. 177. From 1959 to 1970 the military consistently received over 10 percent of the annual national budget, while the army almost doubled in size from 10,000 to 18,000 men. The figures are derived from *The Statesman's Yearbook* (New York: St. Martin's Press), 1959–1960, 1970–1971.

24. Herman, *Christian Democracy*, pp. 128–29.

25. Gene E. Bigler, "The Armed Forces and Patterns of Civil-Military Relations," in *Venezuela: The Democratic Experience*, eds. John D. Martz and David J. Myers (New York: Praeger, 1977), p. 131. Betancourt consistently denounced Cuban subversion as the major threat to the country. Leoni also treated Fidel Castro as an international delinquent.

26. *Latin America Weekly Report*, January 17, 1971, p. 186.

27. Judith Ewell, *Venezuela: A Century of Change* (Stanford, Calif.: Stanford University Press, 1984), p. 171.

28. Herman, *Christian Democracy*, p. 124.

29. Ibid., pp. 133.

30. *Latin America Weekly Report*, March 12, 1971, p. 86. Pérez was especially critical of Lorenzo Fernández, Caldera's minister of the interior and principal architect of his pacification policy. At the time, Fernández was already touted as the likely COPEI presidential candidate in 1973.

31. Marvine Howe, "Venezuela Opens Cuban Contacts," *The New York Times*, April 22, 1973, p. 17. Venezuela resumed full diplomatic relations with Cuba on December 30, 1974.

32. *Latin American Weekly Report*, June 1, 1979, p. 1; also *Yearbook on International Communist Affairs*, ed. Richard F. Starr (Stanford, Calif.: Hoover Institution Press, 1980), p. 400. Ex-President Pérez also renewed his denunciation of COPEI's "indiscriminate" amnesties for former guerrillas.

33. *The New York Times*, February 20, 1984.

34. David J. Myers, *Venezuela's Pursuit of Caribbean Basin Interests:Implications for United States National Security* (Santa Monica, Calif.: Rand Corporation, 1985), pp. 15, 35.

35. It is ironic that on the same day that Gaitán was assassinated, Manual Marulanda Velez, alias Tirofijo, escaped from prison in Ibague, Tolima. Marulanda became well known as a bandit leader during the early years of violence. He later became and still remains the principal leader of the Revolutionary Armed Forces of Colombia (FARC).

36. By 1946, the army had succeeded in staying out of active politics for over forty years. For the most part, it had avoided being used for political ends by the successive civilian administrations during that time. Its gradual development and acceptance as a national force, as opposed to political or regional, and its abstention from direct intervention, had firmly established the military's tradition as a nonpolitical institutional force in Colombian society and its subordination to civilian authority. For an overview of the Colombian military, see the author's "The Colombian Armed Forces in Search of a Mission," in *New Military Politics,* ed. Wesson; also J. Mark Ruhl, "The Military," in *Politics of Compromise: Coalition Government in Colombia*, eds. R. Albert Berry, Ronald G. Hellman, and Mauricio Solaún (New Brunswick, N.J.: Transaction Books, 1980).

37. James M. Daniel, *Rural Violence in Colombia Since 1946* (Princeton, N.J.: Special Operations Research Office, Washington, D.C., 1965), p. 7.

38. The classic study of La Violencia is that of Monsignor Germán Guzman, Orlando Fals Borda, and Eduardo Umana Luna, *La Violencia en Colombia: Estudio de un Proceso Social*, Volume 1, second edition, and Volume 2 (Bogotá: Ediciones Tercer Mundo, 1964).

39. For an assessment of the National Front, see Harvey F. Kline, "The National Front: Historical Perspective and Overview," in *Politics of Compromise*, eds. Berry et al., pp. 59–83.

40. See Gott, *Guerrilla Movements*, Chapter 4, for a description of the fall of one such "independent republic," Marquetalia.

41. For an evaluation of Colombia's early civic-action program, see Edward Glick, "The Nonmilitary Use of the Latin American Military," *Background* 8 (November 1964):161–73. The military's initial involvement in a developmental role appears to have been well received within the officer corps, despite some concern that civic-action programs were incompatible with the military's primary functions and its professional status.

Indeed, it was Ruíz Novoa's insistence on a larger role for the armed forces in Colombia's socioeconomic development that led to his dismissal in January 1965.

42. For an interview of the insurgent groups of the 1960s, see Richard Maullin, *Soldiers, Guerrillas, and Politics in Colombia* (Lexington, Mass.: D.C. Heath, 1973).

43. Ibid., p. 82. The prolonged existence of guerrilla movements in Colombia has undoubtedly made it easier for the military to justify its demands for greater autonomy in areas of professional concern affecting personnel, budget, and organization, and to maintain a viable institutional role in a system in which civilian political elite have been traditionally antimilitary. Despite the military's continuous involvement in counterinsurgency activity, the size of Colombia's armed forces has remained relatively stable since the late 1960s at approximately 65,000 to 70,000 men. The most recent figures for 1984 list the army with 57,000, the navy with 9,200 (including a brigade of marines with 2,500 officers and men), and the air force with 4,000, for a total 70,200. In addition, the National Police, which has been under military control since 1960, presently has an estimated 56,000 men, compared to 35,000 in 1975 and only 10,000 in the mid–1960s. *The Statesman's Yearbook* (1966–67, 1975–76, and 1984–85).

44. In a recent comparative study of guerrilla warfare, Brian Loveman and Thomas Davies noted that like their FALN counterparts in Venezuela, some FARC leaders resigned from the PCC in the period from 1967 to 1970, when the party deemphasized the armed struggle and returned to electoral politics. See *Che Guevara: Guerrilla Warfare* (Lincoln: University of Nebraska Press, 1985), P. 278. PCC candidates were required to run under the banner of the Liberal Revolutionary Party in 1970 but were allowed to campaign under their own party label in the April 1972 elections for departmental assemblies and municipal councils.

45. Estimates of membership early in 1972 ranked the ELN first with about 250 men, followed by the FARC with 150, and the People's Liberation Army (EPL), a pro-Chinese group that began operations in 1967, with 80 members. *The New York Times*, January 23, 1972, p. 18.

46. *El Siglo*, October 10, 1973, p. 2.

47. *El Tiempo*, March 3, 1974, p. 6.

48. Ibid., May 17, 1976, p. 4.

49. Ibid., June 2, 1979, p. 6.

50. The M–19's shift in strategy occurred after its urban network was disrupted by massive arrests from January to August 1979. The military retaliated swiftly and with little restraint in its embarrassment over the M–19's theft of arms from the Usaquen barracks on December 31, 1978.

51. *Revista Militar del Ejército*, April 1, 1981, as cited in Foreign Broadcast Information Service *Daily Report: Latin America*, April 3, 1981, p. VI.

52. For Carlos Lleras's explanation for the dissolution of the Peace Commission, see *El Tiempo*, May 18, 1982, and *El Espectador*, May 19, 28, 1982.

53. *Latin America Regional Reports, Andean Group*, June 24, 1983, p. 4. Carlos Toledo Plata, ex-ANAPO congressman and one of the founders of the M–19, was among the more prominent amnestied guerrillas assassinated in 1984.

54. *El Siglo*, January 5, 1984, p. 4.

55. Betancur's admonition provoked the resignation of four other senior generals, including the chairman of the joint chiefs of staff, General Bernardo Lema Henao. Lema was among those officers who argued that the signing of the peace agreements was a

grave political mistake. They contend that at the time the agreements were signed the army was on the verge of eliminating the guerrilla movement.

56. For a recent discussion of the truces, see Harvey F. Kline, "New Directions in Colombia?" *Current History 84* (February 1985).

57. The armed forces commander, General Augusto Moreno Guerrero, announced in August a "total war against the M–19." See *El Tiempo*, August 9, 1985, p. 7. Colombia's new defense minister, General Rafael Samudio, reaffirmed on August 11, 1986, that Colombia's pacification requires "fighting with the full vigor of the law those who refuse to return to normal life." *El Espectador*, August 14, 1986, p. 6. This sentiment is echoed by Third Brigade commanders in the Valle del Cauca region, where military and police officials are determined to eradicate the M–19 once and for all.

58. *El Espectador*, July 21, 1985, p. 6. The "cost" is still high. Colombian security sources revealed in May 1986 that since the first peace agreement was signed on May 28, 1984, a total of 1,191 guerrillas, 392 peasants, and 477 soldiers and policemen have died (*El Siglo*, May 5, 1986, p. 1).

59. After his inauguration Virgilio Barco indicated he would continue the peace process initiated by Betancur but through more "institutionalized" means. The Peace Commission will now operate in the office of the president under the direct supervision of the minister of government. The new president rejected the possibility of talks with the M–19 but stated that his government would continue an "honest and open dialogue with the FARC's top command" (*El Espectador*, August 10, 1986, p. 1). [Editor's note: During 1987 the truce between the government and the guerrillas seemed to be unraveling. The military began arming peasants into "self-defense units," and six guerrilla organizations, including the FARC, M-19, and ELP formed a united front called the Coordinadora Simón Bolívar. Violent clashes between the army and the guerrillas increased.]

60. Colombians will be able to elect their mayors beginning with the March 1988 elections. The FARC, for example, can be expected to gain from direct elections in such areas as Meta and the middle Magadalena region, where they enjoy strong popular support. Similarly, should the M–19 survive to join the electoral struggle, it might reasonably expect to capitalize on political support in the areas of Valle, Cauca, and Caqueta.

61. Steve Ellner, "Review Essay: Diverse Influences on the Venezuelan Left," *Journal of Interamerican Studies and World Affairs* 23 (November 1981):489.

62. One begins to suspect that guerrilla movements have lost some of their revolutionary fervor when leaders develop a sense of their place in history—and have the time to write about it. See, for example, Jacobo Arenas, *Cese el fuego: Una historia política de las FARC* (Bogotá, Colombia: Editorial La Oveja Negra, 1985).

63. Betancur's humble origins and reputation as a political maverick enhanced his image as a peacemaker in the eyes of guerrilla leaders. He challenged the traditional political elite in 1970 when he ran against Pastrana and again in 1974 when he briefly considered ANAPO's invitation to be its presidential candidate.

12

Colombian and Venezuelan Foreign Policy: Regional Powers in the Caribbean Basin

William A. Hazleton

In the search for a comprehensive settlement to the Central American crisis, the participation of Venezuela and Colombia as members of the Contadora Group illustrates an attempt by regional powers to assume a more active and independent role in international affairs. The fact that Venezuela and Colombia have consciously sought a greater voice in determining the region's future through the Contadora initiative reflects a number of internal and external developments during the last twenty years. The first is a trend toward greater activism in international affairs. As relatively mature democracies committed to the principle of democratic pluralism, they believe that the preservation of their own political systems is tied to political stability and progress toward democratic reform in other parts of Latin America. The second development is that foreign relations are now viewed from several perspectives reflecting the different factors and interests involved. For example, Venezuela and Colombia contend that the complexity of the situation in Central America, and particularly the relationship between poverty and political instability, make a strictly East–West perspective shortsighted in that it ignores what are essentially the North–South roots of the problem. The distinction between socioeconomic and security interests, and the realization that different foreign-policy strategies are required to achieve these ends, have led Venezuela and Colombia to identify increasingly with the Third World issues, while not foregoing their traditional security ties with the West. The final change relates to the decline in U.S. influence within the Caribbean Basin. Although this provides Latin American states a greater opportunity to act, the more important development for Venezuela and Colombia is that both have gained the maturity and confidence necessary to adopt a stand independent of the United States. But given the hierarchical and decentralized nature of the international environment within which they must operate, and their limited foreign-policy resources, how much independence and what degree of influence can these two Latin American countries exert, both within the Caribbean Basin and in the world at large?

The scope of Venezuelan and Colombian interests in Central America and the Caribbean ranges from territorial disputes and economic markets to more overriding concerns about the region's political instability. To address the latter, Caracas and Bogotá have promoted international cooperation to facilitate socioeconomic development, political reform, and the pacific settlement of conflicts. With military capabilities that are relatively modest, even by Latin American comparisons, Venezuela and Colombia are cognizant of the danger that revolutionary forces in Central America present to their external security and, even more directly, to their domestic tranquility. Seeing little chance of isolating themselves, either diplomatically or physically, from the violence that is affecting parts of the Caribbean Basin, Venezuela and Colombia have chosen to become actively involved in the search for a negotiated settlement.

To succeed in this search, however, would require a degree of influence and status that has generally not been accorded to Latin American nations in the global community. Major international developments still remain largely beyond their influence, even though many external decisions have a significant impact on their internal affairs. In Colombia the situation has reached the point described by analyst Fernando Cepeda Ulloa as the "internationalization" of the country's economic decision-making process.[1] Frustration with this and similar developments was also evident during Venezuelan president Jamie Lusinchi's 1984 Washington visit when he said, "We cannot and shall not be indifferent to world issues on which we Venezuelans do not exert much influence, but which affect us to a high degree."[2] Ironically, Venezuela and Colombia have discovered that as efforts toward national development advance, so does the sensitivity of domestic structures to external decisions and constraints, thus requiring more government resources to be devoted to foreign policy.

Although virtually all states attempt to respond to external forces that adversely affect them, only a relative few are in a position to affect changes within the international environment. In this chapter the term "regional power" is used to distinguish Venezuela and Colombia, along with Mexico and Cuba, from other states in the circum-Caribbean region. Certainly, even the smallest island nations in the Caribbean see themselves as international actors, but what makes such states as Venezuela and Colombia regional powers are their capabilities and conscious determination to influence international events. The important distinction of regional powers is not comparative size, but instrumental size; that is, their outward sense of direction and purpose, along with the scope and degree of influence they can exert. Although the classification of regional powers tends to be subjective by nature, there are three characteristics that set Venezuela and Colombia apart from the majority of their neighbors in the Caribbean Basin: capabilities, degree of activity, and intentions.

The growing influence of Latin American states has been attributed to the reduced presence of the United States within the hemisphere. But although the United States' lower profile changes the regional setting, the physical and intellectual capabilities of Venezuela and Colombia are even more critical determinants of how this change will be reflected in their foreign policy behavior. For Caribbean Basin countries living in the shadow of a superpower, military strength plays less of a role in determining regional-power status than does the level of national integration, abundance of economic resources, degree of organizational efficiency, or the quality of political leadership.[3] For example, Demetrio Boersner cited January 1, 1976, as the date Venezuela achieved regional-power status, for it officially marked the nationalization of Venezuela's foreign-owned oil industry.[4] Moreover, as recently seen in the dynamic diplomacy of Colombian President Belisario Betancur, a regional power's physical limitations can be partly offset by skilled leadership and a strong sense of mission.

A second characteristic is a relatively high level of foreign-policy activity. For regional powers this activism involves more than merely speaking out or what Venezuela's Lusinchi has referred to as cultivating "the right of dissent," that is, the right of Latin American states to disagree publicly with the United States so as "to highlight the existing difference between them or simply to reaffirm their wish to exercise autonomous thought and action."[5] Foreign-policy activism is the opposite of passivity and resignation. It involves the formulation and use of foreign-policy instruments in attaining national goals. For example, until the 1960s Colombian leaders sought comfort in the belief that what in essence amounted to a foreign nonpolicy was actually in the country's best interest because it avoided a possible conflict of interests with the United States. Only when this attitude of subordination and resignation was overcome did Colombia begin to chart a semiautonomous foreign policy and extend its political and economic horizons to the rest of Latin America and the world.[6]

Wolf Grabendorff noted that a "willingness to experiment," reflected in sudden swings or shifts of policy, may accompany increased activity and make the foreign policies of regional powers rather unpredictable at times to outside observers.[7] Although discontinuities and inconsistencies are found in the foreign policies of Venezuela and Colombia, such problems are inevitable given their expanding international interests and, in fact, appear no more disoriented or confusing than the foreign policies of larger states that pursue a variety of national objectives. Moreover, elements of continuity, such as a commitment to democracy, are present in Venezuelan and Colombian foreign policy, and these principles and interests, rather than strictly pragmatic considerations, provide part of the internal context within which policies are formulated.

Finally, a regional power demonstrates not just the capability to exercise influence, but also a clear determination to do so. Specific foreign policies derive largely from domestic sources and in response to critical developments or trends in the external environment. In the case of regional powers, there is an important psychological dimension that makes foreign-policy elites think that they should respond to certain situations because their actions may have a positive impact.

Moreover, their intention is not just to react, but rather to respond in ways that change the international environment. Thus, flexibility and change, or the "willingness to experiment," indicate that foreign-policy makers in regional powers feel that they do have choices, that they can "make" foreign policies.

But how much choice do such regional powers as Venezuela and Colombia have, given their sensitivity, or even vulnerability, to external decisions largely beyond their direct control? *Dependencia* theorists have emphasized the role of external constraints and have viewed the foreign-policy behavior of regional powers as primarily a reaction to or reflection of events abroad. In other words, external dependency results in the absence of actor autonomy. Yet, Venezuela and Colombia, states that evidence a strong economic and military dependence on the United States, have repeatedly demonstrated their noncompliance with the latter's wishes. Usually, the nature, scope, and degree of a dependency relationship affects only the broad outlines of a state's foreign policy, not necessarily its position on specific issues. Moreover, the line beyond which a dependent state is not permitted to pass is rarely clearly demarcated, even when it involves relations with a superpower.

National sovereignty and freedom of action, though often treated for analytical purposes as if they were absolutes, are in practice always subject to some kind of external constraint. In determining domestic policy, certain conditions and groups affect the government's range of choice, particularly in such democracies as Venezuela and Colombia, but this does not lead analysts to conclude that these governments have no choice or cannot act independently. An independent foreign policy, then, involves both choices and constraints. Although the degree of choice may be considerably less for Venezuela and Colombia than for the United States, foreign-policy makers in regional powers see themselves as having alternative choices with regard to influencing international environment.[8]

This chapter focuses on the internal and external variables that have influenced the foreign policies of Venezuela and Colombia. More specifically, it examines the foreign-policy objectives and decision-making processes of two different democratic regimes. Venezuela and Colombia have made a commitment to democratic pluralism an essential part of their foreign policy, but advancing the cause of democracy remains only one goal among several they seek to attain. This means different, and not always compatible, objectives compete for attention on their foreign-policy agendas. The choice as to which objectives to pursue, though primarily determined by the chief executive, occurs against a background of popular elections and involves the participation of government ministries, political parties, and different interest groups. The first issue this chapter addresses is the priority that Venezuela and Colombia have accorded to political stability and the maintenance of democracy, and how these goals are reflected in their foreign policies. The second issue is the effect that their domestic political arrangements have had on foreign-policy making. Finally, recent developments in the Caribbean Basin are discussed in terms of the choices and constraints facing Venezuela and Colombia as these two regional powers seek to advance their interests and prestige through a more highly visible international role.

MOVES TOWARD AN ACTIVIST FOREIGN POLICY

Venezuela and Colombia are nations that have multiple identities when it comes to international relations. On the one hand, their historical development causes them to identify with the West in terms of political orientation and national security. On the other hand, both are developing countries that identify with the Third World's position on most social, economic, and resource-related matters. Their major source of identity, however, is that of Latin American states. They have consistently endorsed principles of hemispheric cooperation and regional solidarity, and incorporated these ideals in their subregional roles as Andean nations and, more recently, participants in the Caribbean Basin. Finally, Venezuela, as an oil-producing state, has pursued a commonality of interests with other members of the Organization of Petroleum Exporting Countries (OPEC).[9] Whether Venezuela and Colombia regard themselves as part of the western bloc or the Third World, as Andean or Caribbean nations, depends principally on the external and internal circumstances involved. As Venezuela and Colombia became more concerned with foreign affairs, they expanded their range of activity by developing links with the Group of 77, the nonaligned bloc, the *Sistema Económico Latinoamericano* (SELA), and the Andean Pact. Through these multiple contacts each country has sought to protect its political system by exploiting diplomatic alternatives that are available to it, rather than relying exclusively on its continuing ties with the West.

Venezuela

The emergence of Venezuela as an active participant in hemispheric affairs followed the overthrow of the Pérez Jiménez dictatorship in 1958. The democratically elected president, Rómulo Betancourt (from 1959 to 1964) of the social democratic Acción Democrática (AD), attempted to secure the future of his multiparty coalition government through a foreign policy of defending democracy throughout Latin America. The Betancourt Doctrine, as the policy became known, denied recognition to de facto regimes that had usurped power from constitutionally elected governments. The policy had several intended targets. It was aimed at right-wing authoritarian governments, most notably that of Rafael Trujillo in the Dominican Republic who had sponsored an unsuccessful assassination plot against Betancourt. The primary purpose of isolating military dictatorships abroad was to deter rightist military leaders at home from overthrowing the new government through a coup of their own. The Betancourt Doctrine was equally uncompromising in its condemnation of the Cuban dictatorship of Fidel Castro. Here, too, the policy was designed to serve domestic ends by combating

Cuban support for leftist guerrillas and winning the allegiance of conservative elites who had been forced to accept a democratic regime more or less by default.

With the focus on Cuba, the preservation of Venezuelan democracy evoked a concomitant position of strident anticommunism, placing most foreign policy issues within an East–West framework. Under Betancourt's leadership Venezuela was in the forefront of the movement to expel Cuba from the Organization of American States (OAS). Such actions were not without domestic costs, as the smaller Unión Republicana Democrática (URD) withdrew from the government in protest of the hard line taken toward Cuba. The benefits, however, included forging an even closer relationship between Venezuela and the United States, which further helped to discourage a military coup against the government. Although Venezuela ultimately failed to make democratically elected governments compulsory for OAS membership, the Betancourt Doctrine did provide an impetus for inter-American sanctions against the Dominican Republic and Cuba's suspension from the organization.

Under Betancourt's successor and fellow *adeco* (AD party member), Raúl Leoni (from 1964 to 1969), domestic instability became less of a problem, thus allowing the new government to concentrate on foreign economic issues. During this period, Venezuela joined the Latin American Free Trade Association (LAFTA) and seriously considered participation in the Andean Pact. As economic questions assumed precedence, Venezuela's foreign policy took on more of a Third World orientation. Venezuela sought to diversify its trade patterns, became more active in OPEC, and voted with the Third World Group of 77 on most socioeconomic issues before the United Nations. Despite unsuccessful efforts to internationalize the Betancourt Doctrine, Leoni refused to abandon "this cornerstone of AD thought," even if it meant Venezuela's isolation from the rising number of military dictatorships in Latin America.[10]

The peaceful transfer of power to the opposition social Christian Comité de Organización Política Electoral Independiente (COPEI) candidate, Rafael Caldera (from 1969 to 1974), after his narrow electoral victory, reflected the maturity and growing stability of Venezuela's democratic system. The international situation had also changed in the sense that the world was no longer perceived as being divided into two exclusive spheres of superpower dominance. Under Caldera relations worsened with Washington over U.S. petroleum and tariff policies, and his government prepared to embark on a more independent and active foreign policy designed primarily to advance Venezuela's economic interests and counter potentially dangerous diplomatic moves from neighboring Brazil.[11]

Underpinning Venezuela's identification with the Third World was the notion of social justice, a credo of Christian democratic parties throughout the world and a theme that had been developed by Caldera and his able foreign minister, Arístides Calvani, before they assumed office.[12] Giving international application to what had been a guideline for domestic reform, Caldera criticized the exploitative nature of the existing system and called for a more equitable distribution of power and wealth among nations of the world. Willing to tolerate different variations of social justice for the sake of Third World unity, Caldera replaced the Betancourt Doctrine with Venezuela's recognition of "ideological pluralism." The ideological content of Venezuelan foreign policy was partly aimed at enlarging COPEI's domestic base of popular support and at giving it a claim to the leadership of the Christian democratic movement in Latin America after the Chilean party's electoral defeat in 1970. Moreover, ideological pluralism raised the possibility of a rapprochement with Cuba, but the real incentive for such a move was its attractiveness to leftist voters and its appeal to nationalist sentiments by breaking with the United States on this issue. In the end, rather than serving as rigid principles, international social justice and ideological pluralism provided a flexible framework and justification for a more autonomous foreign policy that was shaped largely by pragmatic considerations.

The return of AD under President Carlos Andrés Pérez (from 1974 to 1979) failed to bring about the restoration of the Betancourt Doctrine. Rather, Pérez chose to recast the concept of international social justice into a Third World call for a new international economic order. Adopting an ambitious and energetic foreign policy that hinged on a highly personalized form of presidential diplomacy, Pérez set out to catapult Venezuela into a position of international leadership. Fortunate to have inherited an expanding economy due to rising oil prices, Pérez was anxious to reduce Venezuela's foreign dependence. He nationalized the extraction of iron ore and the petroleum industry, while carefully preserving the confidence of the United States so as not to deter the continued flow of foreign capital and technology to Venezuela's industrial sector. Themes of Third World unity and South–South cooperation were evident in stronger ties with OPEC and Latin America. Rising oil revenues allowed Venezuela to participate in foreign-assistance programs sponsored by OPEC and United Nations agencies, and even to inaugurate its own assistance programs in the Caribbean Basin.[13] With Mexico's President Luis Echeverría, Pérez created the Sistema Económico Latinoamericano (SELA), which was subsequently headquartered in Caracas. On another front, reestablishing diplomatic relations with Havana had become an important step for Latin American countries wishing to join ranks with the Third World. Despite Betancourt's disapproval, Pérez renewed ties with Cuba and advocated Castro's readmission into the Latin American fold.

Pérez's image as a globe-trotting statesman did not always endear him to his constituents, but his personal visibility and activist foreign policy did enhance the prestige of his party, both at home and within the Socialist International. Pérez's commitment to western representative democracy was akin to that of social democrats like West Germany's Willy Brandt and Sweden's Olaf Palme. He supported popular liberation movements so long as they were not firmly entrenched in Moscow's camp, hoping that western tolerance and understanding would encourage the growth of democratic pluralism.[14] After retiring from office, Pérez was rewarded for these efforts with a vice-presidency of the Socialist International. Even within the Andean Community, political goals tended to eclipse lagging efforts at economic integration as Venezuela joined other Andean nations in providing diplomatic and material support to those struggling to liberate Nicaragua from the control of Anastasio Somoza.

The election of COPEI President Luis Herrera Campins (from 1979 to 1984) ushered in a more conservative outlook and a brand of presidential diplomacy that was much less dynamic than that of Pérez. For largely partisan reasons Herrera and COPEI set out to modify Venezuelan foreign policy by turning more to the United States and away from the Sandinista regime in Nicaragua.[15] Though less willing to embrace revolutionary change than his predecessor, Herrera was hesitant to abandon the autonomous Third World orientation advocated by COPEI's liberal wing and the noncommunist left. The result was a foreign policy that tended to swing back and forth between a western or anti-Marxist posture and one of solidarity with the Third World.

Herrera restored the traditional *copeyano* (COPEI-party) themes of social justice and democratic pluralism to Venezuelan foreign policy. In strife-torn Central America the government emphasized electoral solutions to internal conflicts and respect for democratic guarantees. Herrera's open support for fellow Christian democrat José Napoleón Duarte included sending military advisers to El Salvador, which severely undermined Venezuela's bipartisan foreign-policy tradition. Elsewhere in the Caribbean Basin Venezuela's relations with Nicaragua and Cuba cooled. Although Herrera refused to endorse U.S. measures aimed at countering Soviet–Cuban influence in Nicaragua, he publicly criticized the Sandinistas for failing to fulfill their earlier commitments to democracy. He strongly encouraged political pluralism and moderation on the part of the Sandinista regime by holding out promises of Venezuelan economic and financial assistance. But as the Sandinistas turned more toward Cuba and the regime became increasingly anticlerical, antidemocratic, and repressive, Venezuelan aid diminished and diplomatic pressure against Managua increased.

Relations with Cuba also worsened during this period due to two controversies. The first is a still unresolved dispute over the judicial procedures employed by Caracas in prosecuting a group of Cuban exiles, who, while carrying Venezuelan passports, sabotaged a Cuban airliner in 1976, with the loss of seventy-three lives. Castro's public demands that the perpetrators be punished have been interpreted as unwarranted interference in Venezuela's internal affairs. The second occurred in 1980, when disenchanted Cubans sought diplomatic asylum in the Venezuelan Embassy in Havana. Castro's refusal to allow them safe passage out of Cuba resulted in a mutual recall of ambassadors. Absence of diplomatic relations, however, did not rule out all cooperation. In the wake of the Malvinas crisis, for example, Herrera Campins saw the possibility for a rapprochement with Havana, particularly when Cuba endorsed Venezuela's admission into the Nonaligned Movement and condemned third-party intervention in the Essequibo dispute.[16]

The U.S. decision to support Great Britain in the 1982 Malvinas/Falkland conflict brought a swift reaction from Caracas that caught Washington off guard. With all the passion of an antiimperialist crusade, Venezuela condemned the United States for turning its back on the hemisphere and defended Argentina's position in the United Nations and the Group of 77.[17] Caracas explored membership in the Nonaligned Movement, only to be rebuffed by the threat of a Guyanan veto because of Venezuela's claim to the Essequibo region. Herrera also raised the possibility of creating a political SELA as an exclusive Latin American alternative to the OAS.[18] He even accepted an invitation to the Sandinista's third anniversary celebration in Managua and used the occasion to try to improve relations with both Nicaragua and Cuba.[19] Many interpreted Herrera's shift away from the United States as not only an attempt to regain popular support in light of the country's faltering economy, but also a recognition of the need to have the Third World's diplomatic backing in pressing Venezuela's own territorial ambitions.

During his campaign for the presidency, AD's Jamie Lusinchi (from 1984 to the present) spoke sympathetically of Venezuela's position as a "small, developing country" in a world controlled by the superpowers and the international financial centers. His foreign-policy outlook echoed such familiar themes as democracy and human rights, Third World solidarity, Latin American integration, and closer relations with OPEC in the face of falling energy prices.[20] In office Lusinchi has actively supported the Contadora peace initiative, undertaken by Herrera and other Latin American leaders, which seeks to exclude superpower involvement from the Central American conflict. A lasting solution to the crisis, he told President Reagan during a state visit to Washington, required the formulation and implementation of "a policy of democratization, pluralism, social justice, and economic development for all the countries of the region to the exclusion of none, and without exerting any imposition."[21] The Lusinchi government has been highly critical of U.S. policies toward Nicaragua but at the same time has condemned the Sandinistas for their unwillingness to cooperate in the search for a regional understanding. Moreover, Acción Democrática and the Socialist International have made open and free elections a prerequisite for renewing support to the Sandinista regime.[22]

Meanwhile, Venezuela's relations with Cuba have yet to be normalized. After the election there was speculation that Lusinchi and AD would have a better chance of success, especially if Pérez's personal influence was used.[23] More speculation followed the appointment of Simón Consalvi as foreign minister in 1985, since he had played an instrumental role in the original restoration of relations under Pérez. Yet, continual delays and Consalvi's own references to "special conditions" that must be met indicate that significant internal obstacles remain.[24] Thus, Lusinchi's foreign policy, despite claims that it is different, has basically followed the same course as that pursued during the last years of the Herrera administration, with one exception that it is less outspoken in its support of the Duarte regime in El Salvador.

Colombia

Unlike Venezuela, Colombia's efforts to preserve its fragile democracy had led it, until quite recently, to forego an activist foreign policy in favor of a low international profile. The traumatic loss of Panama at the beginning of this century "fostered a climate of historical introversion," which resulted in widespread suspicion, if not outright rejection, of foreign political entanglements and a noticeable lack of ambition to extend Colombia's influence much beyond its immediate borders.[25] After relations improved with the United States, Conservative President Marco Fidel Suárez (from 1918 to 1922) enunciated the doctrine of the "polar star"; namely, that Colombia's socioeconomic and political development required the country to look northward to the United States.[26]

Allying itself firmly with Washington, Bogotá pursued a pragmatic foreign-trade policy that sought to avoid controversies that might jeopardize relations with its major trading partner, the United States. A second reason for Colombia's low profile, and its close association with the United States, has been a continuing problem of domestic instability. La Violencia of the late 1940s and its legacy of partisan unrest remain a source of great concern for political and military elites, causing them to look to Washington for security guarantees and military assistance.

In the late 1950s the Liberal and Conservative parties reached a consensus on supporting a foreign policy that was generally pro-United States, prowestern, and prointegrationist.[27] During this period, national economic development was a major foreign-policy objective, with trade expansion and foreign investment providing attractive alternatives to domestic economic reforms that might weaken the position of the governing elites. Colombia, for example, was an early proponent of regional economic integration. When the Latin American Free Trade Association (LAFTA) failed to meet Bogotá's expectations, it helped to establish the Andean Pact in the hope of eliminating subregional trade restraints at a faster rate. Colombia also began to scale back its economic dependence on North American markets by emulating the foreign-trade policies of neighboring Latin American states. These attempts resulted in a policy of *aperturismo* (opening) in which Colombia sought to expand its commercial and diplomatic links with western and eastern Europe and Japan.

Despite these initiatives, conscious efforts to remove Colombia from the shadow of the United States only began to emerge during the administration of Liberal President Alfonso López Michelsen (from 1974 to 1978). Having characterized his Andean nation as the "Tibet of South America," López Michelsen endeavored to advance Colombia's international status by pursuing a more independent foreign-policy course. Among his initiatives were establishing diplomatic relations with Cuba, participating in discussions on a new international economic order, joining with Venezuela and Costa Rica in the negotiation of a new canal treaty between Panama and the United States, and forcing foreign-owned banks to become 51 percent Colombian.[28] Although these developments naturally complicated Bogotá's relations with Washington, they were not intended as a radical break with the past; rather, these changes, both in their formulation and implementation, were largely seen as incremental and, if anything, being more adaptive to evolving internal and external conditions.

López Michelsen's successor, Liberal Julio César Turbay Ayala (from 1978 to 1982), continued efforts to enhance Colombia's international position, particularly with regard to the Caribbean and Central America. Joining other members of the Andean Pact, Colombia called for Somoza to step down in Nicaragua and, as if to demonstrate a growing independence, participated as an observer at the 1979 nonaligned summit in Havana. Events during the second half of Turbay's administration, however, caused it to back away from earlier initiatives and adopt a foreign policy that was more closely attuned to that of the Reagan administration.

Relations with Nicaragua suddenly became strained when the Sandinistas reasserted their country's claim of sovereignty over two Caribbean islands, San Andrés and Providencia, and the uninhabited keys of Quinta Sueno, Roncador, and Serrana that had been under Colombian administration since 1803.[29] This development, along with evidence of a growing arms buildup in Nicaragua, caused Turbay to look northward for diplomatic and military support. What made the situation even more alarming was that it coincided with a new wave of guerrilla activity at home. Turbay's view of the Central American crisis began to reflect the domino theory being employed by the Reagan administration, with the addition of Colombia as the southern target of a Soviet–Cuban destabilization plan.[30] Turbay's anticommunist sentiments were widely shared by many of Colombia's ruling elite, who supported a hard-line approach to antisystemic challenges, both internally and externally. What ensued, according to one observer, was the "militarization" of Colombian foreign policy, with the armed forces gaining an upper hand due to increased security concerns.[31]

Relations with Cuba soured in 1979 when Turbay befriended the United States by offering Colombia as an alternative to Cuba's election to one of the Latin American seats on the United Nations Security Council. Two years later, U.S.-supplied evidence of Cuban support for M–19 guerrillas led Turbay to break diplomatic relations with Havana. In 1982 Colombia sent observers to the Salvadoran elections at Washington's request. During the South Atlantic conflict, Colombia refused to endorse Argentina's attempt to regain the Malvinas by force, fearing such an action would create a dangerous precedent for Colombia's territorial disputes with Nicaragua and Venezuela. By echoing the United States' calls for a peaceful resolution to the conflict, Colombia became increasingly isolated from the rest of Latin America, which, in turn, caused Turbay to rely even more heavily on Washington. Sensitive to criticism regarding the government's subservience to U.S. interests, Turbay's foreign minister, Lemos Simmonds, responded that he did not "think it was a disgrace to be a friend of the United States" and claimed that the government had an independent foreign policy in the sense that the foreign ministry did not consult or seek Washington's permission in advance of any key decisions.[32]

Shortly after Conservative candidate Belisario Betancur (from 1982 to 1986) was sworn in as president, Colombia's position on several important foreign-policy issues changed. Seeking greater diplomatic maneuverability through a closer alignment with other Latin American states, Betancur lost little time in publicly supporting Argentina's Malvinas claim. In addition, he joined Venezuela's Herrera Campins in suggesting the possible restructuring of the OAS to make it more representative of Latin American interests.[33] Anxious to benefit from not only Latin American cooperation but also Third World solidarity, Betancur followed in Venezuela's wake by announcing Colombia's intention to seek admission to the Movement of Nonaligned Nations. While claiming that membership would symbolize Colombia's transformation from a "passive to an active role in world affairs," Betancur downplayed the effect it would have on existing foreign relations by stating that membership merely formalized Colombia's Third World position on most international issues and strengthened the country's "independence in dealing with large blocs."[34] Betancur later used President Reagan's stopover in Bogotá to present personally some of the Third World's grievances. He lectured his North American guest on Latin America's severe economic problems, the dangerous consequences of restricting Third World imports from U.S. markets, and the waste incurred by the superpowers in the nuclear arms race.[35] During his first few months in office, the message that Betancur clearly wished to convey, both to President Reagan and the world, was that Colombia would no longer reflect the foreign policy interests of the United States.

Colombia's new-found activism and independence were also a response to the political system's eroding legitimacy in the face of escalating political violence. Turbay's hard-line tactics had failed to stem the guerrilla threat, and his close association with the United States offended the nationalist sentiments of many Colombians.[36] Betancur abandoned military measures in favor of establishing a truce and general amnesty with domestic guerrilla groups. Moreover, he sought to insulate Colombia from the Central American conflict through a joint diplomatic undertaking with Mexico, Venezuela, and Panama in what become known as the Contadora Group. Direct U.S. military intervention in Central America was one possibility that Betancur definitely wished to avoid, for fear that it would produce a wave of new recruits for the guerrilla groups operating in Colombia. Betancur, unlike his predecessor, also believed that the time had come to improve relations with Castro and the Sandinistas, especially if he wanted to bring Colombia's guerrilla leaders to the negotiating table. Although a plan was supposedly formulated for normalizing relations, it was never implemented because of strong opposition from the armed forces.[37] Nevertheless, the president continued to court the assistance of Cuba and Nicaragua through informal contacts. In fact, he relied on the services of Gabriel García Márquez, Colombia's Nobel prize-winning author, whose personal ties with Castro, the Nicaraguan junta, Mexico's López Portillo, and leading European socialists made him quite valuable as a confidential, ad hoc presidential emissary.[38]

As with the case of restoring diplomatic ties with Cuba, Betancur's efforts to chart a more independent course met with strong opposition. Concern was expressed in the Colombian press, and particularly within the military, over the decision to join the Nonaligned Movement, which was seen as extremely damaging to Colombian relations with the United States.[39] The foreign minister, Lloreda Caicedo, however, argued that the government had no hostile intent toward the United States, and he went on to assert that rather than weaken Colombia's position, the independent line pursued by the government had already enhanced the country's reputation as a "responsible" and "respected" international actor.[40]

The degree to which President Betancur became personally involved in foreign affairs was virtually unparalleled in the history of Colombia. His unique mix of populism and conservatism, combined with an engaging personality and proven negotiating skill, allowed him to assume the role of "go-between" in a variety of diplomatic contexts. In promoting his country's Third World and nonaligned ties, Betancur did not forget the importance of the United States in Colombian foreign policy, especially its economic impact. In a 1985 visit to Washington Betancur raised the issue of the need to strengthen the international coffee agreement, expand trade relations between Colombia and the United States, combat drug trafficking, and ease the burden of foreign indebtedness by softening the macroeconomic adjustment programs proposed by the Reagan administration. But rather than simply indict U.S. policies, Betancur called for a "new understanding" through "open, constructive, and fruitful cooperation" with Washington.[41]

A PRESIDENT-CENTERED FOREIGN-POLICY-MAKING PROCESS

Given the few detailed case studies or insider accounts of the foreign-policy decision-making process, the internal variables most widely used to explain and predict Latin American foreign-policy behavior are presidential perspective, charismatic leadership, and regime orientation. Although there is no denying the central role played by Latin American chief executives in foreign affairs, nor the importance of regime characteristics, these factors are often considered apart from the overall domestic context within which decisions are made. Historically, Latin American constitutions have given chief executives almost unchallenged authority in this area, largely because foreign policy was seen as having few domestic political implications. But times have changed in that international economic and political trends have become major factors affecting the course of national development, and various groups in the public and private sectors have developed important external links. Thus, in countries like Venezuela and Colombia where there are institutionalized bureaucracies as well as established interest groups and competitive political parties, the view of presidential predominance in foreign affairs is not so much inaccurate as it is oversimplified and unnecessarily restrictive.[42]

Bureaucratic organs and special-interest groups in Venezuela and Colombia have long been interested in external issues affecting trade and development, while the national legislatures have been more willing to acquiesce to presidential leadership on foreign-policy matters. More recently, Venezuela's broad-based political parties have sought to strengthen their position through international affiliations. The result has been closer Venezuelan ties with other social democratic or Christian democratic governments, depending whether AD or COPEI is in power. Also among the expanding cast of domestic actors involved in foreign affairs are distinguished citizens, who do not hold public office. Though such cases remain relatively rare, former Venezuelan President Pérez's activities with the Socialist International and Colombian author García Márquez's previously mentioned diplomatic missions provide two notable examples.[43] Thus, although the foreign-policy-making process is president centered, it is by no means the totally exclusive preserve of Venezuelan and Colombian chief executives.

Venezuela

Responsibility for foreign affairs has traditionally rested in the hands of Venezuelan presidents, with all major decisions being made at the presidential level. While more responsibility has gradually been delegated to the foreign ministry (Casa Amarilla), recent presidents have wanted to remain directly involved in important foreign-policy decisions and, at times, have even acted as their own foreign ministers in league with a small cadre of political advisers. The presidential style of Carlos Andrés Pérez is an oft-cited example of how Venezuelan foreign policy can become highly personalized. However, the tendency toward tight executive control was also found among Pérez's predecessors. Betancourt, Leoni, and Caldera frequently appointed close political allies to top foreign-policy posts in order to insure that foreign relations would be managed from the presidential palace.

One explanation for this presidential preoccupation with foreign policy is that Venezuelan party bosses have been reluctant to place these matters in the hands of outsiders and thus have opposed institutionalizing the process or giving Casa Amarilla a larger role. Not surprisingly, a foreign minister's influence has depended on his status within the party and personal relationship with the president. Two foreign ministers who were fortunate to have presidential access were Calvani under Caldera and Consalvi under Pérez, and both played instrumental roles in shaping policy. Two who tended to remain outside the president's immediate circle were Herrera Campins' foreign minister, José Alberto Zambrano Velasco, and Lusinchi's first foreign minister, Isidro Morales Paúl. Zambrano Velasco was reportedly under the control of Calvani, the former COPEI foreign minister who during the Herrera presidency was the head of Organización Christiana Democrática de América (OCDA). Similarly, Morales Paúl, a highly respected expert in international law, was pushed into the background by Venezuela's headline-making vice-president of the Socialist International, Carlos Andrés Pérez.[44] The importance of party connections and presidential trust was reaffirmed in July 1985 when Lusinchi replaced Morales Paúl with Consalvi, who moved from his post as general secretary to the presidency to Casa Amarilla.

The involvement of the presidential palace in the foreign-policy process is both an important cause as well as an effect of the structural weaknesses that plague the Venezuelan foreign ministry. Foreign ministers have traditionally enjoyed little bureaucratic support from experts with international-relations backgrounds, causing one critic to allege that the ministry is staffed by individuals who view foreign affairs as "recreation."[45] Beginning with Betancourt, repeated attempts have been made at reorganization and upgrading the level of professional competence. After 1958 businessmen, engineers, and officials from the trade unions replaced the lawyers and colonels appointed by the military regime. The spoils system, however, remained basically intact, which meant that the foreign service was staffed by "generalists" of uneven quality, while appointment and advancement continued to be highly politicized.[46]

During the 1983 presidential campaign, Lusinchi spoke of strengthening the role of the foreign ministry.[47] The Pedro Gual Diplomatic Academy was created in 1984, and the foreign minister, Morales Paúl, announced plans to automate the ministry's information and documentation services, expand educational and training programs for the foreign service, and institute competitive examinations and a rating system for promotion.[48] Most agree that such reforms are long overdue in that the lack of professionalization has caused the ministry to stagnate.

At the cabinet level the foreign ministry's internal weaknesses have been compounded by jurisdictional encroachments by bureaucratic rivals. The growing importance of foreign affairs has led a number of ministries and government offices to become actively concerned about particular aspects of Venezuela's external relations, resulting in the bureaucratic diffusion of policy-making responsibilities at the expense of the foreign ministry. Among Casa Amarilla's most formidable competitors are the ministry of mines and hydrocarbons regarding oil policies and relations with Arab nations; the advisory body, Comisión Asesora de Relaciones Exteriores (CARE), on Central America; the Foreign Commerce Institute (ICE) concerning Andean integration; along with Oficina Central de Coordinación y Planificación (CORDIPLAN), the ministry of finance, and the president of PETROVEN on a variety of important international economic issues.[49] These organs have capitalized on their technical expertise in certain areas and utilized contacts established with foreign counterparts. For example, the foreign ministry was unable to formulate an economic assistance program for the Caribbean Basin, with the result that the joint San José oil accord with Mexico was largely the product of the ministry of mines and hydrocarbons.[50] The elimination of the ministry for international economic affairs at the beginning of 1986 may indicate future consolidation, but for the moment administrative compartmentalization and overlapping areas of bureaucratic jurisdiction ensure that coordination and direction of the foreign-policy process can only come from the highest executive levels.

The Venezuelan military has not played a major role in the formulation of foreign policy. After the overthrow of Pérez Jiménez civilian and military elites reached an understanding that assured the armed forces autonomy in dealing with professional matters (*cuestión militar*) in exchange for their noninvolvement in politics. Although there is a fine line separating civilian and military responsibilities in the area of national security, the Venezuelan armed forces have defined their mission within rather narrow limits and concentrated their attention on external threats affecting the country's geopolitical position and, more specifically, on disputed border claims. The president and civilian officials regularly consult with the military, both formally and informally, on these and related matters, but the armed forces have demonstrated little interest in becoming more directly involved in determining Venezuelan foreign policy.[51]

The Venezuelan Congress has also shown respect for the executive's authority to conduct foreign relations. With power to designate diplomatic chiefs of mission, conduct ministerial inquiries, ratify international treaties, and appropriate funds, Congress is primarily intended to monitor the execution of foreign policy—in other words, play a "watchdog" role. The foreign-relations committee in the Chamber of Deputies, for example, is divided into the following six subcommittees, which reflect both a mix of functional interests and the importance accorded to multilateral diplomacy: (1) border questions, (2) human rights, (3) energy and oil, (4) the Andean Pact, (5) inter-American organizations, and (6) international organizations. According to Dr. Oswaldo Alvarez Paz, the committee's head, Congress in recent years has been most concerned about Central America and the Contadora process, as well as the executive's handling of the Guyanan and Colombian border questions.[52] The oversight responsibilities of the foreign-relations committees in the Chamber of Deputies and Senate are hampered, however, by severe understaffing and inadequate funding. More important, the wide discretion traditionally granted to chief executives would indicate little interest on the part of national legislators in assuming more responsibility for Venezuelan foreign policy.[53]

Special-interest groups have at times left a mark on Venezuelan foreign policy. Perhaps the most publicized incidents involved the Federation of Chambers of Industry and Commerce (FEDECAMARAS) and other business interests opposed to Latin American economic integration. Although they failed to prevent Venezuela's participation, they did manage to delay its membership in LAFTA and the Andean Pact. Recognizing the potential costs of excluding special interests, Pérez sought to short-circuit domestic concerns regarding the nationalization of the oil industry by engaging FEDECAMARAS, along with representatives of the labor unions, in an advisory commission. But since most of the proposals were formulated in private by the president's personal advisers and the foreign oil companies, the commission's major purpose, or so it seemed, was to keep these groups preoccupied and out of the way of the real negotiations.[54] Overall, special-interest groups have tended to have a moderating or restraining effect, especially when it comes to implementing new foreign-policy initiatives, because they are far more concerned about limiting any adverse economic or social impact on their members than in achieving possible, but uncertain, gains through international cooperation.

Venezuela's two main political parties have assumed a greater role in foreign affairs. Both are members of international associations, with AD a member of the Socialist International and COPEI a member of OCDA and the International Christian Democratic Movement. They each have pressed for foreign policies that are sympathetic to the goals and objectives of these international bodies. Of the two, COPEI has been more strongly influenced by ideological principles and philosophical tenets such as international social justice, while ideological considerations have been less important for AD. But even in the case of COPEI, ideological orientation has traditionally been blended with political realism and adjusted to meet concrete calculations of national interest.[55]

When the government's position is challenged, the foreign-policy advisory body CARE provides a platform from which COPEI and AD loyalists can raise disagreements with Casa Amarilla. Venezuelan foreign policy has generally reflected copeyano–adeco cooperation, but revolutionary movements in El Salvador and Nicaragua, along with changing attitudes toward Cuba, called this bipartisan consensus into question at the beginning of Herrera's administration. In particular, AD officials questioned Herrera's strong support of fellow Christian democrats in El Salvador. Dr. Efrait Schacht Aristeguieta, a former foreign minister under Pérez, warned against government actions that would endanger Venezuela's relations with other Central American countries, charging that the assistance given to El Salvador had gone beyond ''the limits of bilateral cooperation and touch[ed] upon the ideological affinities of the presidents of the two countries.''[56] Strong partisan divisions remain the exception, however, with AD and COPEI tending to follow a moderate, incremental approach to foreign relations, if for no other reason than to avoid controversial issues that might divide the nation and weaken their hegemonic position in the political system.

Although the Venezuelan system cannot be accurately described as pluralist, existing structural arrangements do afford opportunities for participation by government ministries, Congress, and representatives from business groups, organized labor, the military, and political parties. Succeeding presidents have embraced the concept of consultation, and several advisory commissions and boards have been created to facilitate official contacts with special interest groups. Formal and informal consultation, however, provides no guarantee of arriving at a consensus, nor is it a particularly efficient or expeditious way to make foreign policy.[57]

Colombia

Colombia also has a strong tradition of presidential autonomy in foreign affairs, with the Constitution and the courts recognizing the chief executive as the head of the country's foreign relations. Moreover, the weak and diffuse nature of the Colombian foreign-policy apparatus caters to strong executive leadership. Few presidents have used their powers either as much or so effectively as Belisario Betancur. He jealously guarded his presidential prerogatives in foreign affairs from encroachments, especially from the military. He looked to political associates for counsel and, in June 1984, placed the foreign ministry in the hands of Augusto Ramírez Ocampo, the Conservative mayor of Bogotá, described as "one of the president's most trusted men."[58] In the end, Betancur greatly enhanced his political stature, both nationally and internationally, becoming widely recognized as a leading advocate of Latin American cooperation in Central America and the international debt crisis.

Within the executive branch the foreign ministry occupies a secondary role, concentrating its attention primarily on issues relating to border conflicts with neighboring countries. The ministry's approach has been criticized as overly technical and legalistic in the sense of formulating positions that are either too narrow or too inflexible to accommodate meaningful political negotiation.[59] Under Betancur efforts were made to modernize the foreign service and improve its quality and efficiency through the better training of personnel. However, political criteria have always played a major role in appointments and advancement, with a recent foreign minister remarking "our foreign service smacks of holiday."[60]

The foreign ministry's position has also been undercut by an increased "division of labor" whereby foreign-policy responsibilities have yielded to other, more professional ministries and semiautonomous government agencies, and influence has simply been lost due to the ministry's own inertia.[61] For example, questions relating to international loans fall under the jurisdiction of the ministry of finance, while most trade issues are handled by the Export Promotion Fund (PROEXPO) and the Colombian Foreign Trade Institute (INCOMEX), with the latter being largely responsible for import policies as well as serving as Colombia's representative to the Andean Pact Commission. Meanwhile, matters relating to the country's leading export, coffee, are in the hands of the Federation of Coffee Growers (FEDECAFE). Increased specialization has meant that the foreign ministry is often not directly involved in important foreign-policy issues, including drug trafficking, which has become a major problem in Colombia's relations with the United States.[62]

Given Colombia's recent history of political violence, more weight has been given to the military's views on public policy, both foreign and domestic, than has been the case in Venezuela. The armed forces officially define their role as apolitical guardians of the Constitution, but their ideology can be characterized as staunchly anticommunist, their orientation as pro-United States, and their politics as leaning toward the Conservative party. Like other segments of the executive branch, the armed forces have cultivated their own network of foreign contacts. However, because of a long-standing preoccupation with internal security, the military has failed to formulate a coherent geopolitical outlook beyond its general orientation toward the United States and has thus paid relatively little attention to Colombia's foreign affairs, except for territorial disputes and relations with Cuba.

Under Turbay an upsurge in guerrilla activity and Nicaragua's claim to Colombian island territories in the Caribbean led the armed forces to seek a strong voice in national security matters. Reportedly, the military conducted secret talks with the Pentagon over granting the United States access rights to the Colombian naval facilities on San Andrés, without ever informing Turbay's foreign minister.[63] Facing what was seen as a growing Marxist threat at home and abroad, the armed forces wished to draw the country closer to the United States diplomatically. Caught off guard by Betancur's decision to join the Nonaligned Movement and his diplomatic feelers to Castro, the military questioned the government's "neutralist" policies and the wisdom of restoring diplomatic ties with Cuba. Tensions mounted as foreign-policy differences and the military's criticism of Betancur's amnesty program for Colombian guerrillas resulted in a direct confrontation with senior officers. In 1983 the defense minister, General Fernando Landazabal Reyes, was forced to resign. Betancur used the occasion to reassert his control over the military as commander-in-chief, reminding the members of the national security council that under the Constitution "the armed forces are not a deliberative body and are not to become involved in politics."[64]

Several large producer and commercial associations, *gremios*, maintain an active interest in Colombia's foreign economic relations. The National Association of Financial Institutions (ANIF) and the National Association of Industrialists (ANDI), for example, have been highly critical of U.S.-imposed restraints on Colombian exports. In retaliation, ANDI asked the Betancur administration to protect local industries by making government contracts with foreign enterprises, as well as the granting of import licenses, conditional of foreign purchases of local goods. Moreover, ANDI attacked the country's coffee mentality and called for an updated and more flexible foreign-trade policy that promoted nontraditional Colombian exports.[65]

Coffee, however, still occupies a privileged position, and FEDECAFE, founded in 1927, remains the political and economic vehicle of large coffee growers. A prime example of what Kline described as the "privatization" of Colombian politics, FEDECAFE has been granted extensive authority to regulate, tax, invest, and even act as a diplomatic representative.[66] The minister of foreign affairs is one of five ex-officio members of FEDECAFE's national governing committee, and the association's manager serves as Colombia's representative to international coffee negotiations. Although the interests of the gremios do not always coincide, they have succeeded in making their opinions heard, not so much with regard to initiating new policies, but rather in criticizing existing situations that are deemed detrimental to association members.

Historically, the Congress has confined its role in the foreign-policy process to legitimizing the decisions and actions taken by the president and executive agencies. Moreover, unlike Venezuela, foreign-policy issues have not gained a prominent place in Colombian party politics. Since the creation of the National Front, a tacit consensus has existed between the principal factions of the Liberal and Conservative parties in support of a foreign policy that can broadly be defined as pro-United States and committed to advancing Latin American cooperation. Foreign-policy issues have not figured significantly in political campaigns, although three recent ambassadors to Washington have left their post to pursue actively the presidency.[67] Most often, presidents are criticized for devoting too much time to foreign affairs, while neglecting urgent domestic problems. One development that might move Colombian partisan politics more in the direction of Venezuela would be the affiliation of the Liberal party with the Socialist International, an idea that López Michelsen proposed during his unsuccessful bid for reelection as president in 1982.[68]

Presidential consultation with representatives from the political parties and major interest groups does occur on certain foreign-policy issues, although the practice is far less common than in Venezuela. For example, Betancur promised that the decision to join the nonaligned bloc would be made in consultation with the Foreign Relations Advisory Committee, but he was careful to add that this was a "presidential decision and a totally valid one because the president is the country's foreign policy maker."[69] How much consultation took place and to what end remains in doubt since only a few days before the decision was announced, Foreign Minister Lloreda Caicedo was quoted as saying that nonaligned membership would only be achieved through a "process of national unanimity."[70] When the decision subsequently came under fire, Betancur insisted that he had consulted and justified his nonaligned foreign policy on the grounds that it was "multipartisan and reflect[ed] the consensus of the former presidents and of the parties on the Foreign Relations Advisory Committee."[71]

Border controversies are especially sensitive issues, and diplomatic efforts to resolve them require popular support and a favorable endorsement by the main political parties. In the case of an ill-fated attempt to settle the disputed Venezuelan border through direct negotiations with the Herrera government, the Colombian foreign minister charged that the talks had failed, not because of a lack of willingness on the part of the governments, but due to political problems within both countries.[72] Thus, although one cannot say that Colombian executives are isolated from political pressures or institutional constraints, they do enjoy greater autonomy and maneuverability in determining foreign policy than do Venezuelan presidents, though until Betancur they tended to exercise these powers much more sparingly.

DEFENDING DEMOCRATIC PLURALISM IN THE CIRCUM-CARIBBEAN

In a broad sense, the motivation and outline of Venezuelan and Colombian foreign policy in the Caribbean Basin are quite similar. Although it is possible to detect different military, political, economic, and geopolitical objectives in their respective foreign policies, both countries share a mounting concern over the revolutionary violence that afflicts several states in the region. According to Venezuela and Colombia, the Caribbean Basin's economic and political problems are interrelated in the sense that respect for democratic guarantees is an essential component in the region's future economic growth and political development. As an important first step, there needs to be a negotiated settlement to restore order and a massive influx of external economic assistance in order to build the foundations necessary for democracy.

Broadly defined security concerns have drawn these two Andean nations into the Caribbean Basin. Although Venezuela has traditionally focused its attention on the West Indian islands and Guyana, rather than on Central America, there is little doubt as to the region's geopolitical importance. The islands off its shore play a vital role in guaranteeing the safe passage of oil bound for U.S. ports. In fact, Venezuela's recent decision to help rescue Curacao's ailing economy by taking over Shell's abandoned refinery was motivated far more by geopolitical considerations than by thoughts of future economic rewards. Yet, given its experiences in the early 1960s with Castro and Trujillo, the need to protect Venezuela's political system even more than the Caribbean's strategic significance has led successive governments to be concerned about revolutionary forces in the region.

Colombia's active involvement in the Caribbean Basin, though much more recent than Venezuela's, reflects many of the same political and security concerns. In response to a growing Cuban and Soviet presence in Central America, President Turbay in early 1982 suggested joint Venezuelan–Colombian cooperation against "forces from outside the continent, entirely alien to Bolivar's ideology, the ideology of democracy."[73] Bogotá, more than Caracas, appears convinced that should the crisis lead to open warfare, Colombia would be unavoidably drawn into the fray. In hopes of containing the conflict, each has warned Washington and Moscow that "Central America must not become the backyard for an East–West confrontation," turning the region into another Middle East, and fragmenting their countries like Lebanon.[74] One of their primary objectives, then, has been to place the Central American crisis outside of an East–West context; or in the words of the Venezuelan government, to make the Caribbean Basin "a zone of peace" that is free from "the global strategies of domination by hegemonic powers."[75]

In early January 1983 the foreign ministers of Mexico, Venezuela, Colombia, and Panama met on Contadora Island to discuss ways of helping to restore peace to troubled Central America. The Contadora Group has taken the position that the revolutionary violence in Central America has evolved from long-standing economic, social, and political inequities, rather than has simply resulted from recent acts of Soviet–Cuban penetration. The long-term solution to the crisis, therefore, demands political negotiations and programs for socioeconomic and political reform. In advocating autochthonous solutions for Central America's problems, the Contadora Group has sought to insulate the region from East–West competition and a possible superpower confrontation. Neither Venezuela nor Colombia welcomes the prospect of increased Soviet and Cuban influence in the Caribbean Basin, but they are equally concerned that growing U.S. military involvement might play into the hands of the radical left and threaten to divide their own countries along ideological and political lines.

The Contadora Group also believes that Latin American nations are in a better position to mediate a Central American settlement than is the United States or the United Nations. "We wish to speak our own language," Betancur has said, "to make our own diagnosis, and invoke our own values with regard to Central America and the Caribbean."[76] Being actively involved as part of the Contadora peace process has taken on a great deal of symbolic significance in terms of the international recognition it has brought Venezuela, Colombia, and Mexico as regional powers. In fact, they have deliberately pursued a "subregional" solution that seeks to limit participation from outside the circum-Caribbean so as to maximize their positions of influence.

The Contadora process serves as a forum for consultation, both among the four-member Contadora Group and with the five Central American states. It hopes to provide a basis for peaceful settlement in the form of a mutually acceptable treaty, along with additional arrangement for mediation, good offices, and/or peacekeeping forces. According to Betancur, the principles guiding his exercise in multilateral diplomacy are self-determination, nonintervention, and the peaceful resolution of international conflicts.[77] Contadora's objectives are the implementation of an immediate ceasefire, the withdrawal of all foreign military advisers, a reduction in the level of offensive arms, and the creation of regional measures to guarantee the integrity of Central American borders.[78] In other words, external security is regarded as the essential key in restoring stability to the region.

Outside the Caribbean Basin the response to the Contadora initiative has generally been quite favorable. Contadora's negotiating proposals have won the public endorsement of the United Nations Security Council, the OAS, the European Community, Japan, the Soviet Union, the Peoples' Republic of China, Cuba, and the majority of Latin American states. At the instigation of Peruvian President Alan García, a Contadora "support group" has been formed by Argentina, Brazil, Peru, and Uruguay, each of which has returned to democracy in the 1980s. The United States has praised the Contadora members for their dedication to the cause of peace, but Washington has been reluctant to press acceptance for an agreement because Contadora's "independence" makes it an uncertain vehicle for protecting U.S. interests in the region.

The international recognition attained by the Contadora states has legitimized their role as regional peacemakers. However, a negotiated peace settlement has always depended on the group's ability to fashion a consensus from different ideological perspectives and foreign-policy interests. Since the beginning of 1984, Contadora has been unable to reconcile the demands and objections of the so-called Tegucigalpa group (Costa Rica, Honduras, and El Salvador), which has the backing of the United States, and those of Nicaragua. All parties endorse a comprehensive peace accord in principle, but in practice each has raised objections to particular points or questioned the means of implementation. The effect has been that each participant is in a position to veto the entire agreement because one segment is seen to benefit rival interests.

Given the stalemate that has developed, Contadora's future is in no way assured. Although its original intentions were to exclude the United States, Contadora's leaders have encouraged direct talks between Washington and Managua. In February 1986 the Contadora foreign ministers, plus those of the "support group," called on Secretary of State Shultz in Washington to urge that the administration withhold proposed aid to the contras and instead reopen negotiations with Nicaragua as a step toward a peaceful settlement. Shultz responded that no discussions with Managua would take place until the Sandinistas first agreed to negotiate with the contras.[79] Two months later in Panama, the Contadora Group failed to gain Nicaragua's adherence to a Central American peace treaty because of the Sandinista's insistence on an end to all U.S. support for the contras. With their initiative stalled once again, the Contadora Group decided to further extend the deadline for signing the treaty, rather than abandon their effort on behalf of a negotiated settlement.

With little likelihood of bridging the difference separating Nicaragua from its neighbors, how much more time is the Contadora Group willing to invest? For Colombia, at least, the 1986 presidential elections may well provide an answer. Betancur's early diplomatic efforts to bring the Salvadoran government and Marxist guerrilla groups together led to the adoption of a similar approach for negotiating an end to guerrilla activity in Colombia. When the government's negotiations with the major guerrilla factions resulted in a ceasefire in March 1984, Betancur proudly reaffirmed the links between the Colombian peace process and Contadora.[80] With Betancur's attempt to incorporate the guerrillas into the political process breaking down at home, conservative and military circles are openly pessimistic about Contadora's chances of success. For internal and external reasons the lagging Contadora process may shift from center stage of Colombian foreign policy, with Liberal President Virgilio Barco Vargas (from 1986 to the present) indicating that he intends to exercise a firmer hand with the guerrillas and concentrate his attention on improving relations with Colombia's immediate neighbors.[81]

CONCLUSIONS

For the past twenty years successive Venezuelan and Colombian governments have sought to diversify their international relations in order to achieve greater foreign-policy influence. For Venezuela this process began with the gradual demise of the Betancourt Doctrine, and it continues today as witnessed by Caracas's modus vivendi with Havana. Because of its oil-based economy, Venezuela was one of the first Latin American states to become associated with the Third World movement. But although supportive of proposals for a new international economic order, Venezuela remains firmly committed to the promotion of western-style democracy.

Colombia also assumed a more active foreign-policy posture primarily for the internal reasons of promoting economic growth and combating political instability. Expended international cooperation has been used to enhance the government's position at home, as in Betancur's efforts to strengthen his hand in negotiations with Colombian guerrilla leaders. As in Venezuela, the future of democracy is seen as threatened not only by revolutionary violence, but also by steadily worsening economic conditions. Fearful of the politically explosive nature of the international debt crisis, Colombia has urged cooperation among Latin American debtor states, with Betancur stressing that if the ''international indebtedness timebomb'' is not deactivated, the consequences would be similar to the political instability of the 1930s.[82]

This connection between democracy, development, and stability, found in both Venezuelan and Colombian foreign policy, draws on Third World as well as western perspectives. They firmly believe that the roots of the current Central American crisis are anchored in endemic poverty and in the refusal of governments to institute badly needed socioeconomic and political reforms. What concerns them most, however, is safeguarding their own democracies from the influences of leftist revolution and/or repressive militarism that have led to instability in the Caribbean Basin. To forestall this danger, Venezuela and Colombia helped initiate the Contadora process, improved relations with El Salvador, Honduras, and Guatemala after they had open elections, and have been strong advocates of political pluralism in Nicaragua.

With different, though not necessarily contradictory, foreign-policy objectives stemming from their Third World and western perspectives, it is important that the Venezuelan and Colombian governments establish priorities to provide guidelines for formulating foreign policies. The lack of an overarching foreign-policy framework is explained in part by their desire to maximize diplomatic flexibility as well as avoid internal controversy. But unfortunately, ''independent'' foreign policies frequently confuse ends and means in the sense that more attention is paid to developing different diplomatic options than to the relative importance of the choices involved. This issue was at the heart of Colombia's debate over joining the Nonaligned Movement. Despite the perception of reducing the country's reliance on the United States by acting more independently, the nature of the issues that had to be addressed required Colombia to look to the West and remain on good terms with Washington. Venezuelan and Colombian participation in the Contadora Group appears to be an exception to this trend, however, for not only have the members sought to provide a regional alternative, but they have done so to make a pointed statement that Latin American states have a role to play in the Central American crisis without the United States.

An effective foreign policy also has to be able to convert different internal demands and needs into national objectives. Linkages between domestic politics and foreign policy do not necessarily mean that the decisions reached are the products of bureaucratic infighting or interest-group politics. Latin American presidents, including those who are democratically elected, have retained a significant degree of control over the foreign-policy process because of their constitutional authority and ability to influence public opinion. They are careful to consult with interested parties about foreign-policy matters when the situation demands and to preserve a consensus among the dominant political factions so as not to endanger national unity. Foreign-policy decision making, then, tends to be highly centralized and subject to presidential discretion and direction. Even in the case of Venezuela and Colombia the process can hardly be described as pluralist in the sense of popular participation or strict political accountability, but neither is it immune to domestic influences or public scrutiny.

The divergence of opinion among domestic groups is often reflected in the government's tentative approach to important foreign-policy problems. In such cases "consultation" and the need for public deliberation serve as pretexts for government delay or postponement. However, in such highly controversial areas as border negotiations, government attempts to circumvent popular participation for the sake of expediency have occasioned a public outcry. When the Herrera government proceeded to draft a secret agreement for a Colombian border settlement, after it had promised a national bipartisan discussion on the subject, there was such widespread condemnation that the government was forced to abandon its proposal.[83] The cautious foreign-policy path followed by most Latin American governments is as much a function of the domestic political considerations as it is a function of the presence of international constraints. But even though executive discretion is far from open-ended, when Venezuelan or Colombian presidents have felt the need to act on a particular foreign-policy matter, they have generally been able to do so without encountering serious domestic opposition.

In the future, foreign-policy making in both countries will remain primarily president centered, with a need for improving the institutional elements of the process if public opinion and special interests are to be accorded a greater role. The Colombian political system is not yet strong enough to accommodate the democratization of the foreign-policy process given the risk of internal dissension, but Venezuela has already made some progress toward this goal through the increased activity of the AD and COPEI and more formalized arrangements for domestic consultation.

The international prestige that comes from a larger and more influential role in the Caribbean Basin is extremely important for each country. Venezuela had firmly established itself as a leader in the region, before Colombia's Betancur sought to attain this status. In the 1970s oil-rich Venezuela was able to utilize "petroleum diplomacy" to enhance its standing, both within the region and in the Third World. Ironically, Colombia's initial entry into the Caribbean was prompted largely by the rising stature of Venezuela and Nicaragua, just as

Venezuela's expanded presence was said to be partly an attempt to emulate Mexico's independent foreign policy. At first, Colombia was anxious not to overextend itself or offend the United States, with Turbay's foreign minister cautiously suggesting that Colombia might serve as a model for "development within a democratic system."[84] Though never possessing the economic resources of Venezuela, Betancur's dogged efforts to bring peace to Central America eventually pushed Colombia on to the center of the Latin American stage.

In several respects Contadora's members have a larger stake in avoiding a collapse in negotiations than have the Central American countries, who are the victims of the conflict. For Venezuela and Colombia the significance of Contadora has not been its success or failure as a negotiating instrument, but rather the special status it has conferred on its participants. The Contadora Group has been described by Carlos Andrés Pérez as a "symbol of the new Latin American consciousness," in which the members have "rescued the right of [their] own voice, [their] own solutions."[85] This view was frequently echoed by President Betancur, who warned that if Contadora was ignored by the major powers, the members would know that they "were looked on as second-rate countries, without the material or intellectual capacity to act on [their] own."[86]

Yet, the expectations aroused by the initial flurry of diplomatic activity, and the worldwide attention it received, have often turned to frustration. In Colombia influential groups like the National Federation of Merchants (FENALCO) have questioned why Betancur could not take advantage of the influence he gained from Contadora to hammer out a better loan agreement with the International Monetary Fund.[87] In Venezuela, too, the Lusinchi government had hoped that Venezuela's democracy, its prowestern orientation, and geopolitical position would pay important dividends in debt negotiations.[88] In actuality, Colombia with its limited capabilities and problems of internal unrest, and Venezuela with a large foreign debt and declining energy prices, have little in the way of leverage except prestige, or ironically the threat of their own political and/or economic collapse, that can be used to make the United States, and the West in general, more responsive to their needs.

Beside recognition and prestige, Venezuela's and Colombia's status as regional actors, along with their wider involvement in the global political arena, have produced few concrete results. Because so many issues are resolved outside of the public glare of international forums, there has been some disenchantment with multilateral approaches and a tendency toward direct negotiations.[89] Venezuela, for example, distanced itself from cooperative ventures that might have been mistaken for a Latin American debtors' cartel and even assumed a lower profile regarding the Central American crisis for fear of antagonizing its foreign creditors. Now that its debt negotiations are behind it, Venezuela is expected to play a much more assertive role in Latin America. Meanwhile, Colombia, despite growing internal problems, reportedly has its sights set on the leadership of the Nonaligned Movement when the presidency shifts to Latin America in 1989.[90] Thus, although their diplomatic approach and level of activity may change in the future, the reasons for their participation in foreign affairs, namely, the consolidation of democracy and the advancement of economic development, make it highly unlikely that either Venezuela or Colombia intends to retreat from the international scene.

NOTES

1. Fernando Cepeda Ulloa, "El Proceso de Paz en Colombia y la Política Internacional," *Estudios Internacionales* (Chile) 71 (July–September 1985):441.

2. "Visit of President Lusinchi of Venezuela," *Weekly Compilation of Presidential Documents* 20 (December 10, 1984):1873.

3. Wolf Grabendorff, "The Role of Regional Powers in Central America: Mexico, Venezuela, Cuba, and Colombia," in *Latin American Nations in World Politics*, eds. Heraldo Muñoz and Joseph S. Tulchin (Boulder, Colo.: Westview Press, 1984), p. 84; Alberto van Klaveren, "The Analysis of Latin American Foreign Policies: Theoretical Perspectives," in *Latin American Nations*, eds. Muñoz and Tulchin, p. 6.

4. Demetrio Boersner, "Venezuelan Policies Toward Central America," in *Political Change in Central America*, ed. Wolf Grabendorff, Heinrich-W. Krumwiede, and Jorg Todt (Boulder, Colo.: Westview Press, 1984), p. 250.

5. *Weekly Compilation of Presidential Documents* 20 (December 10, 1984):1873.

6. Gerhard Drekonja-Kornat, "Colombia: Learning the Foreign Policy Process," *Journal of Inter-American Studies and World Affairs* 25 (May 1985):229.

7. Grabendorff, "Role of Regional Powers in Central America," pp. 85–86. For a more general treatment of this subject, see K. J. Holsti, *Why Nations Realign: Foreign Policy Restructuring in the Postwar World* (London: George Allen and Unwin, 1982).

8. Kenneth M. Coleman, "On Comparing Foreign Policies: Comments on van Klaveren," in *Latin American Nations*, eds. Muñoz and Tulchin, p. 22; Bruce E. Moon, "Consensus or Compliance? Foreign-Policy Change and External Dependence," *International Organization* 39 (Spring 1985):311.

9. For a discussion of Venezuela's multiple foreign-policy identity, see Eva Josko de Gueron, "La Política Exterior: Continuidad y Cambio, Contradicción y Coherencia," in *El Caso Venezuela: Una Ilusión de Armonía*, eds. Moisés Naim and Ramón Pinango (Caracas: Ediciones IESA, 1984), p. 351.

10. John D. Martz, "Venezuelan Foreign Policy and the Role of Political Parties," in *Latin American Nations*, eds. Muñoz and Tulchin, p. 135.

11. Donald L. Herman, "Ideology, Economic Power, and Regional Imperialism: The Determinants of Foreign Policy under Venezuela's Christian Democrats," *Caribbean Studies* 18 (April–July 1978):60–69.

12. Charles D. Ameringer, "The Foreign Policy of Venezuelan Democracy," in *Venezuela: The Democratic Experience*, eds. John D. Martz and David J. Myers (New York: Praeger, 1977), pp. 348–49; Herman, "Ideology, Economic Power, and Regional Imperialism," p. 78; Martz, "Venezuelan Foreign Policy," pp. 135–36.

13. Winfield J. Burggraaff, "Oil and Caribbean Influence: The Role of Venezuela," in *The Restless Caribbean: Changing Patterns of International Relations*, eds. Richard Millett and W. Marvin Hill (New York: Praeger, 1979), pp. 195–98.

14. Boersner, "Venezuelan Policies Toward Central America," p. 251.

15. Ibid., pp. 253–54.

16. "Friends and Foes in Caracas," *Latin American Regional Report*, August 13, 1982, p. 5.

17. Interview with José Alberto Zambrano Velasco by Eugenio Gutiérrez, *Cosas* (Santiago), June 17, 1982, pp. 28–29.

18. *El Diario de Caracas*, May 4, 1982; *Latin American Weekly Report*, August 13, 1982, p. 5.

19. "Un Análisis de Nuevas Direcciones en la Política Exterior," *Zeta* (Caracas), July 25, 1982, pp. 60–61.

20. "Lusinchi Delinea Objectivos de su Política Exterior," *El Nacional* (Caracas), October 7, 1983.

21. *Weekly Compilation of Presidential Documents* 20 (December 10, 1984):1867–70.

22. "Government Communique," U.S. Foreign Broadcast Information Service (FBIS), *Daily Report: Latin America*, May 8, 1985, p. L2.

23. Demetrio Boersner, "Cuba and Venezuela: Liberal and Conservative Possibilities," in *The New Cuban Presence in the Caribbean*, ed. Barry B. Levine (Boulder, Colo.: Westview Press, 1983), pp. 102–3.

24. *Latin American Regional Report*, July 26, 1985, pp. 4–5.

25. Drekonja-Kornat, "Colombia," p. 230.

26. Gerhard Drekonja-Kornat, *Colombia: Política Exterior* (Bogotá: Fundación Friedrich Ebert de Colombia, 1983), pp. 72–73.

27. David Bushnell, "Colombia," in *Latin American Foreign Policies: An Analysis*, eds. Harold Eugene Davis and Larman C. Wilson (Baltimore: Johns Hopkins University Press, 1975), pp. 410–11.

28. Drekonja-Kornat, "Colombia," pp. 229–30 and 237–38.

29. Harvey F. Kline, *Colombia: Portrait of Unity and Diversity* (Boulder, Colo.: Westview Press, 1983), pp. 132–33.

30. Grabendorff, "Role of Regional Powers in Central America," p. 95.

31. Drekonja-Kornat, "Colombia," p. 245.

32. Interview with Carlos Lemos Simmonds by María Jimena Duzan, *El Espectador* (Bogotá), July 22, 1982.

33. Germán Santamaría, "La Decisión del Gobierno Reunir con los Países Noalineados," *El Tiempo* (Bogotá), October 11, 1982; FBIS, *Daily Report: Latin America*, May 16, 1983, p. F1.

34. Jairo Sandoval, "Betancur Defends Decision to Join Nonaligned," Bogotá, U.S. Joint Publication Research Service 83093, March 17, 1983, p. 71; *The New York Times*, January 9, 1983.

35. FBIS, *Daily Report: Latin America*, December 6, 1982, pp. F1–3.

36. Bruce Michael Bagley and Juan Gabriel Tokatlian, "Colombian Foreign Policy in the 1980s: The Search for Leverage," *Journal of Inter-American Studies and World Affairs* 27 (Fall 1985):36.

37. "Foreign Minister Comments on Relations with Cuba," FBIS, *Daily Report: Latin America*, January 12, 1983, p. F1; *Latin American Regional Report*, January 27, 1984, p. 3.

38. Fernando Cepeda Ulloa, "Contadora, Colombia y Centroamérica," paper presented at a conference on Regional Approaches to the Central American Crisis, May 1985, Toluca, Mexico, pp. 25–28.

39. Editorial, "Relaciones con los Estados Unidos," *El Tiempo* (Bogotá), August 25, 1982.

40. "Press Conference with Foreign Minister Rodrigo Lloreda Caicedo," *El Siglo* (Bogotá), June 10, 1983.

41. *Weekly Compilation of Presidential Documents*, 21 (April 8, 1985):413–16.

42. van Klaveren, "Analysis of Latin American Foreign Policies," pp. 10–15.

43. Carlos Andrés Pérez and Gabriel García Márquez have been involved in the establishment of a South American commission for peace, regional security, and democracy, which is a geographically expanded, nongovernmental version of the Contadora Group; see "Peace Commission," *Latin American Weekly Report*, February 7, 1986, p. 12.

44. Manuel Malaver, "Quién es el Ministro Extranjero Verdadero?" *Resumen* (Caracas), October 21, 1984, p. 4.

45. Luis Esteban Rey, "La Política Exterior de la Administración," *El Universal* (Caracas), June 25, 1984.

46. Judith Ewell, *Venezuela: A Century of Change* (Stanford, Calif.: Stanford University Press, 1984), p. 144; Ameringer, "Foreign Policy of Venezuelan Democracy," p. 336.

47. "Lusinchi Delinea Objetivos de su Política Exterior," *El Nacional* (Caracas), October 7, 1983.

48. Interview with Foreign Minister Isidro Morales Paul by Nestor Mora, *El Nacional* (Caracas), December 20, 1984.

49. Gueron, "Política Exterior," pp. 370–71.

50. Robert D. Bond, "Venezuelan Policy in the Caribbean Basin," in *Central America: International Dimensions of the Crisis*, ed. Richard E. Feinberg (New York: Holmes and Meier, 1982), p. 194.

51. Gene E. Bigler, "Professional Soldiers and Restrained Politics," in *U.S. Influence in Latin America in the 1980s*, ed. Robert Wesson (New York: Praeger, 1982), pp. 176–84; Diego Abente and William A. Hazleton, "Civil Military Relations and the Formulation of Foreign Policy: The Cases of Venezuela and Colombia," paper presented at the meeting of the International Studies Association's Section on Military Studies, November 8, 1985, Urbana, Illinois.

52. Interview with Dr. Oswaldo Alvarez Paz by Paula Giraud, *Bohemia* (Caracas), January 28–February 3, 1985, pp. 12–14.

53. Eva Josko de Gueron, "El Congreso y la Política Exterior en Venezuela," *Politeia* (Caracas) 7 (1978):329–441.

54. José Antonio Gil Yepes, *The Challenge of Venezuelan Democracy*, transl. Evelyn Harrison I., Lolo Gil de Yanes, and Danielle Salti (New Brunswick, N.J.: Transaction Books, 1981), p. 211.

55. Martz, "Venezuelan Foreign Policy," pp. 142–45.

56. Nestor Mora, "Un Análisis de Areas Sensitivas en Relaciones Exteriores," *El Nacional* (Caracas), November 22, 1981; Boersner, "Cuba and Venezuela," p. 98.

57. John D. Martz, "Policy-Making and the Quest for Consensus: Nationalizing Venezuelan Petroleum," *Journal of Inter-American Studies and World Affairs* 19 (November 1977):483–508.

58. "Few Surprises in Cabinet Changes," *Latin American Weekly Report*, July 6, 1984, p. 9.

59. Drekonja-Kornat, "Colombia," p. 230.

60. "El Ministro de Relaciones Exteriores Mira la Nación como sin Defensa," *El Tiempo* (Bogotá), October 25, 1982.

61. Drekonja-Kornat, "Colombia," p. 243.

62. Daniel L. Premo, "Colombia: Cool Friendship," in *U.S. Influence in Latin America*, ed. Wesson, pp. 102–3.

63. "Caracas Seeks Visible 'Peace' Role," *Latin American Regional Reports*, January 27, 1984, p. 4.

64. *El Tiempo* (Bogotá), January 19, 1984.

65. José Fernando Corredor, "ANDI Expresa Interes sobre los Países con Quenes Comercia Colombia," *El Tiempo* (Bogotá), September 10, 1982.

66. Kline, *Colombia*, p. 81.

67. Conservative National Front candidate Misael Pastrana Borrero in 1970, Liberal Julio César Turbay Ayala in 1978, and Conservative Alvaro Gómez Hurtado in 1986.

68. Bagley and Tokatlian, "Colombian Foreign Policy," p. 30.

69. Germán Santamaría, "La Decisión del Gobierno Reunir con los Países No-alineados," *El Tiempo* (Bogotá), October 1, 1982.

70. Leonel Fierro T., "No-alinearse es solo una Propuesta," *El Tiempo* (Bogotá), October 4, 1982.

71. *El Tiempo* (Bogotá), January 19, 1984.

72. "Lloreda on Venezuela, Nicaraguan Disputes," FBIS, *Daily Report: Latin America*, August 19, 1982, p. F1.

73. Jesús Medina S., "El Presidente Turbay Pide Cooperación Militar con Venezuela," *El Tiempo* (Bogotá), March 1, 1982.

74. Interview with Belisario Betancur by María Jimena Duzan, *El Espectador* (Bogotá), August 15, 1983.

75. "Venezuelan Government Expresses Views on Central American Situation," JPRS 28, 1983, p. A3.

76. FBIS, *Daily Report: Latin America*, July 28, 1983, p. A3.

77. FBIS, *Daily Report: Latin America*, July 18, 1983, p. F1.

78. These items were first spelled out in Contadora's ten-point Cancún Declaration; see Bruce Michael Bagley, Roberto Alvarez, and Katherine J. Hagedorn, eds., *Contadora and the Central American Peace Process: Selected Documents*, School of Advanced International Studies Papers in International Affairs No. 8 (Boulder, Colo.: Westview Press, 1985), pp. 170–74. Later they were incorporated into the twenty-one-point "Document of Objectives," which has been subscribed to by the five Central American governments; see Bagley, Alvarez, and Hagedorn, eds., *Contadora*, pp. 176–80.

79. Tom Wicker, "The Last Chance," *The New York Times*, February 11, 1986.

80. Cepeda Ulloa, "Contadora, Colombia y Centroamérica," pp. 35–37. [Editor's note: The 1987 Central American peace plan of Costa Rican President Oscar Arias, for which he received the Nobel Peace Prize, has upstaged the Contadora proposals.]

81. "Barco, with an Improved Economy, Will Pursue Less Activist Role," *Latin American Regional Report*, June 26, 1986, p. 1; *International Herald Tribune*, May 27, 1986; Bradley Graham, "Liberal Victorious in Colombia," *Washington Post*, May 26, 1986. During the presidential campaign, Conservative candidate Alvaro Gómez Hurtado distanced himself from Betancur, and though not openly attacking the internal peace process, he left little doubt that the guerrillas were a matter for the military; see Geoffrey Matthews, "Elections under the Volcano," *South*, January 1986, pp. 33–34. Barco, the preelection favorite, appeared more sympathetic to Betancur's domestic and foreign ini-

tiatives, but he leaned toward a more active role for the military in dealing with the guerrilla problem and was skeptical of "spectacular" maneuvers on the international front; see "Two Peace Bids Are Faltering," *Latin American Regional Report*, October 4, 1985, p. 2; "Colombian Election Profiles," *Latin American Weekly Report*, February 28, 1986, p. 6.

82. Felio Augusto Plazas, "El Presidente Betancur Empuja Desarmar la Bomba de Relogería de la Deuda Exterior," *El Tiempo* (Bogotá), August 31, 1984.

83. Gueron, "Politica Exterior," p. 367.

84. Interview with Carlos Lemos Simmonds by María Jimena Duzan, *El Espectador* (Bogotá), July 22, 1982.

85. Carlos Andrés Pérez, "Respect for Latins," *The New York Times* August 14, 1983.

86. Interview with Belisario Betancur by Patricia Lara, *El Tiempo* (Bogotá), May 29, 1983.

87. "FENALCO: Compliance with IMF would Raise Social Costs," JPRS LAM 85–39, May 7, 1985, pp. 24–26.

88. Interview with Jaime Lusinchi by Jean-Claude Buhrer, *Le Monde* (Paris), February 3, 1984.

89. Colombia's Conservative Party presidential candidate, Gómez Hurtado, while ambassador to Washington, expressed this view; see Interview with Alvaro Gómez Hurtado by ALDIA in *El Siglo* (Bogotá), November 4, 1983.

90. See Bagley and Tokatlian, "Colombian Foreign Policy," pp. 48–49; *Latin American Weekly Report*, January 31, 1986, pp. 6–7; "PLO Seeks Stronger Presence in the Region," *Latin American Weekly Report*, January 31, 1986, pp. 6–7.

13

The Influence of the United States on the Course of Colombian and Venezuelan Democracy

David J. Myers

During the early 1960s, the United States became increasingly concerned with threats to its position in Latin America. Not only was Fidel Castro maneuvering Cuba into the Soviet orbit, but revolutionary nationalism in a number of countries assumed an increasingly anti-U.S. flavor. Washington's Latin American policy of the 1950s—benign neglect coupled with a willingness to support any government that would maintain order and support the United States in the Cold War—was being interpreted throughout the hemisphere as opposition to democracy and indifference toward economic development. The stronger this perception became, the greater was the probability that revolutionary nationalists might seek out cooperation with Moscow in order to diminish Washington's influence. For the first time since the beginning of World War II, the special position of the United States in Latin America was encountering a strong challenge.

President John F. Kennedy intended that his Latin American policy, the Alliance for Progress, would demonstrate that imitating the Soviet path to modernization, the choice of Fidel Castro, was unnecessarily costly for Latin America and destructive of the human spirit. Under Kennedy's leadership the United States set out to prove that regulated private enterprise, along the lines practiced in North America, offered the best hope for creating a livable future.

In Colombia and Venezuela the United States observed fledgling democracies attempting to establish themselves following years of military dictatorship. The Kennedy administration concluded that the democratic elites in these countries represented an attractive alternative to the Cuban revolution. Especially given hemispheric trends during the early 1960s, Venezuela and Colombia's "limited"[1] democracies were viewed as perhaps the only kind of regime likely to emerge in Latin America that was both viable and compatible with U.S. interests. Consequently, Washington mobilized important political, economic, and cultural resources on behalf of democracy in Venezuela and Colombia.

To the extent that survival is the ultimate measure of success, Washington was more successful with Colombian and Venezuelan democracy than in its efforts during the 1960s to institutionalize any other of the newly established Latin American democracies.[2] Although numerous disagreements have surfaced subsequently between Washington and Bogotá, and between Washington and Caracas, the United States never has wavered in its support for democracy in either country. In Colombia, as has been discussed at length throughout this volume, the historically antagonistic Liberal and Conservative parties cooperated to monopolize politics. Venezuelan democracy polarized around the social democratic (Acción Democrática, AD) and social Christian (COPEI) political parties. The dominant political parties in both Colombia and Venezuela cooperated to weaken or coopt other political forces.

Radicals, particularly on the left, argue that Colombia and Venezuela's governing political parties, as well as the democratic rules of the game they imposed, perpetuate transnational capitalistic domination in general and U.S. imperialism in particular. Colombia and Venezuela's pluralistic democratic leaders answer by portraying themselves as nationalistic managers, seeking by increments to reduce a dependency on the North Atlantic that has been the lot of Latin America since colonial times. They proclaim that under their leadership, Venezuela and Colombia have experienced some upward international mobility; in addition, they point to significant progress in controlling the foreign interests that operate inside of their respective countries. This chapter will examine many of the policies that are at issue in relation to the exercise of U.S. influence.

It is always difficult to measure influence, even when the action networks being analyzed are compact and the data about how they operate have been collected in accord with methodologically rigorous standards.[3] When influence networks involve relations between several countries over three decades and available data are of widely varying quality and reliability, the most that can be hoped for is to arrive at nonobvious conclusions and tentative hypotheses. This is the intent here as regards the structures, processes, and impact of U.S. influence on Colombian and Venezuelan democracy since 1960.

Three themes or questions orient our efforts. The first asks what the United States sought to accomplish with its Colombian and Venezuelan policies. The second focuses on how the United States implemented its policies toward Venezuelan and Colombian democracy. The third looks at the impact of U.S. policies, especially their political and economic dimensions, on the political evolution of Colombia and Venezuela. Addressing these questions leads to conclusions about how the influence process operated; it also suggests directions for future research in assessing how countries influence each other.

U.S. INTERESTS AND OBJECTIVES

The interests and objectives of the United States in regard to Colombian and Venezuelan democracy, like its broader Latin American policy, display three basic dimensions: strategic, political, and economic. From the strategic perspective Colombia and Venezuela's Caribbean Basin location is decisive. The Caribbean Basin serves as a buffer to protect the southern United States. Sunbelt states are especially sensitive to threats emanating from the Basin. Domestic politics alone insure that Washington will do all in its power to keep Caribbean Basin countries from slipping out of its orbit. Not only does the Caribbean regional international system lie along the southern border of the United States, throughout the twentieth century it has been a secure bastion from which Washington projected power into western Europe and the Middle East. Should conflict break out in these regions, and the United States has declared that it has vital security interests in both, more than two thirds of the material shipped to allied or involved U.S. forces would pass through or skirt the Caribbean Basin.[4]

Caribbean Basin security for the United States also involved defense of the Panama Canal. While the canal is highly vulnerable to sabotage and nuclear attack during war, prior to the initiation of hostilities it remains a critical link in any strategy for positioning naval forces. Both Colombia and Venezuela lie astride the critical southeastern approach to the canal. Finally, the United States possesses a number of important military bases in the Caribbean Basin. These bases provide listening posts vital for the conduct of submarine warfare in the Atlantic, and staging areas for the rapid deployment of combat troops in case of a military emergency in the Basin.[5]

The strategic location of Colombia and Venezuela suggests that Washington will perceive a need to integrate them into planning the defense of Caribbean sea lanes of communication (SLOC) and the Panama Canal. Joint military planning requires that friendly and politically stable regimes remain in power. Support for the post–1958 Colombian and Venezuelan democracies, therefore, is strongly linked to U.S. perceptions of potential threats to its strategic interests in the Caribbean Basin. This was true in 1958, and it continues to be so in 1987.

The overriding political interest of the United States in Colombia and Venezuela derives from the pluralistic democratic regimes that have taken root in these countries. As suggested earlier, the democratic pluralism of Colombian and Venezuelan democracy, despite its "limited" nature, is perceived in Washington both as viable and ideologically compatible with U.S. democracy. Within the Caribbean Basin the United States views Colombian and Venezuelan democracy as an attractive alternative to the Marxist–Leninist regimes of Fidel Castro and Daniel Ortega.

Pluralist democracy in almost any form has been the first preference of both Republican and Democratic administrations since 1945. Until 1960, however, the United States remained more or less indifferent to the emergence or overthrow of democratic governments. Conventional wisdom in the United States held that

Latins would not sustain democracy, that as long as Caribbean dictators respected their country's international obligations and supported the "West" in the Cold War, they should be treated as trusted allies. Correspondingly, Washington's preference for liberal democracy in countries under authoritarian rule was not to go beyond paying lip service to the desirability of eventually restoring elected government.

Revolutions during the late 1950s against Generals Batista (Cuba), Rojas Pinilla (Colombia), and Pérez Jiménez (Venezuela) cast doubts on the viability of military dictatorship in Latin America. Fidel Castro's subsequent institutionalization of "Latin-style" Marxism-Leninism demonstrated that with Soviet assistance one of the governmental forms most at odds with that of the region's hegemon, the United States, had become an attractive and viable option. Given this challenge, the United States reinterpreted its political interest so as to mandate active support for democracy in Colombia and Venezuela, as well as throughout all Latin America. This shift did not so much indicate the presence of a coherent Colombian or Venezuelan policy as it reflected Washington's perception that the fledgling Colombian and Venezuelan democracies were for Latin Americans an attractive alternative to Castro's Cuba. In other words, the shift to active support for Colombian and Venezuelan democracy was a consequence of the United States adjusting its Latin American policy to a new reality; after 1960 the most urgent component in this policy involved containing or rolling back Fidel Castro's Revolution.

The political interests of the United States in Colombia and Venezuela since 1960 have encompassed more than actively defending the newly established democratic regimes. They included encouraging these regimes to evolve along certain lines favored by Washington. The first of these lines involved the attitude of political elites toward the strategic position and economic influence of the United States in the Basin. Those favoring neutrality in the East–West struggle, and a reduction in the economic presence of the United States, were to be influenced to alter these positions; when there was no response to Washington's efforts, the United States would act to strengthen the more sympathetically disposed political elites. Finally, since the early 1960s the United States has defined its political interests in Colombia and Venezuela to include the strengthening of political institutions and procedures that would increase respect for human rights.

U.S. economic interests in Colombia and Venezuela include the following: (1) maintenance of access to critical minerals, (2) stimulation of healthy economies to support democracy, and (3) encouragement of fair treatment of direct U.S. private investment. Washington views its Colombian and Venezuelan economic interests primarily within the context of more encompassing interests in the Caribbean Basin. The Caribbean Basin, after Canada, is the United States' second most important supplier of raw materials. Although in peacetime most of these raw materials represent merely a "convenience" to the United States, in the event of a major conflict they would be vital. Should a conflict break out, Venezuelan petroleum, along with Mexican petroleum and Jamaican bauxite, could become especially important.[6] At present, no Colombian mineral appears critical for the United States in time of war, although from the western European perspective, Colombian coal might fall into this category. Nevertheless, preventing the loss of the cumulative conveniences of Caribbean Basin raw materials, under any circumstances, represents a real interest for the United States.

Economic dynamism in Colombia and Venezuela since 1958 has depended largely on the export of raw materials, especially coffee and petroleum. In order to better manage this dependence, Bogotá and Caracas have launched major programs to create domestic manufacturing industries. They have succeeded in substituting some domestically produced light industrial goods for ones that traditionally were purchased abroad. Employment provided by these import-substituting industries has helped to create internal domestic support for democracy; it also has permitted Colombia and Venezuela's limited pluralism to appear throughout the Caribbean Basin as a viable alternative to Cuba's command economy. Nevertheless, while Colombian and Venezuelan industrial development conforms with the U.S. government's perception of its interests, that perception does not include encouraging either Colombia or Venezuela to export manufactured goods to the United States.

Per capita income in Colombia and Venezuela has risen significantly over the past quarter century, although Venezuela remains far wealthier than Colombia, and Venezuela's standard of living has yet to approach that of western Europe and North America. Although the United States wishes Colombia and Venezuela well, assisting either to achieve increases in its standard of living to OECD (Organization for Economic Cooperation and Development) levels is not high on the list of its Caribbean Basin priorities. In contrast, the United States has been diligent in seeking fair treatment for direct foreign investment in Colombia and Venezuela. Between 1960 and 1981 total U.S. private investment in the former almost tripled. Nevertheless, it remains modest: 1.2 billion U.S. dollars in 1981. In 1960 U.S. private investment in Venezuela totaled 2.6 billion U.S. dollars. Two decades later, only 2.2 billion U.S. dollars was invested. This decline reflects Venezuela's nationalization in the middle 1970s of foreign petroleum and iron mining holdings; the value of these nationalized enterprises was far greater than subsequent transfers of private U.S. capital.[7]

THE STRATEGY AND TACTICS OF IMPLEMENTATION

The strategy and tactics for implementing U.S. policy toward Colombian and Venezuelan democracy are best understood in terms of how general U.S. interests were prioritized during two distinct periods. In the first period, the years of regime institutionalization between 1959 and 1974, all concerns were subordinated to strengthening democratic institutions and norms against authoritarian challenges, both from the left and right. Although "political development" concerns[8] remained just below the surface throughout the second phase, 1975 to the present, the United States was more aggressive in pursuing a broad range of interests, even when pursuit led to open disagreements with the Colombian and Venezuelan governments. When differences did surface, however, Washington carefully portrayed them as minor difficulties among friends.

U.S. interests in relation to Colombian and Venezuelan democracy were pursued along four dimensions: (1) military/strategic, (2) political, (3) economic, and (4) cultural/educational. The military/strategic dimension focused primarily on strengthening the counterinsurgency capabilities of Colombia and Venezuela's armed forces. In addition, the United States helped in weapons modernization, most notably with the sale of F–16 fighter aircraft and their supporting logistics to Venezuela.[9] Finally, the United States Navy continued to train the Colombian and Venezuelan navies through joint participation in exercises such as UNITAS.

Twentieth-century Colombian violence has been more widespread and persistent than the violence in any other Latin American country. Because rural violence has been a major cause of political instability, its elimination was assigned a high priority by the United States once the strengthening of Colombian democracy became an important goal of the Alliance for Progress. On July 1, 1961, with full U.S. backing, the Colombian military initiated Plan Lazo, a coordinated effort to pacify the countryside.[10] Although initially concerned with eliminating guerrilla units, Colombia's military soon found itself involved in large-scale civic-action programs. Winning the "hearts and minds" of the peasantry, the primary source of guerrilla recruits, became almost as important as closing with and eliminating insurgent military units.

Plan Lazo's civic-action dimensions, however, always commanded greater support within the U.S. Military Assistance Group than from the Colombian congress. Consequently, emphasizing developmentalist goals led to several unanticipated difficulties: (1) The Colombian military found itself locked into a politically sensitive role in which it was essentially dependent on the heavy financial sponsorship of the United States; this offended nationalist sensibilities. (2) If the Colombian military had chosen to concentrate on the civic-action dimensions of Plan Lazo, relying exclusively on available local resources, it would have been necessary to curtail strictly military activities; this would have left the fighting capability of guerrilla units intact. (3) Alternatively, if the military high command attempted to wrest more money from an unsympathetic Congress, the effort would have inserted the armed forces—which only recently had been withdrawn to the barracks—back into the politics of resource allocation; given the institutional stresses experienced by the military during the government of General Rojas Pinilla, this was unacceptable to the generals. The dilemmas associated with funding military civic-action programs were resolved by asking those most identified with the Plan Lazo to resign from the armed forces.[11]

While developmentalist civic-action programs initiated during the early 1960s incurred higher institutional costs than their worth to the armed forces, they were never entirely abandoned. The Colombian military implemented them on a limited scale from the middle 1960s into the late 1970s, a period during which low-intensity conflict continued in a number of rural areas. However, the United States maintained its distance from Colombian counterinsurgency operations. Only in 1978, after Fidel Castro agreed to train such guerrilla groups as M–19, did the United States again become an actor.

U.S. involvement in the face of strengthened links between Castro and the Colombian guerrillas remained at a low level, limited largely to providing specialized weapons and military technology for use against irregular military units. Between 1976 and 1984, for example, U.S. military sales to Colombia were a relatively modest 65 million U.S. dollars. Nevertheless, this amounted to three times the value of Colombia's total military purchases from the United States between 1950 and 1975.[12] Also, Washington mobilized its sophisticated surveillance capabilities to identify and trace the movement of men and material from the Caribbean Basin into Colombia.

Two factors explain this modest level of involvement. Most important, it was all that counterinsurgency experts considered necessary. Washington calculated that Colombia's democratic leaders, more securely entrenched than during the early 1960s, could handle this threat without major U.S. assistance. Second, in the aftermath of Vietnam, this was but one of many U.S. experiments with minimal involvement when defending its interests in the Third World, especially when confronted with guerrilla warfare. Washington's approach reflected concern with potential opposition within the general population to U.S. military involvement in the Third World; it also recognized that there was no consensus inside of the traumatized officer corps about what changes the Vietnam experience mandated in its unsuccessful low-intensity conflict doctrines.

The Venezuelan democratic revolution, like its Colombian counterpart, was forced to consolidate in the fact of low-intensity warfare waged by radical guerrillas. The Venezuelan countryside, however, especially in comparison with rural Colombia, had experienced little organized violence during the twentieth century. Also, where Colombian peasants divided their political loyalties between the violently antagonistic Liberal and Conservative political parties, Venezuelan peasants, except in the Andes, supported the social democratic Acción Democrática (AD) political party. In the Andes, while many peasants did back the rival social Christians (COPEI), the peasants joined with AD to defend pluralistic democracy. Finally, the guerrilla bands challenging Venezuela's post–1958 democracy were composed largely of middle-class urban youth intent on recreating the Cuban Revolution. They never gained the support of either peasants or slum dwellers.

Because the AD political party of President Rómulo Betancourt (from 1959 to 1964) had its roots in the countryside, there was no need for the military to engage in developmentalist civic action. Bentancourt initiated and oversaw programs to improve rural living conditions and integrate AD's peasant supporters into both a party and a government hierarchy, each controlled from Caracas.[13] The Venezuelan military, therefore, unlike its Colombian counterpart, was able to focus exclusively on the insurgents. Because the Venezuelan armed forces were not asked to design civic-action programs, the U.S. military mission in Venezuela did not become involved in this dimension of low-intensity conflict.

In 1960 Venezuela was the source of almost 45 percent of the petroleum imported into the United States.[14] Consequently, the radical leftist insurgency against Venezuelan democracy during the governments of Rómulo Betancourt and Raúl Leoni was perceived in Washington as a threat to vital U.S. interests. Substantial military aid was channeled to the Venezuelan military; an elite counterinsurgency group, the Cazadores, received special training and equipment.[15] Cooperation between the AD party and the Cazadores left few safe havens to the guerrillas. In frustration they turned to indiscriminate terrorist acts that eventually cost them the minimal support they enjoyed in the slums of Caracas, Barquisimeto, and other cities. An overwhelming turnout for the December 1963 elections, coupled with the strong showing made by AD and COPEI, demonstrated that Venezuelan democracy was acquiring legitimacy.

The Leoni government (from 1964 to 1969) undercut remaining support for the insurgency and captured most guerrillas who persisted in armed struggle. As during the Betancourt government, the United States continued to supply equipment. However, the need for training by U.S. advisers declined. Amnesty offered by President Rafael Caldera (from 1969 to 1974) reincorporated most former guerrilla leaders and their followers into competitive party politics. Since the Caldera amnesty, despite intermittent guerrilla activity, there has been no serious armed insurgency against the Venezuelan democratic regime. The U.S. government has responded to the success of AD and COPEI in defusing insurgency and integrating the former guerrillas into the legal political process by treating the one-time insurgents as legitimate participants in the Venezuelan democratic experiment.[16]

During the Alliance for Progress, the United States pursued several basic political strategies to influence Colombian and Venezuelan democracy. Although these remain operative to this day, the relative importance assigned to each, and the intensity with which they were pursued, have fluctuated since the Alliance for Progress. In general, strategies during the alliance were intended to shape and strengthen pluralistically democratic "rules of the game." The political strategy initially assigned the highest priority, because arbitrary military rule had been the norm in Colombia and Venezuela during the 1950s, sought to build a consensus around the idea of civilian political supremacy and constitutional guarantees.

After the threat of military intervention lessened, the U.S. government devoted relatively few resources to strengthening the aforementioned. In contrast, Washington gave priority to a second political strategy, building up the status and prestige of political parties and leaders perceived as favorable to the United States. Of course, this also received high priority between 1959 and 1974, the years of democratic consolidation. Finally, on a more or less sustained basis since 1960, the United States has sought to strengthen the capacity of Colombian and Venezuelan government to penetrate aereally and shape the political behavior of all classes. Increasing these capabilities was viewed as central to political stabilization.

The return to civilian rule in Colombia and Venezuela during the late 1950s and early 1960s came as the consequence of internal revolts that stopped just short of civil war. As analyzed elsewhere, consolidation of these civilian regimes was by no means assured. The political traditions of Colombia and Venezuela included positive assessments of many charismatic leaders who used military force to take and hold power. U.S. public opinion, in contrast, indicated that U.S. citizens were very uncomfortable supporting rule by military strongmen. Enthusiasm within the United States for the Alliance for Progress correlated with perceptions that "progress" involved political evolution in the direction of pluralistic democracy. Also, because military regimes appeared vulnerable to popular insurgency, President John F. Kennedy decided that supporting the democratic left was the United States' best defense against communist penetration in the Caribbean Basin and South America. Correspondingly, during the 1960s, the United States extended the assistance it viewed as helpful in strengthening Colombian and Venezuelan democracy.[17]

Early in his administration President John F. Kennedy visited both Venezuela and Colombia. He publicly praised their fledgling democracies, expressed his admiration for their popularly elected presidents (Alberto Lleras Camargo and Rómulo Betancourt), and endorsed newly initiated programs to democratize their economies. Subsequently, Kennedy demonstrated his opposition to military rule by attempting to withhold diplomatic recognition from military regimes that seized power by overthrowing elected governments. For reasons beyond the scope of this essay, Kennedy's policy quickly proved unworkable. Five years after the United States proclaimed the Alliance for Progress, Latin America boasted few democratic governments; however, Colombia and Venezuela were important exceptions. More than ever, the United States sought to portray Colombia and Venezuela as showcases of what was desirable and possible: functioning liberal democratic alternatives to Cuban communism and military dictatorship.

During Richard Nixon's administration, the United States became ever more disillusioned with the activist vision of its global role that John F. Kennedy had proclaimed in his 1961 inaugural address. Official Washington interpreted the "lessons" of Vietnam as demonstrating that the United States could only marginally influence the course of political development in the Third World. This included nearby Latin America.

The journey to pluralistic democracy was viewed simplistically during the halcyon days of the Alliance for Progress. When its tortuous and tenuous character became undeniable, enthusiasm gave way to disillusionment. In its pragmatic neglect of Latin America, Richard Nixon's "low profile" foreign policy strongly paralleled that of his mentor, Dwight D. Eisenhower. The only vital U.S. interest involved minimizing the Soviet Union's Latin American influence.[18]

This orientation continued during the presidencies of Gerald Ford, Jimmy Carter, and Ronald Reagan, except that Carter pursued an activist human-rights policy. Carter, however, presided over an accelerating decline of U.S. influence throughout the Western Hemisphere.

Most observers of Latin America did not expect that democracy would thrive in Colombia and Venezuela. Nevertheless, the U.S. government has come to take for granted these countries' democratic regimes. President Nixon, as well as Presidents Ford, Carter, and Reagan, occasionally made public statements of support for their democratic rulers. They were praised for having consolidated representative governments and for safeguarding human rights. Nevertheless, expressions of approval and compatibility translated into few if any substantive advantages or concessions for Colombia and Venezuela.

Washington's efforts to create good will in Colombia and Venezuela have included arranging for exchanges and visits by influentials to the United States. Colombian and Venezuelan politicians, and other leaders supporting democracy, have been introduced to their counterparts in the United States. Not only has every Colombian and Venezuelan president journeyed to Washington, the United States has funded travel by a steady stream of labor leaders, businessmen, promising youth, and other opinion makers. Visitors have been encouraged to transplant to their countries the institutions and behavior observed in the United States.

The U.S. government has funded technical assistance toward the end of modernizing government institutions and strengthening activities that support participatory democracy. The Inter-American Foundation in Washington has sponsored community development projects that encourage the grass-roots presentation of political demands and reinforce the search for local solutions to political and economic problems.[19] The United States also has facilitated the transfer of advanced accounting procedures to Colombian and Venezuelan local governments. These procedures were viewed as enabling municipal councils to assemble and maintain the records necessary for assessing and expanding local sources of revenue.

Finally, U.S. assistance has been channeled through the private sector and foundations. Organized labor in the United States has sent advisers to assist noncommunist unions in both Colombia and Venezuela. Philanthropic institutions, such as the Ford and Rockefeller foundations, have sponsored technology transfers and made major investments. Colombian agriculture has benefited from foundation-sponsored research, and in Venezuela funding was made available to establish a graduate school of administration (Instituto de Estudios Superiores de Administración, IESA) and train its faculty in the United States. IESA's primary mission involved integrating training and business and public administration toward the end of producing the kind of manager needed by the state and private corporations on which politically stabilizing economic growth depended.

The Alliance for Progress assumed that the viability of Latin American democracy depended on modernizing the blend of feudal and capitalistic institutions that prevailed in mid-twentieth-century Latin America. Alliance advocates saw this blend as responsible for the region's continuing and pervasive poverty, and for Latin America's failure to industrialize. In this context the Alliance sponsored two broad kinds of economic activities. The first sought to soften the most brutal aspects of poverty. It took shape in programs to redistribute national income, build low-cost public housing, provide such amenities as running water and electricity, and increase health benefits. The second was to attack the underlying causes of poverty. Here the emphasis was on stimulating economic growth, diversifying economic activity, aiding land reform, controlling inflation, and pushing for a regional common market. In addition, the Alliance for Progress encouraged the creation of national planning bureaucracies capable of coordinating and supervising these transformations.[20]

Colombia and Venezuela, as indicated earlier, were to be showcases of the Alliance for Progress. Official Washington mobilized on behalf of the former; the latter, as has been pointed out on numerous occasions, received massive infusions of dollars in the form of payments for exported petroleum and petroleum products. This difference is profiled in Table 13.1. Between 1962 and 1978 Colombia obtained more than 1.3 billion U.S. dollars in loans and grants from the United States, roughly 13 percent of all funds that Washington allocated to Latin America during these years.

In addition to being a democracy, Colombia boasted many of the prerequisites that Alliance for Progress planners considered critical for success.[21] These included a vigorous private sector, a large industrial infrastructure, a sound tax base, and incipient land-reform programs. Colombia also was wrestling with many typical Latin American problems that the Alliance for Progress was intended to attack: rapid population growth, feudalistic attitudes toward education, reliance on one crop for a disproportionate amount of foreign-exchange earnings, and a maldistribution of income and land. Finally, Colombia's public administrators, many with U.S. training, possessed the technical expertise to produce the basic document on which Alliance for Progress funding was contingent: a comprehensive development plan. Colombia's plan became the basis for interaction between official Bogotá and the U.S. Agency for International Development (AID), the bureaucracy responsible for supervising implementation of the Alliance for Progress.

Alliance for Progress assistance to Colombia, in the main, was focused on the public sector. It necessitated the strengthening and creation of bureaucracies to formulate and implement developmental plans: agrarian reform, tax-base strengthening, health-care improvement, and peasant technical assistance.[22] These plans guided land reform, school construction, health-care expansion, housing, transportation, and rural electrification. Planning bureaucracies also became an important source of patronage for government supporters.

The Agency for International Development's (AID) administration of the Alliance for Progress generated tensions between the U.S. and Colombian gov-

Table 13.1
U.S. Overseas Loans and Grants: Obligations and Loan Authorizations (U.S. fiscal years, millions of dollars)

Destination	Mutual Security Pact	Foreign Assistance Act					Total Loans and Grants
	1953–1961	1962–1978	1979	1980	1981	1982	1953–1982
Total Economic Assistance							
to Colombia	106.50	1,343.40	8.90	23.10	5.70	3.00	1,490.60
Loans	64.60	1,041.00			*		1,105.60
Grants	41.90	302.40	8.90	23.10	5.70	3.00	385.00
Total Economic Assistance							
to Venezuela	16.30	56.80					73.10
Loans	15.10	40.00					55.10
Grants	1.30	16.80					18.10
Total Economic Assistance							
to Latin American region	1,552.20	10,289.00	449.40	498.20	610.90	839.80	14,239.50
Loans	633.20	6,641.20	231.90	263.30	358.00	480.40	8,608.00
Grants	919.00	3,647.80	217.50	234.90	252.90	359.49	5,631.50

*less than 50,000 U.S. dollars.
Source: U.S. Overseas Loans and Grants, and Assistance from International Organizations: July 1, 1945–September 30, 1982 (Washington, D.C. CONG-R-0105).

ernments. It was a classic example of clashing cultural norms and styles. AID officials sought to minimize what they viewed as questionable clientelistic and political practices in Colombia's development policies and projects. AID's efforts were resisted by Colombian politicians and bureaucrats; they were portrayed as interference. Eventually, a U.S. congressional investigation into the use of Alliance for Progress funds in Colombia concluded that Colombia's political elite had taken advantage of the Alliance for Progress merely to buy time, rather than to undertake structural reform.[23] Soon afterwards, in 1975, President Alfonso López Michelsen announced that Colombia no longer required economic assistance from the United States.[24] The role of AID became to wind down, in an orderly manner, programs already under way.

During the late 1970s and early 1980s, there was a small increase in U.S. economic aid to Colombia. Most of this increase was directed toward strengthening Colombian capacity to control the increasing flow of drugs into the southern United States.[25] As in earlier Alliance for Progress assistance, however, Washington's efforts to oversee implementation led to tensions with Bogotá. The United States again appeared to be interfering in Colombia's internal affairs. In addition, Colombian politicians stated that the core of the drug problem was the consumption of marijuana and cocaine within the United States, not its production and distribution by Colombians. Since February 1982, however, the United States and Colombia have cooperated to seize substantial quantities of drugs bound for North America's Gulf coast.

Washington also has used trade, foreign investment, and banking policies in its efforts to influence Bogotá. Throughout the democratic period, the United States has remained Colombia's single most important trading partner; however, Colombia now exports more to the European Economic Community than to North America. One indicator of the declining importance of the U.S. market is that whereas, in 1960, 65 percent of Colombia's exports went to the United States, by the middle 1980s, this proportion hovered around 20 percent.[26] Periodic negotiations over price supports for coffee continue to generate tensions between the United States and Colombia, as does the former's reluctance to lower tariff barriers on a broad range of light industrial goods produced by the latter.

During the past twenty years, U.S. foreign investment in Colombia has not been an important source of tensions between Washington and Bogotá. Colombia is a founding member of the Andean Pact. Decision 24 of the Andean Pact's board of governors regulates foreign investment so as to discourage all foreign investors. Therefore, in spite of being Latin America's third most populous nation, Colombia ranks seventh as a recipient of U.S. direct foreign investment. Only in 1980 did the book value of U.S. direct foreign investment accumulated in Colombia surpass 1 billion U.S. dollars.[27] However, Colombia's increasing appetite for capital is causing the government to explore arrangements that could circumvent those Andean Pact restrictions on foreign investment that the multinational corporations have found objectionable. If circumvention without modifying Decision 24 is attempted, the possibilities for conflict over which regulations actually apply to foreign investment in Colombia would be endless. Whatever its initial benefits and terms of transfer, therefore, an increase in U.S. foreign investment in Colombia, given the aforementioned situation, would carry with it the seeds of confrontation.

Finally, among South American countries, Colombia has been one of the more prudent in contracting foreign debt. In 1983 loans by large U.S. banks to Colombia totaled only 3.3 billion U.S. dollars. Colombia's debts to other OECD countries, and to international lenders such as the World Bank—roughly 6.7 billion U.S. dollars—were also less burdensome than those of all but a few of its neighbors.[28] Nevertheless, the Colombian government under both Liberal and Conservative administrations, like more heavily indebted Venezuela under AD and COPEI, has supported the efforts of Third World countries to soften the terms of debt repayment.

The economic role of the United States in Venezuela during the democratic era, as throughout most of the twentieth century, has been closely linked to the international petroleum market and to perceptions in Washington about the reliability of Caracas as a source of oil. Nevertheless, during the political and economic turmoil of the Betancourt government, the Alliance for Progress made several important loans to Venezuela. Funds went for urban renewal, low-cost housing, and local self-help projects.[29] As in Colombia, implementation of the Alliance for Progress guidelines in Venezuela involved officials of the Agency for International Development in local politics. Similarly, they became vulnerable to charges of interfering in the host country's local politics. Neither Washington nor Caracas, however, envisioned a major role for U.S. developmental assistance in Venezuela. As early as 1966, the Agency for International Development was quietly disengaging from Venezuela.

Purchases by the United States of Venezuelan petroleum long has been the most important economic activity linking the two countries. During the past two decades, however, Caracas and Washington have implemented policies that reduced the magnitude of their interdependence. Washington would not accept significant dependence on a country whose petroleum pricing and production policies were determined by an international cartel; Venezuela, of course, helped to found OPEC (Organization of Petroleum Exporting Countries). Caracas, on the other hand, calculated that its economic bargaining power would increase if it diversified its customers. Correspondingly, economic relations between the two countries changed. In 1962 the United States imported over 900,000 barrels a day of Venezuelan petroleum; this was 44 percent of total U.S. petroleum imports. By 1979 U.S. purchases of Venezuelan petroleum had fallen to 691,000 barrels a day, only 8 percent of total U.S. petroleum imports. However, this new economic relation proved more asymmetrical than the one it replaced. Even though Venezuela found new customers, the United States still purchased one third of Venezuela's total petroleum exports.[30] The dollar value of Venezuelan petroleum imported into the United States remained substantial; in 1982 it exceeded 4.5 billion U.S. dollars.[31]

In 1976 President Carlos Andrés Pérez nationalized the Venezuelan subsidiaries of all foreign petroleum companies. Transnationals and their subsidiaries had developed and managed Venezuela's petroleum industry for more than half a century. The most important subsidiaries belonged to Exxon, Shell, and Gulf, corporations owned by investors residing preponderantly in the North Atlantic region. Caracas and Washington each made major efforts to minimize the political fallout of nationalization. Venezuela paid the transnationals significant compensation—1 billion U.S. dollars. In turn, the transnationals agreed to continue purchasing petroleum from their former subsidiaries. Washington, "blessed" this agreement, taking pains to point out that all parties had accepted as fair the amount of compensation paid by the Venezuelan government. With this "blessing" Washington hoped to minimize potentially adverse reaction to nationalization within the OECD financial community. The U.S. government did not want entrepreneurs and bankers making punitive decisions that would create economic difficulties for Venezuelan democracy.[32]

Petroleum nationalization, however, set in motion a chain of events that led to economic paralysis and confrontation between Venezuela's democratic government and the OECD financial community. Ironically, an important factor in the aforementioned chain was President Carlos Andrés Pérez's decision to divert an important amount of Venezuela's petroleum income to the exterior, into a specially created Venezuelan investment fund. The expansion of this fund caused Venezuela's international credit rating to soar. It became so strong that banks in the OECD countries asked few questions when Venezuelan state corporations, usually without approval from the central government, began requesting loans.

Indebtedness increased dramatically during the final year of the Pérez government and escalated during the first half of the Herrera administration. Subsequently, declining petroleum revenues reduced available capital below the level envisioned by President Luis Herrera's Sixth National Plan (from 1981 through 1986).[33] In the wake of this reduction the government also "discovered" that it was obligated to repay, in a very short period, large loans taken out by the state corporations. Confidence in the Venezuelan economy plummeted, and capital flight increased. Consequently, on February 18, 1983, President Luis Herrera imposed controls on foreign exchange and declared a moratorium on the payment of Venezuela's foreign debt.

The ministry of finance initially claimed not to know how much Venezuela owed. When the total debt of all state enterprises was consolidated, it came to roughly 28 billion U.S. dollars; an additional 8 billion U.S. dollars was owed by the private sector. In light of declining petroleum revenues, and given the unanticipated magnitude of its foreign debt, Venezuela's only choice was to seek renegotiation of the terms for repayment.

Because the financial crisis became critical during the early stages of the 1983 election campaign, immediate political considerations strongly influenced all efforts at crisis management. Neither of the major democratic political parties was willing to negotiate seriously until after the December presidential balloting.

Following the inauguration of social democrat Jaime Lusinchi, in February 1984, the new administration continued to resist repayment terms as austere as those demanded by its creditors. Throughout the bargaining, official Washington remained in the background, preferring to have Venezuelan frustrations and antagonisms directed toward the consortium of banks holding the Venezuelan debt and the International Monetary Fund. This refusal by the Reagan administration to pressure Venezuela into agreeing to terms demanded by the banks strengthened the hand of Venezuela in negotiations with them.[34]

Cultural strategies, although less prominent than their military, political, and economic counterparts, have played an important role in U.S. relations with Colombia and Venezuela. Culturally, the United States begins with some disadvantages; Simón Bolívar, the hero of Colombian and Venezuelan independence, was an early voice urging his countrymen to keep their distance from the United States. Bolívar viewed Anglo-American and Latin American culture as antithetical in many important dimensions.[35] Nevertheless, U.S. popular culture is much imitated and its technology is much desired in contemporary Colombia and Venezuela. Students eagerly have sought out the hundreds of scholarships to U.S. universities that official Washington and the private sector have made available. In the case of Venezuela, however, the oil-financed Gran Mariscal de Ayacucho program has proved the single most important source of scholarships facilitating study in the United States. Finally, some attention has been given to strengthening ties between the Colombian and Venezuelan, and U.S. academic communities. Here Washington has moved with great care. Since the end of World War II, U.S. academics, more often than not, have been in opposition to the Latin American policies of their own government.

To summarize, the economic strategies by which the United States implemented its policies in Colombia and Venezuela during the democratic era were designed to achieve three goals: political stabilization, continuing access to critical raw materials, especially Venezuelan petroleum, and modernizing economic growth. The core intentions that underlay Washington's military, political, and cultural strategies were essentially the same as those behind its economic strategies. Within Colombia and Venezuela strengthening political stability became support for sui generis democratic regimes and their supporting political parties. In Colombia the Liberals and the Conservatives were the "anointed" supporting political parties. In Venezuela it was AD and COPEI. Washington's treatment of other political leaders and parties ranged from occasional acknowledgment of their "contributions," when they supported democracy, to thinly veiled hostility, when they did not.

The U.S. government viewed Colombia and Venezuela's democratic political leaders as its best hope of keeping these countries within the western orbit internationally. Washington also perceived them as willing to provide critical raw materials and to preserve their countries as markets for U.S. manufactured goods. However, the democratic leaders of Colombia and Venezuela remained apprehensive of Washington's embrace. Military interventions against the Dominican Republic in 1965 and against Grenada in 1982 reminded them that regardless of public pronouncemems, the United States would resort to armed force when defending its Caribbean Basin interests. Also, United States' administration of its foreign aid, whether military or economic, constituted an unwelcome intrusion into Colombian and Venezuelan domestic affairs. Finally, the democratic leaders of Colombia and Venezuela saw Washington's support for them as a two-edged sword. They remembered that during the 1950s, while in the underground, they had played on suspicions that the then ruling military had sold out to the United States. These suspicions had helped to discredit authoritarian governments backed by the armed forces and to pave the road to revolution.

CONCLUDING COMMENTS: THE IMPACT OF U.S. INFLUENCE AND DIRECTIONS FOR FUTURE RESEARCH

Whether post 1958 Colombian and Venezuelan democracy would have disintegrated without support from the United States is unknowable; however, Washington's support contributed to democracy's institutionalization. During the years immediately following the overthrow of General Rojas Pinilla in Colombia and General Pérez Jiménez in Venezuela, the Colombian and Venezuelan armed forces were disspirited, disorganized, and suspicious of civilian democratic rule. U.S. military assistance helped to create highly motivated and trained army units in both countries. It modernized a counterinsurgency capability that reduced in each the costs of defending pluralistic governments against the low-intensity conflict mounted by radical leftists and their Cuban allies. Also, the training of Colombia and Venezuela's most talented military leaders by the United States exposed them to an enormously prestigious military that historically subordinated itself to popularly elected civilian politicians.

A Cuban-style victory by guerrillas in either Colombia or Venezuela during the early 1960s was by no means assured, even had the United States decided against military assistance. Although on the defensive, these countries' armed forces, unlike their Cuban counterpart, remained intact. Also, in contrast to the situation in Cuba, civilian traditionalists in Colombia and Venezuela had been able to disassociate themselves from the disastrous dictatorial rule that terminated in revolution. Colombian and Venezuelan elites retained substantial political and economic power, and they were violently anticommunist. Indeed, throughout much of the 1960s there was concern in Washington that pressures from the guerrillas in Colombia and Venezuela might persuade traditionalists to use their influence with the armed forces to overthrow democracy, replacing it with modernizing rightist authoritarianism, along the lines of Spain under General Francisco Franco.

The persistence of low-intensity conflict had an unanticipated consequence in Colombia and Venezuela; by creating a community of interest between the military and liberal democrats, it caused the former to become more favorably disposed to rule by the latter. The armed forces worked closely with such popularly elected presidents as Lleras Camargo in Colombia and Betancourt in Venezuela. Increasingly, the generals viewed their civilian presidents as brave anticommunists. Washington shared this perception and did all in its power to foster cooperation. Nevertheless, given the confluence of domestic and international currents that occurred during the 1960s, a military alliance with democratic pluralists might have crystallized regardless of U.S. policy. There is little doubt, however, that without U.S. encouragement cooperation between democratic politicians and the generals in Colombia and Venezuela would have been more problematical and tenuous.

Counterinsurgency and other military assistance immediately raise the human-rights issues. In this context, it is important to point out that historically the human-rights record in Colombia and Venezuela is mixed. While political culture affirms the importance of individual liberty, it also provides multiple justifications for and examples of human-rights violations. During the Rojas Pinilla and Pérez Jiménez regimes, respect for human rights reached one of the low points that have been all too common in the Bolivarian republics.

Alberto Lleras Camargo and Rómulo Betancourt came from traditions that affirmed the importance of human rights. They began their presidencies determined to strengthen that heritage. However, as has been discussed at length, Lleras Camargo and Betancourt quickly found themselves involved in the kind of low-intensity conflict that has proved so destructive of individual rights and liberties. While defending their governments against leftist revolutionary violence, they and their successors were sometimes responsible for some human-rights violations. Nevertheless, in the context of Colombian and Venezuelan history, recent democratic governments have made unprecedented efforts to limit abuses. When previously violent groups sought admission to the loyal opposition, Colombian and Venezuelan democrats gave them full constitutional guarantees and civil liberties.

This treatment of political opponents was viewed in Washington as vindication of U.S. efforts to promote respect for human rights. However, linkages between U.S. policy and political styles that safeguard human rights and liberties are difficult to demonstrate. Decisions to respect rights and liberties in Colombia and Venezuela seem most directly traceable to the values held by these countries' pluralistic democratic elites, rather than to the intrusive influence of the United States.

The impact of Washington's economic policy on Colombian and Venezuelan democracy is similarly complex and difficult to assess. Underlying this policy has been an assumption that the United States should stimulate the transformation of Latin American society, viewed by North Americans as that sui generis blend of feudal and capitalist institutions responsible for Latin America's continuing poverty and failure to modernize. Also, Alliance for Progress planners believed that in the short run foreign aid could soften the more dehumanizing dimensions of poverty that appeared responsible for the appeal of Fidel Castro and his Cuban Revolution.

Alliance for Progress loans and grants to Colombia and Venezuela during the

1960s did finance some housing that might not otherwise have been built. However, most Alliance for Progress-constructed apartments were occupied by families who could afford the rents on which loan amortization depended. This condition made it impossible for low-income families, those often displaced to make way for Alliance for Progress projects, to qualify for the newly constructed apartments. Occasionally, the relocated poor actually ended up with worse living arrangements because of Alliance for Progress investments. Even when subsidies did enable Colombian and Venezuelan slum dwellers to occupy housing built by the Alliance for Progress, these exceptional projects were little more than symbolic gestures by the United States and allied local elites. Alliance for Progress funding was not on a scale large enough to influence appreciably the availability of housing in either Colombia or Venezuela. The same was true of other Alliance for Progress investments initiated to ameliorate the more dramatic manifestations of Latin American poverty; in summary, this dimension of U.S. policy had little or no impact on the course of democratic institutionalization.

The United States viewed its efforts at transforming Latin America's traditional social and economic structures as central to eliminating the causes of poverty and unrest. The modern Latin American state was to be the engine of change; Alliance for Progress advocates placed great faith in the central bureaucracy's capacity to plan rationally. Modern techniques and technology were transferred by making advanced training in the United States and western Europe available to promising university graduates selected by the Colombian and Venezuelan governments. Newly trained civil servants were to serve as catalysts upon their return. The United States anticipated they would manage public-sector industries, oversee agrarian reform, transform education, modernize banking procedures, plan cities, and develop national communications networks. Personalistic and clientelistic criteria for resource allocation, long viewed as perpetuating underdevelopment, were to be replaced by the legal and rational norms learned abroad.

In order to be effective, the structural reforms envisioned in the Alliance for Progress required increases in the capacity of Latin American state bureaucracies to gain compliance at all levels for decisions made at the center. Otherwise, the technology mastered by those trained abroad would have little practical impact. Unfortunately, social science has learned very little about the impact of overseas training on the performance of Colombian and Venezuelan bureaucracy.

Some changes in the structure of these bureaucracies are easy to document. Most obviously, Colombia and Venezuela developed central planning agencies modeled on their counterparts in France and Great Britain. They also created or modified institutions dedicated to industrialization, agrarian reform, banking, and other developmental activities. In addition, technology transfer increased the capability of Colombian and Venezuelan bureaucracies to undertake such sophisticated projects as highway construction, irrigation, and telecommunications. However, neither the newly created institutions nor the modernizing projects they initiated operated like their counterparts in the United States or western Europe. They mixed the technology and legal and rational norms learned abroad with historic Latin American clientelism and personalism, behavioral patterns that can be traced to the colonial era. Unfortunately, in-depth studies of how foreign training influenced traditional bureaucratic behavior in Colombia and Venezuela are not available.

To summarize, the Alliance for Progress and successor policies intended to reform social and economic structures strengthened the central governments of Colombia and Venezuela. Since these governments were in the hands of democratic leaders, this contributed to institutionalizing democracy. Here U.S. policy also assisted Colombian and Venezuelan bureaucracies in acquiring modern forms and increased technological capabilities. However, many traditional patterns of behavior persisted. Clientelistic practices remained the norm, and politicians applied performance criteria selectively. For some, this represented reasonable progress, given the burdens of history and tradition. For others, these changes were ill-conceived efforts that postponed the necessary and inevitable revolutionary processes that some day would transform these countries.

Finally, the aforementioned lack of information about the consequences for bureaucratic performance of mixing training in the developed world with traditional Latin American values and procedures suggests a priority area for future research. Bureaucracies will remain pivotal agents for initiating and managing change, not only in Colombia and Venezuela, but throughout Latin America. If the United States continues to view the capability to channel socioeconomic change as important to the pursuit of its interests, resources will have to be allocated toward understanding the consequences for Latin American bureaucracies of training their young executives in western Europe and the United States during the 1960s and 1970s. Measuring and interpreting consequences will be difficult, time consuming, and demanding of cooperation between North American and Latin American social science. For the United States, however, the failure to sponsor such research perpetuates ignorance about the impact of a long-term, costly effort undertaken to advance important national interests.

NOTES

1. José Antonio Gil, *The Challenge of Venezuelan Democracy*, transl. Evelyn Harrison I., Lolo Gil de Yanes, and Danielle Salti (New Brunswick, N.J.: Transaction Books, 1981), Chapter 7.

2. Robert J. Alexander and Charles O. Porter, *The Struggle for Democracy in Latin America* (New York: Macmillan, 1961).

3. For a rigorous discussion of influence, see Robert A. Dahl, *Modern Political Analysis*, third edition (Englewood Cliffs, N.J.: Prentice Hall, 1976), Chapter 3.

4. David Ronfeldt, *Geopolitics, Security, and U.S. Strategy in the Caribbean Basin*, R–2997-AF (Santa Monica, Calif.: The Rand Corporation, 1983), pp. 48–56.

5. Margaret Daly Hayes, "United States Security Interests in Central America in Global Perspective" in *Central America: International Dimensions of the Crisis*, ed. Richard Feinberg (New York: Holmes & Meier, 1982), p. 92.

6. John M. Hunter and James W. Foley, *Economic Problems of Latin America* (Boston: Houghton Mifflin, 1975), pp. 113–25, 177–78, 204–07.

7. James Wilkie and Adam Perkal, eds., *Statistical Abstract of Latin America*, Vol. 13 (Los Angeles: UCLA Latin American Center Publications, University of California, 1984), pp. 699, 701.

8. Samuel Huntington, *Political Order in Changing Societies* (New Haven, Conn.: Yale University Press, 1968).

9. David J. Myers, *Venezuela's Pursuit of Caribbean Basin Interests: Implications for United States National Security*, R–2994-AF (Santa Monica, Calif.: The Rand Corporation, 1985), pp. 37–38. Between 1975 and 1984 Venezuela purchased 758 million dollars in military equipment from the United States. Most of these sales involved the F–16 and its logistic support. Defense Security Assistance Agency, U.S. Department of Defense, *Foreign Military Sales, Foreign Military Construction Sales, and Military Assistance Pacts as of September 30, 1984* (Washington, D.C.: Data Management Division, Comptroller, Defense Security Assistance Agency, 1984), p. 7.

10. Richard Maullin, *Soldiers, Guerrillas, and Politics in Colombia* (Lexington, Mass.: Lexington Books, 1973), pp. 69–71.

11. Ibid., pp. 71–72. An informative summary of the state of Colombian guerrilla activity during 1978 appears in "Colombia" in *Annual of Power and Conflict 1978–79*, ed. Brian Crozier (London: Institute for the Study of Conflict, 1980), pp. 182–90.

12. Defense Security Assistance Agency, U.S. Department of Defense, *Foreign Military Sales*, pp. 6–7.

13. For a comprehensive analysis of the Venezuelan insurgency, see Richard Gott, "Revolutionary Failure in Venezuela," in *Guerrilla Movements in Latin America* (Garden City, N.Y.: Doubleday & Company, 1971), pp. 121–22. Cf. John D. Powell, *The Political Mobilization of the Venezuelan Peasant* (Cambridge, Mass.: Harvard University Press, 1971).

14. Jorge I. Domínguez, *Economic Issues and Political Conflict: U.S.-Latin American Relations* (London: Wiltshire, Butterworth & Company, 1982), p. 130.

15. Myers, *Venezuela's Pursuit of Caribbean Basin Interests*, pp. 26–27.

16. For example, on the tenth anniversary of the Eurocommunist Movement Toward Socialism (MAS), William Luers, the U.S. ambassador to Venezuela, not only attended the celebration but acted in a way that demonstrated his government's acceptance of MAS as a legitimate participant in Venezuelan democracy.

17. William F. Furlong, "Democratic Political Development and the Alliance for Progress," in *The Continuing Struggle for Democracy in Latin America*, ed. Howard J. Wiarda (Boulder, Colo.: Westview Press, 1980), pp. 167–84.

18. Luigi Einiudi, "U.S. Latin American Policy in the 1970s: New Forms of Control," in *Latin America & the United States: the Changing Political Realities*, eds. Julio Cotler and Richard R. Fagen (Stanford, Calif.: Stanford University Press, 1974), pp. 250–55.

19. Ildemaro Jesús Martínez, "The Performance of Local Government in Democratic Venezuela," in *Venezuela: The Democratic Experience*, eds. John D. Martz and David J. Myers (New York: Praeger, 1977), Chapter 15.

20. Furlong, "Democratic Political Development," p. 170.

21. Harvey F. Kline, *Colombia: Portrait of Unity and Diversity* (Boulder, Colo.: Westview Press, 1983), pp. 126–27.

22. Howard I. Blutstein, J. David Edwards, et al., *Area Handbook for Colombia*,

third edition, DA PAM 550–26, (Washington, D.C.: American University, 1977), pp. 321–22.

23. U.S. Senate, Committee on Foreign Relations, *Survey of the Alliance for Progress in Colombia: A Case History of USAID*, a staff study prepared at the request of the Subcommittee on American Republic Affairs, 91st Congress, 1st session, Document 91–17 (Washington, D.C.: U.S. Government Printing Office, February 1, 1969).

24. Blutstein et al. *Area Handbook for Colombia*, p. 307.

25. Kline, *Colombia*, pp. 131–32.

26. Between 1970 and 1981 Colombian exports experienced a sustained expansion, from a little over 790 million U.S. dollars in the former year to nearly 4.1 billion U.S. dollars in the latter. Economic Commission for Latin America, "Colombia," in *Economic Survey of Latin America—1981* (Santiago, Chile: United Nations, 1983), p. 229. The importance of the United States is noted in *Area Handbook for Colombia*, p. 321. Compare with Thomas O. Enders and Richard P. Mattione, *Latin America: The Crisis of Debt and Growth* (Washington, D.C.: The Brookings Institution, 1984), p. 54.

27. Kline, *Colombia*, p. 135; James Wilkie and Adam Perkal, eds. *Statistical Abstract for Latin America*, Vol. 23 (Los Angeles: UCLA Latin American Center, 1984), p. 694.

28. Bruce Michael Bagley and Juan Gabriel Totkatlian, "Colombian Foreign Policy in the 1980s: The Search for Leverage," *Journal of Inter-American Studies and World Affairs* 27 (Fall 1985): 43–44. Compare with Economic Commission for Latin America, "Colombia," in *Economic Survey of Latin America—1983*, (Santiago, Chile: United Nations, 1985), p. 238.

29. David J. Myers, "Eliminating the Committee to Remodel the Barrios," in *The Political Process of Urban Development: Caracas Under Acción Democrática*, Ph.D. dissertation, Department of Political Science, UCLA, 1969, Chapter 3.

30. Domínguez, *Economic Issues and Political Conflict*, p. 130; Compare with Economic Commission for Latin America, "Venezuela" in *Economic Survey of Latin America—1981*, pp. 779–80.

31. James Petras, Morris Morley, and Steven Smith, *The Nationalization of Venezuelan Oil* (New York: Praeger, 1977).

32. For an informative discussion of the role of the U.S. government in relation to Venezuela's oil nationalization, see Franklin Tugwell, *The Politics of Oil in Venezuela* (Stanford, Calif.: Stanford University Press, 1975).

33. Economic Commission for Latin America, "Venezuela" in *Economic Survey of Latin America—1981*, pp. 782–84. Compare with John D. Martz and David J. Myers, "The Politics of Economic Development" in *Venezuela: The Democratic Experience*, second edition, eds. John D. Martz and David J. Myers (New York: Praeger, 1986).

34. Eduardo Mayobre, "The Renegotiation of Venezuela's Foreign Debt During 1982 and 1983," in *Politics and Economics of External Debt Crisis: The Latin American Experience*, ed. Miguel S. Wionczek (Boulder, Colo.: Westview Press, 1985), pp. 325–47. Compare with "Venezuela" in *Lagniappe Quarterly Report* (New York: Latin American Information Services, January 31, 1985), p. 19. Compare with Joseph M. Martin, "Economic Analysis and Outlook" in *Country Analysis and Outlook: Venezuela*, ed. Rosemary H. Werrett (New York: Fund for Multinational Management Education, January 1985), Chapter 2.

35. Simón Bolívar's skepticism is encapsulated in his often quoted warning that the United States was destined to "plague" Latin America in the name of liberty.

14

Reassessment and Projection

Donald L. Herman

The chapters in this book are selective, and admittedly, additional topics might be explored in analyzing Colombian and Venezuelan democracy. During the past several years, however, an important development has taken place the effect of which is of such significance that future studies of Latin American democracy, in certain countries, will be required to examine the problem. Before we reassess the earlier hypotheses and look to the future, let us consider this most important variable.

DRUG TRADE

Any analysis of democracy in the two countries must address the question of the drug trade, particularly in Colombia. The thousands of families involved in production, and the billions of dollars exchanged in marketing, impinge on the Colombian political–socioeconomic structure and thereby affect the very nature of the regime. Drug trade is a dangerous research topic, however, and at best we can only speculate as to its real impact. It is clandestine and illegal and, of course, reliable statistical evidence is scarce. Nevertheless, enough has been written on the subject to allow us to appreciate the influence of the ''narcodollar'' on the substantive and procedural norms of democracy.

The three principal drugs that emanate from Colombia are marijuana, cocaine, and methaqualone. (Rohrer's methaqualone is the primary source of Quäälude tablets.)[1] The success of Mexico's massive herbicide program in 1975 provided an opportunity for Colombian *traficantes* and their U.S. counterparts, and within a few years Colombian marijuana replaced that from Mexico and soon dominated the U.S. drug market. In 1984, not only was Colombia the largest supplier to the U.S. market of the three previously mentioned drugs, but it was also the principal refining source for cocaine.[2] The following year the Federal Drug Enforcement Agency reported that Colombia supplied the United States with approximately 74 percent of its cocaine and 80 percent of its marijuana.[3] Thus, Colombia controls the entire trafficking cycle. Not only is its climate ideal for growing marijuana, principally in the northeastern part of the country, but its geography facilities the smuggling of coca leaf from Peru and Bolivia via Ecuador into Colombia. There clandestine laboratories process the paste into base and the base into cocaine for the domestic and foreign market.

Economic Implications

In December 1970 former U.S. Ambassador Diego Asencio reported to the U.S. Senate:

Colombia has been facing a severe economic challenge from narcotics traffickers. The integrity of its financial institutions has been placed in jeopardy. A growing inflation rate has been accelerated by illegal monies. Legitimate business enterprises have had to defend themselves from absorption by criminals. Land values, both agricultural and residential, are soaring, leaving farmers and middle-class home buyers in a quandary.[4]

Professor Craig pointed out other negative effects on the economy. For example, the government must divert large sums needed elsewhere in efforts to suppress growing and trafficking. Narcodollars contribute substantially to the country's increasing dependence on food importing through the conversion of crop lands to marijuana fields and the recruitment of peasants to grow marijuana instead of staples. The additional illegal funds add immeasurably to a flourishing internal market in a variety of contraband imports.[5]

It stands to reason that drug money is destabilizing the economy. It creates an extralegal banking market while contributing to a currency black market. Furthermore, large foreign-exchange surpluses of billions of dollars in illicit funds, not linked to the productive process, threaten economic development and make rational planning all but impossible.

Political Implications

With enormous sums of money at their disposal, the drug dealers wield considerable power and affect politics at all levels: international, national, regional, and local.[6] On the international level one can argue whether the U.S. market demand or the Colombian "mafia's" desire to reap enormous profits is basically at fault; nevertheless, drug traffic is currently the major issue between the two countries.

Within Colombia high-ranking police and judicial officials, including several Supreme Court justices, have received threats from the drug cartel. In 1984 Justice Minister Rodrigo Lara Bonilla, who was investigating the Colombian drug trade, was assassinated. Furthermore, drug money has influenced various elections, and some observers believe that by 1980, 10 percent of the deputies and senators had been elected with "partial or total drug funded campaign contributions."[7] Their influence is even greater on the regional and local levels.

There is convincing evidence of a tie-in between the drug traficantes and some of the guerrilla movements. Although the army has repeatedly accused the guerrillas of providing drug gangs with armed protection in return for funds and weapons, the M–19 attack on the Palace of Justice (November 1985) convinced many doubters that this indeed might be true.[8] Government troops and police broke the siege by storming the building, and in the ensuing battle more than one hundred people died, including several judges and the president of the Supreme Court.

Two principal facts support the theory of a drug smugglers–guerrillas alliance: the guerrillas destroyed files relating to Colombians the United States was seeking to extradite on narcotics charges, and they murdered at least four judges who had heard, or were about to hear, cases involving drug smugglers. Furthermore, a significant fact that has been overlooked is that the M–19 guerrillas attacked the court building on the day the judges were to hear submissions challenging the constitutional validity of the Colombian–U.S. extradition treaty. Despite heated opposition by Andean drug barons, the treaty was signed in 1979 as part of the two countries' effort to suppress the smuggling of cocaine and marijuana from Colombia to the United States. Though M–19 denied it has links with drug traffickers, the late guerrilla leader Alvaro Fayad, in a recording sent to local newspapers, attacked the "unpopular and scandalous" extradition treaty. Colombian Foreign Minister Augusto Ramírez revealed that abrogation of the treaty was one of the demands M–19 presented to the government after the court-building seizure.

Social Implications

Many of Colombia's impoverished peasant families have discovered that marijuana cultivation provides an income source five to ten times greater than any competing crops, and for the first time they are living above the subsistence level. In many areas along the north coast and in the eastern Llanos, marijuana cultivation provides jobs and a decent income for more than 200,000 people who previously had known only abject poverty.[9] Although the drug smugglers run a risk in marketing the crops, extremely low salaries make judges, local politicians, and penal officials susceptible to bribes. Those who do not "cooperate" are assassinated. Thus, the traficantes have decided advantages operating within a poor society. The more successful they are, the more likely that bribery, violence, assassinations, and corruption will continue to spread. The multimillionaire traficantes have bought respectability by financing social welfare and slum-clearance programs, and acquiring soccer teams and radio stations.

In addition to increasing crime related to drug trafficking and contributing to a moral decline in public administration, the drug trade has infected the highest levels of government. Cocaine shipments through the Colombian Embassy in Madrid led to the arrest of the presidential press secretary and the implication of the vice-minister of foreign relations.[10] The press secretary and two subordinates were charged with participating in two drug shipments made through the foreign ministry's diplomatic pouch.

Colombia now recognizes that it faces a serious drug-abuse problem of its own. Consumption of a coca-base substance known as "bazuco" has spread from low-income groups into middle-class and professional circles. Cocaine has also replaced marijuana as the fashion among the affluent, and narcotics operators are reportedly trying to introduce poor urban youths to heroin, which was previously unavailable to them. According to several directors of the numerous private rehabilitation centers that have sprung up, the problem is taking on the proportions of an epidemic.[11]

Efforts to Control Drug Traffic

Beginning in 1984, and coinciding with the death of Justice Minister Lara Bonilla, the government intensified its effort to institute an eradication program. According to the U.S. Department of State "Strategy Report,"

The government of Colombia has sustained a very impressive campaign against narcotics. The campaign moved into a decisive new phase on July 5 [1984] when the National Police began to test the aerial eradication of marijuana with the herbicide glyphosate. More than 4,000 hectares were eradicated in 1984, including 3,000 by aerial spraying of glyphosate; and the Colombians, who anticipate an even more comprehensive eradication program in 1985, are well on their way toward achieving control of cannabis production.

The Colombians are continuing their strong effort to control cocaine production as well, and have recently begun the testing of several herbicides in search of an aerially applied method of eradicating the coca bush. The Colombians have made a strong effort to suppress cocaine refining, including the major raid at Caqueta last March [1984] which resulted in the seizure of 10 metric tons of cocaine and the destruction of 14 laboratories. Since the assassination of Justice Minister Lara last April, Colombian police have staged more than 1,500 raids resulting in 1,425 arrests and the destruction of about 50 cocaine laboratories.[12]

The U.S. Department of State believes that the Colombian effort is emerging as one of the increasingly effective international control programs. It may well have eradicated most of its marijuana crop in 1985, thus giving the very real prospect of reducing availability from what has been the major marijuana source to the United States. The peasants do not appreciate governmental efforts to coerce them into growing less profitable "substitute" crops, however, and they angrily react to raids by U.S.-trained and -sponsored forces against coca fields.

The U.S. State Department also believes that the U.S.-supported interdiction program has been increasingly effective during the last few years. In 1984 the Colombians reported seizing 22 metric tons of cocaine; 2,870 metric tons of marijuana; and more than 500,000 dosage units of methaqualone, the latter figure reflecting an effective clamping down on imports of powder, which Colombian suppliers were using to tablet the pills.

In January 1985 President Betancur fulfilled his promise, taken at considerable political and personal risk, to extradite drug figures to the United States for trial. Four of these traffickers were flown to Homestead Air Force Base and were arraigned for trial in Florida and Washington, D.C. The Colombian Supreme Court ruled that the extradition of Colombians wanted for crimes in other countries is constitutional, thereby destroying the traffickers' hopes that they could avoid extradition on legal grounds. The United States also extradited two U.S. citizens to Colombia. In the summer of 1986 a total of twelve suspected Colombian drug smugglers were awaiting trial in the United States.

Nevertheless, the violence has increased. In August 1986 Supreme Court Justice Hernando Baquero Borda, who had sat on a special judicial panel that ordered the extradition, his bodyguard, and an innocent motorcyclist were killed by a gunman in Bogotá. The following month the chief of security for Avianca, Colombia's largest privately owned airline, was shot to death two days after he led an operation that discovered 5 million dollars of cocaine aboard a cargo jet bound for Miami. The killing occurred the same day that a Colombian senator was slain on his way to pick up his daughter. He was the thirteenth office holder of the leftist Patriotic Union party to be assassinated in a five-month period.[13]

By the end of 1985 the Colombian government's antidrug program—interdiction, eradication, extradition—eliminated nearly 85 percent of the country's marijuana crop. Realizing that drug traffic is a collective problem, the military and police of several South American countries—Colombia, Peru, Ecuador, and Venezuela—have cooperated to limit the drug trade between them. Unfortunately, however, their success in limiting production and trafficking encouraged drug dealers in other countries to fill the void. Mexico once again became the largest exporter of marijuana and heroin to the United States.

In spite of the Colombian government's successful effort against drug traffic, the top drug leaders wield considerable power. In Medellín, the country's second largest city, the U.S. Drug Enforcement Administration closed its office for security reasons, and gunmen killed six police informers there (from December 1985 to May 1986). Evidence is also growing that coca planters and traffickers are being allowed to operate in remote areas of Colombia's eastern lowlands that are controlled by the guerrilla movement, the Colombian Revolutionary Armed Forces, in exchange for what one official described as rent and one guerrilla called taxes.[14]

Venezuelan Drug Trade

The problem of the traficantes for Venezuela is small compared to the Colombian situation. Nevertheless, although the country has adopted stronger antinarcotics laws, it is one of the new "safehavens" that has been sought as a result of the crackdown in Colombia. According to sparse data, drug money has been laundered via real estate investments in Florida. Although they deny it, some members of the influential Cisneros family have been accused of being involved in the drug trade.[15]

From September to November 1985 several events occurred that caused Venezuelan officials to be more concerned. The army confiscated 453 kilos of cocaine in the city of Coro, and military intelligence arrested a retired army general in connection with drug trafficking. Near the northern end of Venezuela's 1,600-mile western border with Colombia—largely unsettled and unguarded—national guardsmen found a remote field containing approximately 12,000 coca plants, said to be the first discovery of coca cultivation in Venezuela. At the opposite end of the country a police spokesman claimed that some 100 kilos of drugs pass through Sucre state each week, making the so-called "eastern connection" with Trinidad.[16]

The minister of justice stated that Venezuela is basically a bridge in the movement of Colombian drugs and a money base for laundering drug dollars, rather than a producer of raw material or refined cocaine. In addition to investments in Florida, he believes the drug traffickers are laundering some of their profits in Venezuela and investing in legitimate businesses. Toward the end of 1985 the armed forces set up a unified command to combat the drug trade, and Venezuela and the United States began to discuss a new extradition treaty to replace the one signed in 1922.

Implications for Democracy

Drug growing and trafficking negatively affect the substantive norms of democracy. Economic development is hindered on two fronts: The infusion of drug money disrupts the overall economy and its financial institutions, and the government is forced to divert scarce capital resources in its war against the growers and traffickers. As a result, the other component of the word "socioeconomic" development is also in jeopardy. For without adequate economic development the government cannot take the steps to realize meaningful social justice. Programs for education, alleviation of rural and urban slum misery, nutrition and health, decent housing, and the like consequently are pared. Although some peasants have improved their lot by growing crops for the drug traffickers, this is not true for the millions who remain destitute in the rural areas and urban slums. Furthermore, the drug-baron multimillionaires have compounded the society's maldistribution of wealth.

The procedural norms of democracy are also negatively affected. Given the impact of La Violencia on the psyche of the Colombian people, the drug traffickers' "problem-solving" through violence and assassinations can strain a society whose wounds might not have completely healed. Furthermore, the populace's cynicism increases with reports of drug-money-induced bribery and corruption. Governmental and political institutions weaken when certain congressmen and other officials owe their elections to traficantes, when "narcodollar's" determine the outcome of certain court decisions, and when governmental officials are either bribed or are directly involved in drug trafficking. In addition, the democratic edifice is weakened when systemic opponents unite in a drug traffickers–guerrillas alliance.

Nevertheless, the government's efforts to control the drug cycle can have a positive effect on democracy and the functioning of governmental institutions. The more effective it is in meeting the challenge to democracy, and to the rule of law on which it is based, the healthier are the procedural and substantive norms of the democratic system. And the easier will be the particular challenge that the democratic regime must answer: to convince a sizable segment of the rural population that democracy and its institutions are more adept at alleviating the misery of their human condition than are the drug traffickers.

DEMOCRATIZATION

Let us now turn to the question of democratization in both countries. In so doing, we will attempt to determine how successful the respective elites have been in their efforts to further democratize the political systems and thereby extend the procedural and substantive norms.

Political Parties and Elections

If we look at the three electoral regimes in Colombia (Kline, Chapter 2, this volume)—sectarian democracy, consociational democracy, and democracy—we discern a progression that strengthens the democratic tradition. The first chapter concluded that the Colombian procedural norms were more limited than those in Venezuela through the National Front and Punto Fijo periods, and one can argue that the same has been true in recent years. If we compare Colombia *to itself*, however, we conclude that democracy has been growing since 1974 (that is, electoral democracy). Nevertheless, because the vestiges of the consociational period prevent the country from being more completely democratic, the pace of democratization, if not further democratization per se, can be retarded. Several examples since the National Front period illustrate the point.

The so-called primary of 1978, in which one's political strength in the prior separate congressional elections determined which Liberal party precandidate would subsequently secure the party's presidential nomination, did not survive the next election. In addition, during the electoral campaigns, Liberal candidates Agudelo Villa (1978) and Galán (1982) expressed a "radical reformism" that would have made substantive norms more attainable and would thereby have extended the process of democratization. Neither candidate received his party's nomination, however, and their programs were cast aside. Furthermore, as the

Turbay candidacy and presidency indicate, campaign rhetoric and governmental policy often have little relationship.

President Betancur's "democratic opening" was proposed to alleviate, if not eliminate, the threats to Colombian "formal" democracy (Hoskin, Chapter 3, this volume). By their very nature the proposals limited themselves to modifications of basically procedural norms, and they did not attempt to deal with the inequities of the socioeconomic structure that are the heart of the substantive norms. Thus, further democratization would at best be partial. The "democratic opening" also challenges the theory that improving economies encourage Latin American regimes to feel more secure and therefore to institute democratic reforms. In Colombia the opposite was true, and the Betancur proposals were introduced to neutralize a perceived threat to the regime caused basically by an economic recession and crisis.

A democratic opening cannot exist in a vacuum, and it must be an integral part of the political system. In Colombia, however, we discern a system that gives rise to high voter abstention rates with a growing urban population that is not adequately mobilized by the two major parties. Indeed, the most serious political challenge to the Conservative–Liberal domination—the increasing number of independent voters who reject party labels—indicates that the political elites have not adequately responded to the Colombian societal transformation. Further democratization also requires that the programmatic appeals of the post-National Front democratic regime be implemented through specific policies. Elite accommodation, however, that was so effective in ending La Violencia, also continues to blur interparty differences and results in a centrism that prohibits meaningful structural change.

Although Colombian and Venezuelan political practices have major differences (for example, Colombian intraparty competition is more openly discernible), the two countries' party systems have much in common (Martz, Chapter 8, this volume). The principal parties and the electorate are at the center of the political spectrum. The elites continue to hold tight reins over the parties, but the Venezuelan version of democratic centralism (authoritarian tradition) incorporates popular sentiment into policy decisions (democratic tradition) to a greater degree than the Colombian example. While Colombian and Venezuelan systemic democracy continues to exemplify two-party domination, Venezuela is also experiencing a situation in which polls indicate that the independents are stronger than any of the major political parties. An increasing number of Venezuelan voters continues to reject party labels for various reasons, including the lack of a meaningful development of substantive norms.

Economic Development

Analyses of the economy more clearly focus on the question of substantive norms. The Colombian economic indicators (Berry and Thoumi, Chapter 4, this volume) are encouraging when compared to the rest of Latin America. The maldistribution of wealth, however, continues to show little, if any, improvement. Although the status of the lower socioeconomic class has improved in an absolute sense, its relative position vis-à-vis the middle and upper classes has remained fairly constant. The efforts of the Alfonso López and Lleras Restrepo administrations to lessen the gap between the rich and the poor did not succeed to any appreciable degree in the long run. We have seen that the root of the problem lies in both internal and external causation.

Although not to the extent as in Colombia, Venezuela's maldistribution of wealth continues in spite of the infusion of petrodollars and statistical evidence of economic and social development (Alexander, Chapter 9, this volume). As in Colombia, increasing inflation adversely affects the poor, and when accompanied by rising unemployment and almost pathological corruption, the raison d'etre of the democratic regime is seriously questioned. Fundamental structural problems continue to frustrate the planners, and for better or for worse, various Venezuelan administrations cannot avoid the linkages among petroleum income, socioeconomic development, and democracy.

The Colombian State

Historically, the Colombian institutional state has been weak, and to this day, the private business–industrial sector and the transnationals remain stronger than the state and the particular government in power (Kline, Chapter 5, this volume). The implications for democratic evolution are manifold. In one sense we might conclude that procedural norms are invigorated because government leaders must consult with organized groups before important decisions are made. The actors in the tripartite give-and-take—a relatively weak state, a dynamic private sector, and the transnationals—insure spirited debate of the issues and a broad consensus reflected in policies that can be more easily implemented. The caveat, however, is that the dominant social class has remained as a strong component of the state. This factor, combined with Conservative–Liberal elite control, insures that any meaningful changes will come from above and reflect elite priorities at a given time. This does not augur well for a serious consideration of substantive norms that can attack the causes of an oppressive socioeconomic structure. President Betancur's "social pact" or additional billions of dollars from El Cerrejón coal contracts will probably not change this pattern. Short of revolution, changes in the socioeconomic structure will occur, if at all, when the domestic bourgeoisie think them necessary.

The Colombian Church

Although the decision of the Colombian church to support oligarchical democracy provides a major institutional underpinning for the regime (Wilde, Chapter 6, this volume), the conservative nature of the neo-Christendom church coincides with the political, economic, and military elites' limited perception of democratization. The church adheres to the procedural norms of the political system, but support for substantive norms receives either ecclesiastical lip service or specific opposition. If the church does not allow priests and nuns to be active in popular social movements and clearly opposes autonomous movements of lay Catholics, it in effect is thwarting further democratization at the socioeconomic level. Appeals to elite-directed initiatives do not lead to the necessary structural changes.

Thus, church influence simultaneously encourages and impedes further democratization. This results in a dilemma, because the decline of the church's social influence leads to a societal vacuum. The Colombian church has abdicated its role as the catalyst for structural change and human betterment. Who will fill the vacuum and become the spokespeople and activists in addressing the society's needs?

The Venezuelan Consociational Regime

While some scholars disagree concerning the relative importance of petroleum or the state in the Venezeulan political system, one of this book's authors contends that the consociational regime and its components are more significant to an understanding of the Venezuelan polity (Abente, Chapter 7, this volume). Although the Venezuelan state is stronger than the Colombian, primarily because of petroleum income, the former's autonomy is not fully exercised because of the limits imposed by Venezuelan democracy's consociational nature. Thus, in a comparative treatment of the state's role in both countries, we must look beyond the question of which state is stronger and consider other variables.

The decision of the post–1958 governments—to insure elite accommodation and systemic legitimacy—meant that the foundation of the democratic regime was laid and strengthened at the expense of meaningful redistributive legislation. As in Colombia, the very nature of the political accord limited significant structural change. Although one might hope that a younger generation of political leadership would some day further extend the substantive norms at a more rapid pace, the success or failure of the democratization process continues to be linked to the requirements of elite accommodation and *elite perception* of regime legitimacy.

Venezuelan Public Opinion

In one sense the 1948 Venezuelan military coup against the popularly elected government was a setback for democratic evolution (Baloyra, Chapter 10, this volume). In the aftermath of the coup, however, during a ten-year military dictatorship, the seeds of future democratization were sown by Acción Democrática (AD) and the Comité de Organización Política Electoral Independiente (COPEI). Whether in exile or in prison, different levels of respective party leadership engaged in dialogues and developed friendships that proved to be a crucial underpinning for the ensuing democratic regime.

In the aftermath of the 1958 coup that overthrew the military dictatorship,

Venezuelan political leaders chose democratic reform rather than revolution. Which alternative provides a greater degree of democratization? The democrat would argue that procedural norms can only be extended through the reforms of the democratic regime. The revolutionary would protest the implication that a revolutionary regime, not necessarily Marxist, must by definition be dictatorial. He would also insist that substantive norms can only be extended through the program of the revolutionary regime.

The survey data indicate the vulnerability of the Venezuelan democratic regime. In a sense the majority's support of a coup under certain circumstances, and increasing disillusionment with the democratic regime, indicate that popular support for democracy over dictatorship is qualified. Can a country have democracy without a democratic regime? Furthermore, the degree of democratization, realized through the extension of procedural and substantive norms, will be affected by *public perception* of regime legitimacy. The political elite's conduct and programmatic implementation are two variables that will influence that perception. In addition, the regime's response to those groups that are predisposed to support a coup—in large part but not exclusively at the lower socioeconomic level—must reflect policies that attempt to alleviate the oppression of the poor.

Insurgency and Pacification

We cannot say with certainty that the Colombian and Venezuelan elites' exclusion of the left from a role in the reestablishment of the respective democratic regimes led to the formation of guerrilla movements and resultant violence. Nevertheless, the insurgencies not only threaten democratic evolution directly through violent confrontation but indirectly because of intrainstitutional and interinstitutional strain and dissension. The recurring disputes within the Colombian Army over the best way to deal with the guerrillas—socioeconomic and political reform or repression of the various groups (Premo, Chapter 11, this volume)—affects the military's stability. Although one can argue that such intrainstitutional debates are healthy, we must remember that we are dealing with the Latin American military whose commitment to democracy is of recent vintage. The question of the most effective strategical and tactical response to the guerrilla movements also affects presidential–military relations. This was less of a problem in Venezuela where AD and COPEI presidents reached agreements with the military to modify tactics from the 1960s to the 1970s that ultimately led to COPEI President Caldera's successful pacification program. In Colombia, however, the increased use of the army to combat the continuing guerrilla movement has not only led to a greater army role in the administration of justice, but it has caused friction between the army and particular presidents. In a recent example, President Betancur apparently bowed to military pressure during the 1985 seizure of the Palace of Justice. Instead of negotiating with the guerrillas to give up their siege and release the hostages, he ordered an attack with troops and heavy weapons. Of course, without a military–presidental understanding regarding basic principles of governmental policy making, efforts to further the democratization process will be thwarted.

If they are not implemented, agreements with the guerrilla movements will lower the frustration tolerance of a substantial sector of the population. This indeed has happened in Colombia. President Betancur's peace proposals committed the government to address the inequities of the socioeconomic structure (for example, agrarian reform). If they had been implemented, the democratization process would have advanced. Unfortunately, however, neither a majority of Congress nor the major presidential candidates for the 1986 election supported President Betancur's program. This can only lead to an increase in violence and a setback for democratization.

Foreign Policy

Colombian and Venezuelan foreign policies reflect the fact that both countries are governed by democratic regimes (Hazleton, Chapter 12, this volume). In one sense the respective elites have concluded that their political systems will be more secure when other Latin American countries emulate the democratic model. This premise gives rise to specific policies and postures, such as *active* membership in the Contadora Group and criticism of the U.S. role in Central America because of the belief that democratic development is thereby thwarted. In another sense the Colombian and Venezuelan elites also recognize that crucial components of democratization within their own borders (for example, socioeconomic progress) are in large part dependent on economic development in the noncommunist industrialized countries, particularly the United States. Although individual presidents may vary concerning their degree of support for or criticism of U.S. policies, all recognize the multiple linkages. Thus, the Colombian and Venezuelan foreign affairs ministries accept the truism that their respective democracies run a risk when existing in a geopolitical vacuum and that internal democratization is inextricably linked to extracontinental developments.

Influence of the United States

Since the reestablishment of the Colombian and Venezuelan democratic regimes, the United States has supported democracy in the two countries (Myers, Chapter 13, this volume). Regardless of U.S. policymakers' motives, the procedural and substantive norms have become more attainable through the influence of the external superpower actor. Not only have U.S. policies strengthened the major democratic political parties, encouraged human-rights advocates, and underlined the need to transform the socioeconomic structures, but they have placed the United States squarely behind cooperative efforts between the liberal democrats and their respective military establishments.

Although the previously cited policies are in accord with the Colombian and

Venezuelan democratic tradition, neither domestic democrats nor U.S. policy makers can bypass the authoritarian tradition. Clientelism, patronage, and other components of that tradition continue to impede or modify policy implementation.

PERSISTENCE OF THE DUAL MODEL

The analyses in this study do not seriously challenge the dual-model hypothesis. Colombia and Venezuela continue to exemplify the coexistence and blending of the democratic/pluralist and authoritarian/monist traditions. However, the analyses do suggest a refinement and expansion of the model. For example, we find both traditions within the political party system. In addition to considering intraparty dynamics, we must discern how the parties extend democracy at the public level while responding to the authoritarian/monist predisposition in the society. Furthermore, not only is an understanding of civilian–military relations crucial to any discussion of the political system, but the impact of drug traffic impinges on our analysis. Thus, any attempt to apply the model to Colombia and Venezuela must consider additional, possibly unforeseen, variables.

We should also point out that the democratic and authoritarian traditions are not only antithetical, but they can reinforce each other as well. For example, the democratic elites' efforts to modernize their countries and enhance socioeconomic development can actually strengthen the societal hierarchical structure.

Modernization has reinforced, not reduced, Venezuelan reliance on traditional values and attitudes because of the uncertainty and insecurity inherent in rapid change. In such a transitional period, individuals have found kinship and patron-clientele groups to be emotional havens. Personalism and particularism have thus become the means by which the individual is integrated into the larger society. Personalism and particularism are especially important because of the ambivalence Venezuelans feel toward authority and status.[17]

Such observations lead to the conclusion that the model is elastic, requiring periodic reexamination.

PROJECTIONS FOR THE REMAINDER OF THE TWENTIETH CENTURY

Rather than allowing ourselves to become bogged down in semantics over whether individual authors are optimistic or pessimistic, let us look at the broader considerations that apply to Colombian and Venezuelan democracy. This final section contends that the current political and socioeconomic patterns and relationships will remain intact through the remainder of this century, short of a revolution or a military–technocratic coup.

Limited Democracy

Colombian and Venezuelan democracy will be limited because of the nature of elite accommodation. The respective elites will continue to provide resources for the loyal opposition through patronage and budget priorities. They will make decisions based on mutual elite consent, with muted appeals to the masses, as exemplified by Venezuelan petroleum nationalization of the past or probable Colombian coal and petroleum policy in the future. The extent of popular participation, although organized from above, may be greater in Venezuela than in Colombia, and the elite controlled masses' organizational apparatus more dynamic, but demand making from below will continue to be filtered through elite accommodation, control, and consent. This will be so even in Venezuela where the private business sector is more autonomous. As one Venezuelan scholar observed,

Limited pluralism is due not only to the prevalence of political parties in government, but also to poor interest articulation by the entrepreneurial sector. A sector that only shows strength when reacting against a measure another sector has already implemented suffers from serious internal organization drawbacks. In an effective pluralism setting, policies are the outcome of the activities of organized, legitimate groups which know what they expect to achieve through the interest articulation process. When pluralism is limited, interest groups are organized mainly to react against public policies.[18]

Democracy will also continue to be limited because of slow progress in the realization of procedural and substantive norms. The Colombian two-party domination will be a greater impediment to the practice of procedural norms because it will continue to be more exclusive. Both systems, however, will disappoint the masses, and the realization of significant substantive norms will not move beyond the realm of the potential. Structural changes require economic development *and* social justice. Without a significant improvement in the latter, further democratization will be limited to procedural norms. Whether it be systemic inertia caused by the shortcomings of the dependent capitalist state or the refusal of the conservative bourgeois elites to consider "radical reform," the inability or unwillingness of the respective democratic regimes to mitigate significantly socioeconomic problems will continue to threaten regime stability.

Driving Forces Influencing Democratic Institutionalization

The salient political variable in each country is that no one elite is strong enough to dominate, and this will continue to be the case. After a relatively violent history, Colombian oligarchical democrats accept this truism. If the Venezuelan political system ever developed into a Mexican-style one-party domination under AD, the social democrats would limit their own power and still provide patronage positions for the social Christians, and perhaps some of the smaller parties, in the governmental and organizational apparatus. Such is the price for sustained support of the democratic regime.

The elites will also continue to encourage debate as a desirable expression of the respective political systems' competitive nature. Debate is more effective in Venezuela, because the procedural norms are relatively more extensive. Colombian mass organizations are less autonomous and participatory; political expression apart from Liberal–Conservative domination is relatively less significant; and some guerrilla groups that feel alienated still turn to violence. Therefore, debate in Colombia will be more constrained.

Varying degrees of two-party domination in the center of the political spectrum will be an important structural factor through the remainder of the twentieth century. The outcome of particular elections will be less important than the overwhelming combined vote totals of the respective two major parties and their policy output consensus. Because they are basically parties of the center, policy will reflect democratic reformism. In socioeconomic terms and relative to human needs, this will range from inertia to incrementalism. We should remember, however, that the majority of the voters and the corporate organizations are basically conservative and the limited nature of democratic reformism reflects these interests.

In the economic dimension, economic development will continue to take place regardless of disappointment in terms of wealth disparity. In the past, petroleum wealth allowed the Venezuelan elites to mobilize the masses to a greater degree. For the foreseeable future, however, the world petroleum situation and its negative effect on Venezuelan national income will limit such mobilization. The Colombian elites have not mobilized the masses as have their counterparts in Venezuela. Nor will the development of Colombian coal and petroleum production lead to mass mobilization in the future. Not only do the elites see no need for taking such a step, but broader participatory politics would weaken the foundation of oligarchical democracy.

Measuring the Move Toward Democracy

This book has hypothesized that the Colombian and Venezuelan political systems exemplify a blending of the pluralist/liberal democratic and monist/authoritarian traditions.[19] In order to avoid a blend with a primarily authoritarian flavor, there must be an *increasing degree of democratization* over a significant period of time that will in turn continue to provide an underpinning of support for the democratic regime. As we have repeatedly emphasized, democratization requires *both* the attainment of procedural and substantive norms. This is particularly the case in Latin American countries, such as Colombia and Venezuela, where the majority of the people comprise the lower socioeconomic class and where upward social mobility is usually blocked.

The degree of democratization will depend on *governmental performance*, a more important measuring rod than the type of regime. In fact, some scholars believe that the Peruvian military dictatorship of the late 1960s and early 1970s was more effective in realizing substantive norms than the constitutionally elected government it had overthrown. Others insist that the nature of the state is a more accurate measurement in determining political–socioeconomic development. Nevertheless, whether we think in terms of regime type or the nature of the state, it is the people who are in charge of the government and their performance with which we are concerned. It is their bureaucracy that will administer the programs effectively or, because of limited training and almost unlimited corruption, ineffectively.

A third measuring device, somewhat intangible but crucial nevertheless, is *the relationship between the constitutionally elected civilian leadership and the military establishment.* In spite of the previously cited Peruvian example, an increase in military influence within a Latin American country usually leads to a decrease in civilian leadership influence. This, in turn, retards the process of democratization, particularly in terms of procedural norms. Budget priorities and certain decision making can reflect the imbalance toward the military. Neither Venezuela nor Colombia is immune from this danger.

[t]he military as an institution has noticeably increased its visibility and influence within the total Venezuelan political picture. *The VI National Plan 1981–85* was the first such four-year planning document to contain a chapter on national security and defense. The National Security and Defense Council, created by law in 1976, has launched an ambitious program of public education on the subject. Venezuela's military has also become a factor in the nation's industrial economy through the establishment of a number of military-run state enterprises that manufacture and maintain weapon systems. . . .

The praetorian subsystem of Venezuela's politics has increased in importance. It has done so, to a degree, at the expense of the representative-democratic subsector. Popular disillusionment with democracy is also on the increase. . . . When faced with a crisis of a national-security nature, the electoral subsystem may decline in influence while that of praetorianism may increase. However, once this crisis has passed, the electoral subsystem in Venezuela has been able to reassert its centrality. Only a major, violent, political breakdown could convince Venezuela's military leaders to end their restraint.[20]

At the beginning of 1986 Americas Watch, a human-rights organization based in the United States, published a report that accused Colombia's armed forces of being responsible for summary executions, torture, and "disappearances" in its campaign against leftist guerrillas.[21] The report also stated that despite President Betancur's good intentions, the army and police continued to violate human rights with impunity. A U.S. State Department report accused the armed forces, police, secret agents, paramilitary groups, and the guerrillas of numerous examples of political killings and violence.[22] Colombia's attorney general subsequently charged that the country's army and police were increasingly using torture and other human-rights abuses in their fight against leftist guerrillas and ordinary criminals. "We must denounce and halt by all possible means the alarming increase in disappearances," he said, adding that democracy could not tolerate "irregular raids, unfair arrests, illegal trials, excessive punishments, physical and moral torture, and disappearances."[23]

The fourth measurement might be a *political-socioeconomic dialectic*. In expanding upon a remark of Venezuelan President Lusinchi, we identify three stages to help us measure Colombian and Venezuelan developmental patterns for the remainder of the twentieth century: dictatorship, political democracy and social democracy. Both countries have emerged from the darkness of military dictatorship into the light of political democracy. As Plato's allegory of the cave tells us, however, the light of truth can be painful. The light will become brighter and more painful for the leadership as they move from elite accommodations of political democracy toward efforts to realize socioeconomic development of social democracy. The effort will be difficult but the goal most noble: to alleviate misery and raise the level of human worth and dignity for the majority of the people.

NOTES

1. Richard B. Craig wrote two very informative articles on the Colombian drug trade. See "Colombian Narcotics and United States–Colombian Relations," *Journal of InterAmerican Studies and World Affairs* 23 (August 1981):243–70; and "Domestic Implications of Illicit Colombian Drug Production and Trafficking," *Journal of Inter-American Studies and World Affairs* 25 (August 1983):325–50.

2. U.S. Department of State, *International Narcotics Control Strategy Report*, Summary, February 1, 1985—hereafter referred to as "Strategy Report."

3. Fox Butterfield, "Dispute Rises in Colombian Drug Extradition Plea," *The New York Times*, May 22, 1985.

4. U.S. Senate, D.C. Asencio testimony before the Permanent Subcommittee on Investigations of the Senate Committee on Governmental Affairs, Illegal Narcotics Profits (Washington, D.C.: Government Printing office, December 12, 1979). Quoted by Craig, "Colombian Narcotics," p. 258.

5. Craig, "Domestic Implications," pp. 328–29.

6. Ibid., pp. 329–35.

7. Craig, "Colombian Narcotics," p. 332.

8. Joseph B. Treaster, "Colombian Troops Are Said to Break Courthouse Siege," *The New York Times*, November 8, 1985; Joseph B. Treaster, "Colombians Debate Handling of Siege," *The New York Times*, November 10, 1985; "Colombian Guerrillas' Drug Connections Crystalize in Shoot-out," *Wall Street Journal*, November 15, 1985.

9. Craig, "Domestic Implications," pp. 338–39.

10. "Colombia—Heads Roll in Trafficking Saga," *Latin America Weekly Report*, February 15, 1985.

11. Alan Riding, "Drug Abuse Catches Up to Dismayed Colombia," *The New York Times*, August 20, 1986.

12. See also U.S. Department of State, Jon R. Thomas, Assistant Secretary for International Narcotics Matters, *Controlling International Narcotics Production and Trafficking* (Washington, D.C.: Bureau of Public Affairs, March 19, 1985).

13. "Airline Aide Killed in Bogotá after Finding Drugs on Plane," *The New York Times*, September 3, 1986.

14. See U.S. Department of State, Elliott Abrams, Assistant Secretary for Inter-American Affairs, *Drug Wars: The New Alliances Against Traffickers and Terrorists* (Washington, D.C.: Bureau of Public Affairs, February 10, 1986); Joel Brinkley, "U.S. Says Mexico Tops Again in Heroin, Pot Output," *The New York Times*, February 20, 1986; Joel Brinkley, "Diplomacy and Drugs," *The New York Times*, March 26, 1986; Alan Riding, "Even in the Face of a Crackdown, Colombia's Drug Traffickers Prosper," *The New York Times*, May 23, 1986. During 1987 the scale once again seemed to tip in favor of the drug traffickers. Although Carlos Enrique Lehder Rivas, one of the leading traffickers, was extradited to the United States to stand trial for various drug-related offenses, more cocaine flowed out of the country than ever and the antidrug campaign appeared to be largely neutralized by the power and violence of the drug rings. From 1986 to 1987 thirteen traffickers were extradited and thirteen justices were assassinated. In spite of President Barco's opposition, the Supreme Court subsequently declared the Colombian-U.S. extradition treaty unconstitutional. Alan Riding, "Colombia Efforts Against Drugs Hits Dead End," *New York Times*, August 11, 1987.

15. "Disip Runs Amok over Drugs Book—Cisneros Group Cited in Exposé," *Latin American Regional Reports: Andean Group Report*, March 1, 1985.

16. *Latin America Weekly Report*, November 22, 1985.

17. David Eugene Blank, *Venezuela: Politics in a Petroleum Republic* (New York: Praeger, 1984) pp. 34–35.

18. José Antonio Gil Yepes, *The Challenge of Venezuelan Democracy* (New Brunswick, N.J.: Transaction Books, 1981), p. 232.

19. Another study suggests a cultural blending of three traditions, including Marxism-socialism. See John D. Martz and David J. Myers, "Understanding Latin American Politics: Analytical Models and Intellectual Traditions," *Polity* 16 (Winter 1983): 214–41.

20. Blank, *Venezuela*, pp. 100 and 102.

21. "Colombia Army Accused of Human Rights Abuses," *The New York Times*, January 5, 1986.

22. U.S. Department of State, *Country Reports on Human Rights Practices for 1985* (Washington, D.C.: Government Printing Office, 1986).

23. Alan Riding, "Colombia Justice Aide Accuses Army," *The New York Times*, June 9, 1986. The violence increased during 1987. In November Jaime Pardo Leal, leader of the Patriotic Union party, was machine-gunned to death by three men. In the riots that followed, at least eleven more people were killed. Mary Williams Walsh, "In Colombia, Killings Just Go On and On," *The Wall Street Journal*, November 17, 1987.

Glossary and Abbreviations

GENERAL

AID — U.S. Agency for International Development

CELAM — Latin American bishops' conference

Contadora Group — Mexico, Venezuela, Colombia, and Panama

DEA — U.S. Drug Enforcement Administration

EEC — European Economic Community

golpe de estado — a coup d'etat

IMF — International Monetary Fund

LAFTA — Latin American Free Trade Association

OAS — Organization of American States

OCDA — Organización Cristiana Democrática de América
(Christian Democratic Organization of America)

OECD — Organization for Economic Cooperation and Development, based in Paris

OPEC — Organization of Petroleum Exporting Countries

S.A. — Sociedad Anónima (incorporated)

SELA — Sistema Económico Latinoamericano (Latin American Economic System)

SLOC — U.S. plans for the defense of Caribbean sea lane of communication

TNE — transnational enterprise

traficantes — drug traffickers

UNITAS — U.S., Colombian, and Venezuelan joint naval exercises

COLOMBIA

ADO   —   Workers Self-Defense Movement, a guerrilla group

ANAPO   —   Alianza Nacional Popular (National Popular Alliance)

ANDI   —   Asociación Nacional de Industriales (National Association of Industrialists)

ANIF   —   National Association of Financial Institutions

ANUC   —   Asociación Nacional de Usuarios Campesinos (National Association of Peasants)

bogotazo   —   explosion of mob violence following the assassination of Liberal leader Jorge Gaitán in 1948

CGT   —   Confederación General de Trabajo (General Confederation of Workers)

CARBOCOL   —   Carbones de Colombia (Colombian Coal Company)

CONPES   —   Concejo Nacional de Política Económica y Social (National Council of Economic and Social Policy)

CSTC   —   Confederación Sindical de Trabajadores de Colombia (Trade Union Confederation of Colombian Workers)

CTC   —   Confederación de Trabajadores Colombianos (Confederation of Colombian Workers)

ECOPETROL   —   Empresa Colombiana de Petróleos (Colombian Petroleum Enterprise)

ELN   —   Ejército de Liberación Nacional (National Liberation Army), a guerrilla group

EPL   —   Ejército Popular de Liberación (People's Liberation Army), a guerrilla group

FARC   —   Fuerzas Armadas Revolucionarias Colombianas (Revolutionary Armed Forces of Colombia), a guerrilla group

FEDECAFE   —   Federación Nacional de Cafeteros (National Federation of Coffee Growers)

FEDEGAN   —   Federación Nacional de Ganaderos (National Federation of Livestock Raisers)

FENALCO   —   Federación Nacional de Comerciantes (National Federation of Merchants)

FUAR   —   United Front of Revolutionary Action, a guerrilla group

gremio   —   producer association

IFI   —   Instituto de Fomento Industrial (Industrial Development Institute)

INCOMEX   —   Instituto Colombiano de Comercio Exterior (Colombian Foreign Trade Institute)

INCORA   —   Instituto Colombiano de la Reforma Agraria (Colombia Agrarian Reform Institute)

INTERCOL   —   International Petroleum (Colombia) Ltd.

INTERCOR   —   International Colombia Resources Corporation, the Exxon subsidiary

La Violencia   —   violence of the late 1940s through the early 1950s, resulting in over 300,000 fatalities

M–19 — Movimiento 19 de Abril (April 19 Movement), a guerrilla group claiming to be the armed branch of ANAPO

MOEC — Workers, Students, and Peasants Movement, a guerrilla group

MRL — Movimiento Revolucionario Liberal (Revolutionary Liberal Movement)

Nuevo Liberalismo — New Liberalism

Patriotic Union — a coalition of leftist parties

PCC — Partido Comunista de Colombia (Colombian Communist party)

PETROVEN — national oil company

Plan Lazo — a coordinated effort to pacify the countryside

PROEXPO — Fondo de Promoción de Exportaciones (Export Promotion Fund)

SENDAS — Secretariado Nacional de Asistencia Social (National Secretariat of Social Assistance)

UTC — Unión de Trabajadores de Colombia (Union of Colombian Workers)

VENEZUELA

AD — Acción Democrática (Democratic Action)

adecos — members of AD

AEROPOSTAL — Venezuelan domestic airline

Bandera Roja — Red Flag, a guerrilla group

bolívares — Venezuela's monetary unit

Bono Alimenticio — food stamp program

BTV — Banco de los Trabajadores de Venezuela (Venezuelan Workers' Bank)

calderista — a supporter of former President Rafael Caldera

CARE — Comisión Asesora de Relaciones Exteriores, an advisory body on Central America

Casa Amarilla — the foreign ministry

CCN — Cruzada Cívica Nacionalista (Nationalist Civic Crusade)

CENDES — Centro de Estudios del Desarrollo, the social science research department at the Central University

COPEI — Comité de Organización Política Electoral Independiente (Committee of Independent Electoral Political Organization), the social Christian party

copeyanos — members of COPEI

CORDIPLAN — Oficina Central de Coordinación y Planificación (Central Office of Coordination and Planning)

CORPOVEN — operating affiliate of PDVSA formed around the former Venezuelan Petroleum Corporation (CVP) and a small former subsidiary of Mobil

CTV — Confederación de Trabajadores de Venezuela (Confederation of Venezuelan Workers)

CVF — Corporación Venezolana de Fomento (Venezuelan Development Corporation)

CVG — Corporación Venezolana de Guayana (Venezuelan Guayana Corporation)

desarrollistas — a conservative group of entrepreneurs

FALN — Fuerzas Armadas de Liberación Nacional (Armed Forces of National Liberation), a guerrilla group

FAS — Frente Américo Silva (Americo Silva Front), a guerrilla group

FCV — Federación Campesina de Venezuela (Venezuelan Peasant Federation)

FDP — Fuerza Democrática Popular (Popular Democratic Force)

FEDEAGRO — Federación de Agricultores (Federation of Farmers)

FEDECAMARAS — Federation of Chambers and Associations of Commerce and Production

FENAGAN — Federación Nacional de Ganaderos (National Federation of Cattlemen)

FND — Frente Nacional Democrático (National Democratic Front)

herrerista — a supporter of former President Luis Herrera Campins

ICE — Instituto de Comercio Exterior (Foreign Commerce Institute), concerned with Andean integration

IESA — Instituto de Estudios Superiores de Administración (Institute of Higher Administrative Studies)

INOS — Instituto Nacional de Sanitarias Obras (National Institute of Sanitary Works)

LAGOVEN — Operating affiliate of PDVSA formed out of Exxon's prenationalization subsidiary

MARAVEN — operating affiliate of PDVSA formed out of Shell's prenationalization subsidiary

MAS — Movimiento al Socialismo (Movement Toward Socialism)

masistas — members of MAS

MENEVEN — operating affiliate of PDVSA centered on the former Venezuelan holdings of Gulf

MEP — Movimiento Electoral del Pueblo (People's Electoral Movement)

mepistas — members of MEP

MIR — Movimiento de la Izquierda Revolucionaria (Movement of the Revolutionary Left)

miristas — members of MIR

OR — Organizaciones Revolucionarias (Revolutionary Organizations), a guerrilla group

PCV — Partido Comunista de Venezuela (Venezuelan Communist party)

PDVSA — Petróleos de Venezuela, S.A. (Venezuelan Petroleum Company)

PEQUIVEN — Petroquímica de Venezuela, S.A. (Venezuelan Petrochemical Company)

perezjimenistas — any supporters of General Marcos Pérez Jiménez

Pro-Venezuela — Association of Industrialists

trienio — the October 1945 to January 1948 period during which AD and the military ruled jointly; the Rómulo Gallegos presidency of January to November 1948

UCV — Universidad Central de Venezuela (Central University of Venezuela)

URD — Unión Republicana Democrática (Democratic Republican Union)

urredistas — members of URD

VIASA — Venezolana Internacional de Aviación, S.A. (Venezuelan International Airlines)

Martz, John D. and Myers, David J. "Understanding Latin American Politics: Analytic Models and Intellectual Tradition." *Polity* 16 (Winter 1983):214–42.

McDonald, Ronald H. *Party Systems and Elections in Latin America*. Chicago: Markham Publishing Company, 1971.

Mecham, J. Lloyd. *Church and State in Latin America*, revised edition. Chapel Hill: University of North Carolina Press, 1966.

Migdal, Joel S. "A Model of State-Society Relations." In *New Directions in Comparative Politics*, ed. Howard J. Wiarda. Boulder, Colo.: Westview Press, 1985.

Moran, Theodore H. "Multinational Corporations and Dependency: A Dialogue for Dependentistas and Non-Dependentistas." *International Organization* 32 (Winter 1978):93.

Muñoz, Heraldo and Tulchin, Joseph S., eds. *Latin American Nations in World Politics*. Boulder, Colo.: Westview Press, 1984.

Payne, James L. "The Oligarchy Muddle." *World Politics* 20 (April 1968):439–53.

Peeler, John A. *Latin American Democracies: Colombia, Costa Rica, Venezuela*. Chapel Hill: University of North Carolina Press, 1985.

Petras, James, ed. *Latin America: Reform or Revolution?* Greenwich, Conn.: Fawcett Publications, 1968.

Philip, George. *Oil and Politics in Latin America: Nationalist Movements and State Companies*. London: Cambridge University Press, 1982.

Powell, G. Bingham, Jr. *Contemporary Democracies: Participation, Stability, and Violence*. Cambridge, Mass.: Harvard University Press, 1982.

Ronfeldt, David. *Geopolitics, Security, and U.S. Strategy in the Caribbean Basin*, R–2997-AF. Santa Monica, Calif.: The Rand Corporation, 1983.

Schmidt, Steffen W. "Bureaucrats as Modernizing Brokers?" *Comparative Politics* 6 (April 1974):425–50.

Schmitter, Philippe C. "Still the Century of Corporatism?" In *The New Corporatism: Social-Political Structures in the Iberian World*, Eds. Frederick B. Pike and Thomas Stritch. Notre Dame, Ind.: University of Notre Dame Press, 1974.

Sloan, John W. *Public Policy in Latin America: A Comparative Study*. Pittsburgh: University of Pittsburgh Press, 1984.

Stepan, Alfred. *The State and Society: Peru in Comparative Perspective*. Princeton, N.J.: Princeton University Press, 1978.

Thomas, Jon R., Assistant Secretary for International Narcotics Matters, *Controlling International Narcotics Production and Trafficking*. Washington, D.C: Department of State, Bureau of Public Affairs, March 1985.

Wiarda, Howard J. *Corporatism and National Development in Latin America*. Boulder, Colo.: Westview Press, 1981.

———, ed. *The Continuing Struggle for Democracy in Latin America*. Boulder, Colo.: Westview Press, 1980.

———. "Toward a Framework for the Study of Political Change in the Iberic-Latin Tradition: The Corporative Model." *World Politics* 25 (1973):206–35.

COLOMBIA

Alfonso, Luis Alberto. *Dominación Religiosa y Hegemonía Política*. Bogotá: Punta de Lanza, 1978.

Arenas, Jacobo. *Cese el fuego: Una historia política de las FARC*. Bogotá: Editorial La Oveja Negra, 1985.

Bagley, Bruce Michael. "Colombia: National Front and Economic Development." In *Politics, Policies, and Economic Development*, ed. Robert Wesson. Palo Alto, Calif.: Hoover Press, 1984.

————, Thoumi, Francisco, and Tokatlian, Juan, eds. *Colombia Since the National Front*. Boulder, Colo.: Westview Press, 1986.

Bagley, Bruce Michael and Tokatlian, Juan Gabriel. "Colombian Foreign Policy in the 1980s: The Search for Leverage." *Journal of Inter-American Studies and World Affairs* 27 (Fall 1985):27–62.

Bailey, John. "Pluralist and Corporatist Dimensions of Interest Representation in Colombia." In *Authoritarianism and Corporatism in Latin America*, ed. James Malloy. Pittsburgh: University of Pittsburgh Press, 1977.

Berry, R. Albert, Hellman, Ronald G., and Solaún, Mauricio, eds. *Politics of Compromise: Coalition Government in Colombia*. New Brunswick, N.J.: Transaction Books, 1980.

Betancur, Belisario. *¡Sí, Se Puede!* Bogotá: Tercer Mundo, 1982.

Botero Restrepo, Juan. *Breve historia de la Iglesia Colombiana*. Medellín, Colombia: Editorial Copiyepes, 1983.

Camargo, Pedro Pablo. *El Régimen concordatorio Colombiano*. Bogotá: Sociedad Colombiana de Abogados, 1971.

Cepeda, Fernando, and Claudia González de Lecaros. *Comportamiento del Voto Urbano en Colombia: Una Aproximación*. Bogotá: Universidad de los Andes, 1976.

Craig, Richard B. "Colombian Narcotics and United States-Colombian Relations." *Journal of Inter-American Studies and World Affairs* 23 (3) (August 1981):243–70.

————. "Domestic Implications of Illicit Colombian Drug Production and Trafficking." *Journal of Inter-American Studies and World Affairs* 25 (3) (August 1983):325–50.

Daniel, James M. *Rural Violence in Colombia Since 1946*. Princeton, N.J.: Special Operations Research Office, Washington, D.C., 1965.

de Roux, Rodolfo. *Historia general de la Iglesia en América Latina*, Vol. 7, *Colombia y Venezuela*. Salamanca, Spain: Ediciones Sigueme, 1981.

Díaz Uribe, Edwardo. *El Carbón en Colombia*. Bogotá: Instituto de Fomento Industrial, 1978.

Dix, Robert H. *Colombia: The Political Dimensions of Change*. New Haven, Conn.: Yale University Press, 1967.

————. "Consociational Democracy: The Case of Colombia." *Comparative Politics* 12 (April 1980):303–21.

Drekonja Kornat, Gerhard. *Colombia: Política Exterior*. Bogotá: Universidad de los Andes, Fundación Friedrich Ebert de Colombia (FESCOL), La Editoria, 1982.

————. "Colombia: Learning the Foreign Policy Process." *Journal of Inter-American Studies and World Affairs* 25 (May 1983): 229–50.

Fals Borda, Orlando. *Peasant Society in the Colombian Andes*. Gainesville: University of Florida Press, 1961.

————. *Subversión y Cambio Social*. Bogotá: Tercer Mundo, 1968.

Galán, Luis Carlos. *Nueva Colombia*. Bogotá: Coeditores Ltda., 1982.

Gómez Buendía, Hernando. "Los modelos del continente y la opción colombiana: reformismos, desarrollismo, y Socialismo." *Conyuntura Económica* 7 (December 1977):47–58.

González G., Fernán. *Colombia 1974: I. La Política.* Bogotá: Centro de Investigación y Educación Popular, 1975.

Guzman, Germán, Fals Borda, Orlando, and Umana Luna, Eduardo. *La Violencia en Colombia: Estudio de un Proceso Social.* Vols. 1 and 2. Bogotá: Ediciones Tercer Mundo, 1963 and 1964.

Hartlyn, Jonathan. "Military Governments and the Transition to Civilian Rule: The Colombian Experience of 1957–1958." *Journal of Inter-American Studies and World Affairs* 25 (May 1984):245–81.

———. "The Impact of Patterns of Industrialization and of Popular Sector Incorporation on Political Regime Type: A Case Study of Colombia." *Studies in Comparative International Development* 19 (1) (Spring 1984).

———. "Producer Associations, the Political Regime, and Policy Processes in Contemporary Colombia." *Latin American Research Review* 20 (3) (1985):119.

Holguin, Andrés. *Análisis del nuevo concordato.* Bogotá: Revista Derecho Colombiano, 1973.

Hoskin, Gary, Leal, Francisco, Kline, Harvey, Rothlisberger, Dora, and Borrero, Armando, eds. *Estudio del Comportamiento Legislativo en Colombia.* Bogotá: Universidad de Los Andes y Cámara de Comerio de Bogotá, 1975.

Jurado, Franklin. "La inversión extranjera en Colombia." *Nueva Frontera* 328 (April 1981):8.

Kline, Harvey F. "Belief Systems of Colombian Political Party Activists." *Journal of Inter-American Studies and World Affairs* 21 (November 1979):481–504.

———. "The Coal of El Cerrejón: An Historical Analysis of Major Policy Decisions and MNC Activities." *Inter-American Economic Affairs* 35 (Winter 1981):69–90.

———. *Colombia: Portrait of Unity and Diversity.* Boulder, Colo.: Westview Press, 1983.

La Campaña por la Presidencia, 1978–1982: Los Temas en Controversia. Bogotá: Tercer Mundo, 1978.

Leal Buitrago, Francisco. *Estado y Política en Colombia.* Bogotá: Siglo Veintiuno, 1984.

Lombard, Francois J. *The Foreign Investment Screening Process in LDCs: The Case of Colombia, 1967–1975.* Boulder, Colo.: Westview Press, 1979.

Martz, John D. *Colombia: A Contemporary Political Survey.* Chapel Hill: University of North Carolina Press, 1962.

Maullin, Richard. *Soldiers, Guerrillas, and Politics in Colombia.* Lexington, Mass.: Lexington Books, 1973.

Medhurst, Kenneth. *The Church and Labour in Colombia.* Manchester, England: Manchester University Press, 1984.

Molina, Gerardo. "Notas sobre el Frente Nacional." *Estrategia económica y financiera* 12 (June 1978):16–22.

Oquist, Paul. *Violence, Conflict, and Politics in Colombia.* New York: Academic Press, 1980.

Peller, John A. "Colombian Parties and Political Development: A Reassessment." *Journal of Inter-American Studies and World Affairs* 18 (May 1976):203–24.

Rama, Germán. *El sistema político Colombiano: frente nacional y ANAPO.* Asunción: Centro Paraguayo de Estudios Sociológicos, 1970.

Rothlisberger, Dora. "La Organización Formal del Congreso." In *Estudio del Comportamiento Legislativo en Colombia*, eds. Gary Hoskin, Francisco Leal, Harvey Kline, Dora Rothlisberger, and Armando Borrero. Bogotá: Universidad de los Andes, 1975.

Ruhl, Mark J. "Party System in Crisis? An Analysis of Colombia's 1978 Elections." *Journal of Inter-American Economic Affairs* 32 (Winter 1978):29–45.

Santamariá S., Ricardo and Silva Luhan, Gabriel. *Proceso Político en Colombia: Del Frente Nacional a la Apertura Democrática*. Bogotá: Fondo Editorial CEREC, 1984.

Schmidt, Steffen W. "Patrons, Brokers, and Clients: Party Linkages in the Colombian System." In *Political Parties and Linkage*, ed. Kay Lawson. New Haven, Conn.: Yale University Press, 1980.

Sharpless, Richard E. *Gaitán of Colombia: A Political Biography*. Pittsburgh, Penn.: University of Pittsburgh Press, 1978.

Ulloa, Fernando Cepeda. "El Proceso de Paz en Colombia y la Política Internacional." *Estudios Internacionales* (Chile) 71 (July–September 1985):440–50.

Urrutia Montoya, Miguel. *The Development of the Colombian Labor Movement*. New Haven, Conn.: Yale University Press, 1969.

———. "Diversidad ideológica e integración Andina." *Coyuntura económica* 10 (July 1980):187–203.

Urrutia Montoya, Miguel, and Villaveces Pardo, Ricardo. "Reseña de las Perspectivas Energéticas de Colombia." *Coyuntura económica* 4 (October 1979):91–125.

Villar Borda, Luis, ed. *Oposición, insurgencia y amnestía*. Bogotá: Editorial Dintel, 1982.

Villegas, Jorge. *Petróleo Colombiano, ganancia gringa*. Bogotá: Ediciones Peñlosa y Cia. Ltda., 1977.

Wilde, Alexander W. "Conversations among Gentlemen: Oligarchical Democracy in Colombia." In *The Breakdown of Democratic Regimes: Latin America*, eds. Juan J. Linz and Alfred Stepan. Baltimore: Johns Hopkins University Press, 1978.

———. "Redemocratization, the Church, and Democracy in Colombia." In *Colombia Since the National Front*, eds. Bruce Bagley, Francisco Thoumi, and Juan Tokatlian. Boulder, Colo.: Westview Press, 1986.

VENEZUELA

Alexander, Robert J. *The Venezuelan Democratic Revolution: A Profile of the Regime of Rómulo Betancourt*. New Brunswick, N.J.: Rutgers University Press, 1964.

———. *The Communist Party of Venezuela*. Stanford, Calif.: Hoover Institution Press, 1969.

———. *Rómulo Betancourt and the Transformation of Venezuela*. New Brunswick, N.J.: Transaction Books, 1982.

Baloyra, Enrique A. "Criticism, Cynicism, and Political Evaluation: A Venezuelan Example." *American Political Science Review* 4 (December 1979):987–1002.

——— and Martz, John D. *Political Attitudes in Venezuela: Societal Cleavages and Public Opinion*. Austin: University of Texas Press, 1979.

Bigler, Gene E. "Professional Soldiers and Restrained Politics in Venezuela." In *The New Military Politics in Latin America*, ed. Robert Wesson. New York: Praeger, 1982.

Blanco Muñoz, Augustín, ed. *La lucha armada, Hablan cinco jefes*. Caracas: Universidad Central de Venezuela-Facultad de Ciencias Económicas y Sociales, 1980.

Blank, David E. *Politics in Venezuela*. Boston: Little, Brown, 1973.

————. *Venezuela: Politics in a Petroleum Republic*. New York: Praeger, 1984.

Bond, Robert D., ed. *Contemporary Venezuela and Its Role in International Affairs*. New York: New York University Press, 1977.

Bonilla, Frank. *The Politics of Change in Venezuela*, Vol. 2, *The Failure of Elites*. Cambridge: Massachusetts Institute of Technology Press, 1970.

Burggraaff, Winfield J. *The Venezuelan Armed Forces in Politics, 1939–1959*. Columbia: University of Missouri Press, 1972.

Cordero Velásquez, Luis. *Gómez y las fuerzas vivas*. Caracas: Lumego, 1975.

Ellner, Steve. "The Venezuelan Left in the Era of the Popular Front." *Journal of Latin American Studies* 2 (2) (May 1979):169–84.

————. *Los partidos políticos y su disputa por el control del movimiento sindical en Venezuela, 1936–1948*. Caracas: Universidad Católica Andrés Bello, 1980.

————. "Political Party Dynamics and the Outbreak of Guerrilla Warfare in Venezuela." *Inter-American Economic Affairs* 34 (Autumn 1980).

————. "Populism in Venezuela, 1935–48: Betancourt and Acción Democrática." In *Latin American Populism in Comparative Perspective*, ed. Michael L. Conniff. Albuquerque: University of New Mexico Press, 1982.

————. "Inter-Party Agreement and Rivalry in Venezuela: A Comparative Perspective." *Studies in Comparative International Development* 19 (4) (Winter 1984–85):38–66.

Ewell, Judith. *The Indictment of a Dictator: The Extradition and Trial of Marcos Pérez Jiménez*. College Station: Texas A & M University Press, 1981.

————. "The Development of Venezuelan Geopolitical Analysis Since World War II." *Journal of Inter-American Studies and World Affairs* 24 (August 1982):295–320.

————. *Venezuela: A Century of Change*. Stanford, Calif.: Stanford University Press, 1984.

Gil Yepes, José Antonio. *The Challenge of Venezuelan Democracy*. Transl. Evelyn Harrison I., Lolo Gil de Yanes, and Danielle Salti. New Brunswick, N.J.: Transaction Books, 1981.

Gilmore, Robert L. *Caudillism and Militarism in Venezuela, 1810–1910*. Athens: Ohio University Press, 1964.

Gueron, Eva Josko de. "El Congreso y la Política Exterior en Venezuela." *Politeia* 7 (1978):329–441.

Herman, Donald L. "Ideology, Economic Power, and Regional Imperialism: The Determinants of Foreign Policy under Venezuela's Christian Democrats." *Caribbean Studies* 18 (April–July 1978):43–84.

————. *Christian Democracy in Venezuela*. Chapel Hill: University of North Carolina Press, 1980.

———— and Myers, David J. "The Venezuelan Election." In *The World Votes*, ed. Howard R. Penniman. Durham, N.C.: Duke University Press/American Enterprise Institute, 1988.

Klette, Immanuel J. "U.S. Assistance to Venezuela and Chile in Combatting Insurgency, 1963–1964." *Conflict* 3 (1982):227–44.

Kolb, Glen L. *Democracy and Dictatorship in Venezuela: 1945–1958*. New London, Conn.: Archon, 1974.

Levine, Daniel H. *Conflict and Political Change in Venezuela*. Princeton, N.J.: Princeton University Press, 1973.

————. "Venezuela Since 1958: The Consolidation of Democratic Politics." In *The Breakdown of Democratic Regimes: Latin America*, eds. Juan J. Linz and Alfred Stepan. Baltimore: Johns Hopkins University Press, 1978.

Lieuwen, Edwin. *Petroleum in Venezuela, A History*. Berkeley: University of California Press, 1954.

de Lourdes Acedo de Sucre, María and Nones Mendoza, Carmen Margarita. *La generación venezolana de 1928: Estudio de una élite política*. Caracas: Ediciones Ariel, 1967.

Luzardo, Rodolfo. *Notas histórico-económicas, 1928–1963*. Caracas: Editorial Sucre, 1963.

Martz, John D. "Venezuela's Generation of '28: The Genesis of Political Democracy." *Inter-American Economic Affairs* 1 (January 1964):17–33.

————. *Acción Democrática: Evolution of a Modern Political Party in Venezuela*. Princeton, N.J.: Princeton University Press, 1966.

———— and Baloyra, Enrique A. *Electoral Mobilization and Public Opinion: The Venezuelan Campaign of 1973*. Chapel Hill: University of North Carolina Press, 1976.

———— and Myers, David J., eds. *Venezuela: The Democratic Experience*, revised edition. New York: Praeger, 1986.

McBeth, B. S. *Juan Vicente Gómez and the Oil Companies in Venezuela: 1908–1935*. Cambridge, England: Cambridge University Press, 1983.

Moyabre, Eduardo. "The Renegotiation of Venezuela's Foreign Debt during 1982 and 1983." In *Politics and Economics of External Debt Crisis: The Latin American Experience*, ed. Miguel S. Wionczek. Boulder, Colo.: Westview Press, 1985.

Muñoz, Freddy. *Revolución sin dogma*. Caracas: Ediciones Alcinoo, 1970.

Myers, David J. *Democratic Campaigning in Venezuela: Caldera's Victory*. Caracas: Fundación La Salle, 1973.

————. "Venezuela's MAS." *Problems of Communism* 29 (September–October 1980):16–27.

————. *Venezuela's Pursuit of Caribbean Basin Interests: Implications for United States National Security*. Santa Monica, Calif.: Rand Corporation, 1985.

Njaim, Humberto et al. *El sistema político venezolano*. Caracas: Editorial Arte, 1975.

Oropeza, Luis J. *Tutelary Pluralism: A Critical Approach to Venezuelan Democracy*. Cambridge, Mass.: Harvard University Center for International Affairs, 1983.

Peattie, Lisa Redfield. *The View from the Barrios*. Ann Arbor: University of Michigan Press, 1968.

Penniman, Howard R., ed. *Venezuela at the Polls: The National Elections of 1978*. Washington, D.C.: American Enterprise Institute, 1980.

Petkoff, Teodoro. *Checoeslovaquia: El socialismo como problema*. Caracas: Editorial Fuentes, 1969.

Petras, James, Morely, Morris, and Smith, Steven. *The Nationalization of Venezuelan Oil*. New York: Praeger Special Studies, 1977.

Plaza, Helena. *El 23 de Enero y el proceso de consolidación de la democracia representativa en Venezuela*. Caracas: Garbizu & Todtmann, 1978.

Powell, John D. *Political Mobilization of the Venezuelan Peasant*. Cambridge, Mass.: Harvard University Press, 1971.

Rangel, Domingo Alberto. *La revolución de las fantasías*. Caracas: Ediciones OFIDI, 1966.

Ray, Talton F. *The Politics of the Barrios of Venezuela*. Berkeley: University of California Press, 1969.

Stambouli, Andrés. "La Crisis y Caída de la Dictadura." *Politeia* 7 (1978):125–79.

———. *Crisis Política, Venezuela 1945–1958*. Caracas: Editorial Ateneo, 1980.

Tarre Murzi, Alfredo. *López Contreras, De la tiranía a la libertad*. Caracas: Editorial Ateneo, 1982.

Taylor, Philip B. *The Venezuelan Golpe de Estado of 1958: The Fall of Marcos Pérez Jiménez*. Washington, D.C.: Institute for the Comparative Study of Political Systems, 1968.

Tugwell, Franklin. *The Politics of Oil in Venezuela*. Stanford, Calif.: Stanford University Press, 1975.

Valsalice, Luigi. *Guerrilla y Política: Curso de Acción en Venezuela, 1962–1969*. Buenos Aires: Editorial Pleamar, 1975.

Index

Acción Democrática (AD), Venezuela: business distrust of, 7, 136–37; Catholic Church and, 8; campaign consultants and, 164; communists and, 220; electoral reform and, 150; foreign policy and, 261; labor unions and, 11; 1948 coup and, 201–2; 1958 coup and, 206–7; 1963 elections and, 161; oil policy of, 135, 178; Punto Fijo Pact and, 2–4; rural support for, 283; Sandinistas and, 253; split in, 140, 159–60, 167

Acción Communal Popular (FANAL), 90, 119

AD. *See* Acción Democrática

Aeropostal, 185

Agency for International Development (AID), 287–89

agrarian reform: Agudelo Villa and, 29; Alfonso Lopez and, 28; Alvaro Gómez and, 27; Betancourt and, 138; Betancur and, 32; democratic populists and, 10; Galán and, 34; guerilla movements and, 234, 238; Lleras and, 30, 70; Pérez and, 190; Rojas and, 11; Turbay and, 31; urbanization and, 66

agriculture, 75, 79. *See also* agrarian reform

Agudelo Villa, Hernando, 28–29

AID. *See* Agency for International Development

Ailanza Nacional Popular (ANAPO), 12, 115; M–19 and, 231; National Movement and, 49; 1969 elections and, 22

Alcalde Alvarez, Humberto, 227

Alliance for Progress: economic programs of, 287–89, 294–95; Kennedy and, 277; Pardo Parra and, 96; political strategy of, 284–86

Alvarez Paz, Oswaldo, 260

American Popular Revolutionary Alliance (APRA), 11

ANAPO. *See* Ailanza Nacional Popular

Andean Pact, 92, 140, 187; business opposition to, 260; foreign investment and, 289; INCOMEX and, 262; LAFTA and, 254

Argentina: Contadora Group and, 266; Malvinas war, 252–53, 255–56; oil income, 134; TNE investment in, 93

Arias Blanco, Rafael, 205

Arias Londono, Gustavo, 236

armed forces: Caldera pacification program and, 224–25; Catholic Church and, 114, 121, 125; Cazadores, 284; civilian leadership and, 314; corpora-

About the Editor and Contributors

DONALD L. HERMAN, Ph.D., University of Michigan. He is the author of *Christian Democracy in Venezuela* and has written extensively on Mexico and Venezuela. Dr. Herman is adjunct professor of political science at the Center for Latin American and Caribbean Studies at Michigan State University.

DIEGO ABENTE, Ph.D., University of New Mexico. He has contributed to scholarly journals and has written chapters on Paraguay, Uruguay, and Venezuela. Dr. Abente is assistant professor of political science at Miami University, Ohio.

ROBERT J. ALEXANDER, Ph.D., Columbia University. He is the author of *Rómulo Betancourt and the Transformation of Venezuela* and has written extensively on Latin American subjects for over thirty-five years. Dr. Alexander is professor of economics at Rutgers University.

ENRIQUE A. BALOYRA, Ph.D., University of Florida. He is the author of *Comparing New Democracies* and has published extensively on the politics of Cuba, El Salvador, and Venezuela. Dr. Baloyra is professor of political science and associate dean in the Graduate School of International Studies at the University of Miami, Florida.

R. ALBERT BERRY, Ph.D., Princeton University. He is coauthor and coeditor of *Politics of Compromise: Coalition Government in Colombia* and has published extensively on a variety of subjects dealing with Colombia. Dr. Berry is professor of economics at the University of Toronto.

WILLIAM A. HAZLETON, Ph.D., University of Virginia. He has contributed to scholarly journals and has written chapters on Colombia, Venezuela, Peru, and human rights. Dr. Hazleton is associate professor of political science and acting director of the International Studies Program at Miami University, Ohio.

GARY HOSKIN, Ph.D., University of Illinois. He is coauthor and coeditor of *Legislative Behavior in Colombia* and has focused on party and electoral behavior and political development in Colombia. Dr. Hoskin is associate professor of political science at the State University of New York, Buffalo.

HARVEY F. KLINE, Ph.D., University of Texas at Austin. He is the author of *Colombia: Portrait of Unity and Diversity* and has also focused on energy development in the Third World. Dr. Kline is professor of political science and department chairman at the University of Alabama.

JOHN D. MARTZ, Ph.D., University of North Carolina. He is coauthor and coeditor of *Venezuela, The Democratic Experience* and has written extensively on Ecuador, Colombia, and Venezuela. Dr. Martz is professor of political science at the Pennsylvania State University.

DAVID J. MYERS, Ph.D., University of California, Los Angeles. He is the author of *Venezuela's Pursuit of Caribbean Basin Interests* and has written extensively on Brazil, Venezuela, and U.S. security interests in Latin America. Dr. Myers is associate professor of political science at the Pennsylvania State University.

DANIEL L. PREMO, Ph.D., University of Texas at Austin. He has contributed to scholarly journals and has written chapters on Colombia, military and insurgency movements in Latin America, and political assassination and violence in Guatemala. Dr. Premo is professor of political science at Washington College, Maryland.

FRANCISCO E. THOUMI, Ph.D., University of Minnesota. He is coauthor and coeditor of *State and Society in Contemporary Colombia: Beyond the National Front* and has written extensively on Colombia, and international trade and industrialization in Latin America. Dr. Thoumi is head of the International Economics Section of the Inter-American Development Bank and professorial lecturer at the Catholic University of America.

ALEXANDER W. WILDE, Ph.D., Columbia University. He is the author of *Conversaciones de Caballeros: La Quiebra de la Democracia in Colombia* and has written estensively on Colombia and Chile. Dr. Wilde is executive director of the Washington Office on Latin America.